Approaches to Catullus

Views and Controversies about Classical Antiquity
General Editor: M. I. Finley

Also published:

Slavery in Classical Antiquity
Edited by M. I. Finley

The Language and Background of Homer
Edited by G. S. Kirk

Alexander the Great: the Main Problems
Edited by G. T. Griffith

Plato, Popper and Politics
Edited by Renford Bambrough

The Crisis of the Roman Republic
Edited by Robin Seager

Essays on Classical Literature
Selected from 'Arion'
Edited by Niall Rudd

Philip and Athens
Edited by S. Perlman

Approaches to Catullus

Selected and introduced by

KENNETH QUINN

Professor of Classics
University College, Toronto

HEFFER / *Cambridge*

BARNES & NOBLE BOOKS / *New York*
(division of Harper & Row Publishers Inc.)

This volume first published in 1972
by W. Heffer & Sons Limited
Cambridge, England

Heffer ISBN 0 85270 063 6
Barnes & Noble ISBN 06-495756X

Photographically reprinted in Great Britain
by Lowe & Brydone (Printers) Limited
London, NW10

Contents

CONTENTS

* In the present volume the article by R. G. C. Levens is reprinted from the unaltered version which appeared on pages 357–78 of *Fifty Years (and Twelve) of Classical Scholarship,* published in 1968. The three articles by Eduard Fraenkel are reproduced from Volume II of *Kleine Beiträge zur Klassischen Philologie* (1964).

The pagination of the present volume is given in square brackets

Errata

Contributors

Wendell Clausen, *Professor of Greek and Latin, Harvard University*

Frank Olin Copley, *Professor of Latin, University of Michigan*

John Peterson Elder, *Dean, The Graduate School of Arts and Sciences, Harvard University*

†Eduard Fraenkel, *formerly Corpus Christi Professor of Latin, Oxford University*

Jean Granarolo, *Professeur à la Faculté de lettres, Nice*

R. G. C. Levens, *Fellow of Merton College, Oxford*

Michael C. J. Putnam, *Professor of Classics, Brown University*

Kenneth Quinn, *Professor of Classics, University College, Toronto*

Niall Rudd, *Professor of Latin, Liverpool University*

Acknowledgements

Acknowledgements for permission to use material reproduced in this volume are due to the authors, and as follows:

Article I: Basil Blackwell (*Fifty Years (and Twelve) of Classical Scholarship*)

II: 'Reproduced from *L'Information littéraire* with kind permission of the author and his publishers, Messrs J.-B. Baillière et Fils, 19 rue Hautefeuille, Paris 6e'

III: 'Reprinted by permission of the publishers from George P. Goold, editor, *Harvard Studies in Classical Philology*, Vol. 60, © 1951 by the President and Fellows of Harvard College'

IV: *American Journal of Philology*, © The Johns Hopkins Press, 1949

V: The Editor, *Didaskalos*

VI: The Clarendon Press (*Greece and Rome*)

VII: *Transactions and Proceedings of the American Philological Association*, © The Press of Case Western Reserve University, 1958

VIII: 'Reprinted from *Classical Philology* by permission of The University of Chicago Press. © The University of Chicago Press, 1962'

IX, XIII & XVII: Eduard Fraenkel's articles are reproduced from his *Kleine Beiträge* by permission of Edizioni di Storia e Letteratura, Rome

X: *Transactions and Proceedings of the American Philological Association*, © The Press of Case Western Reserve University, 1959

XI: *American Journal of Philology*, © The Johns Hopkins Press, 1953

XII: *Transactions and Proceedings of the American Philological Association*, © The Press of Case Western Reserve University, 1956

XIV: *American Journal of Philology*, © The Johns Hopkins Press, 1947

XV: 'Reprinted by permission of the publishers from George P. Goold, editor, *Harvard Studies in Classical Philology*, Vol. 65, © 1961 by the President and Fellows of Harvard College'

XVI: The Editor, *Greek, Roman and Byzantine Studies*.

Introduction

This selection begins with a review of the state of Catullan studies in 1954. In it Mr Levens wrote :

> A generation which has elevated Donne to the status of a major poet, which has produced and accepted Dylan Thomas, and has come to judge poetry more by the energy it transmits than by the polish of its surface, is naturally drawn to a poet whose sense of form was the servant of his urge to express emotion. The present age is all the more at home with Catullus because the feelings he expressed were those of an [individualist clinging, in a disintegrating society, to the one standard he could feel was secure, that of personal integrity.]

beautiful

Some might feel already that Dylan Thomas is lasting less well than Catullus. Mr Levens's last sentence, however, has almost a prophetic ring. Catullus' popularity today is even more assured than it was fifteen to twenty years ago. Scarcely an issue appears of any of the major classical periodicals without at least one article on Catullus; new translations come out almost yearly—each more determined, it almost seems, than its predecessor to make Catullus speak with as contemporary a voice as possible.

Mr Levens's sub-chapter stands as it stood in the original edition of *Fifty Years of Classical Scholarship*; it was not revised when the volume was re-issued. On textual matters it remains a full and lucid statement of the position immediately prior to the publication of Sir Roger Mynors's Oxford text in 1958; the extent to which the new text changed matters is well set out by Professor G. P. Goold in his review in *Phoenix* 12 (1958) 93–116. Professor C. J. Fordyce's commentary (from which thirty-two poems are omitted) appeared in 1961; the most important review is that by Eduard Fraenkel in *Gnomon* 34 (1962) 253–63. Kroll's commentary, Havelock's *The Lyric Genius of Catullus*, Wheeler's *Catullus and the Traditions of Ancient Poetry* and Wetmore's *Index Verborum Catullianus* have all been reprinted and are to be found in most university libraries. For fuller bibliographical details, those interested should refer to Professor H. J. Leon's 'A quarter century of Catullan scholarship (1934–59)', in *Classical World* 53 (1959–60) 104–13, 141–8, 173–80 and 281–2; I understand that this bibliography will shortly be brought up to date in the same journal by Professor D. F. S. Thomson.

Professor Granarolo's review of Catullan studies dates from the same period as Mr Levens's. It presents some of the same problems from a quite different point of view, while offering also, in admirably clear summary, a review of some of the chief areas of controversy in Catullan scholarship.

The remainder of the articles in Part I, and all the articles in Part II represent different (and, I think, healthily divergent) critical approaches and procedures. All attempt to deal with the fundamental paradox of literary criticism. The paradox may be stated as follows : if a poem is any one thing, it is a structure of words; yet all good poems (those that have something more substantial and more valuable to offer than surface meaning) exist completely only in particular readings, to which individuals must make their own varying contributions.

paradox of literary criticism

There can be no question, therefore, of a single right reading. It seems to me sensible, none the less, to assume the existence (it is not something that can be pointed to, as the verbal structure can be pointed to) of a central area, within which the poet decides what we are to make of his poem; inside that area we are responding to the poem, outside that area we are pursuing our own private reactions. Consider the analogy of the dramatic script. If a script is any one thing, it is, like a poem, a structure of words. But it is a structure of words that prescribes as well a sequence of dramatic situations. To claim these are not part of the play because they are not written down on paper would be absurd. How the situations are realized on the stage is the business of the producer of the play, who offers his reading of the play to the public. Different producers produce different plays, or rather different interpretations of the same play. They must go beyond what the playwright tells them in as many words. But again there is a central area. There are things that are not expressed in as many words in the verbal structure but which fall inside the central area, and must be treated as part of the play. To miss the dramatist's intentions (as these are implicit in the structure of words) is to get the play wrong; the producer has failed, we might say, to submit intelligently or responsively to the control exercised by the verbal structure.

"central area"

Likewise with a poem, except that with a poem each reader is his own producer. Disagreement—serious disagreement—about the central area means failure, on the poet's part, or on ours. It is naturally a ticklish business to decide the contours of this central area—what I call in my article 'The commentator's task' the *hypothesis* of the poem; the things we have to supply (from the data provided by the poem) to make the poem work. The central area may not be located where we first expect. The poem may not turn out to be about what we assumed it was about; or would prefer it to be about—the poem, in other words, may refuse to satisfy our curiosity, because our curiosity takes us outside the area within which the poet has decided his poem will move.

Though only the structure exists, therefore, it is not absolutely autonomous: it needs a response to come fully into existence. It may also require knowledge on our part, as well as our willingness and our ability to respond. Our response, in other words, is controlled and guided—not only by the verbal structure, but by what the poet feels he can rely on every reader to know. Professor Copley makes this point in his article 'Catullus c. 4: the world of the poem', and I go into the matter more fully in my article 'Practical criticism'. There is a third way in which a poem is not autonomous: adequate understanding of it will depend often on acquaintance with other poems by the same poet; the more a poet's *oeuvre* hangs together, the more the poet's other poems are present in each of them—they represent, if we like to think of it that way, a special instance of the things the poet relies on us to know. Professor Elder's article 'Notes on some conscious and unconscious elements in the poetry of Catullus' and Professor Copley's article 'Emotional conflict and its significance in the Lesbia-poems of Catullus' are two examples of this kind of criticism which have exercised an important (and thoroughly deserved) influence on Catullan criticism during the past two decades.

The articles reprinted in Part II represent good examples of modern criticism of individual poems. (I include Professor Clausen's article under this heading, though it deals with Poem 95 in a wider context.) I have been fortunate in being able to print the best known to me, and I am grateful to the authors for giving their permission to reprint so readily; it is a particular source of gratification that I was able to obtain the consent of Eduard Fraenkel, shortly before his death, to reprinting the whole, virtually, of his recent important work on Catullus. The articles are in no sense the work of a school; nor can they be said to rest upon anything more than a loose tacit agreement about the basic critical issues as I have formulated them in this Introduction. They are 'approaches to Catullus'. In each case they will help the reader, I believe, to understand the poem better—as often, perhaps, by bringing his awareness of the difficulties of interpretation into sharper focus as by resolving them to his permanent satisfaction. They show competent critics engaged in the job of trying to understand a Roman poem precisely and sympathetically—and getting somewhere useful with that rewarding experience.

Toronto, September 1970   K.Q.

PART 1 GENERAL

I

R. G. C. Levens
Catullus

ii. Catullus

BY R. G. C. LEVENS

Catullus, like Lucretius, is a poet more congenial to the taste of the twentieth century than to that of the nineteenth. A generation which has elevated Donne to the status of a major poet, which has produced and accepted Dylan Thomas, and has come to judge poetry more by the energy it transmits than by the polish of its surface, is naturally drawn to a poet whose sense of form was the servant of his urge to express emotion. The present age is all the more at home with Catullus because the feelings he expressed were those of an individualist clinging, in a disintegrating society, to the one standard which he could feel was secure, that of personal integrity.

This new understanding of Catullus must be recognized at the outset of any survey of his place in twentieth-century studies. But it is in no sense the result of scholarship applied to his poems; it is the product of a changed environment, and can be observed even in the reactions of students introduced to him for the first time. It may, indeed, be said that in appreciation of Catullus the scholar has lagged behind the general reader. To read Lucretius at all requires some study; but all that is most vital in Catullus can be read by anyone with a basic knowledge of Latin. So the common reader has been enjoying Catullus behind the scholar's back, while the latter, as he labours to extricate his subject from the rubble of nineteenth-century scholarship, is often too much encumbered for direct apprehension of the poet's mind and quality.

The study of Catullus has, of course, shared in the general release from those procrustean tendencies to which Dr. Bailey has referred in writing of Lucretius.[1] But in the sections which follow it will be apparent that a survey of work published in the last half-century yields only a very limited sense of achievement and progress. Much has been written, and many a skirmish has been fought; but of all the dust raised more seems to have settled than to have been dissipated. Particularly depressing to British scholars is the fact that no full commentary in the English language has been published for over sixty years; it is hoped that the next decade will see this deficiency repaired.

1. *Editions.* It will be convenient to follow the plan adopted for Lucretius and speak first of complete editions with commentaries.[2]

At the beginning of this century three commentaries on Catullus may be said to have held the field. These were the Latin commentary of E. Baehrens (second edition, 1885), R. Ellis, *A Commentary on Catullus* (second edition, 1889), and the French commentary begun by E. Benoist and completed by E. Thomas (1882-90). The last, which was attached to a verse translation by Eugène Rostand,[3] deserves mention as a work of undoubted scholarship,[4] but it is the first two which have continued to bulk large in the minds of scholars, not because they were of superlative merit, but simply because they have yet to be replaced by commentaries on the same ample scale. Both are storehouses of information, and the mutual antipathy of the two editors at least ensures that both sides of a question are generally represented in their second editions. Neither, however, is serviceable to modern scholars except as source-material. Both editors shared the contemporary passion for imaginative conjecture, and both were capable of manipulating the discussion of evidence so as to prepare the ground for emendations which had occurred to them. Baehrens was handicapped by a literal and prosaic mind which led him to insist that a poet should express himself in terms of standard literary usage; consequently much of his space is taken up with the manufacture of difficulties which would trouble no one nowadays, and the tendency of his solutions is towards re-writing Catullus in a manner which, if he had so written, would have been fatal to his survival as a poet. The principal weakness of Ellis' commentary is that he so frequently fails to reach the conclusion indicated by the evidence he presents, or to achieve consistency between the views he expresses on related topics. Nevertheless this remains, after sixty-five years, the only full commentary in English, and is still spoken of with respect by those who have little occasion to examine it closely. There was also an edition by E. T. Merrill[5] (Harvard U.P., 1893, re-issued 1951), which became, and still remains, the standard edition for the use of American students. Allowing for its small scale and for its date, this must be ranked as an excellent piece of work, and it is a pity that there has never been an English edition to make it available for general use in this country.

The first substantial twentieth-century edition was that of G. Friedrich, with German commentary (Leipzig, 1908). This was an eccentric work, inspired by a romantic temperament sharply contrasted with the general tone of German scholarship. Friedrich devoted much space to elaborate reconstructions of the processes of textual corruption, yet printed his text without *apparatus criticus*; he leapt from problem to problem, leaving many intervening lines uncommented, yet found time to speak of the beautiful peasant girl whom he saw on the peninsula of Sirmione, or to pour scorn on the Italians as no match for the Germans at drinking. It follows that his commentary is best used in conjunction with others; but useful it is, not only because he is the first editor to show a proper understanding of the relation of Catullus' language to popular speech, but because he is a great collector of parallel instances, whether of textual corruptions or of grammatical and stylistic usages. Many of these, especially from authors such as Silius Italicus of whom he had special knowledge, are additions to the common stock, and any grammarian studying a Latin usage of which Catullus affords an instance would do well to consult Friedrich, as his commentary may well furnish the *locus classicus* for that usage.

W. Kroll's edition with German commentary, first published in 1923 (Leipzig, Teubner) and reprinted, with a brief appendix of additional notes, in 1929, was intended to replace that of B. Schmidt (1887) as a students' text-book. For this reason, and because of the exigencies of German publishing after the First World War, its scale was severely restricted, and it may reasonably be described as a major edition compressed into a small volume. The introduction is too brief, the *apparatus criticus* inconveniently sparse, and the notes, printed in small type below the text, have a forbiddingly cramped appearance. But they show a remarkable gift for selecting what is most useful and significant from the mass of available data; in particular, Kroll is the first editor to make a proper use of the remains of Hellenistic poetry, which have an important bearing on the study of Catullus. Though somewhat heavy-handed and inclined to labour obvious points, Kroll is a thoroughly objective, level-headed, and efficient commentator, and his edition is by common consent the most reliable for consultation by scholars.

The edition by M. Lenchantin de Gubernatis, with Italian commentary, first appeared in 1928 (Turin, Loescher-Chiantore). A second edition, identical except for addenda to the introduction,* was issued in 1933, and a reprint in 1953 has made it readily available. This edition is similar in scale to that of Kroll, to whom it is clearly indebted, but its introduction is much fuller and its commentary less closely packed. The introduction shows a fine perspective, concentrating on the literary heritage and environment of Catullus, and adding a lucid and well-balanced survey of the textual tradition. The text is, however, printed without *apparatus criticus*. The commentary allows appropriate space for introducing each poem, and blends exposition with illustration in a just economy. Lenchantin was perhaps closer in spirit to his poet than any previous editor, and if only he were more sound on points of language his edition could be warmly recommended.

2. *Translations.* The English prose translation by F. Warre Cornish, first published in 1904 (Cambridge University Press), was chosen for incorporation in the Loeb Classical Library (London, Heinemann, 1912), and is therefore the one most widely used. The editing of the Latin text is well below the standard of this series, but the translation is accurate and, though somewhat dated, seldom objectionable in style. It is not altogether complete, though modified versions of seventeen lampoons which Cornish did not choose to translate were inserted by the general editor, W. H. D. Rouse. It may be regretted that the choice for this series did not rather fall on the excellent translation by C. Stuttaford (London, Bell, 1912); it would have furnished a far better text, and time has dealt more kindly with its idiom.

Verse translations of Catullus are so numerous that it will be possible here to mention only those which are complete or nearly complete. They are also, for the most part, ephemeral; the versions of R. Kennard Davis (London, Bell, 1913) and Sir W. Marris (Oxford, Clarendon Press, 1924), well-thought-of in their day, are by now sadly out of period, and that of J. F. Symons-Jeune (London, Heinemann, 1923), is only slightly less so. By contrast that of Hugh Macnaghten (Cambridge University Press, 1925), despite some inversions which are no longer favoured, still appears remarkably fresh and well turned; his translation of poem 17 is of a noteworthy excellence. The translation by A. S. Way, though more recent (London, Macmillan, 1936) and more complete, is less to be commended than any of these; apart from the archaism of his poetic style, the translator has paid little heed to the form of his originals, and has even added flourishes of his own to their content. The Australian poet and novelist Jack Lindsay has published two complete translations (London, Fanfrolico Press, 1929, and Sylvan Press, 1948), the second vastly superior to the first. His idiom, modern and informal, hardly captures either the tenderness or the elegance of Catullus, but he is robust and ingenious, notably in places where translators usually fear to tread. He understands Catullus well, and his introduction and notes show him to be a scholar. Readers accustomed to modern poetry may well find that this translation brings them nearer to Catullus than any of its predecessors could.

I will not presume to discuss translations into languages other than English, beyond mentioning the vivid and scholarly prose translation by G. Lafaye in the Budé series. French has certain advantages over English as a medium for the translation of Catullus, and this is a version which can be consulted with profit, especially as it is set opposite one of the best available texts (see below, §5). The text of E. d'Arbela (see below, §5) is likewise accompanied by an Italian prose translation.

3. *Biography*. This must be treated under a separate heading because it is the most controversial aspect of Catullian studies.

Apart from numerous references that associate him with Verona, there are only three external data of any significance for the life of Catullus:

(1) Suetonius (*Iul.* 73) says that Caesar, after exacting an apology from him for lampoons directed at himself and Mamurra, invited him to dinner and resumed friendly relations with his father.

(2) Apuleius (*Apol.* 10) says that the real name of his Lesbia was Clodia.

(3) Jerome says that he died in his thirtieth year, placing his birth in 87 B.C. and his death in 57 B.C. (*Chron. a. Abr.*, 1930, 1960).

Oddly enough, the one chronological fact which emerges with

absolute certainty from the internal evidence of the poems is that
their author was still alive in 55 B.C.[7] So Jerome must have been
wrong, and is generally held to have ante-dated both birth and
death by three years.[8] The poems also tell us that Catullus served
in Bithynia under Memmius, and this period of service can be
dated from the spring of 57 B.C. to the spring of 56 B.C.[9] Even this
is no more than a deduction, and has not always been accepted as
fact.[10] But the evidence for it may reasonably be called 'conclusive'. No such term can be applied to the evidence for dating
any other event in the poet's life prior to 55 B.C.

Yet writers on Catullus, in this century as in the last, have seldom hesitated to give confident accounts of his career, tracing the
course of his love-life and assigning particular poems to particular
dates or phases. Such biographies are too numerous to list, as they
occur not merely in books about Catullus and in introductions to
editions or translations, but in literary histories and works of
reference. At first glance most of them appear to tell much the
same story; but differences apparent on a closer inspection betray
the large part played by fancy in this game of reconstruction.
Catullus was rich because he owned a villa near Tibur and someone owed him 100,000 sesterces; or he was poor because his villa
was mortgaged for a small sum and he told a friend that his purse
was full of cobwebs. As a young man at Verona, before he met
Lesbia, he had had lovers of both sexes; or Lesbia was his first
love, but when she proved unfaithful to him he sought consolation
with these others. Such-and-such a poem is early because it
shows that Catullus is not yet fully accepted by Lesbia; or it is
late because it shows that the rift between them has begun.

Such biographies generally accept without demur the hypothesis that the Lesbia of the poems is none other than Clodia the
wife of Metellus Celer, and that some, though not all, of the poems
mentioning a Caelius or a Rufus refer to the orator Marcus
Caelius Rufus. This hypothesis is the more attractive because it
links Catullus with a social circle which is well documented in
other sources, notably Cicero's speech in defence of Caelius.
Thus, at the cost of treating a plausible hypothesis as an established
fact, it becomes possible for the imaginative biographer to set up
a new framework of data for the life of Catullus, with results
which are best demonstrated by illustration:

U

When Catullus brought his letter of introduction all the way up that steep ramp to the conspicuous palace of the proconsul it is not likely that he expected to be invited to call again, much less to find Clodia all graciousness and eager to listen to his embarrassed sentences.
(Tenney Frank, *Catullus and Horace*, Oxford, Blackwell, 1928, p. 13.)

Catullus also met Cicero, as we learn from a letter of thanks which must be discussed later. Indeed he could hardly have escaped the observant eye of the ex-consul whose splendid palace stood opposite the poet's favourite haunt. But Cicero spares Catullus in his vituperations of Clodia. He had a weakness for young literary men.
(*Ibid.*, p. 32.)

In 62 B.C. a new governor, Metellus, arrived in Cisalpine Gaul, accompanied by his wife Clodia. There was a strict ordinance forbidding wives to go abroad with their husbands when these latter held an official position, but Clodia was not a woman to whom rules were of any importance. She came to Verona and met Catullus there; and that meeting was the turning-point in the young poet's life. In the spring of the next year he followed the lady to Rome.
(F. A. Wright, *Three Roman Poets*, London, Routledge, 1938, p. 102.)

In the seventy-seventh poem again, written 58 B.C., Catullus inveighs against a Rufus, who had stolen from him his dearest possession; and it was in that year, after the death of Metellus, as we know from Cicero's speech *Pro Caelio*, that Marcus Caelius Rufus was living with Clodia in her house on the Palatine.
(*Ibid.*, p. 130.)

This last extract well illustrates the vicious circle to which this type of biography is prone. It suggests a significant coincidence between two independent facts: that poem 77 was written in 58 B.C. and that Caelius Rufus was Clodia's lover during the same year. But the first of these 'facts' is a mere inference from the second; apart from the hypothesis that Catullus and Caelius were lovers of the same Clodia there is no basis whatever for dating the poem.

This hypothesis is, however, by no means so firmly established as to be capable of supporting a superstructure of inference. Nineteenth-century scholars, after weighing the evidence for and against, generally decided in its favour. But in this century, though upheld by Pascal[11] and others, it has been hotly assailed, notably by Giri and Rothstein,[12] the latter holding that the Clodia in question was not the second but the third of the sisters of P. Clodius. This hypothesis is certainly no more plausible than the other, but discussion of it has served to expose the conjectural status of the commonly accepted view, and the downright scepticism of Giri, who concluded that Catullus' Clodia belonged to some obscure branch of the *gens*, has likewise helped to induce a more cautious treatment of the matter. Thus Kroll, though he regards the usual hypothesis as highly probable, abstains from building upon it;[13] and Lenchantin de Gubernatis, though he dissents from his fellow-countryman Giri to the extent of thinking that Lesbia must be *one* of the three sisters of P. Clodius, leaves the question wide open. The commentaries of these two scholars are thus free from the dubious inferences which have cumbered earlier editions, and demonstrate that in studying the poetry of Catullus we are at no great disadvantage in knowing as little about his Lesbia as we know about Propertius' Cynthia. Among recent writers (see below, §4) Wheeler in *Catullus and the Traditions of Ancient Poetry* (1934) showed a caution sharply contrasted with the 'sure historical touch' of Tenney Frank,[14] and Havelock in *The Lyric Genius of Catullus* (1939) exposed the conjectural type of biography in a parody less far-fetched than some of its originals. Yet in the *Oxford Classical Dictionary* (1949) we find A. M. Duff repeating the familiar circumstantial account, and as recently as 1952 it has been demonstrated that this is a subject still capable of causing confusion.[15] The whole controversy has been documented up to 1940 by M. Schuster (RE VII A coll. 2358-60); he considers that there are good grounds for accepting the traditional identification, but like Kroll abstains from basing inferences upon it. The same article deals fully and fairly (coll. 2369ff) with minor questions of prosopography in Catullus.

An even broader issue than that of Lesbia was raised by P. Maas in a brisk article published in 1942.[16] Rothstein, having discarded Caelius Rufus and his Clodia, had dated all the shorter poems after Catullus' return from Bithynia in the spring of 56 B.C. Maas went further and placed *all* the extant poems after that date, supposing that the poet's brother died as late as 54 B.C., and that he himself lived a year or two longer. This article was perhaps not intended as more than a protreptic (or anatreptic?) exercise, and it makes use of some flimsy supports,[17] but its destructive value is considerable; it both exposes and illustrates the hazards of 'biographical criticism' where Catullus is concerned.

4. *Literary History and Criticism.* During the last half-century our knowledge both of early Greek lyric poetry and of the Greek poetry of the Alexandrian and Hellenistic ages has been substantially enlarged. Discoveries of new material have focused attention on these fields, with consequential benefit to the study of Latin poets who were strongly influenced by Greek models. In the case of Catullus this benefit first became apparent in 1923 in the edition by W. Kroll (see above, §1), and about the same time Wilamowitz devoted a chapter of his *Hellenistische Dichtung*[18] to a study of the more formal poetry of Catullus in relation to Greek models. This lead was followed by A. L. Wheeler in *Catullus and the Traditions of Ancient Poetry* (Berkeley, U. of California Press, 1934); what was chiefly interesting about this book was that, while demonstrating how closely Catullus in his set pieces followed in the steps of his predecessors, it yet vigorously asserted his independence and originality.

Surprisingly little general criticism of the poetry of Catullus has appeared in book form in this century, compared with the large amount of periodical literature devoted to particular aspects of his work or to particular poems. D. A. Slater's *The Poetry of Catullus* (Manchester, 1912) was only a single lecture, but it contained many shrewd observations and is still worth reading when obtainable. Tenney Frank's *Catullus and Horace* (Oxford, Blackwell, 1928) was directed mainly to placing Catullus in the context of his times, and lavish use of the author's wide knowledge of the first-century background makes it attractive reading; but its historical and critical methods invite considerable reserve (see above, §3). S. Gaetani's *La Poesia di Catullo* (Rome, Formiggini, 1934) is of interest mainly for its study of Catullus in relation to Lucretius, Horace, and Virgil. F. A. Wright's *Three Roman Poets*

13

(London, Routledge, 1938) is not, so far as Catullus is concerned, a work of any durable value. But in 1939 E. A. Havelock's *The Lyric Genius of Catullus* (Oxford, Blackwell) swept like a gust of fresh air through the stuffy corridors of Catullian criticism. Unfortunately its publication coincided with the outbreak of war, and the not very distinguished English 'imitations' of twenty-six lyrics of Catullus, with which the volume opens, may also have served to distract attention from the excellence and importance of the essays which follow; hence, despite two laudatory notices,[19] it does not appear to have received adequate recognition. Havelock's especial contribution lies in viewing Catullus as a whole, not as two or more poets writing in different styles,[20] and in observing the impact of the Transpadane circle of poets on Roman society and literature, and its bearing on those elements in the Italian heritage which cannot be explained in terms of Roman *gravitas*. His essays act as a powerful corrective to the weaknesses of a critical tradition too closely centred on the Augustan age, a tradition which seems at times to be regarding Catullus as a deviationist because he did not model himself on poets who at the time of his death had not begun to write. Such a challenge to familiar views, even if too provocative for general acceptance, at least earns the credit due to those who refresh the mind by suggesting new answers to old questions. Certainly no teacher could wish for a more stimulating book to put into the hands of present-day students, and a revised edition would be most welcome.

H. Bardon in *L'Art de la Composition chez Catulle* (Paris, Belles Lettres, 1943) develops by stylistic analysis a view which supports both Wheeler and Havelock. He sees Catullus as a poet too profoundly Italian to be significantly affected by foreign influences; metrical tests do not show him following formal Alexandrian patterns, and his debt to Callimachus is negligible. Bardon especially notes Catullus' habit of expressing his emotional mood in the opening line of a poem, and returning to it at the end, as evidence that with him passion prevails over form.

The influence of Catullus on English poetry has been the subject of special studies by three American scholars, E. S. Duckett, J. B. Emperor, and J. A. S. McPeek.[21] His influence on later ages in general has been cursorily traced in a small volume by K. P. Harrington.[22] The material assembled by these writers is sufficient to suggest that G. A. Highet in *The Classical Tradition*

(Oxford, Clarendon Press, 1948) might reasonably have allocated more space to Catullus.

5. *MSS. and Text*. Apart from the codex Thuaneus (*T*) containing poem 62 only, all the surviving MSS. of Catullus, some 120 in number,[23] are believed to stem from a codex known to have existed at Verona in the fourteenth century,[24] and generally denoted by the symbol *V*. The only extant MSS. believed to have been copied within the same century are the Oxoniensis (*O*),[25] the Sangermanensis (*G*),[26] and the Romanus (*R*). None of these was known to Lachmann,[27] whose pioneer edition (1829) was founded on two fifteenth-century MSS., the Datanus (*D*) and the Santenianus (*L*). *G* was first brought into the foreground by Schwabe, *O* by Baehrens;[28] the latter, following Lachmann's principle of concentrating on the best MSS. available, based his text exclusively on *OG*, as did Merrill in his edition of 1893 (see above, §1). The reaction against this principle was led by Ellis, who recognized the superiority of *OG* but thought it worth while to cite a great many other MSS., some for no better reason than that their aberrations afforded a basis for conjecture. K. P. Schulze, re-editing Baehrens's text in 1893, claimed that a Venetian MS., which he called *M*,[29] was the parent of most of the *deteriores*, and associated it with *OG* in his *apparatus criticus*; but he made a breach in this otherwise closed system by giving credit to the variants of Lachmann's *D*. This MS., though copied as late as A.D. 1463, only a few years before the first printed edition,[30] is distinguished by archaic orthography often coinciding with that of *O*, and contains many readings which differ sharply from those of *OG*. Some of these are obvious interpolations, but others have been regarded by many scholars as beyond the inventive powers of fifteenth-century humanists; yet it is difficult to envisage a process by which one late MS. could, in a period of active copying and cross-checking,[31] become the sole repository of an independent tradition. Difference of opinion concerning the value of *D* may be said to constitute the principal line of division between two schools of twentieth-century criticism.

It was not till 1896 that *R* was discovered by the American scholar W. G. Hale.[32] It proved to be so closely akin to *G* that it added little to our knowledge of the tradition, since almost all its readings were duplicated either in *G* or its correcting hand or in *M*, which Hale, much to Schulze's disgust, declared to be a direct

15

copy of *R*. Consequently the interest aroused by its discovery soon gave place to disappointment and, in certain quarters, to a quite irrational hostility provoked by Hale's habit of announcing the results of his research in advance and then failing to produce them. After promising a full collation and a fascimile, Hale published nothing except a series of articles spread over twenty-seven years,[33] during which he and his research assistants collated 115 MSS. with a view to proving that *R* was an elder brother of *G* and the parent of all the *deteriores*. Had this been established, the textual criticism of Catullus would at least have been greatly simplified, even if no substantial improvement of the text had resulted. As it was, the only effect was to divert European palaeographers to other fields, and this frustrating episode helps to explain why most twentieth-century editions are characterized by fog-bound ambivalence and by a tendency to rest content with citations available in printed sources.

The only systematic attempt at rationalization of the MS. tradition since the discovery of *R* has been that of A. Morgenthaler in his dissertation *De Catulli Codicibus* (Strasbourg, 1909). Morgenthaler's conclusion was that *O* and *G* were transcribed from separate copies of *V*, and that *G* had a brother from which three copies were made, *R*, *M*, and a third which became the parent of the *deteriores*.[34] He thus provided a by-pass route which was a boon to the partisans of *D*, though he himself considered this MS. worthless. Morgenthaler, who was twenty-three years of age when he completed his dissertation, relied on the published facsimiles of *G* and *M*[35] and on photographs of *R*, which at that date are unlikely to have enabled a beginner to distinguish accurately between original readings and corrections *in rasura*; and not being well versed in the habits of the fifteenth century he made too little allowance for the likelihood of crossing between families and sub-families. Nor was he free of the thesis-writer's tendency to pick his objective in advance and brush aside evidence pointing elsewhere. Nevertheless his analysis has had great influence, if only because it is so conveniently simple; like Hale's hypothesis, it has been neither verified nor superseded.

If little progress towards a reconstruction of the archetype can be reported, at least much has been gained by a recoil from the *prurigo coniciendi* which vitiated nineteenth-century criticism. Recognition that Augustan canons of language and metre do not apply to Catullus has led to the restoration of MS. readings in many passages formerly molested by editors. Here Schulze set a fine example, and the prevailing twentieth-century tendency has been to resort to emendation only in desperate cases, and even then to prefer conjectures which have stood the test of time. This development can be simply illustrated by reference to hiatus, of which the MSS. exhibit eleven clear instances,[36] excluding those following *o* or *io*, or where there is correption of a long syllable. Not one of these instances survived the attentions of such scholars as Lachmann, Haupt, and Baehrens, to whom hiatus was 'intolerable' or 'inadmissible'. Schulze restored the received text in all eleven places, while Ellis and Merrill accepted it in only three; only one subsequent editor has departed from the MS. reading in as many as three of these passages.

It remains to show briefly how the more important twentieth-century texts[37] compare with one another in regard to the matters discussed above.

To mention Robinson Ellis among editors of this century seems anachronistic, since he first edited Catullus in 1867, but his volume in the Oxford Classical Text series did not appear till 1904, and is still current. Ellis had himself twice collated *R*,[38] and rated it highly, though out of deference to Hale he cited only a limited number of readings from it; some of these were later repudiated by Hale.[39] Apart from this his new edition showed no great advance on that of 1878, and was retrograde compared with such nineteenth-century recensions as those of Riese, Schulze, and Merrill. Many unwarrantable emendations were printed in the text, and still more crowded the critical apparatus, in which as many as twenty-three MSS. were cited, some of them for reasons which did little credit to the editor's judgment.[40]

It will be convenient, and almost in accordance with chronological sequence, to take next a group of editors who reverted to Lachmann's principle. Friedrich (see above, §1) was an unorthodox member of this group: he based his text and critical observations principally on *OG*, but opened the door to *D* alone among the later MSS.;[41] he had inspected *R*, but dismissed it as worthless. Kroll (see above, §1) was a firmer adherent of Lachmann and Baehrens, and his skeleton *apparatus criticus* cited no MS. other than *OG* (and, for poem 62, *T*) except by a general symbol denoting *deteriores*. His text shows every mark of caution, with free use of the |obelus,| yet contains several dubious emendations. In the same year (1923) Merrill edited a Teubner text based on *OGR*. Since he had access to Hale's collation, this should have been the edition to give a true conspectus of the three oldest complete MSS.; but the opportunity was sadly missed. The house of Teubner was working under conditions of austerity, and Merrill's *apparatus criticus* was too sparse to give a clear picture,[42] or even to add greatly to our knowledge of *R*. His text, incorporating numerous conjectures derived from Ellis, was quite out of line with modern trends.[43]

The editors of the remaining group were all to some degree influenced by Morgenthaler. G. Lafaye prepared for the Budé series (Paris, Belles Lettres, 1922) a soundly conservative text, with an *apparatus criticus* in which *OGMD* predominated but sundry other MSS. were cited from time to time, the editor having no very firm view concerning the *deteriores*. *R* was cited only where its readings were already on record, but this is equally true of later editions. The clarity of the *apparatus criticus*, from which rejected emendations are excluded, combines with the soundness of the text and the excellence of the translation (see above, §2) to make this a singularly useful volume. Lenchantin de Gubernatis (see above, §1) showed good judgment in the constitution of his text, but printed it without *apparatus criticus*. Doubtful readings are discussed in his commentary, but his principal contribution to textual criticism is the second section of his introduction. This is far and away the most lucidly condensed account of the MS. tradition yet written, but it amounts to little more[44] than an abstract of Morgenthaler's thesis, from which the supporting evidence appears to be taken on trust.[45] A similar account, less skilfully presented and somewhat inaccurately printed, forms the Prolegomena to an edition by E. d'Arbela (Milan, Istituto Editoriale Italiano, 1947), and is worth mentioning if only because it is in Latin, whereas Lenchantin's is in Italian. This edition resembles that of Ellis more than any other, but is a great improvement on it, having a less interpolated text and a more concise critical apparatus; d'Arbela cites even more MSS. than Ellis did, but saves space by using symbols to denote a consensus, and records the better-known conjectures merely, as he says, to demonstrate the industry of critics. The most recent text is that of Mauriz Schuster, issued in the Teubner series in 1949 to replace that of Merrill. This is a fine specimen of modern editing in that it separates *testimonia* from MS. readings, and by a neat system of abbreviation gives a wide range of bibliographical reference with the minimum expenditure of space. As it includes, besides a documented *Index nominum,* an *Index metricus* and an *Index verborum et locutionum,* it serves many of the purposes for which recourse to a commentary is normally required. From a critical standpoint it is less satisfying. An uneasily written preface leaves no clear impression except that Schuster has contributed no fresh work on the problems confronting an editor. Having been led to the view that other MSS. besides *OG* may sometimes be of assistance in recovering the reading of *V,* he might be commended for his plan of singling out *RMD* and citing them only when the reading is in doubt; but this plan is not consistently followed in the *apparatus criticus.*[46] In constituting his text Schuster is generally so conservative that when he does discard a defensible MS. reading it comes as a shock;[47] it is in poem 66 that his judgment is most seriously at fault. Had Schuster's edition come up to expectations, little need have been said of the text prepared by E. Cazzaniga and revised by L. Castiglioni for the Paravia series (Turin, 1945), since its editor did not attempt to grapple with the problems discussed above. As it is, this unpretentious work is not merely the most inoffensive, but for general purposes the most serviceable, of modern texts. Cazzaniga was consistently level-headed in his choice of readings, and his *apparatus criticus,* firmly based on *OG* with selective reference to *R* (which he inspected in facsimile), is fully adequate for readers who are not concerned with the difference between one fifteenth-century MS. and another; *testimonia* are printed separately, and appendices assemble useful data on metre, language, and orthography.

It is clear that what has chiefly been lacking in recent editions of Catullus, and what must chiefly be looked for from future editors, is independence of judgment based on first-hand study of the MSS.;[48] in particular, the status of *R* needs clarifying by a full collation employing expert diagnosis to identify the readings of its first hand.[49] For the later MSS. the existing American collations might reasonably suffice, especially as most of them were made by B. L. Ullman,[50] whose name now stands high among palaeographers and textual critics; examination of these collations, if only by a post-graduate student, might at least have the effect

19

of consigning all but a few of the fifteenth-century MSS. to oblivion, which was precisely the intention with which they were collated.

Finally, separate mention must be made of the *Coma Berenices*, since it is the only poem of Catullus directly affected by recent discoveries.[51] Its setting belongs to a period of history about which much has been learnt from papyri, and the life-story of Ptolemy III and Berenice II is now much better documented than it was when Ellis wrote his commentary. Further, two papyri[52] containing substantial portions of the Πλόκαμος of Callimachus have shed new light on the text of Catullus' translation. The first of these, published by G. Vitelli in 1929, corresponded to ll. 44-64 of Catullus 66, and its appearance occasioned a fresh outbreak of the *prurigo coniciendi* which extended even beyond the passage directly concerned.[53] Most of the resulting conjectures, and many others of earlier date, were made to look very foolish when within twenty years a second papyrus came to light, over-lapping with the first and corresponding to ll. 43-55, 65-78, 89-94, with marginal scholia which helped to supplement the defective text. It was reconstructed by E. Lobel, who has since edited it, but R. Pfeiffer was allowed to publish it in the first volume of his edition of Callimachus (Oxford, Clarendon Press, 1949), and rendered a great service to students of Catullus by printing oppo-site the Greek fragments (pp. 112-23) a complete text of the Latin translation with its own *apparatus criticus*, and a commentary which takes account of both versions. The general impression resulting from the juxtaposition of these two texts is that Catullus was a less free translator than was formerly believed,[54] closely following the structure and rhythm of his original even where he was unable to reproduce its elaborate conceits. His text was affected in several interesting ways: the two papyri were found to have different readings where the Catullus MSS. exhibit a fusion of these two readings;[55] a winged horse which editors had long striven to expel with a pitchfork was re-installed by the second papyrus;[56] and a couplet which had been exposed to all manner of ingenious reconstructions was found to need a change of only one letter, and that in a word which had never been suspected.[57] This last discovery pointed at least two morals: that corruption does not necessarily reside where the difficulty appears greatest, and that conjectures requiring only a slight adjustment are more likely to be right than those which involve re-writing a whole passage.

6. *Language, Metre, and Style.* As far as concerns these branches of criticism, the early decades of this century are notable only for the process of liberation to which Dr. Bailey has referred in the corresponding section of his chapter on Lucretius.[58] On the completion of this process the scholar and critic no doubt hoped to enjoy the liberated territory on his own terms. But such is not the way of this fast-moving century, and infiltration by the agents of two upstart neighbours, psychology and semantics, has forced him to acquire new techniques and to wrestle with a new critical language which is still in its formative stage. Consequently work published in the 'thirties and 'forties[59] on the language, metre, and style of Catullus is best regarded as transitional, to be superseded when the critical revolution enters upon a more stable phase.

Much of the recent literature consists of articles devoted to the analysis of particular poems.[60] But there have been some more substantial contributions, the best of them forming an intelligible link between the analytical criticism which infers a poet's state of mind from his vowel-patterns and the more general type of modern criticism which is seen at its best in E. A. Havelock's book described in §4 above. The thesis of H. Bardon, mentioned in the same section, is a link of this type.

What is perhaps one of the most enlightening works in the new critical tradition is also one of the earliest, J. van Gelder's *De Woordherhaling bij Catullus* (The Hague, 1933). The author, a disciple on the one hand of de Saussure, on the other of Husserl, here isolates a phenomenon which must be obvious to every reader of Catullus (word-repetition), and after close analysis defines it not as some mechanical neoteric device but as denoting 'linguistic exuberance, created on the basis of the obsessed oscillation of the attention between some conceptions or experiences'. Though the book is written in Dutch, and even the English summary at the end is, as this excerpt shows, rather oddly expressed, it well repays study as illustrating, on a conveniently narrow front, the legitimate uses of a critical method which has since increasingly come to the fore.

A more forbidding side of this method is seen in Ilse Schnelle's *Untersuchungen zu Catulls dichterischer Form* (Philologus Suppl. 25,

1933), a work justly criticized by an Italian scholar for its *eccessiva cerebralità*. Here vowel-patterns and psychology join hands in the most suspect manner, and the authoress herself is in danger of being overwhelmed by her own jargon. It is evident, however, from the minor literature of subsequent years that this work has had considerable influence.

A reminder that the poet's choice of vowels and of words is not entirely a matter of psychology was administered by T. Cutt in a matter-of-fact thesis entitled *Meter and Diction in Catullus' Hendecasyllabics* (University of Chicago Libraries, 1936). Laborious statistics are here used to show how the metre forces on the poet a preference for certain types of word and certain inflexions.

An Italian scholar, A. Ronconi, who uses the modern approach with discretion, has usefully covered several aspects of Catullus' language and style in a series of articles published in 1938-40.[61]

The relation of Catullus' metre and diction to those of his Latin predecessors has received very scanty treatment. R. Avallone's *Catullo e i suoi Modelli Romani* (Salerno, 1944) is limited to Ennius and Plautus, and what useful data it contains are diluted and obscured by the inclusion of such coincidences as no two writers in the same language could well avoid. This work needs to be done again, and continued through the rest of Republican poetry.

M. N. Wetmore's *Index Verborum Catullianus* (Yale University Press, 1912) is a useful instrument for workers in this field.

---

[1] See above, p. 280.

[2] The scope of this chapter is taken to exclude selections edited for use in schools, and commentaries appended to translations for the enlightenment of the general reader, such as the second volume of V. Errante's *La Poesia di Catullo* (Milan, Hoepli, 1945), which is frankly derivative and popular. The edition by C. Stuttaford (London, Bell, 1909) was very slight and has long been out of print.

[3] Not to be confused with the dramatist Edmond Rostand.

[4] French reviewers still complain (RPh 1950, 223, REL 1950, 384) if this commentary is neglected, but it is none too easily come by; there is not even a complete copy in the Bodleian Library.

[5] Not to be confused with W. A. Merrill, the editor of Lucretius.

[6] These addenda were occasioned mainly by the Vitelli papyrus of Callimachus, which outdated the commentary on poem 66. Since the addenda have themselves been outdated by the discovery of a new papyrus and by Pfeiffer's *Callimachus*, it is a pity that the edition was not revised before reprinting in 1953. See §5, *MSS. and Text*, ad fin.

[7] Catul. 55.6, 113.2; cf. also allusions to Britain at 11.12, 29 passim, 45.22.

[8] The notion, said to have been first advanced by Gibbon at the age of nineteen, that C. must have been alive in 47 B.C. because he refers to Vatinius as swearing by his consulship (52.3) has long since been exploded; Cicero made a similar jest at V.'s expense (*in Vat.* 11), alleging that as early as 62 B.C. he was talking about his *second* consulship; and anyway there were no curule aediles in 47 B.C. (52.3, cf. Dio. xlii. 20.4,

27.2, 55.4). Yet it was recently revived, in complete innocence of its previous history, by two Belgian scholars (P. Gilbert and M. Renard in AC 1942, 93-6).

[9] Catul. 10 and 28. Memmius was praetor in 58 B.C., and is likely to have governed a province the following year, while L. Calpurnius Piso Caesoninus, cos. 58, was governing Macedonia (a chilly province, cf. 28.5).

[10] See Ellis, *A Commentary on Catullus*, pp. lvff.

[11] C. Pascal, *Poeti e Personaggi Catulliani*, Catania, 1916.

[12] G. Giri, *Riv. Indo-greco-ital.* 1922, 161ff, *Athenaeum* 1928, 183ff, 215ff; M. Rothstein, *Philologus* 1923, 1-34, cf. 1926, 472f.

[13] Surprisingly, Kroll (p. 253) refuses to identify the Lesbius of Catul. 79 with P. Clodius, though this is usually the trump card of those who wish to identify Lesbia with a sister of this Clodius.

[14] K. P. Harrington in AJPh 1935, 182 points this contrast, evidently intending it to the disadvantage of Wheeler.

[15] Cicero, *pro Caelio*, ed.[2] R. G. Austin (Oxford, Clarendon Press, 1952), App. III, pp. 148ff. Austin appears to regard the identification of Lesbia with the Clodia of the speech as established fact, that of the Rufus of the poems with Caelius Rufus as conjecture. But the first identification can hardly stand unless supported by the second; cf. n13 above. Possibly Austin shared the delusion of H. J. Rose (*Handbook of Latin Literature*, p. 140, n. 64) that Apuleius specified the Clodia who was concealed by the name Lesbia.

[16] CQ 1942, 79-82.

[17] Maas finds it easier to believe that C. made a second journey to Asia Minor than that Veranius and Fabullus twice went on foreign service together; and he represents C. as saying, in effect (68.15ff): 'I used to compose love poetry as a lad, but that was over ten years ago, and since my brother's recent death I have written nothing'; yet Maas attributes most of the extant poems to the two years preceding the brother's death. For a criticism of Maas by a supporter of the traditional chronology see R. J. M. Lindsay in CPh 1948, 42-4.

[18] U. v. Wilamowitz-Moellendorff, *Hellenistische Dichtung in der Zeit des Kallimachos* (Berlin, Weidmannsche Buchhandlung, 1924), vol. II, pp. 277-310.

[19] By M. B. Ogle (CPh 1940, 440-2); and by C. J. Fordyce (CR 1941, 36-7), who described it as 'a book of extraordinary freshness and vitality' and 'one of the most interesting and stimulating studies in Latin literature which have appeared in this country for a long time'.

[20] For a further study along similar lines see J. P. Elder in HSPh 1951, 101-36.

[21] E. S. Duckett, *Catullus in English Poetry* (Northampton, Mass., Smith College Classical Studies No. 6, 1925); J. B. Emperor, *The Catullian Influence in English Lyric Poetry ca. 1600-1650* (New York, Columbia U.P., 1928); J. A. S. McPeek, *Catullus in Strange and Distant Britain* (Harvard U.P., 1939).

[22] *Catullus and his Influence* (London, Harrap, 1923).

[23] See the list given by W. G. Hale, CPh 1908, 236ff.

[24] See R. Ellis, *Catullus in the Fourteenth Century* (Oxford U.P., 1905); W. G. Hale, 'Benzo of Alexandria and Catullus', CPh 1910, 56-65; B. L. Ullman, 'Hieremias de Montagnone and his citations from Catullus', CPh 1910, 66-82.

[25] *O* is now generally held to be older than *G*. It used to be vaguely assigned to the latter end of the century; Hale at one time thought it might be up to fifty years earlier (CR 1906, 164), but withdrew this estimate on the ground that the ornamentation of the first initial could not be much earlier than A.D. 1400 (CPh 1908, 243). But the illumination may be of later date than the MS.

[26] An adscript at the end of this MS. gives A.D. 1375 as the date of copying; but an 'etc.' at the end of this adscript has led some scholars to believe that the scribe of *G* copied out part of a longer adscript which he found in his exemplar, and that it was the latter which was transcribed in 1375. See E. Châtelain, *Paléographie des Classiques Latins*, vol. I (1884-92), p. 4, and Hale in CR 1906, 162, where Lindsay is said to support this view.

[27] Attention had been called to *O* in 1822 by A. J. Valpy in an appendix to his London edition of Doering's *Catullus* (vol. II, p. 837), but this can hardly have come to Lachmann's notice. *G* was first mentioned by Sillig a year after the publication of Lachmann's edition.

[28] Ellis made use of it in his edition of 1867, but without realizing its importance.

[29] *Ven.* in the *app. crit.* of Ellis's O.C.T.

[30] The earliest dated edition is that of 1472, but there is an undated one which may be earlier; see Ellis, *Catulli Veronensis Liber* (Oxford, 1878[2]), p. lix.

[31] As early as A.D. 1375 the scribe of *G* (or of its parent MS., see n26 above) had apologized for being unable to check his copy against a second exemplar, implying that this was already customary.

[32] It had been concealed in the Vatican Library by faulty cataloguing.

[33] CR 1896, 314; TAPhA 1897, liii-v; CR 1898 447-9; H. 1899 133-4; CR 1906, 160-4; CPh 1908, 233-56; TAPhA 1922, 103-12. See also B. L. Ullman in AJPh 1917, 98-9. One of Hale's most significant claims was that the second hand in *R* was that of Coluccio Salutati, whose ownership of the MS. was attested by a legend on its first page. This is confirmed, in a private letter, by Professor Ullman, who has examined over 100 MSS. owned by Coluccio.

[34] His *stemma codicum* is reproduced by M. Schuster on p. vii of his Teubner text and in RE VII A col. 2400.

[35] *G* was published in facsimile by E. Châtelain (Paris, 1890), *M* by C. Nigra (Venice, 1893).

[36] 11.11; 38.2; 66.11; 66.48; 67.44; 68.158; 76.10; 97.2; 99.8; 107.1; 114.6.

[37] I have not had access to the editions of F. Ramorino (Florence, 1912), E. Stampini (Turin 1921), on which see Hale, TAPhA 1922, 103ff, W. B. MacDaniel (New York, 1931), and G. Bonazzi (Rome, 1936). Nor have I thought it necessary to mention texts devoid of both *apparatus criticus* and commentary. For the Loeb text see §2, *Translations*.

[38] In 1897 and again in 1901. He noted the variants of *R* in his copy of Schulze's text, which is now in my possession.

[39] CR 1906, 160. Five readings attributed to *R* by Ellis were described by Hale as corrections made a century after the MS. was copied. Hale may have been over-anxious to protect his beloved *R* from the charge of harbouring 'good' (i.e. deviationist) readings; but Ellis's skill in distinguishing between original and correcting hands has more than once been called in question (see below, n48).

[40] E.g. at 38.4, where a line longer than its neighbours was split in two by one late copyist, Ellis comments: 'quo indicio mancum declaratur poema'. At 66.15-16 he claims support for a conjecture not even from an aberrant MS. of Catullus, but from an aberrant MS. of a work written A.D. 1329 by Hieremias de Montagnone, in which Catullus is quoted.

[41] Friedrich might perhaps have pleaded, as Ellis had done, that he valued *D* out of respect for Lachmann, since it was one of the latter's two MSS. But A. E. Housman (CR 1905, 21-3) had made short work of this plea: 'Parisians ate rats in the siege, when they had nothing better to eat: must admirers of Parisian cookery eat rats for ever?'

[42] The best source of information about *O* and *G* is still the critical appendix to Merrill's edition of 1893 (Harvard U.P., re-issued 1951), which gives a full and accurate account of the readings of these MSS., marginal notations, ligatures and all.

[43] See A. E. Housman in CR 1924, 25-7.

[44] Lenchantin differs from Morgenthaler in suggesting that the common ancestor of *O* and *G* must ante-date *T*, because *T* and *O* both omit 62.43-4. But since ll. 42 and 44 both end with the words *optavere puellae*, nothing would be easier than for ll. 43-4 to be omitted independently by copyists several centuries apart.

[45] Lenchantin's impressive array of citations is wholly derived from Morgenthaler. On p. xlviii, n2, he says that *M* has *multos* for *multis* at 64.263, where in fact the MSS. generally, including *M*, have *multi* for *multis*. This error is traceable to the following consecutive entries in Morgenthaler, p. 51: '64, 262 *aere*] M *era*; 66, 9 *multis*] M *multos*'.

[46] Schuster, in his list of sigla, commits himself to the view that the reading of *V* is reconstituted by the consensus of *OG*. If this is so, it should follow that where such consensus exists there is no occasion to cite the other MSS.; yet he frequently does so, thus giving the false impression that he considers them independent of *V*. Where the *V* reading is not established by *OG*, it would be logical to cite the readings of all the other three, but this is seldom done. Consequently the *app. crit.* affords no basis for assessing the characteristics and value of *RMD*. Is this merely because full collations are not available in print?

[47] It is surprising to find him reviving Haupt's oxymoronic suggestion *horribile aequor* at 11.11 (where the English Channel is sufficiently described by the graphic hiatus), and printing *ebria acina* at 27.4 on the strength of a text of Gellius incorporating five conjectures by Haupt, four of which are unwarrantable; see Hosius' *app. crit.* to Gellius VI. 20. 6 (Teubner 1903, vol. I, p. 279), and Ellis, *Catulli Veronensis Liber* (1878²), pp. 316-19.

[48] The only recent instance of close study of a Catullus MS., under the improved conditions which palaeographers now enjoy, is the editing by G. B. Pighi (Bologna, Zanichelli, 1950) of the codex Bononiensis (*B*), written in 1412, collated by Ellis, and also cited by Lafaye and d'Arbela. It is disconcerting to note how many of the 'good' readings ascribed to this MS. by Ellis have been found by Pighi to be corrections in a late hand. See his article 'Codex Catulli Bononiensis 2621 cum apparatu Ellisiano minore collatus', RhM 1950, 24-6. This, taken in conjunction with Hale's obiter dicta (see above, n39), suggests that recent editors have been working on data which are overdue for verification.

[49] Another MS. which might well repay careful examination is Parisinus 7989, famed as the sole source of the *Cena Trimalchionis*; though comparatively early (A.D. 1423), it has been strangely neglected since Rossbach's edition of 1860. Hale (TAPhA 1922, 103ff) hinted that it was of greater value than others of which much had been made.

[50] Ullman wrote a doctoral thesis on *The Identification of the MSS. of Catullus cited in Statius' Edition of 1566* (Chicago U.P., 1908). For his later work as a research assistant of Hale see AJPh 1917, 98-9 and CPh 1929, 294-7, where he wrote that he had collated a hundred MSS. of Catullus and that the collations from Hale's collection had passed into his possession.

[51] It would be a pity, however, to ignore the only Soviet contribution to Catullian studies which has come to my notice. This was the publication by A. I. Malein and A. A. Trukhanov (*Comptes Rendus de l'Académie des Sciences de l'USSR*, 1928, 293-7) of a 'sixth-century palimpsest' containing three epigrams of Catullus numbered CIV, CV, CVI, written in uncials and overlaid by a German lyric in a fifteenth-century script. O. A. Dobiash-Rozhdestvenskaya promptly denounced it on palaeographical grounds (*ibid.*, 1929, 59-61), even though it had not struck her as odd that the numeration coincided with that first occurring in printed editions well after 1600 and allowing for three Priapea (nos. 18-20 in old editions) which do not occur in any MS. This was pointed out by E. H. Minns and E. Harrison (CR 1929, 123-4) and by B. L. Ullman (CPh 1929, 294-7); the latter went to the trouble of identifying the text as that printed opposite a German translation in Heyse's *Lyra* (1855). The good faith of the Russian scholars was not in question; but it was evident that the former owner of the palimpsest, the late Fedor Plushkin of Pskov, had been hoaxed by an enterprising German.

[52] *PSI* ix (1929), No. 1092, ed. G. Vitelli; *POxy* xx (1953), No. 2258, ed. E. Lobel.

[53] In these circumstances Lenchantin (in the 1933 additions to his introduction), Cazzaniga, and d'Arbela kept their heads well enough, but Schuster, elsewhere by no means partial to flights of fancy, was betrayed into printing several conjectures of prodigious demerit; for examples see below, nn 56 and 57.

[54] The second papyrus, as reconstructed by E. Lobel, indicates that there was nothing in the Greek to correspond to ll. 79-88 of Catullus; and there are traces of an additional couplet at the end. But Pfeiffer thinks it more likely that the papyrus represents an early version of the poem, later superseded by the version which Catullus translated, than that Catullus departed so far from his original.

[55] Corresponding to 66.54, where *OG* have *elocridicos*, *PSI* 1092 has λοκρικος, *POxy* 2258 λοκ[ρ]ιδος. This is hard on Kroll, whose only change in the text of his second edition (1929) was from *Locridos* to *Locricos* on the evidence of the former papyrus.

[56] In the same line, for *OG alis equos*, generally read as *ales equus*, many scholars including Housman had favoured Achilles Statius' *alisequus*; and Schuster had printed Bickel's outrageous suggestion *alitebos* (supposed to represent *halitibus*). But *POxy* 2258 establishes ἱππος.

[57] 66.77-8, *quicum ego, dum virgo quondam fuit omnibus expers | unguentis, una milia multa bibi.* The end of the hexameter had been much assailed, and Schuster printed . . .

Hymenis expers, | *unguenti cuatum* (i.e. *cyathorum*) . . . But when the new papyrus showed πολλά πέπωκα | λιτά, Lobel was quick to see that *milia* was a corruption of *vilia*.

⁵⁸ Above, p. 280. See also the remarks on hiatus in §5 of the present chapter (p. 296).

⁵⁹ For bibliography up to the late 'thirties see M. Schuster's sections on 'Sprache' and 'Versmasse und Verstechnik' in RE VII A (1948), coll. 2383-98.

⁶⁰ See, for a good example, J. P. Elder, 'Catullus' *Attis*', AJPh 1947, 394-403.

⁶¹ 'Stile e Lingua di Catullo', A & R 1938, 139-56 (see also A & R 1940, 141-58); 'Alliterazione e Stile in Catullo', *Studi Urbinati* 1939, 1-77; 'Quae Catullus ex graeco ascita usurpaverit', AIV 1939/40 717-55.

II

Jean Granarolo

Où en sont nos connaissances sur Catulle?

Où en sont nos connaissances sur Catulle?

Devant la multiplication des études catulliennes les plus diverses au cours du demi-siècle écoulé, quelle eût été, par exemple, la réaction d'un Max Bonnet qui, en 1890, se plaignait déjà de voir le poète de Vérone « inondé de dissertations biographiques, littéraires, grammaticales », et assurait qu'il était devenu « difficile, en parlant de Catulle, d'être original sans tomber dans le paradoxe ou la subtilité »?... Si, en 1903, dans le préambule de sa thèse sur les archaïsmes et les hellénismes de Catulle, A. Dubois pouvait évaluer le volume de la littérature catullienne à quarante fois environ celui du recueil des *carmina*, l'on serait sans doute modeste en l'estimant aujourd'hui quatre cents fois supérieur ! Il n'est pour s'en convaincre qu'à compléter, par exemple, les indications bibliographiques, déjà abondantes, que la recension de N.I. Herescu a arrêtées en 1940 (1), par toutes les références que fournissent E. Bignone (2) ou L. Ferrero (3).

Fait curieux, nos compatriotes sont plutôt rares dans cette masse imposante d'érudits qui ont attaché leurs noms à la critique catullienne de notre siècle, et, depuis la disparition de Lafaye en 1927, c'est tout au plus si l'on peut citer chez nous la traduction de M. Rat (Garnier, 1932), le solide opuscule de H. Bardon, *L'art de la composition chez Catulle* (Les Belles Lettres, 1943), la belle étude (à laquelle vient encore de rendre hommage L.Ferrero, cit., p. 369) de Mlle A.-M. Guillemin sur le poème LXIII (Attis) dans la *Revue des études latines*, tome XXVII, 1949, et, du même auteur, un article sur « Catulle et les jeunes gens » (*Humanités*, novembre 1949) (4); enfin (*Lettres d'humanité*, 1952, pp. 22-54) une étude attachante et personnelle de Léon Catin, « Le roman de Catulle ». Max Bonnet n'aurait-il donc découragé que les chercheurs français? En Allemagne, Belgique, Grande-Bretagne, Hollande, Italie, Scandinavie et aux États-Unis, l'on semble convaincu que le XIXᵉ siècle n'a pas mis un point final aux recherches sur Catulle et son œuvre. L'érudition italienne se distingue tout particulièrement par une ferveur renouvelée dans la restitution d'un Catulle toujours plus vivant, bien qu'on ait pu lui reprocher quelquefois une certaine tendance à moderniser un peu trop la psychologie du poète, ou à juger tout ce qu'il a écrit trop irréprochable !

Cet article ne saurait avoir la prétention de dresser un bilan complet des solutions proposées à tous les problèmes que soulèvent à la fois la personnalité de Catulle et les divers aspects de son œuvre. Son seul but est d'attirer l'attention sur quelques notables changements d'orientation de la critique savante. Nous croyons toujours valable, au demeurant, la remarque de W. Kroll dans l'avant-propos de son édition commentée du *Catulli Veronensis Liber* (1923) :

« Il est impossible d'éclaircir complètement les circonstances qui ont inspiré tous les poèmes du recueil, ainsi que toutes les personnalités, comme s'en targue je ne sais quelle « théologie » catullienne ! Si l'occasion précise de tel ou tel poème demeure souvent tout à fait obscure, c'est tout simplement que Catulle a maintes fois su tirer d'une situation déterminée un poème pour lui-même, et non pour le lecteur. »

Suivant une évolution qui n'est point le fait exclusif des études catulliennes, les préoccupations des éditeurs et commentateurs, après être restées longtemps d'ordre surtout externe et historique (chronologie, prosopographie, etc.), se tournent aujourd'hui plutôt vers la personnalité du poète et ce qui constitue l'originalité de son génie poétique. Sans, pour autant, se désintéresser des influences que ses prédécesseurs grecs et romains, ses amis et émules contemporains ont certainement exercées sur la genèse et le détail de ses *carmina*, les catulliens actuels poussent au premier plan le témoignage de l'expérience propre de Catulle, et ils se montrent très attentifs à tout un faisceau de concordances, d'autant plus probantes peut-être qu'elles ne semblent pas

---

(1) *Bibliographie de la littérature latine* (Les Belles Lettres, 1943), p. 45 sq.

(2) *Storia della Letteratura Latina*, fin tome II (Sansoni, Florence, 1945).

(3) *Interpretazione di Catullo* (Rosenberg et Sellier, 1955), p. 425-454.

(4) Ajoutons un intéressant chapitre de J. Cousin sur l'absence de tout messianisme chez Catulle (*Études sur la poésie latine*, Boivin, 1945, p. 54-63), et, dans la *Revue des Études Latines* de 1945, p. 92 sq., une étude pénétrante de R. Waltz sur le carmen LXIV.

56

toujours avoir été préméditées, entre des mouvements, des formules, des intonations, appartenant, dans son recueil, à des contextes assez dissemblables de prime abord.

Encore cette méthode présuppose-t-elle la restauration d'un texte aussi proche que possible de la rédaction originale, et nul n'ignore les vicissitudes dont a pâti la transmission manuscrite du *Liber!*

TEXTE

Sur ce plan philologique, un remarquable effort a été poursuivi par des générations de savants anglais, allemands et italiens. On peut encore consulter avec fruit les anciennes éditions d'Ellis (1904, mais réimprimée huit fois, dont trois depuis la dernière guerre) avec son riche et scrupuleux apparat critique (Clarendon, Oxford), de Merrill (1893 et 1928) que la *Harvard University Press* a rééditée en 1951 avec un avant-propos du distingué catullien J. P. Elder, de Kroll (Teubner, 1923 et 1929) qui marquait une sage réaction contre les témérités de la « *prurigo coniciendi* » de quelques éditeurs ou commentateurs allemands de la fin du XIXe siècle, sans méconnaître la valeur du travail de clarification des Schwabe et des Schulze. Actuellement, les meilleurs éditeurs de Catulle, au premier rang desquels il faut mentionner M. Schuster (Teubner, 1949 et 1954), auquel on ne peut guère reprocher que d'avoir soudé avec trop d'assurance les c. 68 et 68 b (en reprenant à son compte la conjecture de Schöll, « mi Alli », au vers 11), E. Cazzaniga (1943), E. d'Arbela (1947) évitent soigneusement de risquer des conjectures personnelles, mais s'efforcent de choisir parmi les corrections proposées par leurs nombreux prédécesseurs, sans jamais perdre de vue l'ensemble de la tradition manuscrite : il apparaît, en effet, de plus en plus qu'il ne faut pas faire fi des *deteriores*, dont l'apparentement avec les deux manuscrits essentiels, le *Sangermanensis* et l'*Oroniensis*, et les liens qui les unissent entre eux sont plus complexes qu'on ne le croyait dans le premier quart du siècle, au moment des discussions passionnées qui opposèrent A. Morgenthaler et W. G. Hale (on peut compléter là-dessus les claires indications des p. XXVIII-XXXV de l'Introduction de l'édition Lafaye, aux *Belles Lettres*, mais qui remontent à 1922, par l'excellente mise au point de la *Praefatio* de l'édition Schuster, écrite en 1948). Dans cet ordre d'idées, une mention spéciale doit être accordée à l'humaniste G. B. Pighi qui a collationné plusieurs manuscrits et en a publié des descriptions, entre autres celle du *Codex Bononiensis* 2621 (1950), confronté (*Humanitas*, 1950, p. 37-160) les lectures et corrections du judicieux humaniste portugais de la Renaissance, Achilles Statius, avec celles de ses contemporains Muret, Scaliger, Alexander Guarinus, suggéré dans plusieurs revues spécialisées, italiennes et allemandes, des amendements fort plausibles pour maints endroits du texte.

Néanmoins, comme à part le *Thuaneus* du IXe siècle (mais qui ne nous fournit qu'un poème) tous les manuscrits des poèmes de Catulle sont de date relativement récente, et entachés de multiples altérations et bévues, toutes ces collations, minutieuses confrontations, prudentes suggestions, quelle que soit la sagacité de leurs auteurs, conservent fatalement un caractère en partie conjectural et toujours plus ou moins précaire... Pour tâcher de progresser, malgré tout, dans notre connaissance du texte de Catulle, les latinistes contemporains interrogent en même temps la tradition indirecte : l'un des meilleurs exemples qu'on en puisse donner est formé par le premier des « *Due studi Catulliani* », de F. della Corte (Istituto Universitario di Magistero, Gênes, 1951), qui semble vraiment avoir tiré le maximum, dans l'état actuel de nos connaissances, des citations et allusions que les auteurs, scholiastes, grammairiens antiques et humanistes de la Renaissance nous ont faites des vers de Catulle. Il en résulterait, par exemple, qu'un Pétrarque, et même encore un Guarinus, auraient eu connaissance d'un « *Catullus plenior* », et que les Anciens en tout cas auraient possédé une traduction en vers par Catulle de la seconde *Idylle* de Théocrite, plus probablement qu'ils n'en auraient possédé une adaptation du genre de celle que le poète nous a laissée de la « Boucle de Bérénice » de Callimaque (F. della Corte, *op. cit.*, p. 29 sq.) (1). Et ne citons que pour mémoire les vers priapéens attribués à Catulle (cf. les *fragmenta*).

LE RECUEIL

La question de savoir si Catulle est le propre arrangeur du recueil qui nous est parvenu, prête toujours à controverse. Della Corte (cit., p. 15-20) manie avec ingéniosité une vaste et précise information pour démontrer que cet arrangement serait posthume et imputable à Cornelius Nepos, mais il est permis de ne pas être tout à fait d'accord avec l'interprétation qu'il donne

(1) Birt, auquel renvoie della Corte, avait déjà soutenu cette thèse : *Antike Buchwesen*, p. 405. Elle est fondée sur un mot de Pline l'Ancien, H. N., 28, 19 (cf. p. 99, éd. Lafaye de Catulle, *Belles Lettres*).

du poème dédicatoire et de penser, avec d'autres philologues, qu'on a, jusqu'ici, interprété trop littéralement ce c. 1 (1). Catulle peut fort bien, comme le pensait Wilamowitz (2), avoir eu le temps de ranger, un peu avant sa mort, dans l'ordre que nous voyons, une grande partie, sinon la plupart des *carmina* formant le *liber*. Un classement qui ne serait insolite qu'en apparence, et dont il faudrait peut-être rechercher l'explication dans des raisons d'ordre psychologique et moral, et pas seulement dans des principes esthétiques alors en faveur et se rattachant plus ou moins aux prestiges des *Diegeseis* de Callimaque ou de la *uariatio*. Tout cela n'excluant point absolument la possibilité d'adjonctions ultérieures.

Il convient d'ailleurs de remarquer que, par la force des choses, ce problème préoccupe moins la science contemporaine, dans la mesure où elle est de plus en plus sensible à ce qui fait l'unité profonde de l'inspiration du « divin poète » de Vérone. Déjà en 1928, A. L. Wheeler (*Catullus and the traditions of ancient poetry*, paru en 1934), tout en ne croyant pas que Catulle ait pu être l'arrangeur du recueil, reconnaissait qu'il faut « regarder les différences métriques comme secondaires par rapport aux similitudes de contenu, de ton et d'intention ».

DUALITÉ OU UNITÉ ?

« Le fond des petits poèmes épiques ou lyriques de Catulle est purement conventionnel : le poète ne s'y intéresse qu'aux raffinements de la forme et à l'ingéniosité des détails. »

Ainsi s'exprimaient en 1939 Bornecque, Mornet et Cordier, dans « *Rome et les Romains* » ! Quel catullien, je dirai même quel lecteur de Catulle (même s'il ne peut l'aborder que dans une traduction) serait aujourd'hui de cet avis? Tous les progrès qu'une fervente critique a permis de réaliser dans la connaissance de sa psychologie, s'inscrivent en faux contre cette prétendue indifférence à la matière de son inspiration, quel que soit le poème envisagé. Comment peut-on ne pas sentir la « présence » du poète à travers les plaintes d'Ariane ou les repentirs d'Attis? Autant vaudrait soutenir que Racine était indifférent aux tourments de Phèdre, Chateaubriand à la nostalgie de l'Abencérage !

L'une des plus pertinentes argumentations qui aient été réunies contre la bizarre conception de deux Catulle, un « alexandrin » laborieux et pédant (grands poèmes) et un « primitif » spontané et naturel, se lira avec fruit dans un substantiel article de J. P. Elder (3). Considérant tour à tour la structure, les allusions érudites, l'imagerie, le choix des mots, et présentant une habile synthèse des travaux d'une trentaine de savants de nationalités diverses, le latiniste américain nous démontre que, fondamentalement, Catulle a utilisé de la même façon tous ces éléments de son art dans ses poèmes courts et dans ses plus longues compositions. Il n'est d'ailleurs pas de génération spontanée, quoi qu'en puissent dire certains, dans aucune forme d'art : « Indeed lyric poetry above all other types demands the severe, formal compression of an exacting art. » Qui pourrait se vanter d'être sûr que Catulle n'a aucunement peiné pour écrire tel poème?

Si l'on veut des exemples précis, pour n'envisager que l'architecture des *carmina*, c'est un fait maintenant acquis que nous ne pouvons pas expliquer simplement par « ce sens infaillible des proportions qui est la marque de tout bon artiste » la symétrie rigoureuse des divisions et subdivisions de c. XLV et XLVI, voire de l' « élégie » LXXVI, ou encore la bipartition des huit vers composant l'épigramme LXXII, articulée sur le jeu de « *nosse... cognoui* » et présentant deux séries de deux vers chacune, d'un lumineux enchaînement logique jusque dans leur intensité émotionnelle. Assurément, la construction des petits poèmes de Catulle, qu'il s'agisse des polymétriques ou des distiques, n'est guère moins « savante » que celle des grands poèmes centraux du recueil. Néanmoins, nous le verrons tout à l'heure, cette technique n'est pas, chez Catulle, une pure création intellectuelle, tout au moins dans son principe.

Mais ce problème capital de l'unité du génie poétique de Catulle ne met pas seulement en cause les aspects techniques de son art. Comment concilier avec « the gentle, urbane humor which only a well-educated society can lightly toss about and delight in » (Elder, cit., p. 109), les grivoiseries et les injures obscènes dont notre auteur a truffé ses poèmes satiriques? Est-ce vraiment le même auteur qui a pu écrire le badinage raffiné qu'est le c. VII et les railleries stercoraires du c. XXXIII? la parodie héroï-comique qu'offre le c. XXXVI et les traits répugnants qui s'accumulent délibérément dans le c. XCVII? Quel abîme semble séparer ce scabreux « Rabelais romain » de ce même Catulle que N.I. Herescu a pu appeler « le premier des romantiques » et qui se révèle bien tel par maints élans du cœur et maintes inquiétudes fiévreuses !

(1) F. O. COPLEY, *Transactions of American Philological Association*, 1951, p. 200.

(2) *Hellenistische Dichtung in der Zeit des Callimachos*, Berlin, 1924.

(3) J.P. ELDER, « Notes on some conscious and subconscious elements in Catulllus poetry », *Harvard Studies in Classical Philology*, 1951, p. 101-136.

La plupart des tentatives d'explication de la crudité catullienne peuvent se ramener à deux catégories : celles qui invoquent l'espièglerie et l'insouciance dans la diffamation, propres à la jeunesse; celles qui mettent l'accent sur les lois du très libre genre hendécasyllabique, le prestige des modèles grecs (Archiloque, Hipponax), l'entraînement d'un milieu grécisant et l'affectation de se montrer libéré de l'ancienne pudibonderie des *maiores*. Tous ces facteurs ont pu, en effet, jouer un rôle appréciable, et il est souvent malaisé de faire, chez notre poète, le départ entre les suggestions de sa personnalité profonde et la préoccupation d' « être à la page » et de demeurer à la tête du mouvement littéraire contemporain. Notre Musset n'a-t-il pas souvent témoigné de la même fougue juvénile dans son désir de choquer les lecteurs gourmés? Cette fièvre d'affranchissement de toutes les conventions est un trait constant des révolutions poétiques... et un trait de la jeunesse de tous les temps. Mais, dans le cas particulier de notre Catulle, il ne semble pas qu'il faille être grand clerc pour déceler la primauté d'une appropriation des moyens aux buts énergiquement poursuivis. C'est l'intention bien arrêtée de faire prendre en dégoût aux « multas (mulieres) » (v. 9), parmi lesquelles figurait peut-être Lesbie, un certain Æmilius, qui a manifestement déterminé le satirique à ne reculer devant aucun moyen pour faire de ce rival le plus écœurant portrait qui se puisse imaginer (XCVII). Et nul doute que son acharnement contre Gellius — pas moins de six épigrammes, comme si Catulle ne pensait jamais l'avoir rendu assez immonde ! — ne fasse, lui aussi, partie intégrante d'une stratégie amoureuse où tous les coups semblaient permis pour triompher d'un dangereux concurrent... De même, si, sur un tout autre registre, le preste billet XXXII ne le cède à aucun des petits poèmes de Catulle sous le rapport de cette liberté absolue de langage que les Grecs appelaient παρρησία, c'est, n'en doutons pas, que la destinataire de cette singulière déclaration (si elle n'est pas une pure création de l'imagination d'un adolescent trop ardent !) devait, comme ses pareilles, aimer qu'on lui tînt pareil langage et différer foncièrement à cet égard — autres temps, autres mœurs... mais surtout autre langage ! — de cette jolie femme de la Régence, qui disait que pour toute réponse elle eût envoyé à Catulle un paquet d'émétique ! (mot cité par Pezay : éd. Héguin de Guerle, chez Panckoucke, 1837, p. 232).

En somme, le graveleux n'est jamais, chez Catulle, une fin en soi (ou, comme chez Rabelais, une forme facile de comique); c'est plutôt une manifestation, que nous pouvons regretter, mais qu'il faut définir comme telle, de son bouillant dynamisme, de sa combativité un peu fanfaronne et très ombrageuse, de sa vitalité débordante. Extrême en toute chose, impétueux de cette fougue qui se remarque chez tous les lyriques à courte vie, nous allons le voir apporter la même flamme dans ses ferveurs sentimentales, puis dans ses aspirations esthétiques.

CARITAS, FIDES ET FŒDUS

« Le doux Catulle »! Cette appellation consacrée apparaît, pour peu que l'on songe à la virulence de ses invectives, aussi mal choisie que la formule stéréotypée « le tendre Racine »! Cependant, pas plus que cette dernière, elle n'est complètement erronée, et les travaux de la critique contemporaine s'accordent à mettre en valeur l'éperdu besoin d'attachement qui caractérise au plus haut degré l'âme du tendre poète de Vérone. Attachement au pays natal, attachement à ce frère tant pleuré, attachement à ses amis et compatriotes, attachement désespéré à Lesbie.

L'amour de la petite patrie n'éclate pas seulement dans de célèbres pièces comme XXXI, mais il faut souligner par exemple avec L. Ferrero (*o. cit.*, p. 363, sqq.) les analogies profondes entre l'évolution des sentiments d'un Attis (illusions et désillusions de l' « évasion ») et l'évolution morale de Catulle avant, pendant et après son voyage en Asie : une sorte d'angoisse, un sentiment croissant d'irrémédiable solitude, d'irrémédiable arrachement, prend peu à peu le pas sur l'irritabilité et l'agressivité (dans la mesure évidemment où nous pouvons atteindre quelque certitude sur la chronologie des pièces du recueil !).

Ce n'est pas d'aujourd'hui que date l'importance légitimement attachée, sur le double plan psychologique et littéraire, au deuil cruel dont Catulle semble ne s'être jamais consolé. Mais la critique actuelle, allant encore plus loin dans cette voie, a tendance à prendre très au sérieux l'engagement du c. LXV :

Semper maesta tua carmina morte canam (1)

(v. 12)

_____

(1) Avec Schwabe, Kroll, Schuster, L. Ferrero, Jacoby, Mazzoni, etc., nous pensons qu'il faut lire « canam », et non « tegam » comme le voulaient Ellis et Lafaye.

à telle enseigne que L. Ferrero a finement décelé dans LXVI (« Boucle de Bérénice ») un choix qui tempère l'amertume du « *fratris cari flebile discidium* » (v. 22) par une survivance de cette considération ironique des réalités quotidiennes qui avait jusque-là marqué l'inspiration du poète :

> *Estne nouis nuptis odio Venus? anne parentum*
> *Frustrantur falsis gaudia lacrimulis?*
>
> (vers 15-16)

Même si — ce qui n'est nullement prouvé, dans l'état actuel des découvertes papyrologiques — ces vers sont traduits littéralement de Callimaque (comme le sont, avec d'appréciables variantes, une trentaine de vers jusqu'ici découverts du modèle alexandrin), le mélange des tons n'en est pas moins significatif, et il semble bien que dorénavant un fond de *luctus* assombrira jusqu'aux *nugae* de notre Catulle. Aussi, par son caractère foncièrement distinct des poèmes qui l'encadrent, une « élégie » satirique effrontée comme LXVII semble-t-elle bien appartenir, comme par exemple le c. 17, à la première période de la carrière poétique de Catulle (cf. Ferrero, p. 87 sq.) et non à celle qui suivit la mort de son frère (della Corte, cit., p. 245).

Au surplus, les déceptions iront se multipliant aussi dans le domaine de l'amitié, comme dans celui de l'amour : la *caritas* foncière du poète, en même temps que son culte, bien romain, de la *fides*, seront mis à rude épreuve ! Quelles ivresses pourtant il avait d'abord goûtées dans la chaude affection et l'absolue communion d'idéal littéraire avec ses amis, souvent cisalpins comme lui, du cercle des néotériques ! Pour s'en rendre compte, il ne faut pas simplement invoquer les effusions de IX, l'euphorie malicieuse de XIV, l'admiration de LIII et de XCV (« *Parua mei mihi sint cordi monumenta* [*sodalis*] »), le dévouement de LXVIII, la délicate compassion de XCVI. Il faut mesurer, par exemple, à quel point, dans un poème comme le « L », la plus chaleureuse affection peut s'harmoniser avec l'amour de l'art : alors qu'un Lafaye, dans sa thèse, dont la valeur reste d'ailleurs toujours grande, *Catulle et ses modèles* (1874), ne s'y intéressait guère qu'aux vers 1-6, alors qu'un Ellis, dans son *Commentary on Catullus* (1876), que d'aucuns ont d'ailleurs tort de juger complètement périmé, en retenait surtout l'habile tactique du poète pour se faire à nouveau inviter, L. Ferrero, cit., p. 120-121, va jusqu'à s'écrier : « *esperienza poetica, sodalizio letterario ed affettuosa spontaneità di rapporti si fondono nella calda rievocazione di una testimonianza d'affetto per l'amico e d'amore per l'arte che resta unica nella storia dello spirito umano* ». Au surplus, cette parfaite solidarité se mariait à merveille avec la tendance, instinctive chez Catulle, à identifier l'état d'âme de ses amis avec le sien propre : qu'il suffise de rappeler l'analogie des situations sentimentales définie au début du c. LXVIII, et surtout la communion de sentiments qui donne à l'admirable épithalame LXI une résonance si personnelle.

On ne peut douter, à la lecture de cette pièce justement célèbre, et personne ne semble plus en douter aujourd'hui, que nous ayons affaire non pas à un simple poème de circonstance, ni à une simple imitation de Sapho ou d'autres modèles grecs (1), mais à une véritable profession de foi, à l'exaltation d'un idéal de vie commun à un petit groupe d'amis, pour lesquels la licence de la « vie grecque » n'était nullement une option définitive, mais qui croyaient à la possibilité de satisfaire les besoins de la nature et du cœur dans le cadre même d'une vertueuse vie domestique comme celle des Romains d'antan ou comme celle de maints héros d'Homère, d'Eschyle et d'Euripide. Que l'on rapproche à cet égard les v. 196-225 de LXI des v. 328-336 et 372-374 de LXIV (avec la reprise significative de « *foedere* » à la même place aux v. 335 et 373) et, bien entendu, des leçons qui se dégagent de LXII.

Sous cet éclairage, nous nous expliquerons mieux les rêves chimériques que notre fervent adolescent semble avoir sérieusement fondés (2) sur l' « *aeternum sanctae foedus amicitiae* »

---

(1) N'omettons pas de signaler l'excellente analyse qu'a donnée dans *Humanitas* de 1948, pp. 41-53, G.-B. Pighi, de ce grand poème, sous le titre « La struttura del carme LXI di Catullo » : au lieu de subdiviser à l'excès les deux dernières parties comme on l'avait souvent fait jusqu'alors (v. 126-155, 156-180, 181-190, 191-235); il distingue onze strophes de fescennins (v. 126-180) et onze strophes d'épithalame (v. 181-235); son étude de la métrique fait une bonne fois justice de la bizarre division, proposée par Lachmann, de chaque strophe en deux systèmes (3 glyconiques + 1 glyconique et 1 phérécratien) et elle conclut légitimement que la strophe forme une seule période métrique (« pentastichon glyconeum » comme dit fort bien Schuster dans son Index metricus); enfin les tentatives de restitution des deux strophes mutilées sont ingénieuses.

(2) Voir là-dessus le plus substantiel — et peut-être meilleur — chapitre des *Due studi catulliani*, de F. della Corte, pp. 197-243, « Lesbia illa, illa Lesbia », bien qu'on puisse accueillir avec certaines réserves l'assertion selon laquelle, s'il n'avait pas connu Lesbie, Catulle serait demeuré un « alexandrin » livresque et froid : est-il interdit de penser que la puissante personnalité — à la fois lyrique et satirique — du poète se serait tout de même affirmée? et doit-on juger vraiment « froides » les pièces datant d'avant la rencontre de Lesbie, ou croire qu'aucune des pièces du recueil ne date d'avant cette rencontre?

(CIX, v. 6) romanesquement conclu avec sa Lesbie : bien que sensiblement plus jeune que son amante, Catulle aurait voulu exercer sur elle une sorte de « *patria potestas* » d'un type encore inédit ! Telle serait l'explication la plus profonde d'un vers comme LXXII, 4.

Et à la lumière aussi de ces investigations psychologiques, comme nous saisissons mieux, dans tout son pathétique, l'acuité des désillusions et de l'amertume finales, en amitié, comme en amour, dont nous avons de si poignants échos dans les c. XXX, LXXXIII, LXXVII ! Nous ne pouvons nous y étendre, mais rien n'est plus significatif, par exemple, que la similitude des termes, des tours, des images que nous relevons dans le c. XXX et dans l'épisode des lamentations d'Ariane abandonnée (LXIV, v. 132-201). L'ingratitude, aux yeux de Catulle, est l'*impietas* par excellence, comme suffirait à le prouver le rapprochement de LXXIII, 2-3 et de LXXVI, 9 :

> *(Desine) aliquem fieri posse putare pium.*
> *Omnia sunt ingrata.*
>
> *Omniaque ingratae perierunt credita menti.*

Mais aux sursauts d'indignation, aux violentes invectives, aux appels à la vengeance céleste, nous voyons succéder peu à peu, sinon une calme résignation, du moins une douloureuse acceptation du fait accompli.

CATULLE ÉTAIT-IL UN MYSTIQUE ?

C'est ici qu'il nous faut dire un mot de la tendance observable chez d'éminents critiques contemporains, anglo-saxons ou italiens, à donner à la *fides* catullienne un sens rituel, cathartique, ou bien à déceler dans l'âme de notre poète des aspirations anti-intellectualistes très en avance sur son temps. Le nœud de la question est constitué par le célèbre c. LXXVI, véritable conclusion de l'aventure sentimentale essentielle de la vie de Catulle. Si Benedetto Croce (*Critica*, 1940, pp. 193-197) en minimise l'importance, Herescu (*Catullo*, 1943), Gigante (*Latomus* X, pp. 137-142), Renard (*ibid.* 1946, p. 357), Marmorale (qui la proclame « *la preghiera agli dèi piu bella che di un animo che abbia sofferto ci ha tramandato l'antichita* » : *L'ultimo Catullo*, p. 149, Edizioni scientifiche italiane, Naples, 1952), L. Ferrero, etc. attachent un intérêt extrême à cette émouvante prière. Mais il semble qu'à force d'en scruter les intentions, l'on coure le risque de les fausser quelque peu ! Bien manifestement, Catulle n'aspire ici qu'à une chose : ne plus être hanté de regrets chimériques, cesser une bonne fois d'aimer une ingrate qui ne pourra jamais plus le payer de retour. Avouons qu'il est difficile d'y voir avec F. O. Copley (1) « an ever-increasing loathing of the moral wrong of which he finds himself guilty », difficile de donner avec Marmorale (2) à cette *fides* que le poète affirme n'avoir jamais violée (v. 3) le sens précis que le mot revêtait dans les religions à mystères : respect du secret liant entre eux les initiés; difficile enfin de définir, avec L. Ferrero (3), en Catulle un Antisocrate, voire un précurseur de Saint-Augustin par les intuitions fulgurantes de la *pietas*!... La thèse d'une sorte de conversion de Catulle, en 54, au culte mystique de Dionysos a été soutenue avec brio par Enzo V. Marmorale (*op. cit.*), mais elle a fait peu d'adeptes. Loin de nous écrier avec M. Marmorale, devant LXIV, 200,

> *Orgia, quae frustra cupiunt audire profani,*

« è chiaro che chi scrive questo verso è un iniziato » (p, 198, *op. cit.*), nous inclinons à sentir dans la rutilante évocation du thiase dionysiaque le même sentiment horrifié (cf. particulièrement les vers 254 et 264) que dans la peinture de la course frénétique des Galles (LXIII, 20-34).

---

(1) « Emotional conflict and its significance in the Lesbia-Poems of Catullus », *American Journal of Philology*, LXX, 1949, pp. 22-40.

(2) On lira dans la *Revue des Études Anciennes*, LV, 1953, n° 2, une pertinente critique des thèses de M. Marmorale, sous la plume de M. Boyancé (p. 206, sq.) : peu de vraisemblance d'une restauration par César en 54 des mystères de Dionysos; impossibilité d'attribuer la pureté de la vie passée (LXXVI, v. 19) aux effets d'une conversion actuelle; sens exact des « *multa gaudia* » dont Catulle escompte la récompense « *in longa aetate* »; valeur essentiellement romaine (« loyauté, foi jurée ») de la notion de *fides* dans la dernière partie de la vie de Catulle.

(3) *Interpretazione di Catullo*, capitolo VI, « Dolore e purificazione », 18 : « La raggiunta coscienza » : on y trouvera, à côté de subtilités hasardeuses, une analyse serrée de l'oscillation entre le pessimisme et la confiance dans le destin, et une judicieuse valorisation de cette *voluptas* que Catulle avoue savourer dans le souvenir de tous ses *benefacta* (même de ceux qui ne furent récompensés que par de l'ingratitude !)

61

Mlle Guillemin a naguère brillamment démontré (REL, 1949, pp. 149-157) l'angoisse de notre poète devant l'invasion de ces mystiques orientales qui menaçaient la solide armature psychique du Romain, et nous ne devons pas nous étonner que Catulle emploie les mêmes termes (« Thiasus » LXII, 28, et, plus haut, « Mænades, v. 23) pour le pitoyable cortège d'Attis et pour les délirantes Ménades. Cette assimilation, qu'une brève note de Lafaye (p. 51 de l'éd. de Catulle aux *Belles Lettres*) risque de faire attribuer à Catulle (une liberté de poète) est ancienne : l'*Hélène* d'Euripide (v. 1301-1368) et Strabon (X, 469 sqq.) attestent les étroits rapports qui ont toujours existé entre les rites de Cybèle, de Déméter et de Dionysos, dans la Grèce classique (cf. éd. de l'*Hélène* par Grégoire, Méridier et Chapouthier, aux *Belles Lettres*, tome V, p. 13 et p. 105).

Si Catulle avait vécu plus longtemps, ce n'est pas un mystique, mais peut-être un moraliste qu'il serait devenu, tout au moins un poète de plus en plus sensible aux répercussions de notre conduite sur le bonheur individuel et collectif. Les patientes analyses de la critique contemporaine tendent de plus en plus à mettre en valeur, par exemple, le contenu éthique de ses idées religieuses. Il suffit, pour s'en convaincre, d'observer cette nostalgie de l'âge d'or et de la présence familière des dieux parmi les hommes aux temps héroïques, qui ferait, si nous en croyons R. Waltz (REL, 1945, pp. 92-109), l'unité des deux épyllia enchâssés l'un dans l'autre et formant le c. LXIV. Nul ne croit plus, aujourd'hui, que le finale — où cette nostalgie est particulièrement sensible — des « Noces de Thétis et de Pélée » puisse simplement s'expliquer par une imitation d'Hésiode ou une polémique contre Lucrèce. Des vers appartenant à d'autres pièces du recueil, tels que

> Huc addent diui quam plurima, quae Themis olim
> Antiquis solita est munera ferre piis

(LXVIII, 155-156)

montrent assez combien cette équation de la *pietas*, de la justice et du bonheur était chère au cœur du poète. Un poète qui ne semble pas du tout avoir cru comme Lucrèce les divinités indifférentes aux souffrances humaines, mais les a vues se refusant à épargner aux hommes les maux que leur attirent divers manquements à cette FIDES déjà chère à un Plaute, et qui ne le sera pas moins à un Horace; à cette FIDES qui avait à Rome, et à Rome seule, son temple.

HELLÉNISME OU ROMANITÉ?

De toutes les considérations précédentes il se dégage déjà la figure d'un Catulle beaucoup plus romain que ne l'estimait encore le siècle dernier. Bien rares seraient aujourd'hui ceux qui souscriraient sans réserve à ces mots de l'historien du XIXe siècle J. Naudet : « *Catullus ita Graecorum disciplinis imbuit animum, et eorum in se succum et sanguinem transfudit, ut ipse Graecus in Italia natus graeco ingenio latine scribere videatur* » (p. IX de la *Praefatio* de son éd. de Catulle).

Mais gardons-nous de l'erreur opposée, et ne méconnaissons pas — ce serait nier l'évidence ! — la dette de Catulle envers les poètes grecs, aussi bien envers Archiloque et Sapho qu'envers Callimaque et Apollonius de Rhodes (ces deux derniers se réconcilient dans son œuvre !), envers les épigrammatistes qu'envers Homère, Aristophane, Euripide, Théognis, Théocrite. Pas plus qu'il n'acceptait une radicale séparation des genres, Catulle, et c'est là le point important, n'opérait une discrimination entre ses divers modèles, qu'ils appartinssent à l'époque hellénistique ou aux siècles classiques de la littérature grecque. S'il a préféré aux ambitieuses compositions les ouvrages d'une étendue limitée et d'une économie savamment préméditée, ce n'est point tant, peut-être, par docilité envers les Alexandrins que pour avoir pris assez tôt conscience de ses propres aptitudes et avoir compris que son inspiration ne pouvait, dans un poème déterminé, se contenter d'un seul modèle, mais devait travailler à marquer de sa forte empreinte personnelle des emprunts bien choisis et en nombre relativement restreint. La meilleure mise au point, au cours de ces derniers temps, des rapports de Catulle avec ses « sources » grecques est représentée par l'étude de Domenico Braga, *Catullo e i poeti greci*, Casa Editrice G. d'Anna, Messina-Firenze. 1950. Également éloigné des illusions romantiques et des préventions de plusieurs générations de critiques aux yeux de qui Catulle devait tout aux Grecs, le savant italien ne s'écarte pas de la ligne objective qu'il s'est tracée : sans refuser au génie grec une supériorité en ce qui concerne la spontanéité de l'inspiration, la richesse de l'imagination, la variété de ton et de motifs, il rend pleine justice à ce qui fait l'incontestable grandeur du génie latin et de la lyrique catullienne en particulier : sens marqué de réalisme, capacité d'assimilation, profondeur de sentiment. Et au terme de son étude très précise, D. Braga parvient à une solide définition, qui ne peut qu'obtenir l'assentiment unanime des Catulliens d'aujourd'hui, de ce qui fait l'originalité de notre poète, à savoir la fusion de l'esprit hellénique avec la forme hellénistique :

62

« *Lo spirito ardente di Saffo nelle forme vivide di Asclepiade o di Meleagro, l'impetuosità di Archiloco un pò temperata dalla 'αστειότης di Callimaco, la forza drammatica di Euripide raddolcita dalla pienezza psichica di Apollonio: questa è la lirica di Catullo, emullo dell' antica Ellade nel soffio che anima, seguace della nuova nel tocco che plasma.* »

Dans cet ordre d'idées, et sans pouvoir entrer dans le détail de la discussion (1), ne manquons pas de signaler aux lecteurs d'éditions commentées de Catulle (Bährens, Ellis, Friedrich, Riese, Kroll, etc.), éditions au reste de grand mérite et appelées à rendre toujours de réels services, mais qui datent toutes soit de la fin du siècle dernier, soit du premier quart de ce siècle, que l'érudition contemporaine ne croit plus à l'existence de modèles hellénistiques précis dont les deux grands poèmes centraux du *Liber* catullien (*Attis, Noces de Thétis et de Pélée*) ne seraient qu'une traduction ou une transposition. Le mérite essentiel de l'invention, dans ces *docta carmina*, revient, selon toute vraisemblance, au seul Catulle si, dans le détail des épisodes, l'ornementation, l'expression, le poète latin peut s'avérer tributaire des Alexandrins ou d'Euripide; — encore peut-il s'agir assez souvent, dans ces rencontres de détail, d'une similitude de goûts, de tempéraments, de réactions, et non d'une imitation à proprement parler.

PROBLÈMES DE FACTURE

Technique de la composition, art du trait, usage de la langue, stylistique, relation entre le dessein du poème et la forme métrique, autant d'aspects de l'œuvre catullienne dont l'étude a été reprise à la lumière des progrès des sciences philologiques, esthétiques, psychologiques. Nous ne saurions prétendre les passer tous en revue de manière détaillée.

Les types dominants de structure ont fait l'objet d'intéressants travaux de Ramain, Jachmann, Hezel, Weinreich, Friess (2), Bardon, Elder. Ils semblent, malgré quelques divergences, s'accorder sur un fait capital : la composition, chez Catulle, loin d'être, comme chez les Alexandrins, une pure création intellectuelle et le fruit d'un calcul, traduit surtout une sensibilité, en admettant même que le poète ait pu en venir assez vite à appliquer consciemment, assouplir et perfectionner, par exemple, les deux tendances — ne disons jamais « procédés » en parlant d'un poète aussi impétueux ! — fondamentales définies par H. Bardon, à savoir la « composition embrassée » et la « composition énumérative » (qu'il vaut mieux appeler « directe » ou « rectiligne »); des carmina tels que XVI, XXXIII, XXXVI, LII, LVII appartiennent au premier type, tandis que le second est représenté par II, III, VII-XIV, XXVIII, XXXV, etc., et par toutes les épigrammes. Mais Catulle est-il vraiment l'inventeur de l'agencement « embrassé » (qui atteint une complexité peu commune dans les *Noces de Thétis et de Pélée*, et que Virgile, peut-être sous son influence, reprendra dans l'épisode d'Aristée)? La disparition de la majeure partie des recueils de poésie mélique et la mutilation des débris qui nous en restent, les fragments également trop courts, parvenus jusqu'à nous, des « petits lyriques » romains antérieurs à Catulle, tel Laevius, ne nous permettent certes pas de affirmations trop tranchées ! Soulignons toutefois que ce mode de composition circulaire devait vraiment plaire à notre poète, puisqu'il l'a étendu, en le compliquant, aux grands poèmes LXIV, LXV, LXVIII a et b, et ce malgré l'exemple des Alexandrins, qui n'ont jamais beaucoup aimé, comme le rappelle H. Bardon, cette disposition. M. Boyancé (3) y verrait volontiers quelque héritage du *carmen* latin, associé à un goût d'équilibre qui ne contredirait point l'impétuosité foncière, mais traduirait tantôt un plaisir de virtuose (dans les pièces polymétriques), tantôt (grands poèmes susdits) la fermeté, bien romaine, d'une conception ne perdant pas de vue le but essentiel qu'elle se propose.

Quoi qu'il en soit, les deux sortes de compositions présentent, de l'aveu général, un trait

---

(1) Par exemple, le Commentaire, par ailleurs excellent, de Kroll, adopte encore (il date de 1923) la thèse de Wilamowitz (1879) d'après laquelle l'*Attis* ne serait qu'une traduction d'un poème de Callimaque (dont il ne nous est parvenu qu'un court fragment, d'authenticité assez suspecte) : voir une réfutation détaillée de cette thèse aux pages 145 sqq. de l'ouvrage précité de D. Braga.

(2) *Beobachtungen über die Darstellungskunst Catulls*, Diss. München, 1929, qui est la seule étude d'ensemble de la question ayant paru avant l'opuscule de H. Bardon cité au début de cet article : trop systématiques, les vues de Friess méconnaissent un peu la liberté d'allures du poète et sont grevées par la préoccupation de déterminer le noyau générateur de chaque pièce, au point qu'Elder a pu dénoncer chez lui « a sort of ὀμφαλός-obsession » !

(3) *Revue des Études Anciennes*, mars 1944, compte rendu du livre de H. Bardon.

commun : la fréquence des répétitions, des leitmotive obsédants, qui, naturellement, sont le fait d'une âme hypersensible et passionnée, mais où il convient aussi de voir, avec J. van Gelder (*De Woordherhaling bij Catullus*, Den Haag, 1933) un élément constitutif de la personnalité de « musicien » du poète. Celui-ci utiliserait en quelque sorte des groupes rythmiques ou sonores bien définis et les ferait osciller entre deux ou trois points essentiels de son thème. Tel serait notamment le cas des pièces VIII et CVII. On pourrait à ce sujet, avec prudence, invoquer un Verlaine (cf. *Suppl. Crit. au Bull. de l'Assoc. G. Budé*, 1934, p. 140 sqq.).

N'abandonnons pas ces problèmes si importants de structure sans attirer, avec J. P. Elder (cit. pp. 124-126), l'attention sur l'habitude de Catulle d'ouvrir ses poèmes par une question et réponse (cf. pièce liminaire, VII, XXIX, XL, CIV), ou par l'exposé du thème (très fréquemment), ou encore par une condition (XIV, XIV b, LXXI, LXXVI, XCVI, CII, CVII, CVIII), et ensuite d'introduire l'*explicatio* par un *nam*, de conclure enfin par *quare*, ce schème logique souffrant, bien entendu quelques variantes dans le choix des particules. On ne trouve cet ordre réflexif qu'en prose à la même époque. Le savant américain incline à y déceler une habitude logique, peut-être inconsciemment héritée d'une lecture assidue des grands maîtres du lyrisme grec, chez lesquels la plus violente franchise et le mouvement le plus fougueux n'étaient pas exclusifs d'un appel sous-jacent à la raison; mais, il y insiste, ne pensons point, pour autant, à quelque emprunt direct ! simplement à un tempérament identique, fortifié par une assimilation en profondeur.

En se gardant de toute idolâtrie et sans vouloir surfaire les mérites d'une œuvre forcément imparfaite (mais sans laquelle les chefs-d'œuvre de l'âge augustéen seraient difficilement concevables !), il est permis de la juger attachante en fonction même de tout ce qui concourt à en assurer l'originalité. A ce titre, l'association d'une brûlante spontanéité et d'une ironie ou parodie à laquelle les contemporains devaient être plus sensibles que nous ne pouvons l'être, lui confère une particulière saveur. Dans la virulente invective contre Mamurra, XXIX — qui devait, avec la fabuleuse richesse due aux largesses de César et de Pompée, ravager les cœurs dans ce monde galant de l'Urbs que hantait Lesbie : et ce doit être l'explication de maint poème « anticésarien » !... — dans cette pièce injurieuse que Quintilien, IX, 4, 41, considérait comme le type même de l'iambe satirique, le « aut Adoneus » (v. 8) ne prend toute sa valeur bouffonne que si l'on se souvient avec E.-F. d'Arms (AJPh, 1932, p. 165 sq.) de l'insistance que mettait César à affirmer sa parenté avec Vénus : l'assimilation de son favori à Adonis n'est-elle pas logique ? Et le « putissimei » (qu'il faut préférer à toute autre leçon ou correction) du v. 23 *(ibid.)* n'est pas moins railleur, César et Pompée n'ayant guère les mains propres ! cependant que « *socer generque* » du dernier vers est un trait contre la complication des liens de famille qui unirent successivement les deux personnages (Herescu, R Cl, XIII-XIV, 1941-1942, p. 128 sqq.). Quant aux parodies de divers genres littéraires, elles ne manquent pas : A. Ronconi (A et R, 1940, pp. 141-158) n'a pas eu de peine à le démontrer par une analyse de la composition, du style et du vocabulaire des c. XI, LV, XXXVI, XXXIX, XLIV, XVII, XIII, XXVI; — Herescu (REL, 1947 : « Un écho des Nénies dans la littérature latine »), faisant valoir d'incontestables similitudes de mouvement et d'ordonnance entre le c. III — que les humanistes appelaient très justement « *Epicedium de morte passeris* » — et l'*Apocoloquintose* de Sénèque, en a conclu que le célèbre poème de Catulle se présente comme une imitation de la nénie populaire, mais réalisée, cela s'entend, avec les lois et les moyens de la poésie cultivée.

Si notre « *doctus poeta* » pourrait, tout aussi bien, prendre place parmi les « poètes populaires », ce n'est pas seulement à cause de la popularité immédiate de nombre de ses chants, les « anticésariens » en particulier ! Le caractère peut-être fondamental de la langue de Catulle, et même de son style, c'est la familiarité. Là encore, nous devons rendre hommage aux travaux des philologues italiens : Ronconi (A et R, 1938 et 1940) et Vaccaro (GIF, 1951) entre autres ont montré le caractère en grande partie erroné de la distinction qui avait cours au siècle dernier (et dont Schulze, dans le Bursian de 1920, se fait encore l'écho) entre la langue savante, jugée très hellénisée, des poèmes centraux du recueil et la langue familière des poèmes de circonstance. En effet, les hellénismes de vocabulaire et de syntaxe montent assez souvent chez Catulle des couches inférieures de la population, un peu comme chez Plaute, ou encore ils sont entrés en latin par le commerce et désignent des articles d'importation. Et il faut se défier des prétendus hellénismes de syntaxe, de ceux qui concernent par exemple l'emploi du génitif ou du datif, du pluriel pour le singulier, de l'infinitif : ils sont bien attestés en latin même, dans la langue parlée. Toujours est-il que le linguiste doit, évidemment, s'attacher surtout aux *nugae*, qui constituent un document de premier ordre pour la connaissance de la langue de tous les jours à Rome et contribuent à attester la continuité de la langue populaire, des origines jusqu'à nos jours : « *obstinata mente* » (VIII, 11), n'est-ce pas déjà la formation adverbiale qui prévaudra dans les langues romanes ? Qu'il nous soit permis de renvoyer là-dessus au suggestif chapitre « L'art de Catulle dans la métrique, la langue et le style », du second volume de la fervente *Storia della Letteratura*

64

Latina, d'Ettore Bignone (Sansoni editore, Firenze, 1945). Sur la variété, le mordant, la véhémence, mais la perfection par le travail, les celticismes, les diminutifs (1) et les composés, la préférence donnée à certains termes (par exemple à *natus* sur *filius*) et à certains tropes en raison de leur valeur affective, la transmutation en valeurs passionnelles des procédés les plus raffinés de la technique des Alexandrins, il y a d'excellentes remarques dans cet ouvrage.

Nous manquons encore d'un travail définitif sur les relations entre la tonalité émotive et le choix de la forme métrique dans les petits poèmes de Catulle. Sans doute la force des distinctions métriques paraît-elle s'être considérablement affaiblie depuis l'époque grecque classique, où déjà l'élégie, semble-t-il, ne se différenciait guère de l'épigramme que par la longueur (l'originalité de Catulle paraît bien avoir été d'orienter l'élégie vers la conception moderne que nous en avons, ouvrant la voie à Tibulle, Properce, Ovide). Sans doute est-ce aussi une illusion que de conclure à un renversement total d'inspiration quand on passe des polymètres aux épigrammes, comme le soutenait en 1933 Mlle Ilse Schnelle (*Untersuchungen zu Catulls dichterischer Form*, Philologus, Suppl. xxv) en opposant trop systématiquement à la subjectivité des premiers l'objectivité des secondes. Néanmoins, en dehors de toute considération de thèmes et de pure versification, il entre ici en jeu de notables différences stylistiques, certainement familières à Catulle, et qui ont dû guider, plus ou moins intuitivement, son choix entre les hendécasyllabes par exemple et les distiques élégiaques : c'est ainsi (voir J. Svennung, *Catulls Bildersprache* I, Uppsala Universitets Arsskrift, 1945) que la métaphore est deux fois plus fréquente dans les épigrammes que dans les pièces polymétriques, tandis que les diminutifs apparaissent au contraire sept fois plus nombreux dans ces dernières, les hapax dix fois plus. Il y aurait beaucoup plus de laisser-aller, en somme, dans les pièces lyriques que dans les épigrammatiques. Mais, encore une fois, ces recherches statistiques sont loin de présenter un caractère définitif, et l'on ne saurait être trop circonspect... surtout pour les conclusions à en tirer !

CONCLUSION

Quand bien même « *il piu audace lirico romanzo di vita giovanile che abbia la poesia* » (E. Bignone) serait moins pratiqué des écrivains et du public lettré d'aujourd'hui qu'il ne l'a été du XIVᵉ au XIXᵉ siècle, le monde savant continuerait, on le voit, à assurer une magnifique relève !...

Notre propos ne tendait qu'à rendre un modeste hommage à la somme de savants efforts destinés à nous restituer un Catulle intégral et authentique dans son texte comme dans sa psychologie, dans son art comme dans sa sensibilité. Mettant en œuvre toutes les ressources qu'offrent les techniques modernes des sciences critiques, les études catulliennes ont fait un grand pas dans la connaissance de ce qui constitue l'unité profonde du génie poétique du Véronais. Fait remarquable, l'étude même de ses « sources » met maintenant en pleine lumière son originalité. Si l'affectivité et le subjectif semblent avoir été chez lui primordiaux, cet adolescent fut doué d'une précoce maîtrise pour tout ce qui concerne les vues d'ensemble, la sûreté des buts à atteindre, l'intuition des plus efficaces moyens logiques. Retenons surtout que dans aucune de ses productions il n'apparaît avoir obéi à des mobiles inspirés exclusivement de l'art pour l'art. Attachant mélange d'énergie romaine et de délicatesse transpadane, il n'a rien d'un dilettante, et le labeur, très variable sans doute suivant les poèmes, qui fut le sien, ne répond jamais à des aspirations purement esthétiques.

Nous sera-t-il simplement permis de faire quelques réserves sur certaines tendances qui se dessinent chez d'éminents érudits, entraînés peut-être soit par un excès d'admiration, soit par la tentation d'appliquer à un poète du siècle de César certaines normes critiques (ésotérisme, poésie pure, subconscient, etc.) valables seulement pour la poésie moderne? Nous ne pensons pas qu'il faille subtiliser à l'excès les états d'âme du moins sophistiqué des poètes, ni rechercher un message occulte dans l'élan direct de son effusion. La seule philosophie qui s'en dégage — quand il y en a une ! — est la morale romaine traditionnelle.

Jean GRANAROLO.

(1) Sur la question, nullement négligeable, des diminutifs, on peut consulter, outre l'étude déjà ancienne de Labriolle (Revue de Philologie, 1905) : Ernout, *Aspects du vocabulaire latin*, Klincksieck, 1954, pp. 189-191 (précises références bibliographiques).

III

J. P. Elder

Notes on some conscious and unconscious elements
in Catullus' poetry

NOTES ON SOME CONSCIOUS AND SUBCONSCIOUS ELEMENTS IN CATULLUS' POETRY

By John Petersen Elder

IN the first part of this essay the writer has an axe to grind; the second part, on the other hand, is meant merely to be suggestive, and nothing more. The first section argues against the conception of two Catulluses — the one a genius who wrote the short poems with an easy inspiration and no thought of his craft, and the other the *doctus poeta* of the longer works — and instead would maintain his poetic unity throughout all his poems. The second section, recognizing however that poetic composition does indeed embrace both conscious and subconscious elements, suggests some features in Catullus' poems which may belong to the latter class.

I

The order of Catullus' poems in the manuscripts has been the subject of much discussion.[1] Did the poet himself determine this arrangement, or does it merely reflect a later compilation, perhaps no earlier than the time of Isidore? Though the question is indeed a matter of first importance in understanding how Catullus felt toward his art, it will not be dealt with here. Rather, this paper will comment on an effect which this discussion, as well as perhaps nineteenth-century romanticism, has had on our appreciation of the qualities of Catullus' poetic spirit. I refer to the division of the poems into three groups, with the coloring which such a formal division casts upon our picture of the poet. One may group the poems partly on the basis of metre and partly on length, and come out confidently with 1–60, 61–64, and 65–116, or else partly on the basis of metre and length and partly according to subject, and emerge with a tidy 1–60, 61–68, and 69–116. Then one can handily juggle about such ancillary considerations as attention to structure, amount of lyrical feeling, Alexandrian elements, and the like, and, with not too much Procrustean effort, fit these into the preconceived tripartite division. In the end, Catullus is nailed down with philological neatness, and becomes not one poet but two! On this side is the Catullus who writes spontaneously, with an effortless art and a

41

Rousseau-like "naturalness," pouring out his soul in faultless verse. (But it is momentarily forgotten that one cannot just state an emotion simply and directly and produce poetry. Indeed lyric poetry above all other types demands the severe, formal compression of an exacting art.) This is the *Naturbursche* who spun off the lyrics and the epigrams. But then there is the other Catullus, the one who generally is made to stand shamefully in the corner, the painfully technical composer of the long poems, the pretentious *doctus Catullus* who labored hard at structure, learned allusions, and traditional themes in the most elegant modern style.[2]

Such a cavalier splitting of a poetical psychology is, at the least, probably artificial and unjustified. Few poets, if indeed any, exhibit such a duality of artistic temperament. More than this, as Professor Havelock pointed out,[3] such a superimposed dichotomy is harmful to sound criticism. To assume that there are two Catulluses, one an unconsciously artful poet of lyrics and epigrams, and the other a stiffly conscious pedant in verse, will certainly inhibit one's appreciation of both of these two hypothesized sections of his poetry. One cannot "partition a poet's Muse" without evil consequences. Partitioning will blind one, for example, to such elements as the elaborate artifices of the lyrics or to the lyrical and dainty rococo notes in the longer poems.

In this study it will be argued that, indeed, there are not two Catulluses, since fundamentally Catullus handles such matters as structure, allusions, imagery, and the like, in the same fashion in both short and long works. The differences that bred such an apparent but false division are actually merely differences in what the poet hoped to do in this or that poem and in what techniques he deemed suitable, and were not owing to any basic poetic fission. If, then, Catullus' aesthetic unity can be established on this score, we may then approach in Section II a more delicate dichotomy — not, perhaps, ultimately a very real one either — the question of what a poet does consciously and what, on the other hand, he unthinkingly draws from his subconscious.

To begin with the matter of the presumed two Catulluses (as opposed to the Catullus who now is a conscious artist and now works with the stuff his subconscious sends him), let us consider the structure of the poems. One is accustomed to think of the Catullus who fathered the long poems as a fairly consummate, if a sometimes obvious and mechanical, master of this technique. One recalls the elaborate balances of No. 62. And No. 63, as was recently pointed

out to me,[4] can perhaps be broken down into such minute, counter-
balancing sections as would warm the heart of the most avid searcher
for recondite Alexandrianism. No. 64 needs no comment here in
this regard. The architectonics, real or assumed,[5] of No. 68 are
famous: the "Chinese ball" arrangement of Allius — Lesbia — Laodamia — Troy — Brother — Troy — Laodamia — Lesbia — Allius.
(For the moment one forgets the diverse elements which have here
their uneasy *rendezvous* — the gobs and chunks of poetry, the out-
rageously long and often unclear comparisons, not to mention the
ludicrous tastelessness in comparing the depth of Laodamia's love to
oozy soil or possibly a drainage channel. All these lie restlessly in
their proper compartments dictated by *alexandrinische Spielerei*.)

Yet the same carefulness in structure is to be seen, if we look
closely, in most of the little poems. Nor need one hesitate to look
closely or fear to break a butterfly upon a wheel. One is not thus
violating any sanctity, save possibly that of the Temple of Ignorance.
The incense and holy-water school of literary criticism which re-
joices in a well-bred "charming" and forbids dissection neither edu-
cates nor stimulates. Let us look, then, at No. 46:[6]

Iam uer egelidos refert tepores,
iam caeli furor aequinoctialis
iucundis Zephyri silescit aureis.
linquantur Phrygii, Catulle, campi
Nicaeaeque ager uber aestuosae: 5
ad claras Asiae uolemus urbes.
iam mens praetrepidans auet uagari,
iam laeti studio pedes uigescunt.
o dulces comitum ualete coetus,
longe quos simul a domo profectos   10
diuersae uariae uiae reportant.

On examination, this poem is as artfully constructed as any of
the Hellenistic or post-Hellenistic compositions in the *Greek Anthology* which may have consciously or subconsciously influenced Catullus in this poem. Certainly, too, for its length it is as carefully formulated as any of Catullus' longer works.[7] It divides itself into two
parts, 1–6 and 7–11, each with its own mood, with the first two
verses of each part beginning with *iam*. The first part presents the
general background, and hence all the proper names occur in this
part. Spring is here and we shall be off. This part, in turn, divides
itself into two sections, 1–3 and 4–6. The first section, 1–3, sets
the stage by describing the coming of spring; the second, 4–6, ad-

dressed to the poet himself, gives with its subjunctive mood the concrete effects of the first section: the longings that spring arouses to be up and away. The mood of the second part, 7–11, is one of positive reaction to the first part. Here, too, there is a dual division, 7–8 and 9–11. Again the first section, 7–8, sets the stage by describing, this time, the general state of mind, while the second section, 9–11, addressed this time to his friends, gives the concrete effects of the first section: the departure of all the friends.

Or, to look briefly at one or two other of the short poems, let us turn to No. 45. Here there is an even more striking structural arrangement: 1–7 (Septimius), 8–9 (refrain), 10–16 (Acme), 17–18 (refrain), 19–20 (both Acme and Septimius), 21–22 (Septimius), 23–24 (Acme), 25–26 (conclusion: both Acme and Septimius). The division, then, is: 7–2–7–2 — 2–2–2–2.[8] Or consider the function of the refrain in another poem, No. 8.[9] As the recipient of these essays pointed out to me some years ago, lines 1–2 constitute a general introduction; then comes the refrain in 3; then 4–7 describe the happiness of the past; then comes the refrain again in 8, with its significant change,[10] and 9–19 describe the unhappiness of the present. However one interpret this poem, as serious (in which case it has an interesting relationship to No. 76) or, which has been proposed, as humorous [11] or, as seems best to me, as fairly serious with touches of conscious humor, one thing is clear: the poem is built up upon the balancing use of the refrain so that it has the effect of strophe and antistrophe. Here there is no such mathematically exact division of the corresponding lines as in No. 45, and indeed this element of asymmetry is the usual practice with Catullus as with most ancient poets.[12] One has only to think of the irregularly recurring refrains in Nos. 61, 62, and 64. We could go on in the polymetrics to many another poem and point out the careful finish in construction, as careful a finish as one sees or may think he detects in the longer poems.[13]

Turning to the epigrams, one finds that their very form in itself encouraged obvious structural patterns which are immediately apparent.[14] The alternation of the hexameter and pentameter, the poet's habit of closing the thought with the shorter line, the inherent use of antithesis, and the general tendency to anticipate the thought of the last line in the opening one — all these elements contributed heavily toward a more obvious structure, just as they must have subconsciously affected the poet's choice of this metre for the vehicle for some of his emotional expressions. Thus No. 72. to take a random example, is clearly divided into two groups of four lines, each with its own mood — past and present, highlighted by the interplay between *nosse* and *cognovi*.[15] And each of these two groups is in turn composed of two sets of two lines each. In the case of No. 76 several suggestions have been advanced for the structure of the elegy (if it be an elegy [16]) on the basis of moods.[17] For myself the division is attractive which I find appealed to Ellis: 1–6, 7–10, 11–16, 17–22, and 23–26.[18] Now this falls into the sequence of: 6–4–6–6–4. One should not press this too far; this division may well be wrong or, if right, may not be of much moment. And if it should seem correct, one can then speculate endlessly on whether the poet himself was conscious of this pattern, or whether he instinctively hit on it with that unerring sense of proportion which marks every good artist. And one can go on and on in the matter of structure in the epigrams. The upshot surely is this: any division of Catullus into two poets on the score of attention or lack of attention to structure, whether this be done consciously or intuitively, is unjustified.

The same is true, I believe, in all other respects. For example, consider the matter of learned allusions. One cannot prosaically weigh allusions or similar features and, on the sheer basis of quantity, come to any sound conclusions about a poetic temperament. Such a procedure is not criticism at all but only arithmetic. Certainly the longer poems contain many more such learned references than the shorter ones, although even here one must be careful. For it is chiefly on the basis of Nos. 64 and 68 that we ascribe this characteristic to the nine longer poems. But the fact that such a characteristic can be assigned to some poems and not to others is slim reason for postulating two poets out of one. Rather, one should ask what a poet was attempting to do in a given poem — i.e., what emotions and emotions of what sort was he trying to express — and then, what methods and techniques did he think artistically appropriate to his formal expression.

Catullan criticism, to indulge in a digression, is in a somewhat odd state. A deal of work has been done on his techniques, particularly in regard to possible parallels between the poet and Hellenistic and later writers.[19] All this is helpful, indeed necessary, as Wilamowitz, Reitzenstein, Weinreich, and others have seen, for a proper understanding of Catullus' own poetic genius. One must always reckon with tradition, first and last. Therein lies the secret of a poet's appeal — his evocation of common experience in commonly understood terms — and therein lies his originality. As T. S. Eliot

E

45

observes of the poet, "he lives in what is not merely the present, but
the present moment of the past," and "is conscious, not of what is
dead, but of what is already living." [20] And this is as true of a
Catullus as it is of a Dante, and may make one wonder whether
poetry today does not stand in rather desperate need of a livelier
sense of tradition. To return to Catullus, only by such subtraction
and addition can one hope to find out the secret of his poetic genius.
Yet there is danger here, too. Careful seeking for parallels may become an end in itself, and the poet is likely to become imprisoned
in bulky catalogues of pedestrian notes.[21] An ultimate consideration
of Catullus' use of traditional themes and figures, in the light of his
total genius, is always needed. "The first words that should be taught
our students," remarked Albert Guérard, "should be the scholarly
equivalent of 'So What?' " [22] And it is such an attitude, I suppose,
which inspired Yeats' *The Scholars*.

Against such a background Professor Havelock's study of Catullus
is a welcome and much-needed relief. But he has approached the
poems from only one point of view, albeit certainly the most important one: What is their poetic significance? This he finds, as his title
declares, in the lyrical qualities, and he goes so far as to say:
"Catullus, if he is to be read as a poet, and not simply classified
and labelled like some figure in a literary museum, should be interpreted first and last as a lyrist. Even in his longer compositions, his
writing becomes significant and important only in so far as it is
lyrical." [23] This may be true, but the fact remains that Catullus did
not look upon himself as always and only a lyrist. We should, therefore, seek to find out what a poet was hoping and trying to do in a
poem — a matter of emotion — and then, what methods and techniques he thought fit and right for this purpose — a matter of artistic
conventions and revolts.

A poet is indeed a rather Januslike person, facing both toward
life and toward art.[24] The receptive aspect is here, and becomes the
spirit of the poem; the creative is here too, and furnishes the blood
and bones which body the spirit. Professor Havelock holds that
Catullus is poetically meaningful only when he is lyrical. But this
may be unfair to Catullus himself, and to his readers, since with
such an inhibition we may vastly cheat ourselves. Catullus obviously
experimented — dabbled, if you will, with forms and themes for the
expression of all sorts of emotions. The results vary, to be sure. Still,
all his emotions were not personal, save perhaps in a highly subconscious way. It may be that Catullus found the themes of Nos. 61

and 62 congenial out of some vague romanticism hovering in his mind over the figure of Lesbia. Equally, one might argue — and it is a tempting thought — that subconsciously Catullus found the subject of the *Attis* a sympathetic one, since he himself like Attis through excessive devotion to an unworthy love had forever unfitted himself for any other love. Each had lost his faith in his ideal, his *pietas*. I have even heard an interpretation of No. 64 which holds that Catullus, subconsciously musing on Lesbia in the wedding-scene, equally subconsciously identified himself with Ariadne in the other scene. On No. 68, that *Schibboleth des Catullinterpreten* as Jachmann called it, one can speculate a good deal indeed.[25]

But, to work my way back to my point, Catullus apparently did not look upon these long poems chiefly as vehicles for his lyrical feelings. If, then, we try to find out at what he was aiming in this or that poem, we shall probably be fairer to him. And in the course of our inquiries, it will probably become apparent that, as the poet deemed some features, some "tricks of style," appropriate to the treatment of some themes, so, too, his use of these "tricks," the value he gave them, doubtless varied with his purposes. It has already been seen that the concept of two Catulluses breaks down on the score of carefulness in structure. It is my belief that such a concept will also be invalidated on the score of learned allusions, once one considers the specific aims of the poet in a particular poem.

One recalls what a regular part of the general *décor* such allusions were in pretentious Hellenistic art. Catullus lacked the smooth virtuosity of a Callimachus in this respect, just as he lacked the detachment and objectivity of a Virgil in sustaining for long a major theme with its minor notes. Yet he tried, and the results, not always happy, are well known. But too often the question of allusions in the shorter poems has been skipped over. Or it has merely been noted that his shorter works, like most in the *Greek Anthology*, have far fewer such references. The purpose of these allusions in the shorter poems deserves study and consideration in the light of the poet's aims. One or two examples will show what I have in mind:

> quam magnus numerus Libyssae harenae
> lasarpiciferis iacet Cyrenis,
> oraclum Iouis inter aestuosi
> et Batti ueteris sacrum sepulcrum. (7,3–6)

This dainty little poem is a work of dalliance. Catullus is making love to Lesbia by picking up a question which apparently she, in archness and coquetry, had tossed to him. Whether the device of the opening question is a traditional, rhetorical one need not detain us here (see page 124 below). It is enough for the moment to note that the question is so skillfully worked into the fabric of the poem that it has all the ring of a genuine question which Lesbia had flung at him. The poem, then, like No. 51, is a poem of courtship, but the technique of courtship in this society is a delicate and sophisticated affair. The Lesbias were not only beautiful; they were intelligent, well-read, and witty, and one courted them on all counts. Hence the form of this poem, and its symbolism, are all-important. The very question itself — "How many kisses?" — has a slightly intellectual twist, and the poet can play with it and can and should be learned, too, if only his learning is never paraded for its own sake but sits lightly and is used with graceful humor, the sort of humor that often slyly peeps out in Callimachus. Only pomposity and sentimentality would be unforgivable here. In its sentiment, as in its prettiness of form, it reminds one of many an Elizabethan lyric.

The question is answered by two comparisons. The first is impressively learned — all the more so, when one considers the shortness of the line and of the poem. The other one is utterly simple and natural, despite its antiquity. It is about the first one that we shall speak here. How can one reasonably make love by at once dragging in the Libyan desert, the asafoetida-bearing district of Cyrene (with its association of foul odor), the oracle of sweating Jove and, worst, old Battus' tomb? The learning is perfectly correct. Cyrene did export asafoetida, and near by lay the shrine of Juppiter Ammon (and even a god might sweat in the desert's heat). Battus founded Cyrene. All this, then, appears to center around Cyrene. But why? One immediate answer, and the obvious and usual one, is that Callimachus not only came from Cyrene but claimed to be descended from Battus. But does such an oblique reference to even such a brilliant poet as Callimachus belong in a short love-poem? What does it have to do with Lesbia? Perhaps Catullus, whose respect for Callimachus and familiarity with his works is well attested elsewhere (for example, in Nos. 63, 65, 66, 116), is delicately weaving into this poem several arresting reminiscences from a then well-known but now lost poem of Callimachus which dealt with the same subject. Such a technique, of course, would not be similar to that used in No. 51, where the poet wishes to imply that Lesbia in some respects is a modern Sappho and therefore produces a close paraphrase. Yet, even if this guess should seem at all likely, one still must ask what emotional use Catullus sought to make of these learned allusions.

Plainly we must try to put ourselves back into Catullus' own times, and forget that when we first read this poem all these painful references had to be looked up. Time always works against poetry in this respect. "Poetry," claims Professor Havelock, "when it makes romantic use in this way of history, legend or place-names is simply extending the range of the image-associations which it is always manipulating." [26] This observation has much truth to it, as countless passages in Virgil testify, or perhaps even such a Catullan line from the short poems as

Nicaeaeque ager uber aestuosae (46, 5)

where the repeated vowel-sounds create what Marouzeau called "le charme 'exotique'," [27] or again, in the list of far-away places in the *Phasellus* poem. But in the case of Catullus' No. 7, the romantic element is only a small part of the answer. Most of the effect of these references is, I believe, humor — the gentle, urbane humor which only a well-educated society can lightly toss about and delight in. These references are not worked in for a romantic effect; that would be an element too heavy, too serious, in such a delicate trifle as this poem. Catullus, on the contrary, is quite certain that Lesbia will smile when she reads about her kisses in connection with all these monuments of erudition. Surely she would smile at the long *lasarpiciferis* in the little line, and at the picture of a "sweating" Jove and "old" Battus. One may conjecture that subconsciously Catullus' image of the *aestuosi Iouis* appealed to him to suggest indirectly the heat of his own passion. Or one may feel that Catullus, again unthinkingly, liked his *lasarpiciferis* because its very length and sound — and note the many *s*'s throughout the poem — would somehow adequately describe the sort of kiss he had in mind.[28] Still, to keep to the field of the conscious, the whole passage seems to me purely a matter of humor. But then he has had enough of the sport of learning. It must not be overdone. And so he turns to images of the stars, the silent night, and the stolen loves of men, and from this second picture where stars hang as many and shining as kisses one is ultimately left with the feeling that Lesbia and Catullus are to be alone for their *furtiuos amores*.

To pass to another instance, let us consider the purpose of the references in

> nunc o caeruleo creata ponto,
> quae sanctum Idalium Vriosque apertos,
> quaeque Ancona Cnidumque harundinosam
> colis quaeque Amathunta, quaeque Golgos,
> quaeque Durrachium Hadriae tabernam; (36, 11–15)

in which such a grim end is proposed for the *cacata carta* of Volusius.
Surely here, too, the purpose is one of humor. For all this is delight-
fully mock-heroic, a pleasant parody; such rhetorical features as the
quae — quaeque — quaeque — quaeque — quaeque help to show us
this. As Ellis long ago pointed out, Lesbia may indeed be parodying
the vow of Pandarus to burn his bow. Catullus has perhaps twisted
Lesbia's words

> electissima pessimi poetae
> scripta . . . (36, 6–7)

by turning them from himself — possibly she even took them from
No. 49's

> gratias tibi maximas Catullus
> agit pessimus omnium poeta, (4–5)

— and applying them to Volusius.[29] One may trace here the influence of perhaps Sappho, Alcman, and Theocritus, but that is not
enough.[30] In Catullus' hands these references, well-known, become
part of the mock-heroic machinery, just as in the phrase *tardipedi
deo* (36, 7) with its oblique reference to Volusius' limping rhythm.
The whole little picture, with its ridiculously puffed up air, reminds
one of many a quietly humorous passage in Horace. And surely, to
propose a third example, it is again humor that moved the poet to
introduce the references in lines 1a–4a of No. 55.

In general, then, one cannot find support for the concept of the
two Catulluses in the field of learned allusions. There are, to be
sure, many more in the longer works; but they traditionally belonged
there. And his purposes varied with the nature of the poem he set
out to write. Yet once his aims and methods are understood, one
will not split him up on this score.

Finally, I should like to attack the concept of the two Catulluses
from one more point of view. In this concept it is assumed that the
Catullus who wrote the lyrics also did the epigrams, as opposed to
the other Catullus who wrote the long poems. Now this presumes
that there are no significant differences between the polymetrics, i.e.,
Nos. 1–60, and the epigrams, i.e., Nos 69–116. But is this so?

The usual view is expressed by Wheeler: "within certain rather wide limits Catullus did not regard the metrical form of his short poems as a distinction of the first importance," and "It is safe to say that Catullus regarded his little elegiac poems as not essentially different from the little poems in hendecasyllables and choliambics. It is safe to say that any of the themes which appear in hendecasyllabic or choliambic form might have appeared in elegiac form." [31] Reitzenstein, too, was equally cautious in refusing to define the Catullan epigram by metre. [32]

Wheeler, I take it, was right when he was speaking of the "themes," and certainly the force of metrical distinctions does indeed seem to have been weakening considerably since the time of classical Greek letters. But the heart of the problem, however, is the spirit and tone given the themes in this or that poem. One would like to know, for example, why Catullus chose to entrust one mood, one set of feelings, one idea, to one metrical form, and others to other forms. The sane starting point in this investigation is surely Wilamowitz' comment that Catullus did not ask whether the "rules" allowed this metre or that one. [33] But is it not a matter that transcends mere metre? Are there any notable artistic differences between the poems written in, say, hendecasyllables and those in elegiacs, differences in techniques so marked that one may conclude that, when Catullus intuitively selected this or that metre as the vehicle for his self-expression, he subconsciously selected a number of other technical elements which went automatically along with the metre?

A good deal of light has recently been thrown on this question by Svennung in his important study *Catulls Bildersprache*. [34] On the basis of his own investigations and many earlier ones, he has produced some highly useful facts. The metaphor, for instance, in the epigrams occurs once in every two lines; in the polymetrics, once in every four lines. (Callimachus in his epigrams employed this figure much more sparingly: once in every six lines!) Then the epigrams vary a good deal more in their length than do the polymetrics. The former range from two to twenty-six lines (if one may count No. 76 in this group); the latter average about fifteen lines. Then there are such obvious differences as in the use of diminutives (seven words used in nine cases in the epigrams, but about fifty words used in about seventy cases in the polymetrics), of colloquialisms (plainly much commoner in the polymetrics), of antithesis (naturally much more frequent in the epigrams), and of compound adjectives (only one in the epigrams, *sesquipedalis*, in No. 97, 5, and that was common enough to appear in Caesar; ten instances, on the other hand, appear in the polymetrics). Further, while the epigrams reveal only five *hapaxlegomena,* almost fifty occur in the polymetrics.

This whole matter needs further study.[35] But certain conclusions seem obvious even now. The chief one is that Catullus was highly conscious of the traditional elements in the epigram, and, in certain respects in his epigrams, is closer to his usage in the longer poems, whereas in his polymetrics he was far more easy-going and informal. What, in turn, might this imply? Possibly that sometimes he felt that he could best satisfy his need for the expression of some emotion by "packaging" it in the more disciplined, severe form of the elegiac couplet than in the more fluid polymetrics, and so he instinctively chose that form. One would certainly expect him to realize the value of such a compressing, balancing, exacting mold. Still, as was said before, we need a careful investigation of the relation of form to emotional tone in Catullus' shorter works. For the moment, it is safe at least to say that evidence of the sort that Svennung has collected strongly argues against the old concept of the two Catulluses.

II

If, then, we have rid ourselves of this concept, perhaps this discussion may now turn to another division which would seem to have more validity — that of the role of the conscious and of the subconscious in poetic creation. But let us go back for a moment. Earlier it was said that a poet has a Januslike quality. He looks both toward life and toward art, and his creations inevitably reflect this duality. He draws upon his own intense living for an experience to crystallize into a poem, and yet the act of formal composition demands a strict attention to his craft. And the finished product is no exact and faithful reproduction, but only a series of attempts, of suggestions. The entire business is a rather mystical one, and in this sense indeed a poet, to be a good one, needs to be a bit "divinely mad."

For first, the poet deals with matters that themselves lie in the twilight of uncertainty. His subjects are not just ideas or descriptions or arguments or summaries of facts, or even the account of a feeling, but all of these and more — in short, everything that is rolled up in that elusive word "experience," whose fragments may lie high in our consciousness or be buried deep in the mind's subconscious caverns. But in any case, since a poem is a recreation of all that is implied by "experience," we should doubtless agree with MacLeish that in the end

A poem should not mean
But be.

Moreover, poetry is also inexact for another reason: the poet cannot describe everything — not even the most ardent Naturalist would aim at this — but must pick and choose items which, with luck and intuition, may perhaps express what he has in mind. But even then, he can only hope to suggest. And in his chief means of suggestion, i.e., in his images and arrangements of words, there is no precision. Further, language is a proud, individualistic, and living thing, as Humpty Dumpty quite rightly pointed out to Alice, and tradition has freighted words for each of us with many strange powers. If one tries to pluck out the heart of poetic mystery, at once it is plain that both the conscious and subconscious elements nestling there must be considered.

And then there is the other aspect of the poet's act of creation, his attention to his craft, his virtuosity, if you will. He may know that this or that image or collocation pleases him and is "right," — and that is the ultimate consciousness of a poet, to reject or approve — but he might never be able to tell you why he chose this or that. Indeed, he might simply tell you that he had succeeded in "getting together with himself." The part of the subconscious in this act of creation was vividly described by E. M. Forster:

What about the creative state? In it a man is taken out of himself. He lets down, as it were, a bucket into his subconscious, and draws up something which is normally beyond his reach. He mixes this thing with his normal experiences, and out of the mixture he makes a work of art. It may be a good work of art or a bad one — we are not here examining the question of quality — but whether it is good or bad it will have been compounded in this unusual way, and he will wonder afterwards how he did it.[36]

But some qualifications should at once be offered. First, there should be no illusions about our ability unerringly to put our finger on what is conscious in a poet, and on what came up in Forster's bucket, even though Lowes' discoveries about Coleridge inspire much hope.[37] Then — and this is intimately connected with the first qualification — it is not meant to be implied here that the conscious and the subconscious are in any ultimate opposition. In the final act of creation their products are, I take it, intimately fused, and that "fifth essence" which hovers over a poem — its "tone" or "color" — is the child of the union. As was said before, the conscious usually presides over the wares brought up out of the storehouse of the subconscious, examines, tests, casts out, and accepts. There is no basic quarrel here between the conscious and subconscious — a new version of the battle between the One and the Many. But in studying immediate sources and the ways of a poet in creation, it will possibly be helpful to keep such a duality in mind.

Finally, one should be on his guard against assuming too hastily that what looks like an element from the subconscious is not, in fact, the result of highly conscious craftsmanship. This point has already been touched upon in Section I. A poet, for example, may either like what he once did and do it again and again, or he may consciously cultivate a striking pattern of phraseology.[38] For example, Catullus' habit of addressing himself may not be an egocentric reflection of his subconscious at all, but a device for emphasis and realism which he found a handy one. Or his habit of beginning a poem with a question and answer, or with a command, or with a condition, on which more will be said anon, may not innocently reflect the way his mind works, but may have struck him as a useful technical device. So he used it over again. Take, as an instance, Horace's habit of inserting, half or three-quarters of the way through an ode, the personal clause beginning with *me*.[39] Here particularly one suspects, as usually in the case of Horace, that the poet simply liked this usage. And so, perhaps, with the fateful *nequiquam, quoniam* with which Lucretius begins some of his most effective lines.[40] Or Virgil's fondness for starting a verse with *it, fit*, or *stat*.[41] Were they really unaware of such repetitions? Anyone who thinks, to take another case, that Joyce created his strange verbal combinations by putting together fragments in his own subconscious had best think again. As Edmund Wilson points out in his essay on Joyce, these combinations represent the most conscious, objective art — Joyce's careful attempt to supply the subconscious with what it does not have, a language.[42]

With these qualifications in mind, let us turn to possible subconscious elements in Catullus' verse. First, the matter of sounds deserves attention, then other types of imagery, then structural patterns, and finally the domain of temperament and tastes.

Lowes broke down the first line of Collins' *Ode to Evening*,

If aught of oaten stop, or pastoral song,

into the pattern of its consonant sounds, and discovered that it went: f-t-f-t-(n)-st-p-r-p-st-r-(l-s-ng).[43] Lowes much doubted, as I suppose we all should, that Collins consciously designed such a mathematical

pattern, with its effective range of sounds. If we turn to Catullus'
No. 76, and to the line which, above all, carries the theme:

> difficile est longum subito deponere amorem, (13)

one finds here, too, a pattern of considerable effectiveness. *Subito*,
the key, occupies the mid-position; six syllables — *difficile est lon-
gum* — precede it, and six follow — *deponere amorem*. Each of these
two groups of six syllables ends with a syllable containing *o* and
one ending with *m*, the liquid *par excellence* of sadness.[44] And each
group begins with *d*, and each group has the cohesion of elision.
Thus the thought of each group is bound together in a fairly perfect
balance and contrast. No one, surely, would assume that Catullus
consciously worked this out, but that rather he knew, when it had
come out, that it was what he wanted. So, too, it might seem a bit
too much to believe that Catullus deliberately sought all the liquids in

> uae factum male! uae miselle passer,
> tua nunc opera meae puellae
> flendo turgiduli rubent ocelli. (3, 16–18)

although the artist in him, that is, the conscious arbiter in aesthetics,
surely told him that the sounds which had come forth were "right"
for the expression of this particular emotion. Or consider in No. 1
the final syllables of each line: libell*um* — expolit*um* — soleb*as* —
nug*as* — Italor*um* — cart*is* — laborios*is* — libel*li* — virg*o* — saecl*o*.[45]
These fall into the pattern of: a-a-b-b-a-c-c-d-e-e, and even the "d"-
element, *libelli*, is reminiscent of the "a"-element, *libellum*. Again,
one may well doubt that Catullus planned this; rather, it would seem
that he was satisfied with the neat framework which he had unthinkingly but instinctively erected.

On the other hand, a great many repetitions in Catullus may surely
be classified as conscious. In this category belong the refrains, the
lines that begin and end the same poem,[46] such stock phrases as

> non harum modo, sed quot aut fuerunt
> aut sunt aut aliis erunt in annis (21, 2–3)

(with their variations),[47] key words within the same poem (especially
when in the same metrical position),[48] and such obvious, intentional
juggling as

> *unam Septimios* misellus *Acmen*
> *uno in Septimio* fidelis *Acme* (45, 21 and 23)

or

> *Dianae* sumus in fide
> *puellae* et *pueri integri:*
> *Dianam pueri integri*
> *puellae*que canamus. (34, 1–4)

Here, too, belongs a significant word carried over from one poem to another, like the *identidem* of No. 11, 19 and No. 51, 3, or a phrase carried over, like the important *meae puellae*, or a whole line (with perhaps slight variations) like

amata nobis quantum amabitur nulla (8, 5 and 37, 12)

with its memorable wealth of *a*'s and *m*'s. It would seem such repetitions of sound are as consciously aimed at as, say, the recurrent symbols in Yeats, and have something of the same effect. And here, perhaps, belong most of the rhetorical repetitions (geminatio, epanalepsis, paronomasia, anaphora, epiphora, etc.), although one cannot always be sure that Catullus, by such repetitions, was not subconsciously emphasizing his own strong emotions. Doubtless other types will occur to the reader which deserve to be included in this class.

But then, between the sound-effects which appear to have been unconscious on the poet's part and those which appear equally surely to have been deliberately devised and manipulated, there lies a large no-man's land, into which we now perhaps may venture. Still, as was remarked before, one enters with considerable temerity. Yet in many instances it would seem clear that a poet is not managing the sounds, but that actually a sound may be leading him about by the nose. Thus in No. 8 it would seem likely that *puella* is in some occult way responsible for the *nulla* and *bella* and perhaps even *labella*. Indeed, this poem offers such interesting instances that the last part of it merits quotation here: [49]

> sed obstinata mente perfer, obdura.   11
> uale, puella. iam Catullus obdurat,
> nec te requiret nec rogabit inuitam.
> at tu dolebis, cum rogaberis nulla.
> scelesta †ne te†. quae tibi manet uita!   15
> quis nunc te adibit? cui uideberis bella?
> quem nunc amabis? cuius esse diceris?
> quem basiabis? cui labella mordebis?
> at tu, Catulle, destinatus obdura.   19

Is it, perhaps, going too far to suggest that the last line, for example, was actually compounded, for the most part unthinkingly, out of bits of the previous ones? The *at tu* would have been subconsciously suggested by the *at tu* of line 14, the *destinatus* by the *obstinata* of line 11, and the *Catulle — obdura* by *puella — obdurat* of line 12. And surely there is some relationship between *inuitam* of line 13 and *uita* of line 15, and between *dolebis* of 14 and *basiabis* and *mordebis* of 18, just as there is between *uideberis* of 16 and *diceris* of 17. Yet, to be entirely subjective, the repetitions of *obdura* in various forms seem to me intentional and an entirely conscious matter, since this is a dominant theme. On the other hand, the *a*-endings (sometimes the *-lla*-endings) of lines 11, 14, 15, 16, and 19 may be a subconscious matter. At all events, although no two might ever agree on just what in this composition emanated from Catullus' subconscious mind and what was consciously sought and worked over, probably all would agree that in spots here sounds are indeed leading the poet along willy-nilly. So, too, in No. 4, 24 in the phrase *limpidum lacum*, perhaps one word suggested the other, albeit one cannot easily distinguish egg from chicken. So, possibly, with *lepidum nouum libellum* (1, 1). Even, perhaps, with the wary Horace we may see in the *Odes* similar cases: *dulce decus* (I, 1, 2) or, with unconscious balance and contrast, *mercator metuens otium et oppidi* (I, 1, 16) or *Motum ex Metello consule civicum* (II, 1, 1), and suspect that a sound in a word already acceptable had indeed prompted a word conjoined with it. Similarly, to continue for a moment with Horace, one thinks of the considerable amount of internal rhyme in his lesser asclepiads. And Bailey, speaking of Lucretius' repetitions of phrases, notes that "Sometimes words which he had already written seem to stay in his mind and come out in the same collocation in a quite different context; — This semi-conscious running of phrases in the poet's mind may sometimes be adduced to determine the text of a doubtful passage: —." [50]

These suggestions at once prompt other digressive considerations. First, one remembers the fondness which early Latin writers show for repetitions of sounds, and one allows for this innate characteristic of the language. This, in turn, leads to the matter of tradition. From Ennius onward, the literary tradition of alliteration, assonance, and the like, had indeed great force, and Miss Deutsch in her study, *The Pattern of Sound in Lucretius*, while pointing out how much more skillfully Lucretius and Catullus employed their sound-effects than had Ennius or Cicero, was doubtless right in concluding that "the many forms of repetition — cannot be entirely unconscious." [51]

This mention of the force of tradition suggests another aspect of the whole matter which also should be noticed: apparent echoes of one writer in another.[52] Here, again, in many cases we can unhesitatingly call the echoes conscious ones, as in Virgil's tribute to Lucretius (*G.* II, 490–492).[53] But what is one to say of Virgil's

> Inuitus, regina, tuo de litore cessi (*A.* VI, 460)

in relation to Catullus'

> Inuita, o regina, tuo de uertice cessi, (66, 39)

especially when one considers the taste involved in thus mingling hair and hero.[54] Was this consciously done, and are we to call it artful handling, nay even a compliment? Or are we to say that Lucretius in III, 154–156 was consciously imitating Sappho (or Catullus)? [55] To turn to the cases of Lucretius and Horace, it would indeed appear that Horace was consciously recalling Lucretius'

> iuuat integros accedere fontis
> atque haurire (I, 927–928)

when he wrote his

> O quae fontibus integris
> gaudes, (*Odes* I, 26, 6–7) [56]

but what, if anything, can one say of Horace's *frigus amabile* (*Odes* III, 13, 10) beside Lucretius' unimportant and apparently not particularly memorable *manabile frigus* (I, 534)? If there be any connection here, surely it is an unconscious one. On the other hand, Horace's

> o et praesidium et dulce decus meum (*Odes* I, 1, 2)

may be somehow bound up with Lucretius'

> praesidioque parent decorique parentibus esse (II, 643).

But how? Perhaps it has a direct connection, or perhaps the poetic processes are more devious. The preceding line in Lucretius contained the phrase *patriam defendere terram*. If Horace's first ode was written after III, 2, with the latter's

> dulce et decorum est pro patria mori (13)

then possibly the connection was: *patria* to *decorum* to *decori* to *praesidio* and then to line 2 of the first ode.[57] If this case seems shaky, one is perhaps on surer ground when dealing with Horace's

cedat uti conuiua satur (Sat. I, 1, 118)

and recalling Lucretius'

cur non ut plenus uitae conuiua recedis (III, 938).

Obviously Horace had Lucretius' line in mind, but why *satur* instead of *plenus*? We must turn ahead a few lines in Lucretius to

quam satur ac plenus possis discedere rerum (III, 960)

and one may guess that the collocation *satur ac plenus* (with the suggestive *discedere*) caused him probably unconsciously to make the substitution.[58]

Now let us turn to two poems and briefly examine what may be the conscious and unconscious elements out of which they are compounded. First, No. 107:

> Si quoi quid cupido optantique optigit umquam
>   insperanti, hoc est gratum animo proprie.
> quare hoc est gratum †nobis quoque† carius auro
>   quod te restituis, Lesbia, mi cupido.
> restituis cupido atque insperanti, ipsa refers te   5
>   nobis. o lucem candidiore nota!
> quis me uno uiuit felicior, aut magis ab dis
>   optandum in uita dicere quis poterit?

[margin: Superabundance #107]

In a close study of this poem, Van Gelder rightly points out that the words in the first clause fairly trip over each other.[59] Catullus has more to say than the words can express: the "if"-element, then the fulfillment, and finally reverting to the longing, he adds the tag *insperanti*. The rest of the poem tries to work out the superabundance of thoughts in the first clause. Hence line 5 (with its *restituis* from line 4) takes its *cupido* from line 1, and then the tag *insperanti* which was practically an afterthought in line 2 (as a mere amplification of the *cupido optantique*) now comes to his mind and shoves out the *optantique*. Finally, the *ipsa refers te* is a mere repetition of the *restituis*, as if the poet had to repeat it to believe it — as if he were truly *insperanti*. The *si umquam* has become the "now." As for the *optantique* of line 1 which was defrauded of its to-be-expected place in line 5, it pops up in the end of *optandum*.

Now much of this type of repetition would appear to be the work of the subconscious, although some certainly is conscious as the poet deliberately itemizes problems and answers. But it is not wholly of the formal, antithetical sort which one often associates with the epigram, like the lines of No. 70:

> Nulli se *dicit mulier* mea nubere malle
> quam mihi, non si se Iuppiter ipse petat,
> *dicit*: sed *mulier* cupido quod *dicit* amanti,

or the repetitions in Nos. 78 or 86 or 87. Neither does it resemble the gently insistent recurrences of the masculine *-um*, which has all the earmarks of conscious work, in No. 34:

> monti*um* domina ut fores
> siluar*um*que uirenti*um*
> saltu*um*que reconditor*um*
> amni*um*que sonant*um*: (9–12)

— a technique carried to its artful extreme in the hands of such modern poets as Hopkins or Edith Sitwell.

But the role of the subconscious in proposing sound-combinations merits exploration on another score — the degree to which the sound may either suggest the meaning of the words or groups of words, or may serve as a sort of theme-note throughout a poem.[60] The onomatopoetic element needs no detailed study here; nor, of course, should one forget that in a large number of cases poets consciously strove for this effect. But the matter of a sound's acting as a major note reintroducing in subtle fashion the theme does deserve some notice. Thus in No. 46 (given in full on p. 103) the two themes are spring and travel. The opening words bring in this note at once: *Iam uer*. Perhaps it is not utterly fanciful to see in the *-er* sound a subconscious association with "spring." Then one observes that this theme-note recurs in *refert, ager uber*, and finally in full form in *diuersae*, as well as, in reverse form, in *re*fert and *re*portant (lines 1 and 11). This sort of imagery is in its way as effective as the more obvious sort seen in the sympathetic *uigescunt* (even their feet grow green with spring). Then the second theme — the blowing of the spring breezes with its suggestion of ships and home — may be represented in the *-u* (*w*) sound, as in Horace's

Sol*u*itur acris hiems grata *u*ice *u*eris et Fauoni (*Odes* I, 4, 1).

#46 (handwritten in margin)

So in No. 46 one remarks this note in *uer* itself, in *uolemus, auet uagari, uigescunt, ualete,* and in the charged *diuersae uariae uiae* which, with its homoeoteleuta, asyndeton, and the three conflicts between word accent and metrical ictus (i.e., a three-heterodyned verse), certainly adds considerable emphasis.

So far we have been dealing with sound. Now let us pass to a few other types of imagery in which the subconscious may have played a leading role. One which immediately comes to mind is that of color. Catullus outstrips Virgil, Horace, and Ovid in his use of one color (red), — and one must bear in mind that the ancients had no such wealth of words for distinguishing shades as we do — and he even outstrips the natural spectrum itself.[61] If one wishes to avoid the word "subconscious," one may call this a natural expression of Catullus' temperament, just as one may deal with Pindar's "golden." It is all one and the same. On the other hand, save in the line

> tincta tegit roseo conchyli purpura fuco (64, 49)

Poem 64

where the colors progressively deepen, Catullus does not appear to have employed his hues with, say, the conscious artistry of Virgil in the Aristaeus-episode where the first scene gives us bright and splendid colors, the second one grays, and the final tale of Orpheus and Eurydice is swathed in deep black.[62]

The part of contrast and balance in the arts needs no description here. Every work of art that is worth its salt displays both qualities — balance, if it is to be art and not a mere jumble, and contrast, if it is to be interesting. One sees it in the relation of the idea to the image, of consonants to vowels, of past to present, of one line to the next, and so on. It is this that Coleridge had in mind when, speaking of the Imagination, he said: "This power, first put in action by the will and understanding, and retained under their irremissive, though gentle and unnoticed, control, *laxis effertur habenis*, reveals itself in the balance or reconcilement of opposite or discordant qualities: of sameness with difference,"[63] and surely some of the elements that constitute this "sameness with difference" are products of the subconscious. Consider the use of light and dark in imagery. Nothing could be more traditional, more trite, than the use of such contrast. Yet the creative artist may keep these traditions in his subconscious mind, and when he has used the image of light, that of the dark may follow almost automatically and without conscious thought. When Romeo in the first balcony scene says:

balance + contrast

F

> O, she doth teach the torches to burn bright!
> It seems she hangs upon the cheek of night, (I, 5, 46–47)

perhaps both the rhyme and the unconscious instinct to balance light with dark prompted the "cheek of night," just as in the opening lines of Richard III:

> Now is the winter of our discontent
> Made glorious summer by this sun of York;
> And all the clouds that lour'd upon our house
> In the deep bosom of the ocean buried,

"winter" may have brought forth from the subconscious realms the answering "summer" and the element of darkness prompted the element of light, with "summer" unconsciously sponsoring "sun." Indeed, in the case of Lucretius, who makes heavy use of light and dark, one may even be able to discover not a little bit about the subconscious workings of that strange mind.[64] So, trite and threadbare as are the figures of the *soles* and *nox* in Catullus' No. 5,[65] much here may have come out of Forster's "buckets" from the subconscious. The theme is *Viuamus*. What image will effectively body that idea? Suns, the sun of life, the source of warmth.[66] But the poet at the same time wishes to express the idea that Nature can renew her rhythms and pulsations — a favorite image with Horace — but that man cannot. He must die. *Nox* may have suggested itself to the poet as the answer — an answer over which he spent no conscious labor — since here is light and dark, life and death, and the permanence of Nature and the impermanence of man. And similarly we might look at the elaborate comparison in No. 68, 57–62. If one believes that this simile refers to Catullus' tears (rather than to the help which Allius gave him), then perhaps one might argue that the subconscious is again at work, leading the poet unthinkingly from water (tears) to water (stream). Yet the very elaborations within the comparison may suggest nothing so much as the most conscious, if tasteless, craftsmanship.[67]

Now, in our exploration into the possible operations of the subconscious in poetic creation, we might turn to the large sphere of the poet's entire temperament — his tastes, standards, general outlook, and his consequent habits of thought and expression. Within this field, let us first look at the way in which a poet orders and arranges his material. For aspects of his presentation will surely be the result of conscious effort; yet other aspects, equally surely, will unconsciously reflect the poet's nature.

Thus Catullus strikes the reader at once as a direct poet, who proceeds in an a-b-c-d fashion. Horace, on the other hand, is as obviously devious. In the latter's poems, in fact, one often waits until well in the work before a somewhat shy and brief statement of the "theme" appears. Before that, we move from image to image, person to person, place to place. Not that he has the deviousness of a Donne, who could compound poetry out of hypotheses and conditions. But Horace contrasts strikingly with Catullus. Lucretius, on the other hand, also uses the direct method save that, as Büchner has demonstrated, he can suspend his thought with a digression for twenty or thirty lines — and this is not a reference to the consciously poetic passages — and then return with aesthetic complacency to his general thought.[68] And as for Virgil, Henry long ago called attention to his fondness for lingering over a theme and his tendency to restate it several times before dropping it.[69]

subconscious structure

Two matters relating to structure in Catullus' poems seem interesting enough to merit brief notice here. Each, of course, may be a consciously manipulated device. But one might sooner guess that each unconsciously reflects the way in which the poet's mind worked.

The first is Catullus' tendency to state his theme at the start of a poem, in contrast with a Horace, as Keats contrasts in this respect with a Wordsworth. Then comes the imagery which bodies that theme and makes the poem poetry. And this habit, naturally, contributes greatly to the feeling of directness which his poems breathe. This initial expression of the theme may be a direct statement or a question and answer or an exhortation or a downright command, or, which may be of interest to students of Catullan psychology, a condition. In any case, in itself it can rarely be called poetry and must wait for the imagery, that is, the concrete, to support the abstraction. So

>   Viuamus, mea Lesbia, atque amemus

depends on the subsequent imagery of suns and night; so the

>   Quaeris, quot mihi basiationes
>   tuae, Lesbia, sint satis superque

must wait for the two images, just as Shakespeare's

>   Shall I compare thee to a summer's day? (Sonnet 18)

or Mrs. Browning's

>   How do I love thee?

must wait for the answer, cast in images, or T. S. Eliot's prose-like opening of *Burnt Norton*:

> Time present and time past
> Are both perhaps present in time future,
> And time future contained in time past

only becomes poetry when we come to the imagery of:

> Footfalls echo in the memory
> Down the passage which we did not take
> Towards the door we never opened
> Into the rose-garden.[70]

Now the poem has life and power.

The second structural matter to which we now pass and which, in its logical, reflective order, adds to the effect of simple directness and realism is Catullus' habit of opening his poem with a question and answer,[71] or with a statement, or with a condition,[72] and then with an introductory *nam* giving the reason, and finally closing with the conclusion introduced by a *quare*. The first poem illustrates this sequence: first comes the question and answer (*Qui dono* etc., with the reply *Corneli, tibi*), then the reason (*namque tu solebas* etc.), and finally the conclusion (*quare habe tibi*, etc.). So in No. 6, note the *nam* in line 12 and the *quare* in line 15; in No. 21 the *frustra: nam* in line 7 and the *quare* in line 12; in No. 23 the *nec mirum: bene nam* in line 7 and the interrogative *quare* in line 15; in No. 35 the *nam* of line 5 and the *quare* of line 7; in No. 44 the *nam* of line 10 and the *quare* of line 16; in No. 69 the *neque mirum: nam* of line 7 and the *quare* of line 9. Finally, even No. 76 shows the same pattern: *nam* in line 7 and *quare* in line 10.

These eight poems illustrate the pattern in its fullest form. But no less than at least twenty-four other poems reveal the same basic pattern with such variations as a *quod*-clause for the *nam*-clause,[73] or an *at* for *quare*,[74] or the omission of one of the conjunctions, or the omission of one of the three sections.[75] Upon such evidence we may fairly, it would seem, call this a dominant structural pattern with Catullus, rather like the pattern (with variations, of course) which one sees in the Lucretian sequence of: *principio — tum porro — denique — quin etiam — postremo*. Like the Lucretian pattern, the Catullan lends his writing the effects of directness and of logical reflection.

Now comes the question: is this a conscious device of style, that is,

[handwritten margin note: Poem 1, 6, 21, 23, 35, 44, 69, 76 have this structure]

a traditional, rhetorical element, or a subconscious matter, a reflection of the poet's general temperament and outlook, revealing the way in which his mind proceeded between "I, Catullus," and someone or something else.[76] Can one perhaps guess that Catullus' own immersion in physical sensation explains quite adequately such a note of realism, of directness, so that in most of his shorter poems medium and matter are well-nigh perfectly synthesized?

This question is difficult to answer, since so little is left of earlier collections of lyrics which in many respects must have served Catullus as models. Only bits of such early masters as Archilochus or Alcaeus remain, and we are even worse off when it comes to such Hellenistic lyrics as those of Callimachus.[77] Most of the lyric wealth of Meleager's *Garland* was apparently lost to us when that collection was woven into the later ones. As for the short poem in Latin before Catullus, again there is only a small amount, and most of that is in elegiacs. Laevius alone appears to have made a collection entirely in lyric metres, and here too the fragments are too brief to be of much help. The upshot is that, rich as we are in our knowledge of elegiac production from the fourth century up to Catullus' own time, we are lamentably ignorant about the history of the short lyric during this critical period. One gets, then, little light on this structural peculiarity of Catullus by examining the scanty remains of his predecessors. Nor do other Latin authors before Catullus, whether writing in poetry or prose, show this pattern in such a marked way within such definite limits that we may come to any conclusions about Catullus' usage of it on this score.[78]

In such ignorance one can only guess. My own conjecture would be that this was an unconscious habit of his, a matter of psychology, reflecting more his own mind and its ways than any stylistic characteristic of predecessors. As was said before, this pattern is both direct and reflective. That fact, along with others, should remind us that Catullus doubtless owed a great deal more to the classical poets of Greece than we, with our eyes glued too close on Hellenistic productions, are often likely to remember. The debt includes imitation — and Professor Hendrickson has thrown a good deal of light on Catullus' obligation to Archilochus — but it surely was also a debt of general spirit and outlook.[79] Thus Catullus displays much of the quick but reflective tone of such an elegist as Callinus, and this pattern of statement, cause, and conclusion is merely a mechanism for the expression of the same elements of reason, logic, and persuasion that characterize the best writers of Greek elegiac, lyric, and even melic poetry. Like Archilochus, he expressed love and hatred without inhibition; the satire of each was intensely narrow, intensely personal; neither cared to waste time on didacticism. Like Alcaeus, he felt and wrote — one hardly dares say "thought" — in personal terms of a class whose star was waning, and what the one said of Pittacus is not alien in tone from the remarks of the other on Caesar. And so on. My point is that when it is a question of Catullus' relationship to the classical writers, one must think not just of direct borrowings and parallels but also of common temperament and outlook. Indirectly — and this then is a subconscious matter — the freedom of the individual, the directness, at times the violence, and yet the underlying appeal to reason that lies over most of the poetry of classical Greece must have made a deep impress on this rather lawless mind. One commonly speaks of Horace as the writer who returned to the classical period, and Catullus as the one who looked not farther back than to the Hellenistic age. There is much truth in this view if we think only in terms of forms and parallels. If, however, we think in terms of animating spirit — of general tone — it may appear that in many respects it is Horace who thinks like an Alexandrian and Catullus who thinks like the earlier masters.[80]

Finally, in our exploration of a poet's temperament — his general outlook, tastes, standards, and the like — as a possible field in which the subconscious operates in poetic creation, we might turn to that puzzling poem, No. 68, to see if thus any illumination is to be had on its meaning.

It is not proposed here to go into most of the very difficult problems raised by this poem, but merely to propose an interpretation which leans fairly heavily on psychology. At the outset, however, the writer should state certain assumptions upon which he proceeds. First, lines 1–40 and 41–160 are taken as integral parts of the same poem.[81] Second, Lesbia is assumed to be the *domina*. Third, it is assumed that Catullus had been asked by Allius (or however one wishes to spell his name), to write about love, and in the new style. Catullus refuses with the implication that he must be actively engaged in love to write about it, but his brother's death has made this *studium* impossible. But as he thinks on Allius' *officia* (and their associations with Lesbia), he changes his mind after all and in the end grants both requests.

Two strong feelings dominate the poem: grief for his totally lost brother and love for his half-lost Lesbia. The intensity of the first feeling is evidenced by his references to his brother in other poems, as well as the repetitions within this one. The second feeling needs no comment. As for his feelings about Allius, they constitute, it is true, the ostensible motivation for the poem but no dominant note.

Catullus intends consciously to compare Lesbia with three heroines: Laodamia, Helen, and Juno. The connecting links are obvious. But unconsciously, as Ellis hinted and Professor Havelock has recently explained, Catullus identifies himself with two of these three — Laodamia and Juno — in his romantic idealization of Lesbia in his own image.[82] For it was Laodamia who was the passionate and unhappy lover, and it was Juno who had to overlook Jove's *furta* as Catullus did the *furta* (*rara*, he wistfully calls them) of his *verecundae herae*. At this point, however, the unconscious identification ceases, for Catullus goes on to remind himself that Lesbia was not led to him by a father's hand,[83] and so then he looks at the *furta* from her point of view, as *furta* from her husband:

> sed furtiua dedit mira munuscula nocte,
> ipsius ex ipso dempta uiri gremio. (145-146)

And one immediately recalls the *furtiuos amores* of No. 7, 8.

We may go further. For two of these three heroines are also connected with Troy: Laodamia and Helen. But Troy is the concrete symbol which he uses for his brother and his death. Thus in some vague fashion the themes of Lesbia and his brother are commingled. Prescott was aware of this confusion when he spoke of "the theme of love that is not fraternal but sensual," and concluded that "The logical relation of the brother's death to the context is simply that the emotional upset occasioned by the loss of his brother prevents any other emotional activity." [84]

The answer may be that subconsciously Catullus transferred his love for his brother to Lesbia, and in some way mingled the two loves just as the symbols of Laodamia and Helen embrace both Lesbia and the brother. Hence his rather pathetic attempts to make Lesbia appear less faithless than he undoubtedly knew she was. Indeed, does the line (133)

> quam circumcursans hinc illinc saepe Cupido

suggests the romantic desire once again to endow her with the Cupids and Venuses that hovered over her in earlier days?

This brings us squarely up against the question: What was the nature of Catullus' love for Lesbia, for his brother, and for his friends. Recently it has been argued, and most interestingly, that

[margin note: the nature of his love for Lesbia]

Catullus' affection for Lesbia had two quite separate aspects, and that he himself was aware of this dichotomy.[85] He "desired" her and he "respected" her. For the first, the physical feeling, the vocabulary is traditional: the verb is *amare* and the noun *amor*. For the second aspect, the spiritual feeling, he found no adequate vocabulary since his feeling was no usual one. Here he fumbles with *diligere, bene velle, bene facere, fides, amicitia,* and *pietas.* Catullus' realization of Lesbia's faithlessness caused him to lose his "respect" for her, although at the same time his "desire" for her increased. This in turn bred in him a sense of "wrong, of guilt, of unworthiness" and he is filled with an "ever-increasing loathing of the moral wrong of which he finds himself guilty." It is not, then, from love for Lesbia but from a sense of guilt that Catullus in No. 76 prays to be released!

This view, however stimulating, seems to me to have been compounded mostly out of romanticism and New Testament teaching, and to be quite wrong. Without going into detailed criticism here, the present writer protests against reading backward in our ancient authors. Catullus was no sin-racked neurotic. The couplet (85)

> Odi et amo: quare id faciam, fortasse requiris.
> nescio, sed fieri sentio et excrucior

does not mean anything so complicated as: "I spiritually despise you and am a-lusting after you" (which would follow from such a theory), but just what it says: "For you, I have both love and hate." As for

> dilexi tum te non tantum ut uulgus amicam,
> sed pater ut natos diligit et generos (72, 3–4)

an obvious and fair meaning is: "I did not love you as I might an Ipsithilla but with all the tender affection that a father feels." Surely any division of Catullus' love into a physical and into a Platonic-Christian-spiritual aspect rings very hollow indeed beside the metaphor *prati ultimi flos* (11, 22–23).

But now, what about his feelings toward his brother and his friends? The truth may be that Catullus drew no sharp (and false) distinctions such as we in our shyness like to draw. All affection — call it under whatever names you will — came from the same source, albeit naturally it would take different forms of expression. Thus of Lesbia he could use the phrase

> aeternum hoc sanctae foedus amicitiae (109, 6)

and he could call the now faithless Rufus *nostrae pestis amicitiae* (77, 6). In No. 76 it is Lesbia who had now become *hanc pestem* (line 20). In this connection it is instructive to compare No. 30 with No. 76. Alfenus in No. 30 is reminded that *facta impia* (line 4) do not please the gods; he has no *fides*. In No. 76 Catullus sincerely declares that he has been *pium* (line 2), that is, "loyal," as indeed he had been by his standards, and he again appeals to the gods. He has not violated his *sanctam fidem* (line 3). If *inducens in amorem* in No. 30, 8 refers, as it would seem to refer, to a relationship between Alfenus and Catullus, it probably means "friendship" and nothing more sensational. Finally, it is interesting to observe in both Nos. 30 and 76 the same prosaic phraseology, which indicates that Catullus' mind worked in the same symbols and terms in the same circumstances:

ac tua *dicta* omnia *factaque* (30, 9)

and

haec a te *dicta*que *factaque* sunt (76, 8).

Three facts, it would seem, need to be borne in mind when considering Catullus' affection for Lesbia, for his brother, and for his friends. First, he was obviously capable of a great deal of love — he even lavished it generously on himself — and asked for much in return. Second, he demanded in those whom he loved wit, "elegance," charm, grace, and breeding. One need not list the occurrences of *lepor, sal, facetiae, urbanus*, and the like in his poems. Third, he asked for *fides* or *pietas*, in other words, "loyalty." Indeed, apart from the sexual side, he would appear to have sought to establish the same sort of relationship (*amicitia* or *amor*) with Lesbia as he did with his brother and friends.

To return to my proposal that in No. 68 Catullus is subconsciously transferring his love for his dead brother to a "rehabilitated" Lesbia, let us consider the significance of *domus* throughout the poem.[86] Both Lesbia and his brother were associated with Catullus' *domus*, which takes on the meaning of the concrete harbor of his affection and love — a "family-symbol." In lines 34–35 he says:

hoc fit, quod Romae uiuimus: illa domus,
illa mihi sedes, illic mea carpitur aetas:

Now, whatever may be the correct interpretation of the whole passage and of Catullus' lack of *scriptorum copia* (line 33), the two lines quoted above are highly interesting. Rome was where he lived; one may think of *Viuamus, mea Lesbia*; that was his *domus*, and there he plucked the flower of his *aetas*. This *domus* is surely associated with Lesbia, and *uiuimus* with her, too. We may now turn back to the earlier line 16:

> iucundum cum aetas florida uer ageret.

The same metaphor, the same *aetas*! This, too, then may refer to Lesbia. And indeed the next words, *multa satis lusi* (line 17), support this interpretation, and his following explanation for his inability to write love poetry — that he must be actively engaged in love to do that, and he is not so engaged now. Then one may look at lines 22–23 (repeated as 94–95):

> tecum una tota est nostra sepulta domus
> *omnia* tecum una *perierunt* gaudia nostra.

This time the *domus* is associated with his brother, and that *domus* is now gone with his brother. And with the second of these lines, one may compare No. 76, 9:

> *omnia* quae *ingratae perierunt* credita menti,

when, later on, he realizes that his love for Lesbia, too, is finally dead. The repetition of the same words in the same metrical position may be an unconscious reflection of the earlier lines, just as in No. 73 (where he is speaking of friends, as in No. 77, as opposed to the "family-group" symbolized by *domus*, i.e., his brother and Lesbia), along with the pregnant phrases *bene uelle* and *pium* one finds in line 3:

> *omnia* sunt *ingrata*. - - - -.

In No. 65, 10 he had said of his brother *uita frater amabilior* and now in No. 68 he twice (lines 24 and 96) says of his *gaudia* which now have perished:

> quae tuus in *uita* dulcis alebat amor.

But now this *uita*, this *domus* associated with his brother, is gone, and he transfers these concepts and feelings to Lesbia. So Allius' help, his *officia*, the ostensible and conscious theme of the poem, consisted in his giving them a *domus*:

> isque *domum* nobis isque dedit *dominam* (line 68).

In this connection, one thinks of the proposal that Allius is actually the bridegroom of No. 61, and of the line (31):

> Ac *domum dominam* uoca.

And it is the *domus* which Allius furnished them that is the immediate link between Lesbia and Laodamia:

> coniugis ut quondam flagrans aduenit amore
> Protesilaeam Laudamia *domum*
> inceptam frustra, - - - -. (73–75)

But, as was said before, in his wistfulness Catullus actually, though unconsciously, identifies himself with Laodamia. And more than that. For Laodamia suggests, via Troy, his brother, and as Laodamia's *domus* was begun in vain, so the *domus* associated with his brother is now buried (*sepulta*). It is interesting, too, to see that twice later he picks up the *domus*-theme when speaking of Lesbia: in line 144

> fraglantem Assyrio uenit odore *domum*

and in line 156:

> et *domus* in qua olim lusimus et *domina*,

where there is not only the theme of love (*lusimus*; compare *multa satis lusi* of line 17), but again the dyad of *domus* and *domina*. The final line, then, becomes on this interpretation especially meaningful:

> lux mea, qua *uiua uiuere* dulce mihi est.

NOTES

1. For the problems and chief literature, see the detailed discussion of A. L. Wheeler, *Catvllus and the Traditions of Ancient Poetry* (Berkeley, Univ. Calif. Press, 1934) 1-32 (with whose conclusion, however, that Catullus did not himself arrange the collection I do not agree).

2. Thus recently V. Errante, *La Poesia di Catullo* (Milano, Hoepli, 1945) II, 16, observes that the poems fall "in due sole grandi parti diverse, le quali rappresentano, per dir cosí, i due vólti della Poesia di Catullo," and proceeds on the basis of this dichotomy. O. Friess, *Beobachtungen über die Darstellungs-kunst Catulls* (Diss., Würzburg, Memminger, 1929) 18-19, argues eloquently against the "two Catulluses" and indeed that is the chief lesson which his dissertation teaches. On p. 19, note 20, he collects a number of (shocking) statements from earlier studies supporting the conventional division. This apparently dies hard, since more lately it has ben briefly but forcefully attacked by E. A. Havelock, *The Lyric Genius of Catullus* (Oxford, Blackwell, 1939) 75-76 (to which study I am in general deeply indebted). It should be added that in this

paper the term "polymetrics" is used to refer to poems 1–60, and "epigrams" to 69–116, although this convention is not meant to deny that epigrams are to be found among 1–60 (on this point, see R. Reitzenstein, *RE s.v.* Epigramm, elfter Halbband (1907), col. 102.

3. Havelock (cited in note 2) 76 *sqq.*

4. By my friend and student, Mr. Arthur Millward who it is to be hoped will soon publish his findings.

5. G. Jachmann, reviewing Kroll's ed., *Gnomon* I (1925) 212, refreshingly argues against the usual theory of elaborate symmetry. If one wishes, one may make something, too, out of the symmetry in the first section (lines 1–14): waves of misfortune — Venus — Muses — Muses — Venus — waves of misfortune, or out of the fact that this is picked up (see W. Kroll, *C. Valerius Catullus* [Leipzig, Teubner, 1929] *ad loc.*; H. W. Prescott, "The Unity of Catullus lxviii," *TAPA* LXXI [1940] 479) in the order: Venus (lines 15–30 or 32) and Muses (lines 33–36 or 38).

6. The text used throughout this paper is that of R. Ellis, *Catulli Carmina* in the Oxford Classical Texts.

7. For an interesting discussion of this poem, see O. Hezel, *Catull und das griechische Epigramm* (Diss., Stuttgart, Kohlhammer, 1932) 22–26.

8. As often noted, e.g., by R. Ellis, *A Commentary on Catullus* (Oxford, Clarendon, 2nd ed., 1889) 158 and Friess (cited in note 2) 36–37. On the balancing and contrasting elements in this poem, see H. Comfort, "Analysis of Technique in Catullus XLV (*Septimius and Acme*)," *PAPA* LXIX (1938) p. XXXIII.

9. On the structure of this poem see Kroll (cited in note 5) *ad loc.*; Friess (cited in note 2) 21 and 71–72; and especially I. Schnelle, *Catullinterpretationen* (Diss., Gräfenheinichen, Schulze, 1933) 28–31.

10. The *quondam* of line 3, with which cf. 72,1, is now *vere*, with which perhaps cf. 11,19; 87,2; 109,3.

11. See Wheeler (cited in note 1) 227–230, who follows E. P. Morris, "An interpretation of Catullus VIII," *Trans. Conn. Acad. Arts and Sciences* XV (1909) 139–151. But self-irony, petulance, and retaliation are not humor!

12. On Catullus' use of asymmetry, see Friess (cited in note 2) 40–42.

13. Indeed at times one may wonder whether a scholar like Friess (cited in note 2), with a sort of ὀμφαλός-obsession, has not often gone too far in a rather mechanical fashion.

14. On the Catullan epigram, see Reitzenstein (cited in note 2); O. Weinreich, *Die Distichen des Catull* (Tübingen, Mohr, 1926); Havelock (cited in note 2) 134–144.

15. On the structure of this poem, and for its interpretation, see Schnelle (cited in note 9) 31–34.

16. Kroll (cited in note 5) 247–248, sensibly declares "Der Streit, ob wir hier eine Elegie oder ein Epigramm vor uns haben, ist ganz müssig: es ist ein Gedicht, und zwar ein von tiefster Empfindung getragenes, in dem der Inhalt mehrfach die Form gesprengt hat." Wheeler (cited in note 1) 170–171, unhesitatingly calls it an elegy, as does E. Paludan, "The Development of the Latin Elegy," *Classica et Mediaevalia* IV (1941) 208–209.

17. Friess (cited in note 2) 24–25, finds "wenig von einem Schema" here, but notes that lines 13–14 are the ὀμφαλός, with 12 lines preceding and following. See also his remarks on p. 41. Myself, I should call lines 13–16 the "navel," if there be any profit in such isolation.

18. Ellis (cited in note 8) 446.

19. Most of the basic works in this field are cited in the above-mentioned studies by Weinreich, Friess, Hezel, Schnelle, and by A. Ramminger, *Motivgeschichtliche Studien zu Catulls Basiagedichten* (Diss., Würzburg, Triltsch, 1937). For some recent Italian investigations, see the citations given by L. Alfonsi, "Lesbia," *AJP* LXXI (1950) 59, note 1.

20. "Tradition and the Individual Talent," *Selected Essays 1917–1932* (New York; Harcourt, Brace & Co., 1938) 11.

21. Thus Ramminger (cited in note 19) produces a truly formidable list of parallels on No. 7; a chapter on "Soles" and on "Una perpetua nox" and on "Sidera vident" and on "Der Sand- und Sternvergleich" can hardly leave us in much doubt about the history of these themes. It is true that his title limits him to such lists. My complaint is, indeed, against such a limitation, and one could wish for some final synthesis.

22. *Education of a Humanist* (Cambridge, Harv. Univ. Press, 1949) 101.

23. Havelock (cited in note 2) 78.

24. As D. A. Stauffer, *The Nature of Poetry* (New York, Norton, 1946) 230 *sqq.*, points out in an interesting discussion of this matter.

25. See the views given by Prescott (cited in note 5).

26. Havelock (cited in note 2) 125. On the history of the sand and stars comparison, see Ramminger (cited in note 19) 62–67.

27. J. Marouzeau, *Traité de stylistique latine* (Paris, Les Belles Lettres, 2e éd., 1946) 23.

28. For a technical classification of kisses, see Serv. *ad A.* I, 256.

29. Ellis (cited in note 8) 123, but see G. Friedrich, *Catulli Veronensis Liber* (Leipzig, Teubner, 1908) 191–192.

30. Ellis (cited in note 8) 127–128.

31. Wheeler (cited in note 1) 48 and 47.

32. Reitzenstein (cited in note 2) 102.

33. U. von Wilamowitz-Moellendorff, *Sappho und Simonides* (Berlin, Weidmann, 1913) 293. On the encroachment of one literary *genre* upon another, see C. N. Jackson, "The Latin Epyllion," *HSCP* XXIV (1913) 42.

34. J. Svennung, *Catulls Bildersprache* I (Uppsala Universitets Årsskrift 1945: 3, Uppsala) 20–34, who concludes (p. 34): "Aus den obigen Ausführungen dürfte hervorgegangen sein, dass Catulls Epigramme nicht nur durch das Metrum, sondern oft auch durch bewusste formale und stilistische Ausgestaltung von den Polymetra und grösseren Gedichten des Dichters geschieden worden sind."

35. One must remember that the polymetric lines are usually shorter, that there are fewer epigrams, that perhaps the sapphics and asclepiadics should be excluded, and finally that Svennung is contrasting range with average. Perhaps one can add to Svennung's list: types of verbal repetitions (see below p. 134) and structural patterns (see below p. 136).

36. "The *Raison d'Être* of Criticism in the Arts," *Music and Criticism* (ed. by R. French, Cambridge, Harv. Univ. Press, 1948) 21.

37. J. L. Lowes, in his *The Road to Xanadu* (Boston, Houghton Mifflin, 1930).

38. Friedrich (cited in note 29) *ad* 68, 53 *sgg.* (pp. 452–453) and *ad* 68, 157 (pp. 477–478), noting how fond Catullus is of using the same expression over again for the same situation, has collected a useful list of examples.

39. For example, *Odes* I, 1, 29; 5, 13; 7, 10; 16, 22; 31, 15.

40. Lucr. (cited from C. Bailey, *Titi Lucreti Cari De Rerum Natura Libri Sex* [Oxford, Clarendon, 1947] I–III) II, 1148; IV, 464, 1110, 1133, 1188 (and 1239 without *quoniam*); V, 388, 846, 1123, 1231, 1271, 1313, 1332. That these instances occur chiefly in two books probably indicates that during their composition (and perhaps Bk. IV was written directly after Bk. V [Bailey, *op. cit.* I, 32–37]), some unconscious links had been curiously formed in Lucretius' mind between this rather dramatic phrase in this metrical position and the immediate subjects at hand.

41. See A. S. Pease, *Publi Vergili Maronis Aeneidos Liber Quartus* (Cambridge, Harv. Univ. Press, 1935) *ad* I, 130 (p. 180) and *ad* I, 135 (p. 187).

42. In *Axel's Castle* (New York, Scribner's, 1936) 228 *sqq.*

43. J. L. Lowes, *Convention and Revolt in Poetry* (Boston, Houghton Mifflin, 1930) 244.

44. See Marouzeau (cited in note 27) 29. Perhaps Latin letters offer no better example than Catullus No. 101.

45. As Miss R. E. Deutsch notes in her admirable *The Pattern of Sound in Lucretius* (Diss., Bryn Mawr, 1939) 166–167. Although she does not commit herself on the question of how conscious Catullus himself may have been of this scheme, in dealing with longer and more complex ones in Lucretius she concludes (p. 121): "It hardly seems possible that the details of such patterns can have been consciously formulated by the poet, even though he was most certainly aware of the sound of these rhyme schemes as a whole." For a general study of rhyme and assonance in Catullus, see N. Herescu, "L'Assonance Latine," *Lettres d'Humanité* V (1946) 132–148.

46. See Friess (cited in note 2) 33.

47. While one may conclude that such expressions are unconscious habits with a poet, it would seem more likely that he purposely employed such "mock-heroic" touches as his σφραγίς, so to speak.

48. Like those noted by myself, "Catullus' *Attis*," *AJP* LXVIII (1947) 402–403, as opposed to repetitions of unimportant words at the close of lines in No. 64 (see Deutsch, cited in note 45) 157.

49. On the sound-effects of this poem, see Schnelle (cited in note 9) 31; Deutsch (cited in note 45) 168; and especially J. Van Gelder, *De Woordherhaling bij Catullus* (Den Haag, N. V. de Zuid-Hollandsche Boek-en Handelsdrukkerij, 1933) 100–101 and 167–168.

50. Bailey (cited in note 40) I, 145.

51. Deutsch (cited in note 45) 173.

52. See the interesting remarks of E. Löfstedt, "Reminiscence and Imitation. Some Problems in Latin Literature," *Eranos* XLVII (1949) 148–164.

53. H. A. J. Munro, *T. Lucreti Cari De Rerum Natura Libri Sex* (London, Bell, 4th ed., 1929) II, 198–199 (*ad* Lucr. III, 449–451), has collected a long and significant list of Lucretian reminiscences in *Georgics* II.

54. E. K. Rand, "Catullus and the Augustans," *HSCP* XVII (1906) 23 says of this: "Here and elsewhere it is merely the word or the rhythm that he appropriates, with no thought of the original setting — unhappily, sometimes, as in the present case." This comes close to calling this reminiscence an unconscious one!

55. See Bailey (cited in note 40) *ad loc.* Probably this is not a conscious imitation; such descriptions as III, 453–454, 478–480, 487–505, or that on the

plague, may merely indicate a thorough knowledge of (perhaps even training in) medicine.

56. W. A. Merrill, "On the Influence of Lucretius on Horace," *Class. Philol.* (Univ. Calif. Publ.) I (1905) 120–121, concludes that "Probably there is Lucretian influence here," but does not say how conscious he thought it was.

57. Merrill (cited in note 56) 119, citing Lucr. II, 642 and III, 897–898, says: "Here there is nothing common except the thought which is sufficiently trite."

58. Merrill (cited in note 56) 112–113, and C. Brakman, "Horatiana," *Mnemos.* XLIIII (1921), 217–218, avoid any such elaborate guesses. Or did Lucr. and Hor. independently recall Liv. Andron. (Morel, *FPL* 41)?

59. Van Gelder (cited in note 49) 112–114 and 170–172.

60. A quite different but no less interesting matter is the degree to which a chance collocation of sounds may unconsciously suggest to a poet an image.

61. According to my friend and student, Mr. T. Wells, who also finds that: Catullus probably uses as few color-words as any other Latin poet (37 in the 116 poems); hardly any occur in the epigrams, but 35 per cent in No. 64 (which probably means that a good deal of his color usage is forced); Catullus is fond of bunching together two or three color words. For the general subject, see S. Skard, "The Use of Color in Literature," *Proc. Amer. Philos. Soc.* XC (1946) 163–249, reviewed by A. S. Pease, *CP* XLIII (1948) 142.

62. E. A. Havelock, "Virgil's Road to Xanadu," *The Phoenix* I (1946) 6, notes that "The true associative connection," between the three episodes, "resides in the images of shape, colour, sound, and, we should add, temperature," — a subject worthy of detailed investigation (not treated in C. Opheim's excellent "The Aristaeus Episode of Vergil's Fourth *Georgic*," *Iowa Studies in Class. Philol.* IV [1936]).

63. *Biographia Literaria*, ch. 14 *ad fin.*

64. On which see the interesting and curious study of J. Logre, *L'Anxiété de Lucrèce* (Paris, J. B. Janin, 1946). To cite but one example from Lucretius, consider the *dies* (V, 1190) in "natural opposition to *nox*" and picked up below in lines 1192–1193, and the illuminating note of Bailey (cited in note 40) *ad loc.*

65. See Ramminger (cited in note 19) 42–51.

66. Cf. the refrain in No. 8.

67. Ellis (cited in note 8) 413, cites the observation of A. Tartara, *Animadversiones* (Roma, "Dell' Opinione," 1882) 36, that each noun is carefully equipped with a corresponding adjective.

68. See K. Büchner, "Beobachtungen über Vers und Gedankengang bei Lukrez," *Hermes* (*Einzelschriften*, Heft I) 1936, and C. Bailey, "The Mind of Lucretius," *AJP* LXI (1940) 278–291.

69. J. Henry, *Aeneidea* (London, Williams and Norgate, 1873–1889) I–IV *passim*, followed by H. W. Garrod, *The Oxford Book of Latin Verse* (Oxford, Clarendon, 1927) p. xxxv.

70. For permission to quote from "Burnt Norton" (from *Four Quartets*), I wish to express my thanks to Mr. Eliot and his publishers, Harcourt, Brace and Co.

71. On which see Weinreich (cited in note 14) 44–46, who finds: "In der römischen Literatur setzt, soweit ich sehe, diese 'Antwortformel' ein mit Catull, in der Prosa mit Varro und Cicero, wird häufiger bei den Augusteern, von Martial dann als ein wirklich bequemes 'Schema' zu Tode gehetzt. Dagegen

fand ich nichts Entsprechendes bei den Hellenisten oder in älterer griechischer Dichtung." But cf. Ramminger (cited in note 19) 7–10 on the relation of the "Quaerisform" to the dialogue and dialectic of rhetoric. Friess (cited in note 2) 55–57 stresses the air of realism created by such questions and answers.

72. See Friedrich (cited in note 29) 538.

73. On Catullus' use of *nam*, see A. Clemens, *De Catulli Periodis* (Diss., Wolfenbüttel, Zwissler, 1885) 46–47.

74. On Catullus' use of *at*, see A. Reeck, *Beiträge zur Syntax des Catull* (Progr. Nr. 159, Bromberg, 1889) 4. It may be noted here that when Catullus concludes by şending someone or something to an unpleasant end (e.g. 3, 13; 8, 14; 27, 5; 28, 14; 36, 18), an *at* is his favorite conjunction.

75. These poems show this pattern: 3; 8; 12; 13; 14; 16; 27; 28; 32; 36; 39; 68; 71; 72; 74; 77; 78; 86; 88; 90; 99; 100; 107; 114.

76. See note 71.

77. Cf. R. Pfeiffer, *Callimachus* (Oxford, Clarendon, 1949) I, 216–225.

78. For information on *quare* (relative) before Catullus, I am indebted to the ever generous *Thesaurus Linguae Latinae* Bureau (and in particular to Dr. W. Ehlers and Dr. O. Hiltbrunner). I hope to treat this subject more fully in a separate study of structural patterns in Catullus.

79. See G. L. Hendrickson, "Archilochus and Catullus," *Class. Philol.* XX (1925) 155–157, and N. Herescu, *Catullo* (Roma, Ediz. Roma, 1943) 72–73. Archilochus frg. 79 (Diehl, 2nd ed., 1936), for example, in its grim wishes reminds one of a number of Catullus' poems (esp. No. 108) as in its ending, ὃς μ'ἠδίκησε, λ[ὰ]ξ δ'ἐφ' ὁρκίοισ' ἔβη/τὸ πρὶν ἑταῖρος [ἐ]ών, it brings to mind several others (e.g., Nos. 30, 73, 77, 91, 100).

80. For some interesting views on the place of Catullus and Horace in Latin letters, see Havelock (cited in note 2) 177 *sqq.*

81. As argued by Prescott (cited in note 5); but cf. P. Maas, "The Chronology of the Poems of Catullus," *Class. Quart.* XXXVI (1942) 82.

82. See Ellis (cited in note 8) p. lxviii; Havelock (cited in note 2) 118–119.

83. Cf. 72, 3–4: *dilexi — pater ut natos.*

84. Prescott (cited in note 5) 479 and note 12.

85. By F. O. Copley, "Emotional Conflict and its Significance in the Lesbia-Poems of Catullus," *AJP* LXX (1949) 22–40.

86. On the themes of *domus* and "life" and "death," see the interpretation of Van Gelder (cited in note 49) ch. 6, who, however, makes much of *pietas* in this poem.

IV

Frank O. Copley

Emotional conflict and its significance in the Lesbia-poems of Catullus

EMOTIONAL CONFLICT AND ITS SIGNIFICANCE IN THE LESBIA-POEMS OF CATULLUS

Students of Catullus have long been aware of the fact that Catullus' love for Lesbia did not run true to the usual pattern of the ancient love-affair. Even its very circumstances stamp it as unusual, for it is the love of a gentleman for a Roman *matrona,* not the conventional passion of the young man for a *meretrix.* It is, in other words, a love between social equals; more than that, it is, baldly stated, a case of adultery, and stands therefore in open violation of the accepted moral code.[1] This fact has led some commentators to accuse Catullus of blindness and of self-deception when he declares himself *pius,* speaks of his *fides,* and reveals his expectation that Lesbia could reciprocate his own exalted feelings.[2]

It is not, however, my purpose here to deal with these criticisms, which in the end are scarcely more than moral strictures. With Catullus, the fact of adultery must be accepted. To defend it on moral grounds is worse than useless; to attack it on those grounds is to disseminate prejudice and misunderstanding. In the end, Catullus is not the first nor the last man in the world to fall in love with a married woman; it is a common, and tragic, experience, in this day as in that. That Catullus felt himself privileged to carry that love to the point of actual liaison is a condemnation not so much of the man as of the age in which he lived.

Rather, laying aside the moral issue, and laying aside, too, any speculation as to the reasoning, perverted or otherwise, by which Catullus may have justified his pursuit of an adulterous affair, I should like to examine the nature of his love for Lesbia as he himself describes it, with a view to resolving some of the problems it presents and to revealing those of its characteristics which set it apart from the usual Roman or Greek love-affair and give it a special character of its own.

[1] Cf. Plautus, *Curc.,* 37-38: *dum ted abstineas nupta, vidua, virgine, iuventute et pueris liberis, ama quidlubet.*

[2] E. g. E. T. Merrill, *Catullus* (Boston, 1893), Introd., pp. xx-xxi; Gustav Friedrich, *Catulli Veronensis Liber* (Leipzig, 1908), p. 492 (on *c.* 76, 1).

22

As a general rule, the ancient love-affair as we find it in *the ancient love affair* erotic poetry had two outstanding characteristics: it was ephemeral, and it lay almost wholly in the physical sphere. It was not a prelude to marriage, and in fact had nothing whatever to do with marriage.[3] In every case it was coterminous with the physical attractions of the beloved, as a host of passages warning of the ravages of time amply attest.[4] This is not to *physical* say that the ancient lover had no interest in the intellectual or spiritual charms of his lady, but only that any such interest as he possessed was distinctly of secondary importance, and played no real part in his passion. From beginning to end, his love is a glorification of his desire; any spiritual, non-physical elements which may have been in it are no more than incidentals. His attention never focuses upon them long enough to enable him to make of love the mutually interdependent complex of the physical, the emotional, the intellectual, and the spiritual which today we call by that name.

It is precisely an absorption in the non-physical aspects of love that sets Catullus' love for Lesbia apart from the common *Catullus difference* run of ancient affairs and gives to it its special character. It is notable from the very start that nowhere in the Lesbia-poems does Catullus dwell on the joys of physical intimacy—this in the face of his complete lack of reserve in such poems as 32 and 56. Kisses he mentions, of course, but beyond that there is nothing more immodest in the Lesbia-poems than the almost bashful *multa iocosa* of c. 8.[5] This is not to suggest that he practiced any restraint in such matters, or to claim for him a delicacy of feeling that would not merely have set him apart from his

[3] Cf. E. Rohde, *Der Griechische Roman* (Leipzig, 1900), pp. 63-77. The fact that many of the love-affairs of the New Comedy end in marriage is beside the point. Such ending is quite accidental in nearly every case: in the beginning the young man's intentions were merely to win a mistress, not a wife. This fact is clearly signalized by Terence's *Phormio*, in which Antipho finds the marriage which he underwent in order to satisfy his passion highly embarrassing: cf. 173-176, and compare *Andria*, 438-442.

[4] E. g. *Anth. Pal.*, V, 21, 27, 23, 28, 74, 79, 85, 112; Theocritus, VII, 120-121; XXIII, 27-34; Horace, *Od.*, I, 25; Tibullus, I, 1, 69-74; VIII, 41-48; Propertius, II, 18, 19-20; Ovid, *Ars Am.*, III, 69-72.

[5] Contrast e. g. Propertius, I, 3; II, 15. Even the relatively modest Tibullus thinks fondly of the joys of the couch in his idyllic picture of love-in-a-cottage: I, 1, 45-46.

contemporaries but would have marked him as abnormal. It is rather to be taken as *prima facie* evidence that his interest in Lesbia lay elsewhere, that his love, while it had its overpowering physical side, had an even more compelling aspect that was not physical in its nature.[6]

Curiously enough, the earlier Lesbia-poems show no demonstrable evidence of this aspect. They are tender and affectionate (3, 5, 7), full of amatory gayety and enthusiasm (36, 43, 83, 86, 92, 107), occasionally touched with melancholy (2, 70), or with awe (51). Apart from their unique sweetness—a reflection of the man himself rather than of his love—and their surpassing poetic art, they are almost conventional in character. It would appear that as long as Catullus and Lesbia were happy together, as long as he felt that his feelings were reciprocated, he either was unaware that his love for her possessed any special or unusual characteristics, or felt no need to attempt an expression of them. Lesbia apparently was accepting him as he was, and was understanding and appreciating the affection he bore her.

It is only when he began to perceive that Lesbia was not viewing their love in the same way as he was that there began for him the long struggle, never successfully concluded, to give adequate expression to his feelings, to explain the nature of the non-physical side of his love—the very side that had made it significant and worth while to him. Only after we have clearly understood this struggle can we fully understand the Lesbia-poems themselves.

The first hint of the struggle is to be found in *c.* 109, and lies in the contrast between the first and last distichs of the poem.[7] The experience lying behind it would appear to be

---

[6] In point of fact we do not even learn from Catullus' poems anything about Lesbia's appearance. Not a single one of her physical characteristics is ever mentioned. She is *pulcherrima tota* (86, 5); she is *candida diva* (68, 70), both conventional and colorless phrases. Even in *c.* 51, where the overpowering effect of her beauty and charm is described, there is no hint of a single physical trait: cf. E. A. Havelock, *The Lyric Genius of Catullus* (Oxford, 1939), p. 11.

[7] In the following discussion I am laying aside considerations of chronology, and am not suggesting that the poems discussed were written in the order in which I have taken them up. It is convenient to study the development of Catullus' concept of love in a step-by-step fashion;

something of this sort: Lesbia and Catullus have had a discussion of the nature of their mutual feelings; Lesbia has protested undying love on her side, and has offered to Catullus an *amor iucundus perpetuusque*. As Catullus reflects on this discussion, it occurs to him that the phrase Lesbia has used is too hackneyed and ordinary. It does not ring true; more important than that, it does not at all express the feeling that he himself possesses, nor does it describe the kind of love in which he is interested. In legal language, he does not like the terms of the contract she proposes. After, therefore, expressing (vv. 3-4) the hope that, whatever she meant by *amor iucundus perpetuusque*, she meant it sincerely, he goes on to attempt an expression of what he himself desired. What he wants is not *amor*, for that to him means primarily the standard brand of erotic interest. He does not want something merely *iucundus*, for he sees clearly enough that such a feeling is *perpetuus* only as long as it remains *iucundus*. Rather, he wants a love which is not mere physical attraction, but rather has its basis in a harmony of body, intellect, emotion, and spirit. Unfortunately, no word exists in the Latin language which will adequately express this idea. He tries, therefore, to analyze the feeling itself, to break it up into its component parts, and in that way to find expression for it. It is, first of all, something that lasts throughout life, and does not disappear with youth and beauty. It is no mere casual connection; it is a bond, covenant, *foedus*. Perhaps *amicitia* is the right word. But *amicitia* has two faults: it is not normally used of relations between men and women,[8] and it is essentially a cold and formal term.[9] It is adequate only in that it expresses a feeling based on elements that are not physical in nature. To lift it out of its usual formal sphere, Catullus adds to it the epithet *sancta*; this, he hopes, will show that he does not mean the ordinary feeling of friendship, but something more exalted in character.[10] In the end, Catullus' attempt at expression is not

(handwritten margin note: no word can describe his desire)

(handwritten margin note: amicitia — formal — not b/t sexes)

needless to say, his ideas may not have developed in any such orderly way, but may well have undergone periods of regression, as the poet groped for words to express his feelings.

[8] Cf. Kroll on v. 6 (Wilhelm Kroll, *C. Valerius Catullus* [Leipzig, 1929]).

[9] Cf. Oskar Hezel, *Catull u. das griechische Epigramm* (Stuttgart, 1932 [*Tübinger Beiträge zur Altertumswissenschaft*, XVII]), pp. 67-68.

[10] Kroll, *ibid.*: "die Stärke seiner Empfindung hebt C. ganz über die

successful; he succeeds only in indicating that his love is no ordinary love, and that *amor* is not the proper term for it. To the average ancient, as to the modern reader, his *aeternum sanctae foedus amicitiae* must have remained something of a puzzle.

aeternum...
amicitia

One idea which this phrase does suggest rather clearly is that of loyalty, *fides*. This is implied not only by *foedus*, with its hint of contractual obligations,[11] but also by *amicitia*, and by *sancta*, with its connotation of inviolability.[12] As if seizing upon this idea of *fides* as the one phase of his love which he can express with clarity, Catullus, in *c.* 87, tries once again to formulate his concept of the affection he bore Lesbia. Leaving aside the term *amicitia* as essentially unsuccessful, he combines *fides* with a quantitative rather than a qualitative expression, perhaps in the hope that the two together will more nearly express his meaning.

He tells us in the first distich that no woman can truly say that she has been loved *as much as* Lesbia has been by him; then, to show that his love was not merely greater in quantity— or intensity—he adds in the second distich:

> nulla *fides* ullo fuit umquam in foedere tanta
> quanta in amore tuo ex parte reperta mea est.

He bore for her, in other words, not merely a passion (*amor*) that surpassed all others; in addition, his feeling was possessed of a constancy, a trustworthiness, a *loyalty* (*fides*) such as no other had ever known.[13] In this poem, as in *c.* 109, we gain the impression that Catullus first expresses the nature of his love

gewöhnliche Auffassung der Liebe hinaus und lässt sie als *sancta . . . erscheinen . . .*"; cf. Ellis, *op. cit., ad loc.*

[11] Cf. Cicero, *De Off.*, I, 7, 23: *fundamentum autem est iustitiae fides, id est dictorum conventorumque constantia et veritas.*

[12] Cf. Marcian, *Dig.*, I, 8, 8: *sanctum est, quod ab iniuria hominum defensum atque munitum est.*

[13] Propertius also protests his *fides*, and says that it will last to the grave: *ossa tibi iuro per matris et ossa parentis . . . me tibi ad extremas mansurum, vita, tenebras: ambos una fides auferet, una dies* (II, 20, 15-18; cf. *ibid.*, 4 and 34; II, 24b, 26b). But as III, 25 shows, his *fides* proved of much shorter duration. Further, both he and Ovid (*Am.*, I, 3) "protest too much"; their sentiments have a conventional ring, and completely lack the simple intensity of feeling which characterizes Catullus.

82

in more or less conventional terms, and then, finding that expression inadequate, attempts to correct it by adding some element which is unmistakably non-physical—in this case, *fides*. Again, just as in *c.* 109, the amended declaration is unsatisfactory and incomplete: it does not say what Catullus wanted to say. It is no more than a thrust in the right direction, but a thrust that does not reach its goal. *Amor* and *fides* together do not completely define his love.

It is of course possible that in neither *c.* 109 nor *c.* 87 was Catullus attempting to define his love in its entirety. The thought of *fides* may have been uppermost in his mind at the time he wrote both poems, possibly because of some incident, now lost, in which Lesbia had signally indicated her lack of the very quality of loyalty which to Catullus was so important. In spite of this possibility, both poems give the impression of a basic dissatisfaction with the standard erotic vocabulary, of a realization that, for Catullus, *amor, amare,* and the other terms regularly associated with love did not express his own feelings.

This struggle with terms, with a language which as yet possessed no adequate expression of the concept of love as he knew it, becomes more obvious in *c.* 72.[14] He begins, as in *c.* 109, by contrasting Lesbia's words with his own: she had said *solum nosse Catullum, velle tenere,* using phrases both of which lay wholly in the physical sphere and conveyed no hint of anything but the most conventional of carnal passion. To this he offers his own contrasting term, *dilexi,* a word which can refer to the affection of friends as well as to that of lovers. But he realizes at once that *diligere* does not by itself express his meaning, even when he adds *non tantum ut vulgus amicam,* for this could be interpreted as meaning no more than that his love was greater, or more intense, than the ordinary.[15] In the pentameter, there-

---

[14] Cf. Kroll, introd. note: "Er versucht, das Besondere seiner Empfindung für sie in Worte zu fassen und einer Empfindungsweise Ausdruck zu geben, die für die Antike neu war. Dabei ist völlige Klarheit nicht erreicht und konnte nicht erreicht werden, weil die Empfindung selbst unklar war; aber das Ringen mit dem Ausdruck hat hier wie in *c.* 75. 76 etwas Ergreifendes. Die im Inhalt ähnliche Ausführung bei Ovid *Am.* 3. 11. 33 wirkt konventionell." Cf. also Hezel, *op. cit.* (see note 9), p. 65.

[15] Kroll, *ad loc.:* "*dilexi* kann auch von sinnlicher Liebe gesagt werden (wie *amare* von Freundschaft) vgl. 6, 4. 81, 2; dass es hier um etwas Höheres handelt, ergibt sich erst aus dem Folgenden."

fore, he tries to clarify his meaning by adding the simile *sed pater ut gnatos diligit et generos.* This line has only a superficial and accidental resemblance to the well-known words of Andromache to Hector,[16] or of Chrysis to Pamphilus,[17] or to any of the imitations of these passages.[18] All of these latter express primarily, or perhaps exclusively, the idea of helplessness and dependence; they impose upon the one party to the relationship a special responsibility for the welfare of the other.

It is at once apparent that Catullus had no such idea in mind; he is not assuming the rôle of a Hector, much less suggesting that Lesbia might have felt toward him the helpless dependence of a child upon its father. Nor is the line to be interpreted as evidence of naive bewilderment on Catullus' part, as a kind of extravagant expression engendered by hurt and confusion.[19] Rather, it is to be taken as one more attempt to express the non-physical aspect of his love. It is a line deliberately thought out and devised toward this end. In order to convey the idea that his love for Lesbia had a different quality, one completely dissociated from the carnal, different even from the sincere passion which many of his contemporaries must have known, Catullus compares it to the clearest example he can find of love which has no share in physical interest, the love of a father for his sons. Then, as if even that were not sufficiently divorced from the physical—for father and child are, after all, bound by the physical tie of blood-relationship—he adds " sons-in-law." The love which a paterfamilias bore the men who had married his daughters could not by any stretch of the imagination be regarded as having a physical basis: it must have been based exclusively on a feeling of intellectual, emotional, and spiritual sympathy, coupled with that intense community of interest which characterized the Roman family.[20] The *paternal* aspect of such affection is entirely irrelevant; Catullus does not mean that he

---

[16] *Iliad*, VI, 429-30: Ἕκτορ, ἀτὰρ σύ μοί ἐσσι πατὴρ καὶ πότνια μήτηρ ἠδὲ κασίγνητος, σὺ δέ μοι θαλερὸς παρακοίτης.

[17] Terence, *Andria*, 295: *te isti virum do, amicum tutorem patrem.*

[18] E. g. Propertius, I, 11, 23: *tu mihi sola domus, tu, Cynthia, sola parentes*; II, 18b, 33-34: *cum tibi nec frater nec sit tibi filius ullus, frater ego et tibi sim filius unus ego.*

[19] Havelock, *op. cit.* (see note 6), p. 85, has correctly pointed out the error in this view.

[20] Havelock, *op. cit.*, p. 148.

felt as a father feels, *qua* father. He means only that his love had the same spiritual, non-physical quality that a father's love possesses.

[totally free of physical]

In the end, the expression is fumbling. It could scarcely be expected that Catullus' contemporaries would make the correct equation of ideas. The line probably produced some wise nodding of heads and quoting of the Andromache passage, and probably, too, became the occasion for cynical jibes at the poet's naiveté. It is fair to doubt that Catullus was understood—possibly because he himself did not clearly understand his own feelings.[21]

[he was misunderstood]

It is as if in realization of these facts that in this same poem, Catullus goes on to attempt an expression of his love in still other terms. In the last two distichs he proclaims that his affection for Lesbia had two aspects, and that these aspects were totally different in character, one from the other. So different were they that they were capable of being completely separated, in such a way that the one could continue and grow stronger while the other grew ever weaker. In vv. 5-6, he describes the emotional experience which has accompanied this separation:

> nunc te cognovi: quare etsi impensius uror, *[flame]*
> multo mi tamen es vilior et levior.

In other words the flame of passion, representing the physical side of his love, has grown ever hotter, while his spiritual esteem, the non-physical side, has fallen lower and lower: Lesbia is ever " cheaper " and " of less moment (*levior*) " in his eyes.

The contrast in ideas is immediately apparent in these lines; no less apparent is the fact that while Catullus finds no difficulty in expressing the carnal side of his love, for which *impensius uror* is a perfectly clear and understandable expression, he is not so capable of defining its other aspect. In vv. 3-4, he attempted a definition in positive terms; now he tries to phrase one in a negative way, by showing what he has lost now that this side of his love has become weakened. His sense of Lesbia's *value* and *importance* to him, he says, is diminishing. But " value " and " importance " do not suggest love; at best, they suggest the personal esteem which accompanies friendship.[22]

[passion and "value"]

---

[21] Cf. Kroll, above, note 14.

[22] The meaning of the phrase *vilior et levior* is well illustrated by Tacitus, *Hist.*, IV, 80 (of Antonius Primus and Domitian): *Neque ipse*

This may be part of love, just as is the *fides* of which he made such point in *cc.* 109 and 87, but it is by no means the whole story. Standing alone, the definition is quite inadequate, and may have stirred his readers to the same sort of incredulity as did his use of *amicitia* in *c.* 109.

In the light of this fact, one may well imagine that the abrupt question " qui potis est? " expresses the reader's wonder not only at how such a paradox of sentiment was possible, but also at how there could truly be any element of this second kind in a love-affair. What have such colorless concepts as " value " and " importance " to do with love, unless they are associated with the usual, basically physical, interpretation of that passion? And if these concepts do properly belong to this enigmatic " other side " of love, how can they be expressed positively?

Catullus' answer to the question again consists in an attempt to point up a contrast between the two aspects of his love:

> quod amantem iniuria talis
> [cogit] amare magis, sed bene velle minus.

What the *iniuria* was need not concern us at the moment, since it has no bearing on the question in hand.[23] Significant only is the fact that it is forcing (*cogit*) him into a position which must have seemed paradoxical to his readers, but was not so to him. To them, a man " esteemed " (*bene velle*) his mistress only in proportion as he " loved " (*amare*) her; to Catullus, these are two separate emotional phenomenà, and only if he can explain the nature of them both can he reveal the nature of his love. Once more, as in vv. 5-6, he finds no difficulty in expressing the carnal side: for this purpose *amare* serves very well. But for the non-physical side he is thrown back on a flat and almost insipid phrase, *bene velle*. It expresses nothing more than a rather vague feeling of good will, a sort of warm friendliness.[24]

(*sc.* Antonius) *deerat adrogantia vocare offensas, nimius commemorandis quae meruisset. Alios ut imbelles, Caecinam ut captivom ac dediticium increpat. Unde paulatim levior viliorque haberi, manente tamen in speciem amicitia.* (Referred to by Kroll, *ad loc.*).

[23] I shall revert to it later. Ellis (on v. 8) says that it was " doubtless a preference shown by Lesbia to some rival of Catullus." I doubt if it was as trivial a matter as this.

[24] Its meaning is excellently shown by Plautus, *Truc.*, 434-442:

> pro di immortales! non amantis mulieris
> sed sociai unanimantis, fidentis fuit

But the sentiment is at least non-physical in character, and Catullus hopes that by placing it in juxtaposition to *amare*, and thus implying that it was equivalent to *amare* in intensity and importance, he may be able to give some indication of its special meaning to him. Had he been a modern writer, with centuries of romantic tradition behind him, he could have stated his case very simply and clearly: "The hurt she has done me compels me to *desire* her more, but to *love* her less." To us, familiar as we are with the concept of romantic love, it is no paradox to desire without loving; to Catullus' contemporaries "desire" and "love" were scarcely to be dissociated from each other; to Catullus himself they were indeed dissociated, but he had no adequate means of expressing the dichotomy.

This poem also raises another question, which must be answered if the nature of Catullus' love for Lesbia is to be fully understood: why should a "hurt" cause his physical passion to increase, even as it caused his love—to use the modern term—to diminish? The answer is given at least partly by *c.* 75:

> Huc est mens deducta tua, mea Lesbia, culpa,
>   atque ita se officio perdidit ipsa suo,
> ut iam nec bene velle queat tibi, si optima fias,
>   nec desistere amare, omnia si facias.

In this poem we see the same contrast of ideas as in *c.* 72, and in the same terms: *bene velle* and *amare* once more are used to express the twofold nature of his love. The sole difference is that now the "hurt" has gone so deep that love—again in the modern sense—has been completely destroyed, and only passion, desire, remains. Moreover, his passion has reached such a degree that it can never be satisfied. The "hurt" then, must have been of such character that it could enflame desire at the same time that it destroyed spiritual affection; more than that, it must have caused desire to reach its apogee when all spiritual affection was irrevocably dead. It can have been no mere matter

---

officium facere quod modo haec fecit mihi,
suppositionem pueri quae mihi credidit,
germanae quod sorori non credit soror.
ostendit sese iam mihi medullitus:
se mihi infidelem numquam, dum vivat, fore.
egone illam ut non amem? egone illi ut non bene velim?
me potius non amabo quam huic desit amor.

of feminine coquetry or of ordinary *amantium irae*,[25] for Catullus has already shown his willingness—albeit not without some grief—to overlook the occasional deviations of Lesbia from the straight path that he had set for himself,[26] and such incidents, even if they had weakened his feeling of *bene velle*, could scarcely have roused his passions to such an unbearable pitch.

Only one thing, it seems to me, can account for the violence of Catullus' reaction, and this is the realization, brought home to him at long last, of Lesbia's utter profligacy and complete promiscuity. This is what hurt him so deeply, not of course because it convicted her of immorality, but because it made clear to him the fact that she had never really understood or appreciated the quality of the love he bore her. Always dissatisfied with her own interpretations of their love, he has now seen that she was not even honestly attempting to understand what he meant. In brief, she did not care that he felt for her as no other man had ever felt for any woman; if she had, she would not, with such complete disregard for his feelings, have slipped from the *rara furta*, which he could tolerate, to the sexual orgies in which she was now indulging. In *c.* 75, these escapades are only hinted at in the phrases *si optima fias* and *omnia si facias*; the lines *glubit magnanimi Remi nepotes* (*c.* 58), *puella nam mi . . . consedit istic* (*c.* 37), and *cum suis vivat valeatque moechis quos simul complexa tenet trecentos* (*c.* 11) give the true picture of her depravity, and their sorrowful bitterness shows the true depth of the hurt she had inflicted upon him. Not with the best of wills could his *amicitia—fides— bene velle—diligere* survive such an attack. And conversely, her conduct served only to heighten his desire to possess her,

[25] Ellis appears to accept this inadequate explanation (on 72, 8) and follows the younger Dousa in quoting *Anth. Pal.*, V, 256, 3-4: ὕβρις ἔρωτας ἔλυσε· μάτην ὅδε μῦθος ἀλᾶται. ὕβρις ἐμὴν ἐρέθει μᾶλλον ἐρωμανίην. On 75, he quotes Theognis, 1091-1094: ἀργαλέως μοι θυμὸς ἔχει περὶ σῆς φιλότητος· οὔτε γὰρ ἐχθαίρειν οὔτε φιλεῖν δύναμαι, γιγνώσκων χαλεπὸν μέν, ὅταν φίλος ἀνδρὶ γένηται, ἐχθαίρειν, χαλεπὸν δ' οὐκ ἐθέλοντα φιλεῖν. Kroll also uses this latter quotation, but presumably only as a parallel for the mechanical juxtaposition of ideas. Neither passage shows anything approaching Catullus' intensity of feeling.

[26] The lines are almost tearful, and yet resigned: *quae tamen etsi uno non est contenta Catullo, rara verecundae furta feremus erae, ne nimium simus stultorum more molesti* (68, 135-137).

for it showed to what lengths she could go to arouse, enjoy, and satisfy the sexual impulses of men. Catullus knew no squeamishness on this score; her knowledge, openly displayed, of the arts of love tempted and tormented him. As the full extent of her libidinous skill is made clear to him, he feels an insatiable desire to share in it. Thus it is that he can say *ut iam nec bene velle queat tibi, si optima fias, nec desistere amare, omnia si facias.*

Thus far we have dealt only with Catullus' struggle for adequate expression of the nature of his love. Even though he never attained complete clarity of terms, he did succeed in presenting a clear picture of the psychological conflict which that love occasioned. On the one side, Lesbia's physical attractions impel him toward an ever-increasing desire for possession; on the other, his loss of respect, spiritual affection, intellectual and emotional sympathy, drive him ever more to despise her. The emotional conflict itself is evidence of the power and significance that resided in the non-physical side of his love, for if this side had had less power and significance, no such conflict would have resulted. Instead, Catullus would have fallen resignedly into that attitude of mock despair which was canonical for ill-starred lovers among his predecessors and followers.[27] The very fact that he experiences no such shallow emotion, but is instead driven half-mad with heartbreak proves that he had attained to a concept of love unfamiliar to the other erotic poets of ancient times, and far more akin to our modern conception of romantic love.

In spite, then, of the terminological difficulties experienced by the poet, the conflict and the nature and intensity of the feelings that brought it about are clear to see and to understand. But even as Catullus reveals this conflict, a further idea begins to manifest itself, an idea which gives greater point and meaning not only to *cc.* 72 and 75, but even more to *cc.* 85 and 76. This is the idea of guilt, a feeling which arises in Catullus' mind not from any sense of wrong-doing in having participated in an immoral affair[28] but from the very emotional conflict itself.

[27] Cf. e.g. *Anth. Pal.*, V, 256 (above, note 25) ; Theognis, 1091-1094 (*ibid.*), Anacreon, 89: ἐρῶ τε δηὖτε κοὐκ ἐρῶ καὶ μαίνομαι κοὐ μαίνομαι; Ovid, *Am.*, III, 11b, 14.

[28] The simple innocence of 68, 143-146 shows how far he was from any feeling of guilt in this connection.

3

Not only is Catullus torn by two opposing, and to him anti-
pathetic, emotions, and thereby subjected to unbearable tension;
he seems to sense, too, that there is something fundamentally
unsound in the conflict itself.   Nebulously at first, but with
increasing clarity, the idea arises in his mind that he ought
not to continue to desire the woman for whom he has lost all
sense of spiritual and intellectual sympathy.   In other words,
amare and *bene velle* belong together; the one without the other
is wrong.   In making this association he has set up for himself
a moral ideal which has much in common with the modern,
romantic ideal of love.   And in continuing to desire Lesbia, as
he does, he finds himself standing in open violation of his ideal.

The feeling of guilt which results from this violation of his
self-conceived moral principle shows itself at first only in a sort
of vague wonder: in *c.* 72 he is not only describing the emotional conflict which he is experiencing and trying, by describing it, to understand it; in addition, he hints that he is aware
that he is allowing himself to be involved in an unhealthy situation.   The question " qui potis est? " is half addressed to himself; it is as if he were a trifle concerned at his own feelings
and were not entirely satisfied that he is doing right in feeling
toward Lesbia as he does.   And if, in *c.* 72, this inchoate sense
of guilt can only be read between the lines. it becomes much
clearer in *c.* 75, where in the face of the same basic conflict
Catullus remarks that his heart " has destroyed itself in the performance of its native office ": *ita se officio perdidit ipsa suo.*
Its " office " is to love; in loving Lesbia it has been led by her
wrong-doing to a form of loving which consists wholly of physical desire, unaccompanied by spiritual and intellectual esteem.
In so doing, his heart has " destroyed itself "; the poet's concepts of right and wrong are in confusion, and he is caught up
in a situation in which willy-nilly he is pursuing a course which
he knows is wrong.   It is this feeling of guilt, of wrong-doing,
which gives the poem its tragic overtones.   Catullus is not merely
frustrated or stubborn; [29] he is afflicted by a realization that he
has not been true to his own ideal.   It is not only that Lesbia
has not been true to him: he has not been true to himself.   Yet
he persists in his course; he goes on desiring her when he knows

[29] This is Ellis' view (*ad loc.*), which strikes me as essentially shallow.

he should not; he is now even convinced that he can never cease to desire her. This is the guilt which oppresses him and throws him into despair.

The conflict and the guilt which it occasioned are rendered somewhat clearer in *c.* 85. The phrase *odi et amo* is usually translated, "I hate and I love," and it is thereby implied that Catullus meant *odisse* to be the opposite of *amare*. But in the light of *cc.* 72 and 75 it should be clear that this is not the case: *odisse* is not the opposite of *amare*, but of *bene velle*, and the conflict of feeling here is precisely the same as that which is expressed in the *amare magis . . . bene velle minus* of *c.* 72, and the *nec bene velle queat . . . nec desistere amare* of *c.* 75. The emotion expressed by *odisse* is the final revulsion which has filled the gap, so to speak, that was left when all the poet's spiritual and intellectual affection was gone; expressed negatively, it is *bene velle desiisse*.[30] But *odisse* is clear in meaning as *bene velle*, and the various synonyms attempted for it, never could be. It could never be confused with physical passion: one does not "hate" a woman for her physical qualities, nor does "hatred" have a physical basis. "Hatred" is antipathy (as opposed to sympathy), ill-will (as opposed to esteem), revulsion (as opposed to affection). It is thus not the opposite of *amare*, which to Catullus expresses physical desire, but of *bene velle* and its synonyms, by which he tried to express the nature of the non-physical side of his love.[31] If Catullus could have found a word which would adequately express the opposite of *odisse*, he would have been able to say clearly what he tried to say by means of such inadequate terms as *bene velle, diligere, fides,* and *amicitia.*

As for the "torment" of which the distich speaks, this is not occasioned merely by the stress and strain of conflicting feelings, nor is it expressive solely of mental confusion. If it were, we should find Catullus here in no greater danger of real unhappiness than is Terence's Phaedria in the *Eunuchus*.[32] The very

---

[30] Cf. Hezel, *op. cit.* (see note 9), p. 55: "An die Stelle von 'non bene velle' ist 'odisse' getreten."

[31] Ovid has expressed the same conflict of feeling *Am.*, III, 11, 38: *aversor morum crimina, corpus amo.* This comes much closer to Catullus' meaning than do most of the other parallels cited by the editors (e. g. Kroll, Ellis).

[32] 70-73: *nunc ego et illam scelestam esse et me miserum sentio:*

simplicity of the distich, the sharp black and white of its emotions, are enough to prove that no such shallow interpretation may be given it. Catullus' *excrucior* is not to be ascribed to the conventional lover's despair. The distich becomes much clearer in meaning and reveals the true depth of the poet's feeling if we realize that the thing which causes his torment is his sense of guilt, his perception that the desire he feels is wrong. It is wrong because it is accompanied by hatred rather than by sympathy, esteem, and good-will. He sees that under the circumstances he ought not to desire Lesbia, yet in spite of that, he does. At the risk of over-simplification and importing into an ancient author concepts strictly modern, one might say that it is not so much his heart as his conscience which is here putting him on the rack. He is violating his self-imposed and self-conceived moral code; he knows it, yet he cannot help it. It is this which is the cause of his torment. Well might his contemporaries ask " quare id facis? " for they could have had no conception of his feelings. For that matter, Catullus himself does not understand why he suffers so—witness the despairing " nescio " which he offers in reply. He senses only that he is possessed at once by two emotions which he knows, perhaps only by a sort of cloudy intuition, ought to be mutually exclusive. The modern, backed by his tradition of romantic love, can understand Catullus better than could the poet himself, for it is now commonly accepted, at least as an ideal, that desire is right only if it is accompanied by love—using the word again in its modern sense. Unaccompanied by spiritual and intellectual sympathy, physical desire is, if not morally wrong, at least unworthy or improper. Whatever may be modern practice in this respect, the accepted moral code condemns such unrelieved animal feelings, and our ideal of love assumes the justice of this condemnation. Catullus, alone of the ancient erotic poets, has a prevision of this ideal, and *c.* 85 shows that he was scarcely the happier for his deviation from the norm of his times. The modern, at least, could understand the reason for his sense of wrong-doing; Catullus senses only the wrong-doing; the reason is beyond his grasp. To be conscious of doing wrong, but not to know why the wrong *is* wrong—this is indeed *excruciari.*

et taedet et amore ardeo, et prudens sciens, vivos vidensque pereo, neo quid agam scio.

[handwritten margin note: structure of # 76]

The conflict of feeling and the guilt consequent upon it reach their final and much-expanded statement in *c.* 76. The poem may be divided into three parts: *vv.* 1-8 constitute an attempted definition of the poet's love in terms of actions and thoughts; vv. 9-16 describe the destruction of that love, the resulting torment, and the resolution of the poet to rid himself of it; vv. 17-26 are a prayer to the gods to assist him in that resolution. This division has no special significance, but arises naturally from the succession of Catullus' thoughts, which pass in orderly progression from one idea to the next.[33]

In the first eight lines, Catullus returns again to the attempt to define the nature of his love by a process of analysis, by a description of the various types of thought and action which made it up. Very prominent is the idea of *fides*, which is expressed here in much the same terms as those which appear in *cc.* 109 and 87.[34] To this concept, he now adds that of *pietas,* that peculiarly ancient virtue, the definition of which rather escapes any modern tongue, but which means basically the quality of doing the right thing in the right way at the right time. If these two ideas may be classed as feelings or psychological states, Catullus goes on to describe what he *did* in the name of his love. Here he limits himself to rather general terms; he speaks of *benefacta, quaecumque homines bene dicere aut facere possunt*, thus leaving the reader to assume that in response to his love he left no kind or thoughtful word unspoken or act unperformed.

[handwritten margin note: definition of pietas]

His love, then, was characterized by *fides, pietas, bene dicere,* and *bene facere*, all of them either spiritual qualities or outgrowths of spiritual qualities. In the end, they represent only an expansion of the concept which Catullus had expressed by *bene velle* in the earlier poems, and it is obvious that he has been no more successful here than there in making clear the nature of his feelings. For while all the qualities he mentions are indubitably parts of the non-physical aspect of love, they do not completely describe it. An essential element, which might best be called spiritual and intellectual sympathy, has been omitted— for the reason, of course, that although Catullus felt this sympathy, he did not know how to put it into words. That he did

[33] Cf. Kroll, introd. note.
[34] Cf. especially 76, 3-4 and 87, 3-4; 109, 6.

H

indeed feel it is revealed by vs. 9: *omnia quae ingratae perierunt credita menti*: his love perished, he says, when it became clear that the heart to which it was entrusted lacked the power or will to respond to it—lacked, in other words, the very sympathy which alone could have answered and complemented his own. He offered to Lesbia loyalty, constancy, rightness and kindness of thought and deed, and sympathy, that mutual understanding of thought, emotion, and purpose which is the *sine qua non* of love. She scorned them all, either because she was incapable of understanding such a love, or because she did not find it of interest. To Catullus' love she consistently offered nothing but kisses, embraces, the *iocosa* and *iucunda* of the conventional passion of the day. Even her protestations of fidelity were couched in these terms.[35] And when Catullus protests her defection from even this relatively trivial kind of fidelity, she tells him not to be a nuisance and a fool.[36] In the end, her utter lack of appreciation and understanding, demonstrated by her shameless conduct, sends the structure of his love crashing to ruin.

With the loss of his spiritual love, Catullus is left with nothing but a steadily mounting physical desire, and we have already seen the torment to which this passion subjected him, not because it was unrequited—for there is nothing in the Lesbia-poems to indicate that Lesbia was unwilling to continue to entertain Catullus as a lover, and some evidence that she was anxious to do so [37]—but because of his conviction that his desire was wrong. This torturing sense of wrong-doing is the fearful state from which he wishes, in *c.* 76, now to free himself. It should be easy, he thinks: *quare cur tu te iam amplius excrucies?* But it is not. The gods seem to be against him.[38] And his love has lasted a long time; one cannot simply shrug off an emotion so deeply implanted. Yet it must be done, for he can know no

[35] Cf. 109, 1-2; 72, 1-2.

[36] Cf. 68, 137: *ne nimium simus stultorum more molesti.* I feel certain that Catullus is here " quoting " from a passage-at-arms between himself and Lesbia.

[37] E. g. the mission of Furius and Aurelius, *c.* 11.

[38] I interpret *dis invitis* as a concessive: " even though the gods are unwilling " (i. e. to let you cease to be *miser*), in spite of Kroll's note *ad loc.* For if the gods were unwilling that he should *continue* in his misery, why should he feel it necessary, in his prayer, to ask for their mercy (vv. 17-18) and to remind them of his deserts (vv. 25-26)?

peace of mind until he is rid of the oppressing sensation of guilt which his continuing passion occasions.

The last part of the poem, the prayer to the gods, makes it clear that it is indeed from guilt, from a sense of wrong-doing, that Catullus wishes to be freed. If it were merely from the unhappiness consequent upon unrequited love, he would scarcely have described his state of mind as a disease. Unhappiness and disappointment may be bitter, but they are normal feelings, and can hardly be characterized as *pestis perniciesque, torpor, taeter morbus,* all of which suggest that Catullus is convinced of the abnormality, or in moral terms, of the wrongness of his feelings. Nor is the problem solved if we explain his suffering as arising not from disappointment but from the fact that he persists in loving when his love is unanswered. If this were so, then Lesbia's reform, and return to his arms should satisfy him. But he says emphatically that he does not want her now, not even if she could learn to love him as he had once loved her, or could learn to be "chaste" (*pudica*), i. e. could show toward him the loyalty and constancy that he had shown toward her. The poem becomes clear in meaning only if we understand that it is not from love itself that Catullus wishes release, but from the sense of wrong, of guilt, of unworthiness that has arisen from the persistence of his physical passion after his spiritual and intellectual affection has been destroyed. As his thought progresses, he thinks with ever-increasing loathing of the moral wrong of which he finds himself guilty. Starting as *pestis perniciesque* it is next *torpor*, and finally ends as *taeter morbus,* "foul disease," a phrase which can describe only a hideously ugly state of mind. Neither disappointment nor persistence in unrequited love could well be so described; the phrase is apt only if it denotes a sense of wrong, of obliquity, and of shame. Catullus' feeling here shows his conviction that love, to be good and right, must be composed of two mutually necessary parts, desire on the one hand and spiritual sympathy on the other. He does not say what spiritual sympathy alone might be; such a "Platonic" relationship between man and woman would have been quite beyond his comprehension. But he is clear that physical desire alone is not merely empty and meaningless, but— if I may venture to use the anachronistic term—sinful.[39]

[39] A word of caution is needed here, lest I be accused of making a

It is this concept of love as a dual entity made up of aspects one of which is not only incomplete but wrong without the other, that sets Catullus' love for Lesbia apart from the ordinary ancient love-affair and gives it a character approaching more nearly to that of the romantic tradition of later times. Only in the light of this concept do the poems of conflict—*cc.* 109, 87, 72, 75, and 76—become clear in meaning; without it they remain either a puzzle or fall into the class of poetry represented by such poems as Ovid, *Amores*, III, 11 b and 14, pieces the frivolity of which is utterly out of harmony with the passionate sincerity of Catullus. That Catullus himself did not clearly understand the nature of his own feelings, and that, for all his struggle for expression, he never succeeded in formulating them in unequivocal terms, is due to the fact that his concept of love was not only new to him, but was equally new to the world in which he lived and to the language which he spoke. Many centuries before the advent of the poets of romantic love, Catullus foreshadowed the ideal to which they, and the Western European world after them, at least in theory subscribed.

FRANK OLIN COPLEY.

UNIVERSITY OF MICHIGAN.

Puritan of Catullus. I do not mean to imply that he felt this same guilt in his—doubtless countless—casual relations with *meretrices* or other women of easy virtue. It is only when he has *loved* that he can feel as he does here, and he would have been the last to characterize as "love" the fly-by-night joys of the *lupanar* or the *convivium*.

V

Kenneth Quinn

The commentator's task

The commentator's task

KENNETH QUINN

I shall write as though what I was saying were no more than common sense. And so it seems to me. I know there are those who think the job better done in other ways. I can imagine commentaries on Catullus, or Horace, or Propertius, quite different from the one I shall describe. But these would, or should, set out from different sets of prior assumptions. Writing a scholarly commentary for scholars, one might feel obliged to prove everything (if only to prove that one is capable of proving everything), and to gather in all sorts of things from obscure places, however tenuous the thread of relevance, precisely because the facts were only to be found in obscure places, and those who used the commentary mightn't know where to look: it seems to me a wholly praiseworthy enterprise—there should be such books. I can imagine a watered-down version of that, written to introduce sixth-formers and students to the best and austerest traditions of classical scholarship: personally, I should regard this as the kind of misguided enterprise that has contributed a good deal to the prevailing depravity of critical standards in thinking, talking, writing and lecturing about Roman poetry; ideally, however, there should perhaps be a place for that kind of book also. But as things are, we can scarcely hope for three different up-to-date commentaries on each Roman poet, even the major ones. This being so, I think the kind of commentary I shall describe to be of more use than either of the others; more use, certainly, than a jumble of all three.

Take an old school photo (the sort that backed up Minty's impostrous pride in Graham Greene's *England Made Me*), 'rows of boys blinking against the sun'. Who is the little chap with warts, second from the left in the front row? Ten years later the possessor of the photo might not be sure; he might not even care, being concerned only, a little distastefully, with his own smug shining face in the middle of the front row; or, more wistfully, with the young Apollo, 'magnificently unprepared for the long littleness of life', slightly left of centre three rows behind. A hundred years later the possessor of the photo might have no idea who any of these were. But it is normally possible to find out.

How many articles has one read, in CQ and elsewhere, which take the form, 'Who is the little chap with warts, second from the left in the front row?' There is of course nothing wrong with the question. Even if the photo is a little battered, an answer should be possible. Indeed, the answer is very likely worth the trouble it will take to find it—our photo may be the only evidence surviving for something important. This is in short a typical piece of research on a historical document. Documents, like dictionaries, record: their purpose is to satisfy our curiosity, without any attempt at controlling the form it will take.

The trouble is that scholars get so good at this sort of thing, it makes them want to apply the same technique to contexts where the technique is altogether out of place. The man who took the school photo set out to record all the members of a particular group present on a particular day. Suppose instead an artistic photo—a fake school photo, say, in which the hero of a novel or a film is portrayed, recognizably shining out, or ridiculous, among irrecognizable contemporaries. Suppose even a painting.

In a sense the answer to our question, 'Who is the little chap with warts second from the left in the front row?' still makes sense: he is the film extra, or the artist's model, or whoever he chances being, as any Greek would say. A work of art is also a historical document, no less than a poem is a historical document. It cannot help itself. It may even turn out to be an important historical document – the only evidence surviving for a fact we wish to establish; provided he is not just a blob or a blur, we may hope to track our man down. But, though our curiosity about a historical fact may thus be satisfied by the work of art, we should be rash in assuming that the artist's purpose was to record fact, or to satisfy our curiosity about the past. It is much more likely that the artist's purpose was to arouse a rather different kind of curiosity, and to control the form, moreover, which that curiosity would take.

As for our particular question, 'Who is the little chap with warts second from the left in the front row?' the chances are that an answer is not even possible: the focus has indeed been deliberately blurred, the sketch made too sketchy to permit identification. Still, who would want to prevent those so minded from going into this? Clearly nobody, so long as they do not suppose that the answers they find (or don't find) are pertinent answers. Often, however, they are apt to suppose just this. Yet in a work of art filled perhaps with questions which the artist expects us to ask, theirs is a question the artist did not reckon with. Concern with it distracts, uses up intellectual energy to no pertinent end. We should do better to try to discover the area within which the artist's thinking moved; to discover the shape and nature of the curiosity which it was his purpose to arouse; to reconstruct in short, supposing the work of art is a poem, what I shall speak of as the *hypothesis* of the poem.

II

Every commentator is aware of the temptation to say too much, the temptation to satisfy the reader's idle, impertinent curiosity, and many yield to the temptation. 'The charm of a note,' said that great writer of notes, T. E. Page, in the Preface to his Horace, 'often lies in that part which is least strictly relevant.' If one prefers to resist the temptation, some rationalization of the commentator's task is clearly necessary. According to a recent commentator on Euripides' *Orestes*, Professor Biehl,[1] he

[1] Werner Biehl, *Euripides Orestes* (1965), Einleitung.

should concern himself with three things: (1) establishment of
the text; (2) structural analysis (*die Strukturforschung*), including
the relationship of form and content; (3) interpretation ~~*Commentators' task*~~
(*Interpretation*–the German word implies, I think, something
less subjective and more comprehensive than what English-
speaking literary critics call 'interpretation'; it covers the whole
process of making sense of a literary work). The three things,
moreover, should be done jointly: the ideal commentator, like
the bird of popular legend, circles round a problem in circles
of ever-decreasing radius (*sozusagen in zentripetal verlaufender
Bemühung*) until he can settle on a solution; only in this way,
Biehl maintains, can one approach systematically the fundamental unity of form and content which is manifested in the
text (*erst ihre gleichzeitige Berücksichtigung führt ... konsequenterweise
zum Verständnis der im Text selbst manifestierten Einheit von Inhalt
und Form*).

These are surely exemplary sentiments. But they reflect the
fundamental change in emphasis which has taken place in the
past 50 years. By the end of the Victorian age, the textual
critics, as Dr R. R. Bolgar remarks,[2] had won. If asked what a
Latin poem was about, scholars of a couple of generations ago
were apt to say, either that it was obvious what the poem was
about, or that it was impossible to decide–or perhaps simply
that the poem was of course rather poor stuff, but one might as
well settle the text, and clear up such difficulties of interpretation (by which they meant chiefly construing the Latin), and
fact, as the text presented. Because we have escaped so recently
from their clutches, the textual critics are apt to loom rather
larger than life on the horizon behind us, like Polyphemus and
his fellow one-eyed giants against the Sicilian skyline in
Aeneid III. They represent a first, heady infatuation with the
false god of scientific scholarship. Look back a little further
and we shall find better sense talked by the gentleman humanists
of the mid-nineteenth century–men like Jowett, who is said
to have solved his students' textual worries with the advice,
'Buy a good text'.

I set out therefore from Biehl. He talks what we can accept
as obvious common sense. His insistence moreover that the

[2] *Didaskalos* I, 1 (1963), 17.

commentator must tackle his three tasks together represents a wholesome rejection of a misguided passion for neatness which can persuade us we should abandon common sense in favour of a system of logical priorities (first settle the text, then the translation, then the meaning). What he says holds good, whether we are writing a commentary on Aeschylus, or on Valerius Maximus.

Or whether, to make a more instructive comparison, we are writing a commentary on the poems of Catullus or the letters of Cicero. I take these two because they bring me back to the issue with which I began—the need (when our author is a poet) to avoid asking (let alone solving) questions that have nothing to do with the poet's purpose.

For clearly the poems of Catullus and the letters of Cicero have a lot in common. First, length: Cicero, it is true, is apt to be long-winded; but the typical Ciceronian letter, like the typical Catullan poem, is often no more than a few lines, at most a page or so. Second, style: both adopt, usually, the easy, elegant Latin of an educated Roman of their time, as is plain from the letters of Cicero's friends and acquaintances included in the collection. This is what I have called elsewhere the language of conversation improved upon. The Latin of Catullus and Cicero is more consciously urbane than that, say, of Clodia's husband, Metellus Celer (ad fam. 5. 1), but it is basically the same Latin—refreshingly dissimilar from the Latin of our manuals of Latin prose composition. Then, there are obvious structural similarities—Catullus' short poems, like Cicero's letters, normally have an addressee; they are really letters in verse—or so we may be at first tempted to think. One can even venture to point out some similarity of content; both deal with the things that interest the writer, the things that happen to him and his friends and enemies; to some extent the same names, places and events crop up in both.

My concern, however, is with the ways in which the two kinds of text are not alike. Some of the differences are plain enough; the rest are best brought out by careful critical formulation, which involves some recourse to argument and to theory.

III

My *first thesis* is that a Catullan poem is always *about some one* ✕
thing. To work as a poem, it must have some kind of unity. **THESIS**
A letter of Cicero *may* be 'about some one thing' in this sense,
but it is just as likely not to be. For example, *ad fam.* 7. 22, to
Cicero's learned friend, the lawyer C. Trebatius Testa (whom
we meet in Horace, *Satires* 2. 1), which bears an evident and
interesting similarity to Catullus' Poem 50 (*Hesterno, Licini, die
otiosi/multum lusimus in meis tabellis . . .*), has, like Poem 50, an
obvious unity:

*Illuseras heri inter scyphos, quod dixeram, controuersiam esse, possetne heres quod furtum
antea factum esset, recte furti agere. itaque, etsi domum bene potus seroque redieram, tamen
id caput, ubi haec controuersia est, notaui, et descriptum tibi misi; ut scires, id, quod tu
neminem sensisse dicebas, Sex. Aelium, M'. Manilium, M. Brutum sensisse. ego tamen
Scaeuolae et Testae assentior.*

You made fun of me yesterday over our wine for saying it was a disputed point
whether an heir could lawfully prosecute on a charge of theft committed before
he succeeded to the property. So, although I had returned home pretty drunk and
at a late hour, I nevertheless marked the section in which this question is discussed,
and have sent a copy of it to you, so that you may know that the opinion held,
according to you, by nobody, was in fact held by Sextus Aelius, Manius Manilius
and Marcus Brutus. Personally I agree with Scaevola and Testa.

But a letter doesn't have to be, like this, about one thing. A
letter may equally well be about a number of things—and
usually is. And in dealing with them it may leave a number of *letter is
poem
structure*
ragged edges; its structure tends to be linear. The structure of
a poem tends to be circular. Nor does this apply just to the
poems of Catullus; it seems to me true of poems generally:
if a poem develops an argument, or tells a story, the argument
or the story must move within a single self-contained area.

A letter or so of Cicero will show what I mean. First, *ad
Atticum* 12. 8:

*De Cicerone multis res placet. comes est idoneus. sed de prima pensione ante uideamus. adest
enim dies, et ille currit. scribe, quaeso, quid referat Celer egisse Caesarem cum candidatis,
utrum ipse in fenicularium an in Martium campum cogitet. et scire sane uelim, numquid
necesse sit comitiis esse Romae. nam et Piliae satis faciendum est et utique Atticae.*

My plan for Cicero [his son] meets with general approval. A suitable companion
is available. But let us see before that about a first payment [of Tullia's dowry, to
be repaid by Dolabella]. The time is near and he [Dolabella] is in a hurry. Please
write and tell me what Celer says Caesar has settled with the candidates, whether
he thinks of going to the field of Fennel or the field of Mars. I should much like

to know too whether I must come to Rome for the elections. Pilia must not be disappointed, still less Attica [the joke being, as Bailey points out, that Attica was only six years old].

Or take *ad Atticum* 12. 9:

Ne ego essem hic libenter atque id cotidie magis, ni esset ea causa, quam tibi superioribus litteris scripsi. nihil hac solitudine iucundius, nisi paulum interpellasset Amyntae filius: ὦ ἀπεραντολογίας ἀηδοῦς! cetera noli putare amabiliora fieri posse uilla, litore, prosspectu maris, tumulis, his rebus omnibus. sed neque haec digna longioribus litteris, nec erat, quod scriberem, et somnus urgebat.

I should be really happy here, and become more and more so every day, if it weren't for the reason I mentioned in my former letter. Nothing could be pleasanter than this solitude, except for the occasional interruptions of Amyntas' son. How his chatter does bore one! As for the rest, the villa, the beach, the sea view, the hillocks and everything–you mustn't suppose anything could be more charming. But these don't deserve a longer letter, and I have nothing else to say, and I'm very sleepy.

We can imagine a Satire or an Epistle of Horace moving along easily like this from point to point; but not an Ode, or any poem of Catullus.

Our starting point, then, our *a priori* assumption, is that a poem somehow forms a unity. I call this in my commentary the *hypothesis* of the poem–borrowing that term from Dylan Thomas.[3] I see two advantages in the term. First, it invites us to treat a poem like a proposition in logic, or a theorem in geometry. The poem sets out from, builds upon, *makes* something out of a set of conceded data. Second, the term hypothesis warns us that the data may be fact or fiction, or a mixture. We may be asked to assume for the duration of the poem something outside the normal limits of truth or reality. A poem moves, if you like, within a world of its own creation: a world, for example, in which Catullus can round up his hendecasyllabic poems, as an ordinary man might round up his friends, to recover by force from a former mistress a book of verse which she refuses to restore to its author (Poem 42).[4] Similarly in logic or in geometry you may argue out the consequences of a proposition or a set of data plainly false to human experience.

[3] Dylan Thomas, '*A few words of a kind*', an introduction to a poetry reading at the Massachusetts Institute of Technology, 7 March 1952, recorded on Philips B9401C L.

[4] The matter is well dealt with by F. O. Copley in connection with Poem 4 in his article 'Catullus c. 4: The World of the Poem', *TAPhA* 79 (1958), 9-13.

Letters tend to be about facts, poems tend to be about fancies; if about facts, the fact that they are facts ceases, usually, to be very important. This is not true of course of ⌐didactic⌐ poetry, which is why Aristotle objected to calling it poetry.

IV

My *second thesis* is that the data on which a poem rests must be discoverable, incorporated somehow in the text, or deducible from it as a plausible, necessary deduction. Naturally, this does not apply to what the poet feels he can rely on any reader to know—though two thousand years later, it may require some research to discover what was common knowledge at the time; Poem 17 (*O Colonia, quae cupis ponte ludere longo . . .*) poses, it seems to me, this sort of problem: if familiarity with the saying *sexagenarios de ponte* and the picturesque festival ritual to which the saying referred were part of our cultural equipment, we'd have little difficulty with the hypothesis of this poem. Perhaps I may add, however, that I think the extent of this area is commonly exaggerated—classical scholars suffer from a special kind of guilt complex about their ignorance.

It seems to me that what I am talking about is a necessary consequence of a necessary feature of any competently constructed poem of the kind we are discussing: its ability to stand on its own feet, independent of the circumstances in which it came originally into existence, and thus make sense (to the extent the poet chooses) to other people than its original addressee. Cicero's letters are not subject to this structural requirement. They are full of loose ends (as in the letter about Dolabella and the dowry). They move constantly out of the area of common knowledge into important areas private to Cicero and his addressee, where we must follow them as best we can. The fact that Catullus' poems *look* like letters will seriously mislead us, if it causes us to suppose, as many do, without giving the matter much thought, that the poem has come into our hands by accident; that we have, as it were, simply stumbled across an actual letter from Catullus to his friend which just happened to be in verse. It is true that the addressee probably received a fair copy of the poem before it was circulated; but the poem was constructed to be intelligible (to the extent the poet chose) to an audience with no private access to 'the facts'.

I follow of course the precept of Eduard Fraenkel, who puts the matter well, if, to my mind, a shade categorically:

> My interpretations are, without exception, based on the conviction that Horace, throughout his work, shows himself both determined and able to express everything that is relevant to the understanding and the appreciation of a poem, either by saying it in so many words or by implying it through unambiguous hints.[5]

I don't mean simply that a Catullan poem is as it were a letter with the unessential facts left out, though this may be part of the process by which a piece of occasional verse becomes a poem. To quote Professor Fraenkel again:

> Damit ein Gelegenheitsgedicht zum echten Gedicht wird, muss es von seinem äusseren Anlass emanzipiert und so durchgeformt werden dass es geschlossen und autark in sich selbst ruht.[6]

In this process of detachment from what Fraenkel calls the 'external occasion' a poem acquires a kind of independence of the original facts: it passes, as Aristotle might put it, from the particular to the universal. Once this is grasped, we are better equipped to understand how Poem 11 (*Furi et Aureli, comites Catulli . . .*) can utilize events in 55 BC in dismissing a mistress with whom Catullus had broken, apparently, some two years before that; or how Poem 51 (*Ille mi par esse deo uidetur . . .*), having started life as what Mr L. P. Wilkinson calls a 'feeler',[7] may have ended up as a poem–and had the final stanza added, perhaps, years later when Catullus came to knock his collection into shape: even when they are writing about the most intimate secrets of their lives, poets learn the trick of keeping one eye on eternity.

Take a harder case. Did Catullus own the yacht which forms the subject of Poem 4? He could have done, many have therefore supposed he did. Perhaps they are right. But in such matters we do well to be no less cautious than Fraenkel, who remarks, 'I try never to ask a question when I see that the poet

[5] Eduard Fraenkel, *Horace* (1957), 26.
[6] Eduard Fraenkel (on Poem 50) in 'Catulls Trostgedicht für Calvus', *Wiener Studien* 69 (1956), 282. (If an 'occasional' poem is to become a genuine poem, it must be released from the external occasion that gave rise to it and be so transmuted as to become independent and self-contained, relying upon itself alone.)
[7] L. P. Wilkinson, Fondation Hardt, *Entretiens sur l'antiquité classique*, 2 (1953), 47.

is determined not to answer it'.[8] What is more important is that the *speaker* in Poem 4 talks as though he had no personal knowledge of the facts, but had to take them all on hearsay from the yacht. Until we accept this basic hypothesis, we have not tuned in to the poem; once we have accepted it, we are free to make what deductions we think helpful, so long as we make no deduction which does violence to the text. Those which simply do no violence to the text, but for which there is no justificatory hint in the text, we must entertain with caution –we may be losing touch with the poem: the deductions to concentrate on are those which a sensitive reading of the text seems to compel.

The data may be set out at the beginning, more or less as in a problem in geometry: Poem 17, for example, or Poem 50. Catullus will do this even when it means telling the addressee what he must know already–one sign that the poem is only pretending to be a letter. Another sign is that the addressees are often things–a ship, a bird, a peninsula–which do not receive letters from people in their normal prosaic minds. But there is an obvious objection to putting all the data (all the poet chooses to provide) at the beginning: the poem is bogged down just when it should be getting off the ground. In any case it may be more effective to let the reader work out for himself what the poem is about by piecing together the clues scattered through it; this is very much the method of Horace in his Odes.

The reader should not be left guessing of course about anything which is important to the working of the poem. A challenge is extended to him, however, to build up the hypothesis of the poem from the clues provided; the rest is a matter for the reader's private thoughts and reactions, though he may not be able to tune in fully without supplying something from that source: good poems need a responsive reader. But the reader must keep his deductions under stringent control or he will cease to be tuned in to the poem. If the poet is competent, he will provide the clues; he will moreover not confuse the reader by scattering false clues. Does it seem a chancy game for a poet to play with the reader? We must remember how well-

[8] Eduard Fraenkel, 'Two poems of Catullus' [8 and 42], *JRS* 51 (1961), 49.

trained Catullus' contemporaries were by the practice (as writers as well as readers) of epigram—a form so slight that only the absolutely indispensable data could be provided, and these had to be sketched in as quickly and as deftly as possible.

V

My first and second theses have been concerned with positing the consequences of assuming that a short poem, if decently written, is a self-contained, permanently valid entity. My *third thesis* follows naturally from these two: it is that the primary task of a commentator is *to reconstruct the hypothesis of the poem.* It is my argument, first, that he must do this; second that, if the poem is any good, he may do it quite objectively. (With Cicero's letters there is not usually the same need; or, where there is a need, the evidence is often lacking.) The faster a poem works, the more important it becomes to reconstruct its hypothesis carefully, and the greater the risk of getting off the track in over-zealous pursuit of the wrong kind of detail.

As an example of how easy it is for a commentator to yield to that temptation, we may take Gow on Horace, *Satires* 1. 5. 16. Horace and his companions are on the night boat through the Pomptine Marshes:

> . . . *absentem ut cantat amicam*
> *multa prolutus uappa nauta atque uiator*
> *certatim.*

viator. There is some doubt who this person is. Palmer thinks he is a passenger on the boat; Orelli that he stands for all the passengers, since they must all have fallen asleep together (l. 17), else some of them would have noticed at once that the boat was not moving (l. 20). But *viator* naturally means a 'wayfarer', a traveller *by road*, and may have that meaning here. The sailor and the *viator* are both on the towpath. The passengers, sleepy and in the dark, do not notice the stoppage of the boat till dawn.

Would it not be more to the point to remark that Horace, though 'sleepy and in the dark', can still tell that the voice which joins the sailor's is obviously that of a member of the travelling public (not a sailor) and doesn't care who he is, or where he is—he only wishes he would shut up?

My *fourth thesis* brings us from matters of theory to a matter of strategy. It is that, given the highly organized nature of a short poem–it is a structure in which things are apt to happen fast–the commentator must accept stringent rules of relevance. Only so can he hope to unfold ('explicate') the poem successfully.

The old-fashioned commentator regarded it as his function to tell the reader just about anything he thought his reader might not know. Philology, being the love of words, is necessarily promiscuous with its affection. This is the ideal to which commentators on Catullus from Ellis to Fordyce have aspired. I imagine it does not greatly matter if one adopts this approach with a prose text, one at any rate whose structure is fairly loosely organized, one where there is less risk of missing the point. But with a short poem of Catullus, an ode of Horace or an elegy of Propertius, the rambling, gossipy commentary becomes at best an impertinence; at worst, an excuse for what a *TLS* reviewer, in a front-page article on recent work on Donne, called para-scholarship; the difference, says the reviewer, between scholarship and para-scholarship is that 'the one deals with reality, the other with its shadow'.[9] Brevity alone will help, but it is not enough. In that case the commentator is even more likely to evade his main task–the task, often far from straightforward, of making sense of the poem.

A few precepts to conclude. Our ideal commentator will follow Biehl, concerning himself simultaneously with text, structural analysis and interpretation. If his author is Catullus, he will print the whole text. He will make it his object to reconstruct the hypothesis of each poem, providing the reader with the information he needs (and no more) to test this hypothesis and such additional help (and no more) as his readers need to understand the Latin and to enjoy the poem. He will be unobtrusive, not heavy-handed. He will not spoil the effectiveness of his commentary (and the poem) by fussing, by telling his readers things they can easily find out for themselves (from a dictionary, for example). In explaining historical

[9] *Times Literary Supplement*, 6 April 1967.

allusions, he will not pile up irrelevant facts which the curious can easily gather for themselves. Likewise, if his author is one who makes extensive use of myth (Horace or Propertius), he will draw out those details of the legend which underpin the poetic structure, not retell the tale. He will, however, explain, if he can, why, and how, the myth is used. In commenting, for example, on Horace, *Odes* 1. 8. 13-15:

> *quid latet, ut marinae*
> *filium dicunt Thetidis sub lacrimosa Troiae*
> *funera . . . ?*

it is not sufficient to say that *marinae filius Thetidis = Achilles*; one must try to explain why Achilles is so described at this point in the poem.[10]

He will be exceedingly parsimonious with parallels. The function of *literary* parallels is to suggest what the poet's words probably suggested to his contemporaries, what the poet himself had perhaps in mind—not to provide random selections of re-formulations of the same cliché. The function of *linguistic* parallels is to help us sense the flavour of the poet's words: they should therefore be relevant in time and style—I have tried to take mine as far as possible from Cicero's letters. He will list good critical work (where it exists) on each poem. He will cater for a reasonable range of readers, not hesitating to explain (briefly) small things that may trip the reader up, or puzzle him. He will try to draw the reader out, to suggest to him the things he is not likely to think of for himself; often these are best put in question form. Above all he will try to stimulate the reader's response, and not to waste his time.

KENNETH QUINN
is Professor of Classics
in the University of Otago, New Zealand

[10] See my interpretation of the stanza in *Latin Explorations* (1963), 139.

VI

Kenneth Quinn
Practical criticism

PRACTICAL CRITICISM: A READING OF PROPERTIUS i. 21 AND CATULLUS 17

By KENNETH QUINN

IN *Didaskalos* 1968 I have argued that the chief task of the commentator on a short poem (an ode of Horace, an elegy of Propertius, or a poem of Catullus) is to reconstruct the hypothesis upon which the poem rests by piecing together the data actually provided by the text, or deducible from the text as a plausible, necessary deduction; to these data, I argued, one need only add what the poet feels he can rely on any reader to know, though two thousand years later it may of course require some research to recover what was common knowledge at the time. I cited Catullus 17 ⊤-17 as a case in point—a poem where reconstruction of the hypothesis depended on things outside the text, things which, though part of the cultural background of the poet's contemporaries, were hardly part of ours, yet within our grasp if we cast around a little.

I expect some will have felt I was making a concession which invalidated my general thesis—because it forced me to admit either a class of poems, like Catullus 17, which didn't work properly as poems (according to my definition of how poems worked), or a class of readers (ourselves) imperfectly competent, in the case of some poems at any rate which we might be disposed to regard as important, to participate by a response that was adequately informed as well as intelligent and sensitive in the experience of reading and understanding and enjoying the poem. I thought it a good idea, therefore, to attempt an exercise in practical criticism, complementary to the theoretical statement in *Didaskalos*.

We must be clear, however, about the degree of certainty and finality which is appropriate to a task as delicate as that of reconstructing the hypothesis of a poem. Take Propertius i. 21—a relatively simple exercise in reconstruction, provided we are patient and keep our wits about us:

> Tu, qui consortem properas euadere casum,
>   miles ab Etruscis saucius aggeribus,
> quid nostro gemitu turgentia lumina torques?
>   pars ego sum uestrae proxima militiae.
> sic te seruato ut possint gaudere parentes,   5
>   ne soror acta tuis sentiat e lacrimis:
> Gallum per medios ereptum Caesaris ensis
>   effugere ignotas non potuisse manus . . .

113

Whose, for a start, are the parents (5: *parentes*), whose is the sister (6: *soror*)? If the elegy were a message from Propertius to an unknown addressee which we happened to have intercepted, there would be no way of telling. But it is not, so there should be a way of telling. Line 5, given its context in a poem which we are entitled to expect (until proved wrong) to make permanent sense to any reader who takes a little trouble with it, clearly justifies one assumption only—that the parents who will rejoice if the man escapes alive from the siegeworks at Etruria are *his* parents. The sister, too, is likely to be his, though plainly a relationship between her and the dying man is implied as well; the neatest assumption is that she is the sister of both. The two men, in other words, are brothers; that fits in reasonably well with the dying man's reassuring words to the man who is escaping, 4: *pars ego sum uestrae proxima militiae*; the phrase is a puzzling one (what is *uestrae*?), but when we know the poem better I think we shall see that it is *meant* to be less than clear—an ironic meiosis, perhaps, the first hint of an ambivalence in the unlucky brother's feelings toward the lucky one. We may now reconstruct the hypothesis on which these lines rest more or less as follows: During the fighting around Perugia (in the Perusine war of 41 B.C.) chance has brought one brother past where the other lies dying. Hearing the dying man's groans, the survivor turns his gaze in terror toward the sound. The dying man reassures him but in tones in which we detect overtones of irony or bitterness, and in wishing his brother a safe escape he attaches a condition (5: *sic te seruato*): let the survivor spare their sister the truth, let her think her brother was killed by Caesar's army, not by an unknown assailant while running away.

This seems to me a satisfactory reconstruction of the hypothesis of the first eight lines. Of course, the sister of the man running away *might* be the wife or fiancée of the dying man, but I find it neater and more natural to assume that the sister and the parents are those of both men. At a pinch she might be the dying man's sister and the wife or fiancée of the other, but in that case I fancy Propertius would have felt obliged to say *soror mea*. My personal preference is based on a principle of an economy of assumptions. It is not necessary for us, the readers, to agree about every detail. Reconstruction should aim only at that degree of clarity which is appropriate. In a short poem there is not room to clear up every detail. The effectiveness of this poignant *chose vue* is unimpaired, may even be enhanced, if the relationship between the two men is left imprecise. What the relationship was is not really our business; all we have to grasp is that there was a relationship. The data the poet provides, or implies, in short, may properly leave us uninformed about details about which in another context we might feel entitled to information.

These uncertainties are of a different order from those which affect the text. The former are under the poet's control, are calculated by him; the latter are like the crackle on the line which seems often to obscure or drown the speaker's voice at the very point where he is saying something we particularly need to catch if his meaning is to be clear to us. It is infuriating not to know what Propertius actually wrote at the beginning of line 6. Did he write *haec* (as Butler and Barber once thought) and is *ne* (which Barber now prints, returning to the reading of the primary manuscripts) a piece of well-meaning interference on the part of a scribe, or perhaps just a silly mistake? Is it even possible that Camps is right in following Sluiter, who reads *me* for *ne* and baptizes the sister *Atta*, thus removing *acta*? On grounds of neatness and coherence I should prefer *nec*, the reading of the *deteriores*, regarding Barber's *ne* as a second best. It is an awful nuisance not to be sure, since one way (*nec* or *ne*) we have a message that is a mixture of irony and shame, the other way (*haec*), something closer to straight pathos. Reconstructing is made more difficult; but it is hardly the poet's fault.

Quite unlike these accidental uncertainties are the calculated uncertainties of a poetic text, those which are the result of the poet's decision to leave things that way. Because of these, until classicists become better literary critics, the interpretation of a Latin poem is apt to be confused by profitless argument over details. Details are important, people will say, in pained or angry tones, depending on the critic; to disregard them is slapdash, unscholarly. I agree entirely. But we must not expect our willingness to take details seriously to lead us to certain answers. Disagreement about details of interpretation is natural and healthy, provided each of the divergent views takes adequate stock of the data provided or implied by the poet, his practice as a poet, and the potentialities of the Latin language. The critic who does not tackle the task of getting to grips with details will not establish real contact with his author. We tune in to a poem by worrying at details; this is how we train ourselves to notice what will be the important clues; rid ourselves of assumptions which the words will not stand; isolate the areas where the poet does not choose to satisfy our curiosity; discover the areas where he seems concerned to stimulate it.

It follows that the discussion of minor points is often exemplary—an argued demonstration of one way in which the data point, rather than a provocation. One allows oneself no doubt a more provocative tone in a book of essays than in a commentary, but a poem is a complex intellectual and emotional experience, not a mathematical exercise. Though perhaps the difference is not so very great. There is no answer, in the mathematical sense, to the question, what is this poem about? We cannot write down something on a slip of paper which is the final, unchallengeable result of our thinking about the poem, expressible in a few

115

words. But if the poem is competently written, we should be able to restate its hypothesis, and about this there should be reasonable agreement. If you like, you can call that the answer. The important thing, however, is not the answer, but the experience—what corresponds to the working, if you like, in the mathematical sense. Part of the experience comes from trying to fix limits. Which may involve ruling out wrong answers. The most valuable part of the experience, however, comes from the pleasure and exhilaration derived from a complicated process of analysis and synthesis.

[margin handwriting: Finding the hypothesis]

What do we make, for example, of the last couplet of the Propertius? Until Housman, nobody saw any particular difficulty. Since Housman, most continue to see no particular difficulty, but they tend to assume the lines mean something quite different. The discussion turns on the emphasis which we give to 10: *haec*. Does *haec* pick up 9: *quaecumque* (so that the meaning is 'any old bones will do')? Or is *haec* opposed, as Housman argued, to *quaecumque* (so that the meaning is 'sister will find a lot of bones around after today: tell her which are mine')? Our decision is admittedly complicated by the uncertainty about the text of line 6, but it is not, I think, at the mercy of that uncertainty. One feels inclined perhaps at first to side with Housman. His seems the safer meaning. It fits in with what we know about ancient ideas about the importance of burial—Antigone and so on. But then the process of synthesis takes over, or should. We are apt to make nonsense of a poem if we try and make sense of it couplet by couplet. Housman's view of 9–10 really involves monkeying with the text. Either we must turn 9: *et* into *sed* (with Enk), or at any rate *at*, or we must get rid of *ne* in line 6, and go back to *haec*. A decision to play safe, if adhered to, can lead us where it led Camps, into drastic textual surgery. Is it not really safer to stick to the manuscripts (at most accepting 6: *nec* of the *deteriores* in place of *ne*), and admit the possibility that Propertius may have meant something challenging and out of the ordinary? After all Propertius would not be the only Roman poet to make a man in despair reject the hope of burial: what about Virgil's Anchises (*Aeneid* ii. 646: *facilis iactura sepulchri*)? Does not the following elegy talk of the body of a kinsman of Propertius killed in the Perusine war that was not buried? What about the ghastly mix-up of remains that Tacitus describes with such relish in *Annals* i. 62? Apart from the fact that on that occasion five years had gone by, was this so exceptional?

I want one more thing out of Propertius i. 21 before we turn to Catullus 17. For Propertius' poem to have its proper effect on us, we need to know that the occasion for it is the siege of Perugia in 41 B.C.; we need to know something about the peculiar bitterness which that siege and the massacre which followed the taking of Perugia caused; it would help, too, with our interpretation if we knew or could infer something about Propertius' view of the matter. Well, the occasion is indicated by the opening lines, with appropriate obliqueness, and i. 21 is followed by i. 22 to jog our memory; i. 22 also helps us with the way Propertius felt about the siege of Perugia. What happened, however, it is not the business of i. 21 to inform us; i. 22, though more explicit than i. 21, hardly aims at information. We come here into the area of what the poet feels he can rely on any reader to know. Once again, as with the difficulties caused by different readings, we may feel that possession of the poem could easily elude us. But the cases are different. In the matter of his text the poet is pretty much at the mercy of chance; all he can do to forestall corruption is to make his sense absolutely plain and his Latin absolutely conventional in grammar and idiom. It is asking rather a lot of a poet. In the matter of what he relies on us to know, the poet's judgement has some control, provided the reader also exercises control of his judgement, and is willing to hunt around. After all, we do not read a Latin poem written in the time of Julius Caesar or Augustus in utter ignorance of its cultural context.

Now is the moment to turn to Catullus 17. For here is a poem where the text presents no special difficulty (modern editors depart from the reading of V in a score or more of minor points, but none of these seriously affects interpretation). In the matter of what the poet relies on every reader to know, however, it has been touch and go; but that, I suggest, has been more our fault than the fault of Catullus.

The hypothesis upon which Poem 17 rests is set out in suitably poetic terms in the opening 11 lines and amplified in a concluding 4-line footnote. First, 1–11:

> O Colonia, quae cupis ponte ludere longo,
> et salire paratum habes, sed uereris inepta
> crura ponticuli axulis stantis in rediuiuis,
> ne supinus eat cauaque in palude recumbat:
> sic tibi bonus ex tua pons libidine fiat,   5
> in quo uel Salisubsali sacra suscipiantur,
> munus hoc mihi maximi da, Colonia, risus.
> quendam municipem meum de tuo uolo ponte
> ire praecipitem in lutum per caputque pedesque,
> uerum totius ut lacus putidaeque paludis   10
> liuidissima maximeque est profunda uorago.

Poem 17

Let us make a preliminary attempt at extracting the data. In a country-town, possibly Verona, preparations are complete for the fun and games (1: *ludere* paraphrases *ludi*) of a rustic festival. The rickety old bridge, on which the rude dance (2: *salire* paraphrases Salisubsalus, if that is really his name—something like the *tripudium* perhaps of the Salii) is to take place, has been patched up for the occasion (3: *axulis stantis in rediuiuis*); everybody is anxious, however, in case the bridge gives way under the strain and collapses into the marsh beneath. Catullus proposes a propitiatory victim—he knows of a suitable candidate—and goes on to indicate with some gusto how he would like that part of the show to go. Then after a further 11 lines in which Catullus sets out his grievance against his proposed victim, we revert to the theme of the opening lines in the concluding 4; in these, Catullus expresses his willingness to administer the ducking personally, adding that he has some hope that the mud bath will have a beneficial effect.

> nunc eum uolo de tuo ponte mittere pronum,
> si pote stolidum repente excitare ueternum,
> et supinum animum in graui derelinquere caeno,
> ferream ut soleam tenaci in uoragine mula.

The details are somewhat unusual, which may be why Catullus devotes so much space (over half his poem) to them, though plainly his object is imaginative vivacity as much as careful presentation of the basic data; some exuberance of tone is appropriate to match the rollicking metre, and, no doubt, the mood of the occasion. But the imagery is more than embroidery. It conveys obliquely an important detail which I have restated in bald prose. There is nothing in these lines about a propitiatory victim, and you will look in vain for any hint of this in the standard commentaries. Indeed a common assumption is that line 5 refers to a new bridge altogether (so Fordyce); Catullus, the commentators suggest, merely expresses a hope that the townspeople will get their new bridge; far from doing anything in particular about it, he even (like the dying man in Propertius i. 21) attaches a condition to his good wishes.

I think we are entitled to object that this does not make very good sense of Catullus 17. It seems, moreover, to neglect the patent hint of 3: *rediuiuis*, about which more in a moment. Professor Niall Rudd in an astute study of the poem (*TAPA* 90 [1959], 238–42) points out that Catullus speaks of the bridge as though it were an old man shaky on his pins (2–3: *inepta crura*), standing at the moment (3: *stantis*) but likely to collapse full-length on his back (4: *ne supinus eat cauaque in palude recumbat*); in short, the bridge is the symbol of the husband of lines 12–21. But he takes this as part of the imaginative exuberance of the poem, not as something which prepares us for the idea that one can take the place of the other; that the old man flat on his back in the mud will, Catullus hopes, be acceptable to the powers concerned as a substitute for the bridge flat on its back in the mud.

The fact of the matter is that bridges, old men, and propitiatory sacrifices fall within the area of things Catullus relies upon his readers to know something about. He provides what he considers sufficient clues, and leaves it to his readers to apply the familiar material of common knowledge to a situation which is novel, indeed fantastic. As in the case of a mythological allusion, or the unusual meaning of a word, the modern reader must build up by patient research the nearest thing he can manage to the contemporary reader's immediate response: or nearly immediate response, for part of the fun of a poem may lie in the fact that it takes us a moment to put two and two together, or to realize what the poet is getting at.

There are intriguing references in Roman literature to an ancient custom at Rome of throwing sexagenarians off a bridge. By Catullus' time all that remained of the custom, most likely, was a proverbial saying —*sexagenarios de ponte* [*deici oportet*] or something of the sort—and, apparently, a picturesque ceremony in which rush effigies were substituted for living sexagenarians. A remark by Cicero in his first speech in a criminal case (*pro Rosc. Amer.* 100) shows that the proverb, if not the practice, was still sufficiently current to be made the subject of laughter in court: that versatile thug Chrysogonus, adept in all forms of assassination, had even arranged for one of his victims to be bumped off a bridge into the Tiber, thereby offending against the *mos maiorum*, since the man had not reached the qualifying age of 60 years. (*habeo etiam dicere, quem contra morem maiorum minorem annis LX de ponte in Tiberim deiecerit.*) Frazer's 35-page excursus on Ovid *Fasti* v. 621 inclines to the view that the rite was originally a sacrifice to the river god to ensure his continued toleration of the bridge spanning his waters. Th. Birt (*Rheinisches Museum* 75 [1926], 115–26) argues that the dance was a display of military force, a symbolic incursion across the bridge into enemy territory. For ancient references (the main one is Festus 450 L, s.v. *sexagenarios*—a series of guesses about the meaning of a proverbial saying) see Klotz in *RE*, s.v. *sexagenarii*; like Frazer and Birt, Klotz rejects the innocent explanation given by Lewis and Short.

It is true that Catullus seems to be building on, or imagining, a somewhat more picturesque festival, not in Rome, but in a country-town, in which an actual victim will get off with a ducking. Eduard Fraenkel in a brilliant discussion of Catullus 42, in which he shows that poem to be based on the ancient custom of *flagitatio*—a piece of rough justice sanctioned by tradition whereby a complainant sought redress by exposing an offender to public ridicule (*JRS* 51 [1961], 46–53), adds an *obiter dictum* on Poem 17:

Catullus introduces his Roman readers to the strange ceremony which as a small boy he had watched with delight in the neighbourhood of his birthplace Verona. That ceremony had once been part of a serious religious ritual, but, as happens in this world, in course of time it had changed its character to that of a carnivalesque pastime. But whether picturing a well-known and common ceremony or one remote and rare, Catullus always applies to it the care and the skill of a great artist. He makes use of those customs not because he, like a scholarly poet or an antiquarian, is interested in folklore for its own sake. His approach differs widely from that of Callimachus and those other Alexandrian poets who were constantly on the look-out for something refined and recondite. It is not impossible that their example may have encouraged Catullus to treat similar themes. But if so, he did it in a spirit of his own. What primarily seems to have attracted him in what we call folklore was its wealth of realistic and picturesque detail.

All this would be very nice, if there were evidence for it, though Fraenkel's words seem to me to suggest, as I shall argue presently, a false emphasis in reading Poem 17. But it is not necessary to suppose an actual ceremony, ducking and all. Indeed, we should avoid assuming this, since we are then apt to suppose further that the ceremony was sufficiently well known for Catullus to regard it as falling into the area of things which he could rely on his readers to know about; not just a few friends, but that wider and more permanent audience for which any poet worth his salt writes. For Catullus is not *describing* a ceremony, he is at most alluding to one. He takes it for granted that his readers, those at any rate who have their wits about them, will grasp what he is up to. It seems to me more plausible, therefore, and to make a better poem, if we assume Catullus is weaving a whimsical fantasy out of a common saying in Rome and some rustic festival which may or may not have included something like the throwing of effigies into the Tiber, but whose details are quite unimportant and probably not common knowledge.

Fraenkel's reason, I take it, for assuming that Catullus is writing about a ceremony actually involving a ducking is that he takes the ceremony to be the real subject of the poem, Catullus merely permitting himself a diversion or an expansion on the appropriateness of his particular candidate; if describing an actual ceremony, the poet has no call to manufacture the details out of his own poetic imagination. It seems to me however, first, that Fraenkel assumes more than the poem requires (it needs only a general awareness that such ceremonies exist, or once existed, or survive in a popular saying, as a springboard from which to get the poem in the air); second, that preoccupation with an actual ceremony has led Fraenkel away from what the poem is really about.

Let us take a second look at the basic data: lines 1–4 call only for a place that can be addressed as Colonia, a festival involving some pretty energetic dancing, and a rickety patched-up bridge on which the dancing is to take place. We cannot be sure the place was Verona; we cannot even be sure that the festival was that of Salsubsalus or Salisubsalius—the name sounds a little too good to be true; it may be just a name to suggest a *ne plus ultra* of heavy-footed dancing to which, Catullus hopes, the bridge will stand up, provided, of course, his *municeps* has been tipped over the side. Nothing implies that the ceremony involved a ducking. Catullus' offer to supply a suitable candidate, and thus restore to the bridge the desired soundness (5: *sic tibi bonus ex tua pons libidine fiat*), though put in terms that suggest he is claiming an official part in the ceremony (7: *munus hoc mihi maximi da, Colonia, risus*), may be no more than a piece of fantasy, in which the poet's imagination leaps from a rustic festival at Verona (if it is Verona) to a familiar saying (*sexagenarios de ponte*) and a traditional ritual at Rome and what might happen here if that saying were applied in not too grim earnest.

But whether the ceremony is real, improved upon, or imagined, it is surely clear that Catullus is more interested in the victim. He begins with Colonia, its games, and its bridge rather than the victim because a good poem and a good joke demand a measure of obliqueness. It is true that the concluding four lines appear to bring us back to where we started from, so that 1–11 and 23–6 could make up, almost as they stand, a complete poem; but we could do much the same with Poem 44, where 1–9 and 16–17 would give us a complete poem. Poem 17 ends for all that with its true subject, the husband. The bridge, shaky on its pins, no longer fit to play its part in a life of fun and gaiety, is the symbol of the husband, as Rudd has pointed out; if not a sexagenarian, he behaves like one. The bridge, we gather, has collapsed before, has emerged from the bog and been given a fresh lease of life. (This is surely the most natural way to read *axulis stantis in rediuiuis*—more natural than supposing that the bridge had been patched with second-hand material from elsewhere). Let us try, says Catullus, the same treatment on the husband—and at the same time take no chances with the bridge.

The butt of Catullus' righteous indignation is that stock character, the supine husband, the *mari complaisant*, more often treated by the comedians and the love poets with tolerant contempt, though there are interesting parallels between Catullus and Ovid's complaint to a husband, *Amores* ii. 19. Really, says Catullus, the fellow is *such* a fool (12: *insulsissimus est homo*); like Varus' girl-friend, he makes a nuisance of himself by not knowing how to behave in sophisticated society (10. 33: '*sed tu insulsa male et molesta uiuis.*'). The basis of Catullus' condemnation, in other words, is, as usual, social, not moral. The husband is insufferable because he is too innocent to twig what is going on; he has not the gumption, as Catullus puts it, of his two-year-old son asleep in his father's trembly arm (12–13): *nec sapit pueri instar/ bimuli tremula patris dormientis in ulna*). (A passage that has been curiously misunderstood. 'Der Gebrauch des Deminutivums *bimulus*', complains Kroll, 'und die Nennung des Vaters statt der eher zu erwartenden Mutter sind, wie so

vieles in diesem Gedicht, durch metrische Rücksichten mitbedingt.'
'Gentlemen of such advanced years are not usually the fathers of two-
year-old infants', remarks Rudd, 'and even if they were what would this
contribute to the poet's picture?' But Catullus is not talking about what
is usual, but about a particular husband, who *has* a young son and
regarding whose senility exaggeration is excusable.)

For in his innocence, the husband lets his pretty, frisky young wife
gad about as she likes (17: *ludere . . . sinit ut libet*; her fondness for fun
and games corresponds to that of the people of Colonia—*ludere* here
picks up *ludere* in line 1). We are reminded of Ovid's complaint that *his*
husband makes the game too easy (*Amores* ii. 19. 1–2):

> si tibi non opus est seruata, stulte, puella,
> at mihi fac serues, quo magis ipse uelim.

Second, Catullus' husband makes no effort to provide a little competition (18: *nec se subleuat ex sua parte*)—in this way too spoiling the
fun; no man of spirit, complains Ovid, enjoys an affair if the husband
lets him go ahead, adding a sublime sally in which he appeals to the
husband for a healthy spirit of rivalry (ibid. 4–5):

> ferreus est si quis, quod sinit alter, amat.
> speremus pariter, pariter metuamus, amantes.

Catullus sees pretty much eye to eye with Ovid in the matter of husbands, as his angry, contemptuous outburst against Lesbia's husband in
Poem 83 shows:

> Lesbia mi praesente uiro mala plurima dicit;
> haec illi fatuo maxima laetitia est.
> mule, nihil sentis! si nostri oblita taceret,
> sana esset: nunc quod gannit et obloquitur,
> non solum meminit, sed, quae multo acrior est res,
> irata est; hoc est, uritur et loquitur.

His role in Poem 17, however, is not that of the husband's rival. He
adopts instead the pose of the scandalized observer. His object is not
pasquinade, or satire, but poetry. For Catullus there are the makings
of poetry in even the most sordid affair—Flavius', for example, in
Poem 6 (15–end):

> quare, quidquid habes boni malique,
> dic nobis: uolo te ac tuos amores
> ad caelum lepido uocare uersu.

Round the supine husband of Poem 17 he constructs a framework of light-hearted fantasy, in which he leaps from vivid image to vivid image—the luscious description of the bog, for instance (10–11):

> uerum totius ut lacus putidaeque paludis
> liuidissima maximeque est profunda uorago.

In it the husband will, he hopes, shed his supine mind, like a mule its iron sandal (25–6):

> et supinum animum in graui derelinquere caeno,
> ferream ut soleam tenaci in uoragine mula.

Husband and wife are brought to life in a string of images from the Italian countryside. From these Poem 17 largely derives its very considerable poetic stature. At the same time the situation is reinterpreted from another viewpoint, not that of the *urbanus* contemptuous of the provincial, but that of the normal, healthy, vigorous countryman. The girl is so slight and fragile, and yet as frisky as a baby goat (15: *puella tenellulo delicatior haedo*). Goats were proverbial for their amorousness —cf. Horace's *haedus, Odes* iii. 13. 4–5: *cui frons turgida cornibus | primis et uenerem et proelia destinat*; as for *delicatus* ('naughty', almost 'wanton') Augustus is said to have remarked that he had two gadabout daughters to put up with, Rome and Julia (Macrobius ii. 5. 4: *duas se habere filias delicatas, quas necesse haberet ferre*). Any sensible farmer would watch over such a girl more carefully than he would watch over his choicest grapes (16: *adseruanda nigerrimis diligentius uuis*)—to prevent others getting their hands on her. Instead he lies sprawled out like an alder log, hamstrung in the ditch where some Ligurian axeman left it (18–19: *uelut alnus | in fossa Liguri iacet suppernata securi*). If one's first impression from the structure of the poem is that it is about a festival in a country-town, surely the imagery suggests a different emphasis, in which the ceremony provides an appropriately fantastic frame for a witty, shrewd, sensitive, poetic study of country-love.

PART 2 PARTICULAR

VII

Frank O. Copley

Catullus *c.* 4: the world of the poem

II.   Catullus *c.* 4: The World of the Poem

FRANK O. COPLEY

UNIVERSITY OF MICHIGAN

Editors and students of Catullus have found in the *phaselus*-poem a host of puzzling, unanswered, and unanswerable questions. What kind of ship was a *phaselus*?   How big?   If big enough for a sea-voyage, how did Catullus get it up the Po and the Mincio to Lake Garda?   Is the *limpidus lacus* indeed Lake Garda, or is it some other lake; and if so, what lake?   Was the *phaselus* not an actual ship but only a model or picture or carving?   Whose ship was it: Catullus', or somebody else's?   Did Catullus come home from Bithynia in it?   If so, then why in *c.* 46 does he seem to be talking about a return by land?   How many trees is a *silva*? Was the ship built of one tree or many?   If we are to believe the commentaries, these and many similar questions must be answered before we may be sure of having grasped the meaning and intent of the poem.[1]

But a poem is itself.   It presents its own world to its readers and demands that they accept it as true for the purposes of the poem and not for anything else.   The world so created may be factual, but equally it may be completely or partially fictitious.   We have no trouble with those poetic worlds that are patently made up out of whole cloth; we are—at least I hope we are—never so foolish as to ask the geographical location of Coleridge's "Xanadu" or to inquire why the caverns of the river Alph were "measureless to man."   Our trouble comes when the poet, especially if he writes in the first person, tells of experiences and places and persons that seem to have been "real" and speaks of them as if they had been "real."   For then if the world of the poem does not seem to square with external facts as we know them, or think we know them, we are tempted to break the law of the poem and to ask

[1] For a typical discussion of these and other similar questions see Friedrich's notes (G. Friedrich, *Catulli Veronensis Liber* [Leipzig and Berlin 1908]). See also W. Kroll, *Catull* (Leipzig and Berlin 1929), R. Ellis, *Commentary on Catullus* (Oxford 1889), E. T. Merrill, *Catullus* (Boston 1893, now reprinted by Harvard), A. Baehrens, *Catulli Veronensis Liber* (Leipzig 1876–85), M. Lenchantin de Gubernatis *Il Libro del Catullo Veronese* (Turin 1953).

improper questions about it.   And unless we can get answers to
these questions that satisfy us of their objective validity, we begin
to twitch and pull at the poem, to interpret the poet's words to
make them fit our view of the world, to say to ourselves, "The poet
says thus-and-so, but he must be wrong, because we know that
thus-and-so does not fit the facts; therefore he must have meant to
say thus-and-thus."

By all the laws of poetry this is a felony.   Every poet has a right
to say anything he chooses about himself or his world, to present
in his poem any set of assertions that will enable him to say what
he wants to say, and to present them as facts, whether they are or
not.   And we as his readers have no right whatever to question
the validity of the facts so presented: the world of the poem is what
it is, and only if we accept it as such will we ever find out what the
poet wanted us to know.   Only when a given text presents patent
impossibilities may we raise questions about the validity of its
factual content, its "world."   This is obviously an over-
simplification of the critical problem, but this much, at least, I
believe we can accept: we must start our criticism with the
assumption that our poet meant what he said and that the world
of the poem is *for that poem* a real world.   Now what is the world
of Catullus' *phaselus*-poem?   What facts does he ask us to accept?
First: there is a ship present before our eyes (quem videtis,
hospites).   It is a ship, not a model or a picture or a piece of
sculpture, for this is what the language of the poem requires us to
see.   Secondly, the ship has sailed through the Adriatic, the
Aegean, the Propontis, and the Black Sea.   Thirdly, her timbers
came from Mt. Cytorus, and she was launched at or near
Amastris.   Fourthly, she was a fast, seaworthy ship that successfully rode out many storms, handled nimbly under oars, and was
a good sailer, either before the wind or on port or starboard reach.
Finally, she is now moored in a clear, quiet lake, where she is
being dedicated to Castor and Pollux.   This is the world of the
poem, and there is not one single impossibility within it.   Impossible to get a sea-going ship up to Lake Garda?   Does the
poem say anything about Lake Garda?   The world of the poem
contains only a *limpidus lacus*, quite unnamed.   And if we insist
that it must be Lake Garda because Catullus had his villa there,
and insist further that no sea-going craft could possibly have been
gotten up there, either *via* the Mincio or overland, and that

therefore Catullus must have been talking about a model or a picture of his ship—let us grant it all.   Let us imagine Catullus sitting before such a model or picture in his villa on Sirmio and deciding to write a poem about a ship, his or someone else's.   Or let us assume that there was a ship on Lake Garda that attracted the poet's attention—just a ship, any ship, about which he knew nothing at all.   Perhaps it was just an old hulk, rotting and half-full of water.   Somehow the sight stimulated him to write a poem about a ship.   But poems are not written about ships; they are written about *this* ship or *that* ship, a particular ship, and so Catullus particularized this ship by ascribing to it things he had seen and heard and imagined about ships, linking them together in such a way as to create a believable set of circumstances.

In actuality, of course, we have no way of knowing what Catullus saw or did not see or of what it was that prompted him to write his poem.   What we do know is what he wanted us, his readers, to see; we do know the world of his poem, the world that he created for it.   The incident, the ship, the lake, the whole story, may be completely fictitious or made up of a combination of fact and fiction.[2]   For the world of the poem it is all real; and since it contains neither follies nor impossibilities, we are required to accept it and to see in it what our author has put there for us to see.   It requires no additaments on our part to make it either believable or understandable.   In fact, if we try to add anything to it, we are all too likely to obscure its meaning and lacerate its structure.   Was the poem written about Catullus' journey home from Bithynia?   It may have been, but it does not say so, and we do not need to know; nor, if we did know, would the poem be one whit better as a poem.   Was the ship Catullus' own?   It may have been, but the poem does not say so, and we do not need to know; nor if we did know, would the poem be one whit better as a poem.[3]   When was it written?   The poem gives no hint

[2] De Gubernatis (above, note 1) *ad loc.*: "a dire il vero, la lettura del carme insinua il dubbio ch'esso sia tutto frutto della fantasia possente del poeta . . .;" cf. R. Wellek and A. Warren, *Theory of Literature* (New York 1956) 64–5: "One cannot, from fictional statements . . . draw any inference as to the biography of a writer. . . . The relation between the private life and the work is not a simple relation of cause and effect."

[3] In spite of these facts, the commentators and literary historians persist in speaking as if the poem were evidence of Catullus' trip and of his ownership of the *phaselus*: see e.g. Merrill (above, note 1) p. 35; J. W. Duff, *The Literary History of Rome*[3] (London 1953) 228.

whatever of its date. It may have been written after Catullus came back from Bithynia, either immediately thereafter or after a lapse of years; equally well, it may have no connection whatever with Catullus' Bithynian adventure or even with Catullus at all or with any of his friends or anybody else he knew. In short, it is a poem, a skillful and graceful poem, written by a poet of taste, sensitivity, and imagination; it is not a piece of biography, auto- or otherwise. In fact I will go one step further: it is not a piece of autobiography even if it is autobiographical.[4] That is to say, it was not written to recount an incident of the poet's life, even if its data were drawn from his experiences. It is written wholly, simply, and entirely, about a ship, and its poetry is the poetry of ships. This is what Catullus wrote it for; this is what he wanted us to see and understand and enjoy.

And what is the poetry of the ship? The ancient ship was by our standards a clumsy craft, none too seaworthy. It was flat-bottomed and of shallow draft; it had no deep keel or center-board; it had no hinged rudder but was steered by long oars lashed to the rails near the stern. Travel by sea was hazardous and uncertain; it must also have been cold, wet, and un-comfortable.[5] It may well be that the scarcity of poems about ships among the ancients is due not only to their fear of the sea[6] but to the unpoetic clumsiness of the ships themselves and the risks and miseries of travel in them. The double handful of epigrams in the *Anthology* that deal with ships[7] are without exception chilly, mannered performances. In fact, I will hazard a guess that ships are "she" in antiquity solely by linguistic coincidence, and not because the ancients were generally aware of the paradox, so vivid to us, of the inanimate fabric that had life and personality.

It is precisely this paradox that Catullus does see and on it that he builds his poem. His *phaselus* is very much alive, and in a curious and subtle way, her life is made more real to the reader by the poet's device of having her tell her story not in person—for this would have recalled too vividly the speaking tombstones and

[4] Cf. Wellek and Warren (above, note 2) 64–7.

[5] The best account of a journey by sea is St. Paul's: *Acts* 27–8. For the ship itself, see Cecil Torr, *The Ancient Ship* (Cambridge 1894).

[6] O. Hezel, *Catull und das griechische Epigramm* (Stuttgart 1932) 11.

[7] Hezel (above, note 6) 10, and notes 1, 3, and 4.

other similar objects of the *Anthology*—but through a narrator, thus suggesting that her language was not one to be heard and understood by everyone but only by those who had lived on and with her. In other words she is not an inanimate object, conveniently but temporarily granted quasi-human personality, but a creature in her own right, of her own kind, with her own peculiar life and her own special language.

She is alive now; she was alive when she sailed the *impotentia freta* and without a single wasted prayer skirted the reefs; she was alive even before she was a ship, when she was trees on Mt. Cytorus and "talked and whispered when the wind blew in her hair."[8] This is the poetry of Catullus' ship; this is what his poem is about. It is for this that he created the world of his poem; and only if we accept that world, seeing and hearing exactly what the poet's words require us to see and hear, adding nothing to it, inferring nothing from it, will we grasp the meaning of the poem and know its delights.

[8] Loquente saepe sibilum edidit coma.

VIII

M. C. J. Putnam

Catullus' journey

CATULLUS' JOURNEY (*Carm.* 4)

MICHAEL C. J. PUTNAM

RARELY has a poem been subjected to exegesis exhibiting more violent contrasts than Catullus' *Phaselus ille* (*Carm.* 4).[1] Critical approaches toward it, almost Protean in their variety, run the gamut from complete empirical belief in the reality of the ship, that is to say, from unquestioned acceptance of the poet's objectivity, to equally strong partisanship of a quite opposite view, wherein the ship becomes a kind of mystic symbol and the poem, literally considered, scarcely referable to Catullus at all.

Even by those who concede the reality of the ship, it has been debated whether it could, not to say did, make such a journey as the poet describes. To those for whom the journey appears partly fact and partly fiction, the vessel becomes merely the ex-voto model through which the poet offers homage to Castor and Pollux for his safe return. Finally, progressing from thorough involvement on the poet's part with the ship to an equally complete lack of personal interest, the *phaselus* takes on, for some, a purely imaginary character and the poem is considered a sudden *jeu d'esprit*, written solely for the amusement of guests at the poet's Garda villa. Many other positions between these two extremes have also been proposed by exegetes of the poem.[2]

The most compelling argument against the last approach, that the poem is a purely illusory and imagined experience, is the fact that Catullus' mind, as opposed to Horace's, say,

just does not work that way, that tangible, sensory experience was to him the essence of all poetic production. The "symbolic" theory would have had fewer supporters, and there would have been less learned quarreling about the poem, if, in the early stages of discussion, the first explanation had received due attention; if, that is to say, it had been shown that Catullus could have bought a yacht in Bithynia and sailed with it not only to the mouth of the Po but up the Mincio and into the Lago di Garda, on the shore of which Sirmio, the poet's peninsular home, was situated. Yet it is only recently that this route has been authortatively demonstrated by Svennung to be possible, even probable.[3] He has shown that ancient techniques of navigation up a small river made such a trip as this up the Mincio by no means unusual. Therefore, if Catullus says that he made such a voyage and if the ancient evidence supports his statement, we should accept it as true.

Yet, since many of the problems the poem poses are of a practical rather than interpretative nature, the poetic qualities have rarely been allowed to shine through the exegetical haze. Assuming Svennung's conclusions, that it *was* Catullus' ship and that it did make the very journey the poem describes, I propose to examine some of the ways by which the poet elaborates and enhances the literal aspects of the journey, both in 4 itself and in other related poems.

[CLASSICAL PHILOLOGY, LVII, January, 1962]

I shall begin by stressing the fact that no interpretation of 4 which looks to that poem alone can do it justice. It stands, as we shall see, finely unified by itself. But this unity is enhanced by our knowledge and possession of two other poems of Catullus bound closely to 4. These are 46, written before the poet's departure from the east, and 31, the product of his safe and happy arrival back home. Though its quality of reminiscence clearly suggests that it was composed after the address to Sirmio, our poem forms the geographic and literary bridge between these two. It takes the poet from the heat of Nicaea (the setting of 46) into the waves of Lake Garda, translating the eagerness of the mind into the reality of the voyage, the thought into the physical reaction. At the same time it forms the central piece of a lyric trilogy. All three poems complement one another, and each is necessary for the full understanding of the remaining two. Thus the three form a close-knit cycle, the subject of which is the total sweep of Catullus' journey.[4] Literary form is, as a result, perfectly matched with content which, in turn, reflects the rise and fall of an emotion both in and, at the same time, beyond any reference to time and space.

To realize the tight structure of this design, we must first turn away from an examination of the journey itself to the two poems which precede and follow it, 46 and 31. Only when the close connection between these two poems has been demonstrated can it be shown how crucial the position of 4 is in the chain of which they are the beginning and final links. This is not to say that Catullus, writing in Bithynia on the eve of his departure, knew exactly how his imagination would respond when he had finally arrived at his beloved Sirmio, in the same way as Dante, say, was in general aware of the shape and content of the concluding cantos of *Paradiso* as he began the initial part of his *Commedia*. Yet Catullus has given us clear proof that, at his journey's end, his thoughts returned to the manner in which he had expressed his emotion preparatory to taking leave of Bithynia. Let us observe some of the hints he provides.

Poem 46 opens with the coming of spring and continues with a description of the desire for travel which the newborn world arouses in Catullus. Only when we reach the end of the poem and he addresses his companions as those "longe quos simul a domo profectos / diversae variae viae reportant . . ." (10–11) does it become clear that all the initial thoughts, devoted to spring and to the wish to wander, are products of one central desire, to return home. The poet's mind moves swiftly from one thought to the other, so that the coming of spring, which *refert tepores*, leads, in the end, to the devious routes which bring (*reportant*) the poet and his friends back home.[5] And the thought, once conceived, receives immediate physical response as his feet sympathetically absorb the themes of creativity and wandering which spring proposes. Linked as are these ideas, their unity rests with the image of the *domus*. And the *domus*, as we learn explicitly in 31. 14, is, of course, Sirmio.

The poet makes the connection clear when, with appropriate change of mood, he repeats the imagery of 46. 4–5, "linquantur Phrygii, Catulle, campi / Nicaeaeque ager uber aestuosae," at 31. 5–6, "vix mi ipse credens Thuniam atque Bithunos / liquisse campos et videre te in tuto." The emotion first experienced in Bithynia is similar to that which he experiences upon arrival at Sirmio, the only difference being that 46 portrays the birth of yearning, contemporaneous with the coming of spring, while 31 denotes its fulfilment. The feeling of mind which comes to the poet in his faraway province ("iam mens prae-trepidans avet vagari," 46.7), the pent-up tension which must arise when a long road stretches ahead at the conclusion of which lies a destination which symbolizes love, ends only in Sirmio "cum mens onus reponit, ac peregrino / labore fessi venimus larem ad nostrum" (31. 8–9). The happy feet of the poet, in 46. 8, eager to begin their way, become the figure of the poet himself as he looks happily on his beloved peninsula after safe arrival (31. 4).

These two poems, therefore, run on two levels which are so interconnected as hardly to be separable. On the one hand there is the actual description of the journey's beginning and end, but this is also equivalent to the emotion of desire, the journey's cause, which is aroused in 46 and attained in 31. For this reason, it is important to observe carefully the imagery through which the poet conjures up his final picture of Sirmio.

In its careful craftsmanship and balanced structure 31 closely resembles 46, but the emotional content is conveyed in a manner much more complex. Partially this arises from an undercurrent of ambiguity which runs throughout the piece. It appears in the opening lines: "Paene insularum, Sirmio, insularumque / ocelle, . . ." The word *ocelle* produces an inner effect. The commentators tell us that it means "gem" and cite a passage in which Cicero calls his villas *ocellos Italiae*.[6] But Catullus uses this diminutive elsewhere only when addressing a person dear to him. Thus he adjures Calvus "nunc audax cave sis, precesque nostras, / oramus, cave despuas, ocelle, . . ." (50. 18–19). *Ocelle* in 31, therefore, is equivocal. It seems to be directed to the gleaming beauty of the peninsula jutting out into the Garda. Yet it could with equal validity be applied to a person. This inherent ambiguity gathers force from line 4, where the personification becomes more explicit: "quam te libenter quamque laetus inviso." In the intensity of his feelings, Catullus begins to treat Sirmio as if it did indeed momentarily appear to him as his little eye of love. The word *inviso* means not only to "visit," as it should if applicable to a place, but also to "see and look at." The lines which follow clarify still further this double meaning:

vix mi ipse credens Thuniam atque Bithunos liquisse campos et videre te in tuto. o quid solutis est beatius curis, cum mens onus reponit, ac peregrino labore fessi venimus larem ad nostrum, desideratoque acquiescimus lecto [5–10]?

A comparison with similar thoughts in 9, another poem where the focus of attention is on returning home, offers the best commentary on these verses. Catullus asks Veranius

venistine domum ad tuos penates fratresque unanimos anumque matrem? venisti! o mihi nuntii beati! visam te incolumem audiamque Hiberum narrantem loca, facta, nationes . . . [9. 3–7].

We should note that the position of Catullus is different in the two poems. In 9 he is at home, welcoming Veranius from abroad, experiencing the same emotions as does Sirmio in 31, upon receiving the poet back after his prolonged absence. But the scope of imagery common to the two poems shows that in each case the poet's emotional pattern is following the same course. To Sirmio he says, picking up the initial idea of "seeing" (*inviso*), how happy he is to return safe and sound (*videre te in tuto*). Likewise he will now look upon Veranius, returned without misfortune (*visam te incolumem*). Veranius had come safely back to family and friends just as Catullus did to Sirmio. Of his own home the poet states *venimus larem ad nostrum*, while, with the requisite change of person, to Veranius he asks "venistine domum ad tuos penates . . . ?" (9. 3). And the interrogative is changed to the positive *venisti!* in line 5, as if the poet had suddenly become sure that the news was true. Examples could be multiplied.

The point here is that Catullus depicts his own feelings upon seeing Sirmio in the same manner as he does when speaking to the newly returned Veranius. The *domus*, the symbol upon which the strongest of Catullus' emotions always centered, in the long poems as well as short, becomes here not only the old home but its personification, whom Catullus addresses in terms of deep emotion.[7] And so the desire, born in 46, finds its fulfilment, as journey, in the sight of the lake and of the familiar *lar*, as emotion, in line 10 where Catullus asks "desideratoque acquiescimus lecto?" The cycle has been completed.[8]

This brings us to the final lines of the poem, another direct address which balances the opening invocation:

salve, o venusta Sirmio, atque ero gaude:
gaudete vosque, o Lydiae lacus undae:
ridete, quidquid est domi cachinnorum.

The implications of the word *venusta* are not now unexpected. Though such an adjective might well be applied to a geographical spot, it only takes on its full significance if applied to a woman, whose beauty manifests inner charm. Likewise, the *cachinni* suggest the roar which waves make lapping against one another when wind strikes the water (so also in 64. 273), but it may also be the raucous noise of joyous laughter. Both meanings are possible here, both, no doubt, intentional, for the wit which *venusta* assumes may also manifest itself in the *cachinni*. When Fabullus is invited to the poet's for dinner, it is expected that he will bring with him wine, salt, and laughter ("et vino et sale et omnibus cachinnis," 13. 5). And we note the manner in which Catullus addresses Fabullus as he immediately adds "haec si, inquam, attuleris, *venuste noster*, / cenabis bene; . . ." (13. 6–7). And how important the sound of loud laughter is on occasions such as this the poet shows when he begs Sirmio to ring out with shouts of glee. Likewise the intimations of personal beauty which the word *venusta* carries[9] are intensified and further realized in the phrase *ero gaude*, and both reinforce the idea of personification.[10] The power of the poet's emotions finds its ultimate expression in the request he makes of Sirmio to share his feelings of joy.

This heightened emotional diction comes in part from poem 4, to which we now turn. We will assume, at the start, that the poet did indeed make the journey he describes through the world of the Aegean. One main critical objection, however, remains to be countered before this hypothesis can be completely acceptable. It is often assumed, from what the poet says in 46, that he was planning a land journey at least as far as the *claras Asiae urbes* and that, therefore, only some of the places named in 4. 6–9 could have been visited by Catullus, at least on this particular trip. And so, the argument continues, if some of the stops on the itinerary of 4 can be thus called in question, why is not the rest of the catalogue placed in jeopardy, why, in short, is it not easier to call the poem purely imaginative? It is best here to look at the metaphors themselves on which this assumption of a land journey is based. In 46. 8, for example, Catullus states "iam laeti studio pedes vigescunt." Now if the word *pedes* be taken, as it is even by Svennung, as proof of a trip by land, then we may equally well assume that Catullus was going to walk his way down the coast of Asia Minor! But this is a poem describing the coming of spring and what effect this event has on the poet personally. He himself is *laetus*, but his happiness arises from the newly reborn desire for home. And so, understandably enough, he transfers the rebirth of nature and of his own longing to his feet because it is through them, metaphorically, that the desire finds its first impulse to be up and going.[11]

There is one other word, again used metaphorically, which strongly suggests that this interpretation is correct, *volemus*. This, too, has no connection with a land journey. Rather, the tense quality of the poet's emotion leads to a wish for speed, for the speed of flying, in fact, and it is this which the poet, crucially enough, transfers to or, better, concentrates on the *phaselus*, which claims to be the swiftest ever fashioned, a ship which none could surpass "sive palmulis / opus foret volare sive linteo."[12] The transition is now easy to the itinerary of the voyage:

et hoc negat minacis Hadriatici
negare litus insulasve Cycladas
Rhodumque nobilem horridamque Thraciam
Propontida trucemve Ponticum sinum, . . .
    [6–9].

Thus the poem is in a sense the log of a very special and exciting journey. But the boat does more than merely carry its' master (*erum*, 19) home, it *is* his emotion.[13] It is just this sudden wish for speed on his part that the boat can supply. Only through speed will the *quies* for which he yearns be attained. At the moment when the poem was composed, clearly some little time after the return home, the poet relives his past feelings which placed more emphasis on the vessel's speed than on the actual geography of the trip. Indeed, when he does turn to a mention of place names, in line 6, it is only to show that no spot they passed could deny such unusual ability on the vessel's part.

The stress on speed is not the only way in which Catullus betrays his emotional involvement. The description of the journey's excitement is heightened, also, by the personification of the yacht, a device we have seen the poet utilize to great effect in 31. Just as Sirmio seems to be deliberately portrayed for a moment as a person of flesh and blood, so also it is only right that the *phaselus*, which symbolizes the speed of desire, should be treated in the same manner as the end of longing. The boat carries its *erus* to Sirmio; now Sirmio must, in turn, rejoice at his arrival. Indeed, the *hospites* are expected to listen with understanding as the yacht tells its own tale (and to suspend disbelief of such a possibility in order to become willingly involved in the strength of the poet's emotion) and to visualize it not as the poet's pawn but as the possessor, through the poet, of a life all its own.[14]

We begin to sense this in the opening lines. The geographical catalogue adds to the impression. Instead of merely giving a straightforward enumeration of his stopping places, beginning in Bithynia and ending in his beloved Garda, the poet reverses the order, and takes the reader backward, through Adriatic, Aegean, and Black Sea, through the transition from forest to boat, to the crest of Mount Cytorus "ubi iste post phaselus antea fuit / comata silva." Even then the wood whistled and spoke, a clue to its future function as a storyteller. The lines which describe Mount Cytorus (10–16) form the center of the poem (and, in a sense, of the whole cycle from 46 to 31). Since there is a deliberate balance of language and thought on either side of this middle section, the poem manifests what is usually called the ὀμφαλός technique, so common in Alexandrian poetry.[15] Here, as in the poem on Attis, structure and content are unified through the symbol of the mountain which forms not only the rhetorical apex of the poem but the turning point of its emotion as well (and, in the case of 63, the emotional focus toward which desire is heightened only to fall away into despair).

In 4, however, the mountain top is not the goal of sensation but only its beginning. The desire, described in 46, found its start in Bithynia; and, logically enough, if the boat is the personification of desire, Catullus must establish the origin of his emotion at the actual birth of the boat itself. And this he does as he takes the reader back through the turmoil of the seas to the top of Mount Cytorus, to what was and still is most clearly related (cognitissima) to the vessel as it began its progress through the world.

This special use of the symbol of the mountain is not unique in Catullus. The initial section of 64 furnishes another example of the close connection

in Catullus' mind between mountain top, journey by ship, and the birth of desire:

Peliaco quondam prognatae vertice pinus
dicuntur liquidas Neptuni nasse per undas
Phasidos ad fluctus . . .

Except that Pelion replaces Cytorus, and that the mountain-top scene forms the beginning and not the center of the poem, the geographical and emotional situations are closely parallel.[16] The newborn ships each ride with rushing speed toward their destinations. This, in the case of the Argo, changes smoothly from the seamen's search for the golden fleece to Peleus' love for Thetis. Once these two have met, there is no further need for sea journey or ship, and the poem's action, by means of a subtle reference to Tethys and Oceanus, gradually switches from water to land to the wedding itself, where desire, born of the ocean journey and, ultimately, of the mountain top itself, is fulfilled.

From this center in 4 Catullus now reverses direction and, balancing the geographical exposition, gives what might be called a meteorological guide homeward as he puts the emphasis not on the particular place names but on the more universal wind, tide, and shore, until the arrival at Garda. Then in the end, with a temporal change of which Catullus is especially fond,[17] we come out of the violence of the past journey to the calm lake which comprises the quies (26) of the present.

It is, of course, in part to this very quies that Catullus alludes during the course of poem 31, for the limpidum lacum of 4. 24 is surely formed of no other waves than the Lydiae lacus undae which the poet asks to rejoice at the end of 31 and which gain by comparison with all the other liquentibus stagnis (31. 2) through which the

L

poet has passed on his return journey. The poem's opening lines, in which Sirmio stands pre-eminent among all isles "quascumque in liquentibus stagnis / marique vasto fert uterque Neptunus," are but a comprehensive summary of 4, taking the reader along with the yacht "a mari / novissimo hunc ad usque limpidum lacum" (23–24). During the course from Cytorus to Garda, whether through water fresh or salt, nothing equaled Sirmio for beauty, in the poet's estimation. And since the boat is also a reflection of the poet and his yearning for home, nothing equaled the little yacht for speed and intensity as it made its way back to *venusta Sirmio*.

It is not only geographical exposition, however, which joins one poem with the other. The emotional schema, begun in 46 and continued in 4, reaches its conclusion, as we have seen, in 31, a poem which, tightly unified in its own structure, looks to the other poems for completion just as one book of the *Aeneid* looks to another for commentary on its own place in the epic as a whole. The ambiguity of the phrase *solutis curis*, in 31. 7, is a case in point. If *cura* be taken in its usual erotic sense of "longing,"[18] then the words form part of the strand of sensual imagery woven around the figure of Sirmio and hence are to be restricted specifically to the organic aspects of 31. If, on the other hand, the *curae* are "trials" or "cares," in the word's more general sense, then they are synonymous with one aspect of the *onus* of 31. 8 which the poet's mind can now put behind it, namely the *peregrino labore* of lines 8–9. Looking back at 4, the *labor* of journeying embraces the *impotentia freta* through which the poet traveled in such safety (and this fact, too, is reiterated in 31. 6)

that no vows whatsoever had to be made to deities of the shores. Thus there seems to be almost a deliberate analogy between the *quies* of the boat (4. 26) and the joy which the phrase *desideratoque acquiescimus lecto* (31. 10) makes manifest. They are one and the same, since rest at the journey's end postulates fulfilment of the poet's desire.

Likewise the word *vix* in "vix mi ipse credens Thuniam atque Bithunos / liquisse campos et videre te in tuto" (31. 5–6) stresses again the two spheres in which 31 should be interpreted. If the poet is expressing his pleasure at the accomplishment of a journey with a safety for which he had dared not hope—and recalling the yearning for home from which he suffered in Bithynia—then these lines become strictly limited to the context of 31. Yet they can with equal aptness be taken as a reference to the sudden and swift completion of the passage. And this brings the reader's thoughts back not only to 46 but to the whole of 4.

In short, the *phaselus* of 4 is both real and symbolic at the same time. It is real because it accomplished a journey of some difficulty over the Mediterranean Sea, and it is symbolic because it stands for Catullus himself and his desire. Like the poet's yearning for home which the newly reborn spring activates, it grows green with its *comata silva*, is heightened in the *impotentia freta* of the separating sea, and reaching fruition becomes calm as the poet gains the *quies* of Sirmio.

If we consider 4 by itself, it is the sea which is the basic unifying force of the poem, for it is against the background of the sea that the journey of the *phaselus* takes place and against which the scale of its accomplishment is measured. In this respect the poem bears a close resemblance to 63. Attis also is sailing on the swift ship (*celeri rate*) of his desire through the deep floods which part him from his beloved goddess. In his case the change from sea to the place of emasculation is so rapid that no mention of the shore is even been made. When once the basic urge has been accomplished, it remains for him only to climb the mountain to the *domus* of fulfilment on its top. The sea does return for a brief moment in Attis' speech of exhortation to his companions: "rapidum salum tulistis truculentaque pelagi," he says (1. 16).[19] The *truculenta . . . pelagi* correspond to the *impotentia freta* through which the yacht steered an unerring course. But the chief difference between the two poems cannot be observed until Attis reaches the top of the mountain and learns that the *domus* for which he yearned, contrary to the poet's own, has turned out utterly false. From then on the sea becomes one of the crucial images of the poem, not as a symbol of the voyage of desire, as in 4, but rather of eternal separation from true home and true love. At this moment, as at many others, Attis and Ariadne, similarly helpless on the shore, are one and the same. It is only by deliberate and direct comparison with their plight that all the vividness and excitement of Catullus' own journey can be realized and the intensity of their suffering understood.

The image of the *impotentia freta* leads to yet another level of interpretation. The ship now becomes more than an object of special reference to the poet and, if only for a moment, seems to stand as a paradigm for the life of mankind, for the journey of existence, freed from exact reference to the present and looking beyond that to a more universal archetype. From

birth (*origine*, 15) to old age (*senet quiete*, 26) with the roaring floods between, this is the course of the poet's emotion; but it also suggests something apart from and beyond his own particular factual and emotional voyage, namely, the journey of life itself.

In this sense, the course of the *phaselus* is ideal rather than actual, at least in relation to Catullus' own life. In 68 he compares himself, lovesick for Lesbia, to sailors on a storm-tossed sea, for whom a gentle and benign breeze is as welcome as the aid of Manlius to him:[20]

hic, velut in nigro iactatis turbine nautis
  lenius aspirans aura secunda venit
iam prece Pollucis, iam Castoris implorata,
  tale fuit nobis Manlius auxilium [68. 63–66].

On the other hand, the yacht dedicates itself, in its old age, to the Dioscuri, perhaps because it never had to offer them homage during the stress of life. The poet himself has been less fortunate but, with all brevity and within the emotional context delimited by this journey alone, he may have turned his eyes away from any sorrow, past or possibly to come, to look at the untarnished happiness of the present.[21]

To overemphasize any such profound implications in Catullus' lyric is to do its special lightness and charm an injustice. Though the poem runs on many levels, any allegorical interpretation must remain secondary to the pressing emotion which the particular journey presents.[22] The literary tradition, from which this poem evolves, springs from many sources. Catullus certainly must have known, from his Hellenistic background, poems in which ships were offered *ex voto* after a life of service, or poems where the object dedicated tells its own tale.[23] Yet knowledge of a great poet's tradition is of vital service not to offer proof that he borrowed literary motifs but to show how he transposed and changed them in the light of his own creative personality. Much of the poem's power is gained, as we have seen, from the manner in which actual description is enriched by an emotion which symbolizes Catullus' own feelings as well as describing the actual experiences from which they spring. It remains only to stress once more the importance to Catullus of the reality of the ship and its adventures, for, however rich the poem by implication, this alone occasioned the composition of *Phaselus ille*.

BROWN UNIVERSITY
THE CENTER FOR HELLENIC STUDIES

NOTES

1. On the spelling of *phaselus* I follow the edition of R. A. B. Mynors (Oxford, 1958). See also W. V. Clausen, *A. Persi Flacci saturarum liber* (Oxford, 1956) on 5. 136.

2. A brief bibliography of the major writings on this poem since 1900 is offered by M. Schuster in *RE*, VIIA2 (1948), 2372. This may be supplemented by reference to K. P. Schulze, "Bericht über die Literatur zu Catullus für die Jahre 1905–20," *JAW*, CLXXXIII (1920), 1–72 (esp. 3–4, 39, 43); H. Rubenbauer, "Bericht über die Literatur zu Catullus für die Jahre 1920–26," *JAW*, CCXII (1927), 196–97; and H. J. Leon, "A Quarter Century of Catullan Scholarship (1934–59) II," *CW*, LIII (1960), 142–43. See also C. L. Smith (*HSCP*, III [1892], 75–89); C. Cichorius (in *Festschrift O. Hirschfeld* [Berlin, 1903], pp. 467–83); L. A. MacKay (*CP*, XXV [1930], 77–78); L. Herrmann (*RBPh*, XXXIII [1955], 493); and F. O. Copley (*TAPA*, LXXXIX [1958], 9–13).

3. J. Svennung, "Phaselus ille. Zum 4. Gedicht Catulls," *Opuscula Romana*, I (1954), 109–24. The questions which he discusses are: Where did Catullus get the money for such a venture? Was it possible for a private person to buy or rent such a ship? Could a vessel of this sort be sailed all the way up into the Lago di Garda? Only the problem of where the trip began, which is treated below, does he leave unsatisfactorily resolved. Svennung owes much, at least in spirit, to A. L. Wheeler, *Catullus and the Traditions of Ancient Poetry* (Berkeley, 1934), pp. 98–102.

4. Closely connected as these poems are to a single happening, this pattern was not necessarily deliberately planned by the poet. It is not a "cycle" in the sense applied to the writings of the post-Homeric bards or to a group of interconnected shorter poems such as the sonnets of Swinburne or even the "Roman" odes of Horace (on the unity of which see F. Solmsen, "Horace's First Roman Ode," *AJP*, LXVIII [1947], 337 ff.). We might better compare the Oedipus plays of Sophocles or the complex emotional and symbolic unity which exists between Yeats's *Sailing to Byzantium* and *Byzantium*, whose composition is separated by a period of four years. Whether or not Catullus arranged the collection of his poetry as we now have it remains a moot question (see K. Quinn, *The Catullan Revolution* [Melbourne, 1959], p. 106, n. 11), but it is hardly an argument against the type of unity proposed here.

5. The structure of this poem is worked out with extreme care. See J. P. Elder, "Notes on some Conscious and Subconscious Elements in Catullus' Poetry," *HSCP*, LX (1951), 103–4, 121.

6. See, e. g., R. Ellis, *A Commentary on Catullus*[2] (Oxford, 1889), p. 110.

7. The importance in poetry of this metaphorical elaboration of the inanimate in personal terms need not be stressed. It is at the core of the mythmaking process (see the interesting chapter on "Elements of Mythopoesis" in J. Huizinga, *Homo Ludens: A Study of the Play-Element in Culture* [Boston, 1955], pp. 136–45). The tendency to personify is also typical of Catullus' intensity of feeling—he uses the device elsewhere, e. g., in 44—and the combination of life as actuality with life as myth is what gives poem 4 its special power.

8. The sensual imagery is anticipated not only by the word *curis* but in the phrase *labore fessi*, which manifestly refers to the trials of the journey, yet also contains sensual undertones. Thus does Catullus describe his limbs *defessa labore* (50. 14), worn out with desire for Calvus, limbs which, significantly enough for a comparison with 31, *lectulo iacebant*. So also the Gallae and their master are described in 63. 35–36 as *lassulae/nimio e labore*, where *labor*, as in 31, can be ambiguously related either to the actual journey (in 63, over the seas and up the mountain) or to their misdirected passion for Cybele.

9. On the importance of the adjective *venustus* in the vocabulary of Catullus see B. Axelson, *Unpoetische Wörter* (Lund, 1945), p. 61. In *De or.* 3. 180 Cicero speaks of the *venustas* of a ship, a reference important for 4 as well as 31.

10. Outwardly meaning "rejoice upon the return of your master" (which is the obvious sense of *erus* also in 4. 19), the phrase may bear more sensual connotations. *Erus*, or rather *era*, in Catullan usage, is applied to one's mistress, whether she seem true, as in 68. 136 (at least momentarily!), or perversely false, as in 63. 18. (On the poet's use of *erus*, -*a*, and their connection with *dominus*, -*a*, see H. Heusch, *Das Archaische in de: Sprache Catulls* [Bonn, 1954], pp. 42–44). These lines in 31 might well be compared to the description, in 61. 116–19, of the manifold joys which the husband will experience in his marriage to such a bride. The double repetition of *gaudia* and *gaudeat* (as in 31. 12–13, *gaude* and *gaudete*), coupled with the mutual use of *erus*, makes one more than suspect that the poet wished the sensual impressions to carry over to the phrase *ero gaude* of 31.

11. Following the Greek commonplace, Catullus constantly associates the foot with some eagerly awaited occasion. Lesbia appears *molli pede* in 68. 70, and Hymen comes to the nuptial ceremony *niveo pede* (61. 9–10). And how often is the eager desire of Attis manifested in his *citato pede*! Hence the constant association of dancing with a happy occasion, be it marriage, or the coming of spring, as, for example, in Horace *Carm.* 1. 4. 7 or 4. 7. 6 (the last a poem in which Horace was recalling Catullus 46; Horace's *frigora mitescunt Zephyris* [4. 7. 9] is a clear echo of *Zephyri silescit* in 46. 3).

12. The iterative form, *volito*, is also thus used in 64. 9.

13. How very personal is Catullus' emotional involvement may be seen by comparing his treatment of the

phaselus with Ovid's imitation of it in *Trist.* 1. 10 (cf. H. A. J. Munro, *Criticisms and Elucidations of Catullus*² [London, 1905], pp. 10–21).

14. The personification begins in 1. 2 with the word *ait*. It is a most unusual vessel that can tell its own tale (the same thought is carried further by *loquente*, 12, *ait*, 15, *dicit*, 16). Moreover, though it never had to resort to such measures, the inference of 22–23 is that it was capable of making vows to the gods of the shore, should the need have arisen. Other ambiguities, such as *stetisse* (16) or *imbuisse palmulas* (17)—hands or oars?—should be cited. Likewise the course from birth (*origo*) to old age (*senet quiete*) is strange if applied to an inanimate object only.

15. In this regard see O. Friess, *Beobachtungen über die Darstellungskunst Catulls* (Würzburg, 1929), p. 29, and H. Bardon, *L'Art de la Composition chez Catulle* (Paris, 1943), pp. 13–14. A detailed examination of the use of sound values in this poem shows a clear attempt to balance the first half against the second.

16. The similarity of situation is emphasized by the verbal parallels (e. g., *nasse*, 64. 2, and *natantis*, 4. 3; *palmis*, 64. 7, and *palmulis*, 4. 17). See also n. 12, above.

17. Here the change is from *prius* to *nunc*. Usually as in 8. 3–9 or 72. 1–5, it is *quondam* to *nunc*.

18. Cf., for example, the use of *cura* in 2. 10. For a definition of the word which embraces both the facets proposed here see O. Skutsch in *Rh. Mus.*, XCIX (1956), 198–99.

19. Cf. the use of *trux* in 4. 9 and of *truculentus* in 64. 179. Many of the words which give 4 its dramatic power (e. g., *celer*, *impetus*, *minax*) recur in 63 but are rarely used elsewhere by C.

20. The imagery of love as storm is, of course, basic to the whole poem. On the simile, see J. Svennung, *Catulls Bildersprache I* (Uppsala, 1945), 81f., and the more general discussion of J. Kahlmeyer, *Seesturm und Schiff-*

bruch als Bild im antiken Schrifttum (Diss., Greifswald; Hildesheim, 1934), pp. 22–26. E. de Saint-Denis (*Le rôle de la mer dans la poésie latine* [Lyon, 1935]) devotes pages 137–58 to Catullus.

21. For further references to the equation of life and sea journey in ancient literature, see Kahlmeyer, *op. cit.* (n. 20 above), pp. 26–39. The metaphor of life's journey as an ocean voyage is one of the most common imagistic strands in Greek tragedy (it is basic to the structure of the *Suppliants* and the *Antigone*, for example), and, in a form which is almost crystallizing into allegory, offers the background for Odysseus' return home through the world of experience. The analogy between physical movement and any spiritual development outside of space is easily drawn, and Catullus utilizes two of the most common shapes this movement takes—here, the sea voyage, and in 63 the mountain to be climbed, the most well-known literary instance of the latter being Dante's ascent of the hill of Purgatory to the earthly paradise on its top and heaven yet further beyond. It, too, must be taken, in a spiritual sense, as the journey from childhood to age. (This point is finely illustrated by F. Fergusson in *Dante's Drama of the Mind* [Princeton, 1953], pp. 8–10.)

22. For a moment Catullus dips his oars into the main stream of classical Greek poetics wherein life as myth gradually evolved out of life as actuality, as the lyric forms were succeeded by those of tragedy. It was back to this tradition primarily that Horace returned for his inspiration and models, maintaining an aloofness from his Catullan heritage which seemingly borders on disdain. But even without a direct admission of indebtedness, the influence of *Phaselus ille* on Horace is clear beyond a doubt (see C. W. Mendell, *CP*, XXX [1935], 298–99; J. Ferguson, *AJP*, LXXVII [1956], 15–16).

23. On the relation of the tradition of epigram to poem 4 see T. Birt, "Zu Catull's Carmina Minora," *Philol.*, LXIII (1904), 453–58 and O. Hezel, *Catull und das griechische Epigramm* (Stuttgart, 1932), pp. 9–14.

IX

Eduard Fraenkel

Two poems of Catullus

TWO POEMS OF CATULLUS *

*To Miss M. V. Taylor
on her eightieth birthday*

XLII

Adeste, hendecasyllabi, quot estis
    omnes undique, quotquot estis omnes.
iocum me putat esse moecha turpis
    et negat mihi vestra reddituram
    pugillaria, si pati potestis.   5
    persequamur eam et reflagitemus.
quae sit, quaeritis? illa, quam videtis
    turpe incedere, mimice ac moleste
    ridentem catuli ore Gallicani.
circumsistite eam et reflagitate.   10
    'moecha putida, redde codicillos,
    redde, putida moecha, codicillos'.
non assis facis? o lutum, lupanar,
    aut si perditius potest quid esse.
    sed non est tamen hoc satis putandum.   15
    quod si non aliud potest, ruborem
    ferreo canis exprimamus ore.
conclamate iterum altiore voce.
    'moecha putida, redde codicillos,
    redde, putida moecha, codicillos'.   20
sed nil proficimus, nihil movetur.
    mutanda est ratio modusque vobis,
    si quid proficere amplius potestis.
    'pudica et proba, redde codicillos'.

The poem begins with a passionate cry. 'To my aid, little poems, every one, all of you from everywhere, every single one of you, all!' When Catullus says *adeste, hendecasyllabi,* he is not of course summoning representatives of one metrical

* Journal of Roman Studies 51, 1961, 46-53. — I am very grateful to Mr. Frederick Wells for improving the style of this article.

genre only. Since by far the greater part of those short poems
which now make up the first section of his book (I-LX) has as
its metre the hendecasyllable (*phalaeceus*), he can readily use
this name for his short poems in general without excluding an
occasional iambic or choliambic piece. Catullus has to summon
his poems *undique*, for they are scattered over a wide area, which
proves, if proof were needed, that, like other poets in antiquity,
he was in the habit of sending first, before publication, individual
poems to individual addressees.

After the second line we have to imagine a brief pause : the
hendecasyllabi are rushing in. When they have gathered the
poet can tell them why he has summoned them. But he is so
angry that, to unburden his mind, he first bursts into bad language and only then comes to the point,

> et negat mihi vestra reddituram
> pugillaria, si pati potestis.

The reading of the only manuscript that reached the early
humanists, *vestra*, has in many editions, from the sixteenth
century on, been changed to *nostra*. But *vestra* is certainly
what Catullus wrote. Not only does it go much better with
the following *si pati potestis*, where the anger at an intolerable
indignity is marked by the alliteration (as at 29, 1, *quis potest
pati*), but it is required by the legal or quasi-legal fiction on
which the whole poem is based. The poems are themselves
considered the legitimate owners of the *codicilli*, the *pugillaria*,
or, as they more commonly are called, the *pugillares*, the little
writing-tablets, note-books, which you can hold in your closed
hand. These note-books, being a mere instrument for jotting
down the poems, are subordinate to the poems; it is the poems
who are their masters and owners. *vestra pugillaria* unmistakably
47 denotes the ownership | for in the terminology of Roman law
meum est means ' I am the owner ' [1]. Unless we bear this in
mind we shall miss the note of burning indignation in the words
of the wronged farmer (Virgil, *ecl.* 9, 2 ff.) :

> O Lycida, vivi pervenimus, advena *nostri*,
> quod numquam veriti sumus, ut possessor *agelli*
> diceret ' haec mea sunt; veteres migrate coloni '.

[1] Fritz Schulz, *Classical Roman Law*, 339.

' I, I am the owner of this piece of land ' he cries — the strong emphasis is brought out by the wide hyperbaton *nostri ... agelli* [1] — and yet the usurper is shameless enough to claim the owner-ship for himself, *haec mea sunt*, just as he might say in front of the praetor *hunc ego agrum ex iure Quiritium meum esse aio*. But to return to the *hendecasyllabi*. If they went to court, they would appeal to the praetor, *in iure*, for the *actio in rem* known as *rei vindicatio*, and they would have a fair chance of winning afterwards, *apud iudicem*, their case, ' ubi enim probavi rem meam esse, necesse habebit possessor restituere, qui non obiecit aliquam exceptionem ' [2]. However, the *hendecasyllabi* do not go to court but, as we shall see, resort to a more drastic and less tedious expedient. But even so they act as the legitimate owners and it is in this quality that they perform the *flagitatio*.

It is all very well for Catullus to say *persequamur eam et reflagitemus*, but how are the *hendecasyllabi* to do that if they have been given no clue by which they might recognize the woman? They therefore ask for fuller information. Now in a poem like this, only the poet himself can speak directly to his readers. There existed, however, a device, invented by some tragic poet and adopted by several comic playwrights, through which it became possible to acquaint the audience or the reader in an indirect way with what non-speaking persons are saying. It is this device that Catullus uses here [3] : *quae sit, quaeritis*. In answer to the question the *hendecasyllabi* and we, the readers, receive a most unflattering description of the woman and of her behaviour in public :

> illa quam videtis
> turpe incedere, mimice ac moleste
> ridentem catuli ore Gallicani.

turpe incedere : it is the way she walks that more than anything else betrays her. In Petronius 126, 2, a beau is rebuked for his affected gait, *quo incessus arte* [4] *compositus et ne vestigia quidem*

---

[1] An equally emphatic hyperbaton of the same type occurs at Eur., *Alc.* 1072-4, where σὴν ... γυναῖκα is separated by a whole trimeter; for the implications see my note on Aesch., *Ag.* 13 f.

[2] Ulpian, *Dig.* 6, 1, 9.

[3] And afterwards, for instance Horace, *Epodes* 7, 15 f.

[4] *arte* Dousa : *tute* trad. For other possible corrections see Konrad Müller's recent edition.

pedum extra mensuram aberrantia, nisi quod formam prostituis?
and then the speaker adds : *ex vultibus ... hominum mores colligo,
et cum spatiantem vidi, quid cogitet scio.* Perhaps even more
significant, on account of its exemplary conciseness, is the
characterization of a noble *matrona* in the loveliest epitaph that
has come down to us from the Republican age [1], *sermone lepido* [2],
tum autem incessu commodo. People in the south of Europe may
more easily be aware of the importance of the *incessus* as revealing
the character of a man or woman, but such a symptom is no
less obvious to the attentive eye of an observant northerner.
In a poem by Goethe, written at the age of twenty-six, ' Er-
klärung eines alten Holzschnittes, vorstellend Hans Sachsens
poetische Sendung ', a figure which represents at the same time
Honesty, unspoiled Nature and healthy Poetry, is described
thus :

> Da tritt herein ein junges Weib,
> Mit voller Brust und rundem Leib,
> Kräftig sie auf den Füssen steht,
> Grad, edel vor sich hin sie geht,
> Ohne mit Schlepp und Steiss zu schwänzen,
> Noch mit 'n Augen 'rum zu scharlenzen.

48 This young woman is the very opposite of the one *quam videtis
turpe incedere, mimice ac moleste ridentem.*

mimice ac moleste : if we press our lips tightly together to
produce the threefold m-sound, we shall not remain deaf to the
contempt in this half-line. The connotations of the word
mima are well known.

ridentem catuli ore : when she is grinning she looks like an
angry dog showing his teeth. The ancients seem to have been
impressed by this similarity of look. In the *Captivi* of Plautus
the parasite complains that when he is making his usual jokes
no one laughs any more, and then he goes on (485 f.) :

---

[1] *Carm. lat. epigr.* 52, 7.

[2] This recalls the famous remark of the great orator L. Licinius Crassus in
Cicero's dialogue *De oratore*, 3, 45, ' cum audio socrum meam Laeliam (about her
sermo and that of some other ladies of the contemporary aristocracy see also Cic.,
Brut. 211) ... eam sic audio ut Plautum mihi aut Naevium videar audire '. The
sentence by which the remark on Laelia's speech is interrupted, ' facilius enim
mulieres incorruptam antiquitatem conservant ' etc., is a rendering of Plato, *Crat.*
418c αἱ γυναῖκες αἵπερ μάλιστα τὴν ἀρχαίαν φωνὴν σῴζουσι (not noticed in the
commentaries of Piderit-Harnecker and of Wilkins).

> ne canem quidem irritatam voluit quisquam imitarier :
> saltem, si non arriderent, dentes ut restringerent.

The careful description of the woman puts the *hendecasyllabi* on the right track.   After a short pursuit they succeed in hunting her out.   Therefore the poet need no longer say *persequamur eam et reflagitemus*, but can change his command : *circumsistite eam et reflagitate*.   And now the action proceeds with increasing speed.   The crowd of the little poems surround their victim, and with the gusto of Italian youngsters who relish such a game they shout at her :

> moecha putida, redde codicillos,
> redde, putida moecha, codicillos.

When I read these lines aloud I am careful not to lose the effect of the double liquid in the last word and also to give the full volume to this momentous quadrisyllable.   The word-order of the first line, *moecha putida*, *redde*, is reversed in the second line, *redde*, *putida moecha*.   We may call this a stylistic device of popular eloquence.   It serves in a simple yet effective manner to express strong emotion.   In one of the most moving scenes of Menander the young officer who has maltreated his girl so that she has run away from him implores the old gentleman Pataecus to help him (*Peric.* 256 f.) :

> Γλυκέρα με καταλέλοιπε, καταλέλοιπέ με
> Γλυκέρα, Πάταικε.

Here we are listening to the cry of a distressed soul.   At the other end of the scale we find, in the German nursery rhyme, the naughty boy who obstinately refuses to eat his porridge, yelling :

> Ich esse meine Suppe nicht, nein, meine Suppe ess' ich nicht.

In the case of the *flagitatio* the reversal of the word-order, as we shall see, belonged to a very old popular custom as a means of intensifying the demand.

At l. 13, once more, we are made to perceive in an indirect way the reaction of a partner, this time of the woman herself : *non assis facis?*   We see her standing in the middle of the excited crowd, smiling, motionless, quite unruffled.   That is the limit.

The poet, wild with rage, pours out a welter of abuse. He begins with a choice alliterating pair, *o lutum*, *lupanar*, and ends with the comprehensive formula *aut si perditius potest* [1] *quid esse*. In the face of her impudence no weakening must be permitted; the attack has to be renewed in a more powerfulf fashion :

> quod si non aliud potest, *ruborem*
> *ferreo* canis exprimamus *ore*.

If we want to recite these lines properly, the soft backsound of the English R will not do; we have to round our tongue and produce unashamedly a series of rolling and sustained Italian R's. It is this sound above all that here suggests the ugliness of the dog. To the Roman ear the snarling of a dog was disagreeable [2]; at an early stage they called R the ' littera canina ' [3].

49   After this preparation the poet repeats and amplifies his injunction :

> conclamate iterum altiore voce
> ' moecha putida, redde codicillos,
> redde, putida moecha, codicillos '.

This time the unholy chant begins ' forte ' and swells in a steady crescendo to the drawn-out final fortissimo. There follows a long pause, a suspense of hopeful expectation. *Sed nil proficimus, nihil movetur.* So the poet, frustrated, orders a complete change of tactics [4]. After the ear-splitting shouts we now hear the voice of humble supplication, piano, pianissimo :

> pudica et proba, redde codicillos.

We are not told with what measure of success this palinode meets.

Students of ancient literature who are inclined to regard most of their work as an auxiliary branch of prosopography

---

[1] I feel no qualms in accepting the old emendation *potest* (*potes* the Veronensis), which makes the expression much more forcible and idiomatic.

[2] In his *Roman Elegies* Goethe wrote : ' Manche Töne sind mir Verdruss, doch bleibet am meisten Hundegebell mir verhasst; kläffend zerreisst es mein Ohr '.

[3] See Lucilius 2 and 377 with Marx's comments and notice especially Persius I, 109 f.

[4] An attentive fifteenth-century scholar saw that at line 22 the *nobis* of the Veronensis must be changed to *vobis*.

and who, moreover, have a passion for solving puzzles thought up for the purpose have long been busy asking the question ' who is the lady (if that is the right word to use) in Catullus' poem XLII? '. I cannot join them, for I try never to ask a question when I see that the poet is determined not to answer it. Things which a poet worth the name does not mention are always wholly irrelevant to the understanding of his poem. Therefore, instead of indulging in misplaced curiosity I now turn to a different aspect of the poem, one for which some genuine learning, though none of my own, is essential.

That eminent scholar who threw so much fresh light on large areas of ancient thought, religion, and folklore, Hermann Usener, published a few years before his death an article on popular justice in ancient Italy [1]. I must not attempt here to summarize that immensely fruitful article, but shall content myself with reproducing in a very simplified form only those observations which have a direct bearing on Catullus' poem.

In Italy, as in many other parts of the world, there existed certain procedures of popular justice which dated from the time before state-controlled jurisdiction had established its authority. But even after this, people, for obvious reasons, might often prefer to take the law into their own hands. Here we are concerned only with the particular case in which someone who has failed to obtain what is due to him (the most typical instance is that of a debt not repaid), instead of appealing to the praetor for an *actio*, brings a different kind of pressure to bear upon the person who has not fulfilled his obligation. He gathers a boisterous crowd either in front of the housedoor of his adversary or in the market square or some other public place. The crowd is instructed to shout against the guilty man demanding that he should do what so far he has been unwilling to do. The shouting, in the most unflattering language, is performed in concise, roughly rhythmical phrases, the kind of delivery for which the Romans use the word *carmina*. If the man happens to be indoors, his attackers will shout against the house-front (*occentare*); otherwise, they must waylay him in the street or the market square,

---

[1] 'Italische Volksjustiz', *Rhein. Mus.* LVI (1900), 1 ff. (*Kleine Schriften* IV, 356 ff.).

9

surround him, deafen his ears with their incriminations and, in doing so, attract the curiosity of the neighbours and any passer-by.   The fear of defamation — a formidable threat in a relatively small community — is more likely than not to induce the offender to yield to the accuser's demand.   The procedure, however riotous, runs on strictly conventional lines and therefore acquires an almost formal character.   The essential element of the whole action is the insistent demand, the *flagitare*, for the immediate fulfilment of the obligation.   This *flagitare* may, of course, in certain cases be performed not by a crowd but a few persons or even by one only.   In an exhilarating scene of the *Mostellaria* of Plautus (532 ff.) the money-lender, to whom the juvenile ' hero ' owes a large sum, appears in front of the young man's house at the most awkward moment, just when the father of the spendthrift has returned from a journey abroad.   He first attempts to obtain his money by amicable means, but, when 50 that has proved unsuccessful, he not unnaturally | resorts to the customary device of popular justice.   His impressive *flagitatio* culminates in these shouts (603 ff.) :

> cedo faénus, redde faenus, faenus reddite.
> daturin estis faenus actutum mihi?
> datur faenus mihi?

The sequence of *redde faenus, faenus reddite* shows the — in this context apparently traditional — inversion which we have noticed in *redde, putida moecha ... moecha putida, redde.*

conclamate ... altiore voce is the command given by Catullus to his *hendecasyllabi*.   This *convicium* [1], produced in the most clamorous manner, is indispensable to the proper conduct of a *flagitatio*.   In the Plautine *Pseudolus* (555 f.) the slave challenges his master :

> namque edepol, si non dabis,
> clamore magno et multum [2] flagitabere,

and similar expressions are not uncommon.

---

[1] Usener, *Kl. Schriften* IV, 373, and Wackernagel, *Kl. Schriften* 1284, following an ancient etymology, derive *convicium* from *vicus*, but J. B. Hofmann's argumentation (Walde-Hofmann, *Lat. etymol. Wörterbuch* I, 269 f.) has convinced me that a connection with *vox, vocare* is far more likely.

[2] I follow Lindsay in accepting what is to all intents and purposes the reading of the παράδοσις, *multum*. Goetz-Schöll (ed. min.), Leo and Ernout accept Scaliger's *multo*, but I see no valid reason for the change.

We have a glorious representation of a full-sized *flagitatio* in the scene of the *Pseudolus* which first directed Usener's attention to the problem discussed in his article [1]. In enjoying this scene we must not, of course, forget how much it owes to the genius of Plautus [2], who here and elsewhere knows how to blend the *Italum acetum* with Falstaffian self-mockery. But neither should we forget that, quite apart from the rich ornamentation by the comic poet, it is the very nature of this particular act of popular justice to move every now and then on the verge of buffoonery.

Since in the scene of the *Pseudolus* the attackers are only two, the young man and his slave, the *flagitatio* cannot be performed by a full choir, but only by two soloists. We have seen that in many cases the victim will be waylaid in the street or some public square. To prevent his escape, his pursuers have to surround him, *circumsistere*. That is what the crowd of Catullus' *hendecasyllabi* most efficiently achieves. In the Plautine play Calidorus and Pseudolus have to be satisfied with a more modest version. Being only two, they cannot effect the traditional *circumsistere*. Consequently Calidorus gives the order (357) 'Pseudole, adsiste altrim secus atque onera hunc maledictis'. And now we see them standing in a row, the pimp in the centre and Calidorus and his slave on either side of him. What the two attackers lack in numbers, they try to make up for by vocal strength. They shout at him a cataract of breathless abuse, without pause, prestissimo. But after a while they run short of abuse and have to resort to such ordinary

---

[1] On its first page Usener speaks of his 'Beschäftigung mit den Erscheinungen der sogenannten Volksjustiz, zu welcher mich zeitig eine Stelle des Plautinischen Pseudolus (v. 357 ff.) veranlasste'. Had Usener been a Hellenist in the now only too common sense of the word, he would never have been the Usener we know and admire.

[2] In all probability Plautus, and not an Attic playwright. The features common to this scene and to Ar., *Clouds* 909 ff., disturb me now even less than when I dealt with this point in *Plautinisches im Plautus* 401, n. 3. An observation made by Paul Lejay, *Plaute* (published posthumously 1925), 68, n. 1, may be as helpful to others as it has been to me : 'On a comparé Aristophane, *Nuées* 909 suiv. Le point commun est dans les réponses, ici, du leno, là, de l'Injuste. L'idée de ces impudences narquoises a pu venir séparément à deux auteurs comiques, comme on peut les trouver tous les jours dans des querelles populaires. Quoi qu'il en soit, la scène elle-même d'insultes appartient à une tradition nationale, nettement italique '.

M

names as *impure* and *leno* (366). There follows a last effort, a
big insulting phrase, ' verberavisti patrem atque matrem ', but
the pimp is able to cap it : ' atque occidi quoque potius quam
cibum praehiberem : num peccavi quippiam? ' That silences
them; the game is up. They, too, like the attackers of the
moecha putida, have to admit ' sed nil proficimus, nihil movetur '.
The wonderful Ballio [1], who, firm as a rock amidst the raging
seas, has all the time kept his central position, grinning, applaud-
ing, acknowledging the insults, has won the day.

The process of *flagitatio*, which modern learning has had
51 to recover from a few│echoes in literature, was familiar to every
Roman child. Catullus knows that all his readers will gladly
follow him when he transfers this process from the sphere of
everyday life into the sphere of poetry by masking his little
poems as *flagitantes*. With the help of this unusual chorus he
builds up, on a small scale, an enchanting comedy around a
dramatic plot, ending in the poet's failure.

The good grace with which Catullus accepts defeat here,
as in the equally accomplished poem X, is part of his inimitable
χάρις. And here as elsewhere he makes happy use of popular
customs. In his lyric epithalamium (LXI) all the colourful rites
of a Roman wedding come to life, the procession with its torches,
the *flammeum* of the bride, the *pronubae* [2], the *praetextatus* [3], the
lifting of the bride across the threshold, the throwing of nuts
to the guests, the *Fescennina iocatio* with its somewhat coarse
jests at the expense of the bridegroom, the solemn *collocatio*
of the bride in her husband's house. These wedding rites
were as familiar to everybody as the characteristic features of
a *flagitatio*, and perhaps even more so. But on another occasion,
in poem XVII, *O Colonia*, Catullus introduces his Roman readers
to the strange ceremony which as a small boy he had watched
with delight in the neighbourhood of his birthplace Verona.
That ceremony had once been part of a serious religious ritual,

---

[1] It was not for nothing that the greatest actor of the Ciceronian time chose
this part for himself (Cic., *p. Rosc. com.* 20).

[2] 61, 179 f., 'bonae senibus viris cognitae bene feminae', for which see Festus
p. 244 M. (282 Lindsay), ' pronubae adhibentur nuptis, quae semel nupserunt '.

[3] Festus p. 245 M. (282 Linds.), 'patrimi et matrimi pueri praetextati tres
nubentem deducunt ', etc.

but, as happens in this world, in course of time it had changed its character to that of a carnivalesque pastime. But whether picturing a well-known and common ceremony or one remote and rare, Catullus always applies to it the care and the skill of a great artist. He makes use of those customs not because he, like a scholarly poet or an antiquarian, is interested in folklore for its own sake. His approach differs widely from that of Callimachus and those other Alexandrian poets who were constantly on the look-out for something refined and recondite. It is not impossible that their example may have encouraged Catullus to treat similar themes. But if so, he did it in a spirit of his own. What primarily seems to have attracted him in what we call folklore was its wealth of realistic and picturesque detail. He was most sensitive to the exuberant vitality in those homely popular customs. So it is certainly not in the identification of the woman, but rather in the happy conception of the *hendecasyllabi flagitantes* that the poet's chief interest lay and the chief interest of a sympathetic reader should lie.

VIII

Miser Catulle, desinas ineptire,
  et quod vides perisse perditum ducas.

fulsere quondam candidi tibi soles,
  cum ventitabas quo puella ducebat,
  amata nobis quantum amabitur nulla.   5
  ibi illa multa tum ¹ iocosa fiebant,
  quae tu volebas nec puella nolebat.
  fulsere vere candidi tibi soles.

---

¹ An early correction (*cum* the Veronensis). To assume here a conjunctional clause, with the principal clause following at line 8, would destroy the severe structure of the poem which, as will be shown presently, consists of a series of self-contained cola. Moreover, it is necessary to have a full stop at the end of line 7, for the following *fulsere vere candidi tibi soles*, echoing line 3, would lose a good deal of its force if it did not stand in isolation. To these stylistic arguments I would add one derived from Catullus' *usus linguae*. In all his smaller iambic or lyric poems, I-LX — and only these are comparable — Catullus uses the conjunction *cum* twenty times. In fourteen of these cases *cum* stands at the beginning of a sentence or clause. Of the remaining six sentences four begin with a pronoun (in one case two pronouns) which is immediately followed by *cum*: 5, 5, *nobis cum* ...; 17, 14, *cui cum sit* ...; 22, 9, *haec cum legas tu*; 13, 13, *quod tu cum olfacies*. In only two cases is *cum* preceded by a simple noun or adjective: 22, 16, *poema cum scribit*; 39, 5, *orba cum flet*

52   nunc iam illa non volt : tu quoque inpotens noli [1],
            nec quae fugit sectare, nec miser vive,   10
            sed obstinata mente perfer, obdura.

        vale, puella. iam Catullus obdurat,
            nec te requiret nec rogabit invitam.
        at tu dolebis, cum rogaberis nulla.
        scelesta, vae [2] te, quae tibi manet vita?   15
            quis nunc te adibit? cui videberis bella?
            quem nunc amabis? cuius esse diceris?
            quem basiabis? cui labella mordebis?
        at tu, Catulle, destinatus obdura.

The tissue of this poem is so delicate that one is almost afraid of applying to it the scalpel of rational analysis. But its inner life shall suffer no harm from our operation, and after performing it we may hope somewhat better to understand the functions of the organism which we are examining.

Like many of the finest ancient poems, *Miser Catulle*, if it is fully to be appreciated, has to be read aloud. When we are doing that, we cannot fail to notice something unusual : we may safely pause at the end of each line. In other words, enjambment is not to be found in this poem [3]. This is a remarkable deviation from the practice which Catullus employs throughout in his other choliambic as well as in his iambic poems. To take the two iambic poems first. IV : enjambment between 3-4, 4-5, 6-7, 10-11, 11-12 [4], 15-16, 18-19, 19-20, 20-21, 22-23, 23-24, 25-26; XXIX : enjambment between 3-4 [5], 18-19, 21-22 (?),

---

unicum mater. A parallel to *ibi illa multa cum iocosa fiebant* cannot be found in these poems.

[1] Avantius' supplement of the end is certain.

[2] Since ' Meleagri (h. e. Balthazari Venatoris) Spicilegium in edit. Liuineii et Gebhardi Francofurtae 1621 ' is known to me only from Ellis's Prolegomena, p. LXXVII, to the second edition of his Catullus, I assume that that gentleman's claim to immortality rests mainly, if not solely, on his having seen that here the MS reading *ne* means *uae*.

[3] This is true even of lines 4-5, for, owing to both its weighty sense, and its size, ' amata nobis quantum amabitur nulla ' functions not as a mere attribute but as a self-contained clause. It is no accident that this whole line, only the second word being different, recurs at 37, 12. In transplanting it like that, the poet must have felt that the line was an autonomous unit.

[4] Not necessarily between 14-15, see my ' Kolon und Satz, II ', *Nachr. Gött. Ges.*, Phil.-hist. Kl., 1933, 326 f. [see vol. I, p. 101].

[5] Not necessarily between 6-7, for 6 may be regarded as ' enlarged subject ', and so may 13.

23-24. We now turn to the more numerous choliambic poems. XXII : enjambment between 4-5, 5-6, 9-10, 10-11, 12-13, 15-16, 18-19, 19-20; XXXI : enjambment between 1-2, 2-3, 5-6, 8-9, 12-13; XXXVII : enjambment between 4-5 (?), 6-7, 7-8, 9-10, 14-15; XXXIX : enjambment between 2-3, 4-5, 18-19; XLIV : enjambment between 2-3, 6-7, 11-12, 13-14, 16-17, 18-19, 19-20; LII, consisting of only four lines, the fourth of which repeats the first, has no enjambment; LIX (five lines) : enjambment between 2-3, 4-5 (?); LX (five lines) : enjambment between 4-5. It appears that in all these poems, except the shortest, enjambment is, in some measure, admitted, whereas the nineteen lines of poem VIII are all separated from each other by a clear incision at the end of each line. The sustained staccato will not have been lost on the ear of an ancient reader, who would expect, in a poem of this metrical type, a smoother movement, at any rate an occasional overflow from one line into the next. No doubt this staccato is intentional. The hard rhythm, produced by the incision at the end of every single line, is in keeping with the hard tone of the whole poem. Its keynote is the imperative *obdura*, with which the second and the last section conclude and to which we hear the answer, *iam Catullus obdurat*, in the opening line of the last section. The poet's determination appears to be adamant, and adamant is the form which he has chosen for the arrangement of this poem and of this poem alone.

The structure of the whole poem is clearly marked; the reader would probably grasp it even without the help which I have tried to give in the text printed above. The first two lines, a severe self-admonition, prepare our mind for what is to follow. The next part (3-11) starts abruptly with the verb, which is emphatically placed at the beginning. This part is divided into two sections, six lines being devoted to the happiness of the past and three lines to the misery of the present. The *quondam* (3) and *tum* (6) of the former section contrast with the *nunc* (9) at the beginning of the latter. The four | imperatives 53 of this second section vary, and intensify, the two hortative subjunctives of the first part. The third, and last, part is arranged in three sections. The first section opens with a brief farewell; there follows a series of short affirmative clauses, revealing first the poet's present state of mind and then the fate in

store for him and for Lesbia.   She, after being the object in the
second line (13), becomes the subject in the third (14).   Thus
the way is prepared for the second section (15-18), where — so
it seems — everything else is forgotten, nothing exists for him
but the once beloved *puella*.   A storm of passion, sweeping
away the affirmative clauses, brings in a rush of tempestuous
questions.   And then, suddenly, there sets in an ominous calm:
at tu, Catulle, destinatus obdura.   The final verb links the end
of this section with its beginning (12) and also with the end of
the preceding part (11), while the beginning of the last line,
at tu, Catulle, harks back to the first phrase of the poem, *miser
Catulle*.   The circle is complete.

These formal elements, or some of them, will not perhaps be
discerned by every modern reader, and it is certainly not on
their being discerned that the suggestive force of the poem
depends.   It is the essence of this little masterpiece that everything in it sounds as if it could not have been expressed in any
other way, as if Nature herself had guided the poet's pen.   Simplicity, strong simplicity, and unwavering directness govern
every phrase and every line.   Nothing could be simpler than
the manner in which Catullus adopts in the second line a homely
proverb, *et quod vides perisse perditum ducas* [1].   But these simple
words are here a cry of desperation : I will not, I cannot give
up what I know to be lost to me.

As the poem moves on, its intensity increases.   In the series
of passionate questions (15-18), Catullus may be pretending to
himself that he is merely following Lesbia into the future, but
some compulsion forces him to conjure up all his lost happiness.
Deeper and deeper he sinks into these memories.   But his
memories blend with the prospect of pain.   At the end his
imagination is tormented with the vision of the rival, of Lesbia
embracing him.   He attempts to draw away : *at tu, Catulle,
destinatus obdura*.   But neither Catullus nor the reader can be
deceived.

When listening to the beat of another man's heart we may
allow the skill of the poet to recede into the background of our

---

[1] Plautus, *Trin.* 1026, 'quin tu quod periit periisse ducis ? ' has long been quoted by the commentators.

consciousness. But we should not forget it altogether. The truly wonderful thing about the poem which begins with *miser Catulle* is the complete absence of self-pity. The poet describes a most crushing humiliation, describes it with minute precision, but at the same time he accepts it, without whining, as inevitable, as if it were an act of Nature. This supreme detachment in the midst of profound passion is due to the artistic discretion and maturity of the young poet. Part of the poem's secret lies in its form, in the compactness of its language, the severe structure of its sentences and the touching simplicity of its clauses. An experience which might have lent itself to a display of unmanly sentiment has here become the theme of a firm, a virile, a Roman poem.

X

Niall Rudd

Colonia and her bridge

XVIII.   Colonia and her Bridge: A Note on the Structure of Catullus 17

NIALL RUDD

UNIVERSITY COLLEGE, TORONTO

The poem's outer form is quite straightforward. In lines 1–11 Catullus asks permission to throw one of his acquaintances from the bridge of Colonia into the marsh beneath. Why? The answer is given in lines 12–22: the fellow is a laggard in love. The last four verses combine these two themes and so round off the poem. Looking a little closer we find evidence of a more detailed design. The first eleven verses fall into three parts. Lines 1–4 describe the town and its bridge, 5–7 mark a transition ("May you have a new bridge if my wish is fulfilled"), then 8–11 tell us what the wish is. So we are left with a symmetrical pattern of 4–3–4.

The second main division, i.e. lines 12–22, also reveals a pattern though not of a linear kind. The man is stupid (*insulsissimus . . . nec sapit*, 12), he is like a baby (12–13), he neglects his pretty wife (14–18), he is like a fallen tree (18–20), he is stupid (*stupor . . . . nescit*, 21–22). So the chiasmus is arranged thus: stupid husband, simile, neglected wife, simile, stupid husband. If we focus our attention on the lady, we find out three things about her. She is in the prime of her beauty (14), she is more dainty than a kid (15), she is more tempting than ripe grapes (16). We also find out three things about her husband. He lets her play around to her heart's content, he doesn't care a straw, and he refuses to rouse himself (17–18).

The concluding lines combine the two themes already mentioned by taking up words, phrases and ideas from the main body of the poem. Thus *voragine* (26) echos *vorago* (11), *nunc eum volo de tuo ponte mittere pronum* (23) harks back to *de tuo volo ponte/ ire praecipitem* (11), *stolidum* (24) recalls *insulsissimus* (12) and *stupor* (21), and the mule in line 26 is not without significance. All this shows how an apparently simple poem can be a work of careful design and craftsmanship. Yet apart from a little elementary mathematics we haven't accomplished much. The problem of the poem's inner structure still remains. I believe there is such a problem, but scholars have usually been so busy determining the site of Colonia that they have never bothered to formulate it.

Let me put it this way. A student beginning the piece assumes that he is to hear about a country town. By the time he has reached line five he realizes that the town's bridge is going to be just as important as the town itself. He is now more than a quarter of the way through the poem, his mind full of rustic gaiety, when it gradually dawns on him that Catullus is talking about something totally different, namely a lethargic gentleman of Verona. Now granted this fellow deserved to be taught a lesson. If we wish, we can imagine Catullus leaning over the bridge and gazing down on the slime beneath while thoughts of condign punishment pass through his mind. But why do we have to be told so much about the unsteady condition of the bridge? (A strong one would have suited Catullus's purpose just as well.) And why are we expected to take an interest in the town's enthusiasm for festive games, square dancing and other high jinks? These questions cannot be answered by the convenient phrase "local color." For in his *nugae* at least Catullus was not that kind of poet. If we want a solution which will preserve the poem as a coherent work of art, we must look elsewhere. And we must employ a method which, though not available to scholars like Friedrich, Baehrens and Ellis, is now a familiar feature of literary criticism.

As we read through the poem, we are struck by certain peculiarities. The first word we pause at is *inepta* (2). The editors, remembering that *ineptus* is the opposite of *aptus* and that *aptus* means "fitted" or "fitting," give the meaning as "loose." [1] And the Loeb translator renders the word, rather quaintly, as "ill-jointed." Well, the interpretation gives good sense, and etymologically it cannot be faulted. So let us accept it, leaving aside for the moment the fact that such a meaning is quite without parallel. The bridge's legs then are loose and shaky. But that is not all. There is something very strange about *crura*. Merrill tells us what it is. "The noun," he says, "is unique in this humorous application to inanimate objects, *pes* being commonly

---

[1] Ellis, following Munro, cites *quod multo maiorem habent apta vim quam soluta* (Cic. *Orat.* 68.228), *cum sint ex aptis dissoluta* (*ibid.* 70.233) He also mentions *aptissime cohaereant* (*ibid.* 44.149). Baehrens adds *De orat.* 2.4.17.

used in such connections." In other words your legs are *crura*, but the legs of your chair are not.

Turning away from this oddly human bridge, we move on to the description of the lazy husband sleeping like an infant *tremula patris . . . in ulna* (13). This time we must differ from Merrill, for surely *tremulus* cannot refer to "the tremulousness of age." Gentlemen of such advanced years are not usually the fathers of two-year-old infants, and even if they were, what would this contribute to the poet's picture? Friedrich realized the irrelevance of such an interpretation, but he could only suggest that having written *tremulus parens* in 61.51 and *tremuli parentis* in 68.142 Catullus lost command of his pen and automatically used the same word here. Clearly Ellis and Kroll were right to abandon the idea of age and to take *tremula* in the sense of "rocking." Yet it is significant that the only parallel which Ellis could provide from his vast store of learning was a passage of Plato, where *seiô* is used in the same way.[2]

Our last pause occurs at line 19 where the alder tree is said to have been hamstrung—*suppernata*—by an axe. It is a vivid, indeed a unique phrase, and it is clearly related to the less decorous of the two meanings of *se sublevat* in the previous line. Loose legs, unsteady arms, severed hams, nerveless members—they are all connected, and they provide a direct contrast to the idea of strong, vigorous legs implied in *salire paratum habes* (2) and in *Salisubsali sacra* (6).

All this may appear rather fanciful. But is it really? What we are trying to do is to establish a relation between the bridge and the lazy husband. And, as it happens, there is more evidence than this. Let us go back to the beginning. The bridge's legs are so rickety that it is in danger of falling on its back (*supinus*) and wallowing in the mud (*recumbat*). This anticipates the description of Catullus's fellow-townsman, who is like a sleeping baby (*dormientis*), who refuses to stand up (*nec se sublevat*), and who resembles a tree lying in a ditch (*iacet*). The poet hopes that the treatment proposed will rouse him (*excitare veternum*), and that he will leave behind in the mud his indolent character (*supinum animum*). The reference to the man's *supinus animus* reminds us that he is a silly dolt (*insulsissimus, stupor* etc.); and the bridge is

---

[2] *Laws* 790. It will be found, however, that *seiousai* receives a lot of help from its context.

silly too.   In spite of what the editors tell us we cannot ignore the usual, and indeed the only attested meaning of *ineptus*.[3]   As Gertrude Stein would have said, "Stupid is stupid is stupid." Furthermore there is no mistaking the tone of ridicule in the phrase *ponticuli axulis stantis in redivivis*, "the crazy bridge standing on its resurrected sticks."   So much for the first of the poem's two main structural features.

We now turn to Colonia itself—or rather herself, for the town is obviously personified.   Unlike her shaky bridge she is full of vitality and is eager to hold a festival.   When one thinks of the dancing, the drinking, the laughter and the flirting entailed by religious celebrations of this kind, it is easy to see why *ludere* rather than *orare* was the proper word to use.   And it is noticeable that the other words describing Colonia's enthusiasm are not wholly innocent: *cupis . . . salire . . . libidine*.   By all means let us translate them as "want," "dance" and "wish," but the naughty overtones of the Latin cannot be silenced.

All this of course foreshadows the young wife.   She is, we are told, *delicatior haedo*.   The phrase is not a simple one.   The images of flowers and grapes which precede and follow it show that *delicatior* refers primarily to the girl's seductive appearance, not to her temperament and behavior.   To this extent Friedrich and Merrill are wrong, and Kroll's brief comment "rein körperlich," "purely physical," is justified.   On the other hand when we read the poem over again, it is hard not to supply the secondary meaning of *delicatus* as well, i.e. "wanton," and to take it as a preparation for *ludere ut lubet* in line 17.   Unfortunately for the translator there is no English word which holds the two meanings in solution.

Whatever may be felt about the last point, there can be no doubt concerning the implications of *ludere hanc sinit ut lubet*.   I say "implications" rather than "sense," because I do not think that Catullus is being quite so blunt as in 61.204, a passage which Kroll cites as a parallel.   There *ludite ut lubet* is followed by the unvarnished injunction *et brevi liberos date*, whereas the present context seems to suggest a flirt in danger rather than a habitual libertine.   The young wife "amuses herself" with the local lads, laughing, dancing, drinking and kissing, in fact doing all the things that Colonia wants to do.   This is of course a lamentable state of affairs, and Catullus has no doubt where the blame lies.

---

[3] *Ineptus* itself does not appear in any of the passages referred to in note 1.

It is because of the husband's inadequacy that the girl amuses herself elsewhere, just as Colonia's frustration is due to the inadequacy of her bridge.

I hope this analysis has shown that the poem is a single, integrated structure.   Perhaps, however, a word may be added about the bog.   There it lies, waiting for the collapse of the bridge, waiting for the fall of the husband.[4]   At first the punishment seems purely retributive.   The fellow is a silly ass and deserves to be hurled head first into the deepest, blackest and most stinking part of the bog.   It is an appropriate penalty for a sluggard since mud has always been associated with dull insensitivity.   But at line 24 the poet's plan takes on a new quality.   Far from being an impulse of mere exasperation, it aims, we are told, at a wholesome and therapeutic effect.   This is confirmed by a passage of Celsus (3.20) which recommends that lethargic patients should be wakened up by offensive odors and by sudden cold showers.   Later (4.27) the same treatment is prescribed for a woman in a coma.[5]   And yet on closer inspection something appears to be wrong.   The smells enumerated by Celsus include those of burning pitch, a smoldering lamp wick, vinegar, garlic, and onions, not quite of the same order as the foul stench of a marsh.   Nor are showers of cool water exactly comparable to immersion in a stagnant bog.   In fact the element of filth, which is most emphasized by the poet, is entirely absent from Celsus.   So it looks as if Catullus as a physician is not entirely within the tradition of Hippocrates.

But if his methods seem unorthodox and his manner a little disconcerting, there can be no doubt that his aim is a salutary one. So much is clear from the poem's conclusion, and this in turn echos the optimistic note in line 5.   Eventually, one hopes, the old bridge will be replaced or at least thoroughly repaired, so that Colonia may attain her wishes.   So too the lively young wife will receive from the slime a husband who is a new man, a man of spirit, yet of the earth earthy.

---

[4] A corresponding part is played by *fossa* in line 19.

[5] Like Catullus, Celsus uses the word *excitare* in both passages; in the former he uses *repente* as well. Cf. also Pliny, *NH* 19.155 where *nasturtium* is said to be a kind of cress which shakes off lethargy (*torporem excitantis*), and *ibid*. 30.11 where we are told that *lethargus olfactoriis excitatur*.

XI

Frank O. Copley
Catullus 35

The cumulative comment on this poem, although massively learned and very informative, leaves the reader with a sense of disappointment; he feels that he has learned much, but that he still does not know what the poem means, what its author's purposes and intentions were, and what he wished his readers to know and to feel. For the commentaries leave unanswered, or answer only in a hesitating and uncertain way, the questions which are really crucial: why did Catullus invite Caecilius to come to Verona? Why is he so insistent on haste? Why does he allege that a *puella* has been Caecilius' reason for hesitation? Why does he declare that the *puella* conceived her passion for Caecilius upon reading his *incohata Dindymi domina*? Why does he make such a point of the *unfinished* character of Caecilius' work? On these primary questions hang at least two others: what were the *cogitationes* of vs. 5, and who is the *amicus suus meusque* of vs. 6? Until these questions are answered in a sensible and plausible, if not in an authoritative way, we cannot say that we have really understood Catullus' poem; it remains nebulous and vague, and thereby loses much of its charm and its poetic validity.

The reasons for our failure to answer these crucial questions are not far to seek. They lie in our concept of the commentator's task. He has been expected to gather, sift, and record under appropriate lemmata such factual material as will identify persons and places, indicate dates, explain syntactical peculiarities, demonstrate sources and influences, and illuminate style. We have required him to confine himself to that which can be proven or at least substantiated by objective data; we demand that speculation and theorizing be based on such data and kept to a minimum; we frown on flights of the imagination and exclude personal and subjective judgments. By this method we have learned a great deal, and it is probably true that our use of it has given us a vastly clearer and sounder view of ancient literature than was possessed by those who stood much nearer to it in time. Whenever it can answer our questions, it is the method to be preferred above all others.

149

N

Sometimes, however, it falls short of its goal, and, as in the case of the poem we are here discussing, leaves us without the understanding which we need, and which is the ultimate aim of all scholarship. For the factual data on which to answer the questions raised by Catullus' poem are not now available, and in all likelihood never were. They were known to Catullus and to Caecilius, but probably to very few, if any, others. The fact that Catullus included the poem in his published works (or that his literary heirs did so, if we wish to insist that Catullus did not publish his poems himself) shows clearly enough that the poem was expected to have meaning to its ancient readers, even without a background of factual data; the poet felt that his readers should be able to supply out of their own minds the conditions and presuppositions which gave the poem its meaning. In short, he expected them to use their imaginations; he may even have felt that some share of the joy in reading poetry was derived from the creative activity of the reader's own mind.

If the commentators had been willing to accept this view and had truly confined themselves to the listing of appropriate factual data, all would have been well. Unfortunately this is not the case, for they have gone farther and have attempted to answer by the objective method questions which were never intended to be so answered. Their answers, as might have been anticipated, are equivocal, hesitant, and unsatisfactory; far from revealing meaning, they serve only to obscure it. They create problems where none exist; they leave the reader with the discouraging feeling that a lifetime of learning will never reveal meaning to him, that the obvious meaning can never be right, and — worst of all — that ancient poetry had best be laid aside as incomprehensible.

The application of the objective method to the crucial questions raised by Catullus' *c.* 35 has resulted in several confusing and obfuscating answers. We are told that Caecilius may have been a member of the school of *novi poetae*, and that Catullus' invitation had something to do with that fact. This answer is based on an objective study of the adjective *tener*. Since it does not matter whether Caecilius was a *novus poeta* or not, the statement that he "may have been" one only confuses the issue by bringing in irrelevant considerations. No objective answer to the problem of haste can be found other than the suggestion that the poet may have been expressing himself jocularly, a theory based on the obvious hyperbole of vss. 8-15. The best reason that can be adduced for the appearance of the *puella* in the poem is that Catullus wished to pay her a compliment. Here the editors have recourse to a literal reading of *Sapphica puella Musa doctior*, vss. 16-17. One editor, Baehrens, has noted the importance of the word *incohata*, and has suggested that by its use Catullus wished to express his critical opinion of Caecilius' poem — i. e. that it needed more work — but few have followed him in this suggestion, and Baehrens himself, having made it, drops it without carrying it through to its logical conclusion. To most editors, *incohata* presents only a problem in translation: does it mean "unfinished," i. e. a rough draft of the whole, or "just begun," i. e. just the introductory lines. This is a problem which does not even exist, as a study of the dictionaries *s. v. incohare* should have shown. As for *cogitationes*, the objective method has led to some very strange theories — that it means "certain weighty matters" (Merrill), "unbekannte Mitteilungen" (Riese), "progetti poetici" (De Gubernatis) and "something political" (Ellis). The obvious meaning of "thoughts" seems to have been discarded for little reason other than that it was obvious. *Amicus suus meusque*, the editors say, means either Catullus himself, or a third party, some mutual friend of Catullus and Caecilius; parallels are cited in support now of the one, now of the other. When the decision is for the third party, no attempt is made to explain his presence, but much is made of the question of his identity—a question which cannot be answered and does not need to be, since the identity of this putative third party has no bearing on the meaning of the poem.

The insidious aspect of such comment lies in its leaving the reader with the feeling that this is all that can be done; if meaning is not thereby revealed, then he must conclude that meaning cannot be revealed, and that any attempt on his part to discover meaning will be necessarily speculative, subjective, and unscholarly. Yet is this not to deny the very nature of poetry? Is not the poet's chief function to lay before us images and ideas, whether abstract or concrete, which are to have meaning for us, as they had for the poet himself, because of the implications

and associations discoverable in them by the exercise of the two
functions of imagination and reason? And if this be granted,
does it not then become the task of the commentator, after he
has gathered and absorbed all available and pertinent factual
data, to apply his imagination and his reason to the discovery
and revelation of meaning? No doubt it will happen from time
to time that different scholars will come up with different meanings for a given poem. But this is a fault that not even the
objective method has been able to obviate, and in any case is it
true that a poem, like a problem in arithmetic, can have only
one right "answer"? Ideally, we should like to find, finally
and incontrovertibly, the meaning which the poet himself intended, yet how often can we be sure of doing this, even with
our own English and American poets, let alone with an author
some two thousand years dead? If we avoid anachronisms, ab-
surdities, and impossibilities, if we take due account of all facts
that are available, if we conscientiously familiarize ourselves
with our author, his methods and habits of thought and expression, the meaning which we eventually discover cannot in the
nature of things be too far wrong. And if my meaning is different from, or even contradictory to, yours, have we done anything but demonstrate the essential richness of the poem in
question? Certainly a plurality of meanings is better than no
meaning at all.

To return now to our example, Catullus, *c.* 35, let us see what
can be done. We may begin with two facts, both objectively
demonstrable; the first, that this is an "occasional" poem, i. e.
a poem based on an incident of some sort, the second, that the
key to its meaning will probably be found in its concluding line
or lines. For the first fact nothing but an examination of the
poem is necessary; it is an invitation, and an invitation must
always arise from some set of circumstances, or incident. For
the second, a quick glance at almost any group of Catullus' short
lyrics (or "iambics," if we prefer to use his own term) will
demonstrate his habit of placing the key thought, the unifying
idea, at the end. (Rather than list the examples of this practice,
I should challenge the reader to find one in which this is not
the case.) Now it is certainly true that if we are to understand
an occasional poem, we must have a reasonably clear picture of

the occasion on which it is based, or out of which it grew. If we may assume that Catullus had the sound poetic sense to know that a brief lyric must preserve unity of thought — and will anyone deny that he did? — then the key thought or unifying idea at the end of the poem should be related in some logical or at least plausible way to the occasion which suggested the poem.

Let us begin, then, with the concluding thought: *est enim venuste Magna Caecilio incohata Mater*: "It is indeed a charming piece of work, that unfinished 'Magna Mater' of Caecilius'." Now there are only two ways in which we may interpret this remark. It means either that Caecilius sent Catullus the "first draft" of his poem, hoping that Catullus might have some suggestions which would aid him in the writing of a finished version, or that he sent him a version which he (Caecilius) considered finished, but which Catullus felt needed further work. Whichever of these alternative explanations we may eventually adopt, we certainly now know why Catullus invited Caecilius to come to Verona: it was so that he might discuss Caecilius' poem with him. This reason, and only this reason, ties the beginning and end of Catullus' poem together; any other suggestion destroys its unity. There is nothing in the poem which contradicts this reason for Catullus' invitation or makes it improbable or illogical; furthermore, it does not require us to assume the existence of any elements not revealed by the poem as it stands. It presents a plausible connection between the occasion for the poem and the key thought of the poem. Above all, it is simple and natural, and does not require for its apprehension any learned apparatus or collection of factual data — and we must remember that the ancient reader probably knew very little more than does the modern about the special relations or circumstances which prompted the writing of the poem.

The next question — why is Catullus so insistent on haste? — both compels and enables us to make our choice between the two alternative explanations of the concluding line of the poem. For if Caecilius sent Catullus an acknowledged "first draft," why should Catullus have been in such a hurry to discuss it with him? There would appear to be no reason why Caecilius, under such circumstances, should have been told that "if he was smart" (*si sapiet*), he would "burn up the road" (*viam vorabit*) from New Comum to Verona. The admonition, *si sapiet,* with its abrupt hint of trouble if Catullus' invitation is not complied with at once, precludes the supposition that his demand for haste is motivated by his own enthusiasm and excitement: we cannot say that he was so full of ideas that he could hardly wait to impart them to his friend. Furthermore, how are we to account for the repetition of the word *incohata,* and for its presence in the key line of the poem? If Caecilius had represented his work as only an unfinished version, why should Catullus have felt it necessary to remind him twice of something he already knew and had himself acknowledged? And does not the final, critical line of Catullus' poem fall a little flat if it merely records an obvious fact, known to both parties from the beginning?

If, on the other hand, we follow Baehrens in seeing in *incohata* a *tacita censura* of Caecilius' work, we find a ready explanation both for Catullus' haste and for the repetition and critical position of the word *incohata* itself. To take the second, and simpler, problem first, the word is repeated for the sake of emphasis and is placed in the critical final line for the same reason. Thus Catullus tells Caecilius, and also his subsequent readers, that he considers Caecilius' work "unfinished," and that this is to be the main consideration in the conversation which he wishes to have with him. In effect, he is saying, "Your poem is charming, but in its present form, it won't do: it needs additional work. Won't you come and talk this over with me?" Since Catullus was notoriously impatient with "unfinished" poetry (see e. g. *cc.* 17, 95), and since *venustas* was one of the qualities he most prized, the phrase *venuste incohata* becomes a neat and subtle oxymoron, and thus gives excellent point to the concluding line of his poem. If one wonders why Catullus bothered to be so subtle and so indirect — wonders, in other words, why he did not come out flatly with his critical opinion, one may find justification for his indirection in either of two ways: his reason may have been purely literary, in that it gave him the opportunity of creating point in his final line, or, as Baehrens suggests, he may have used indirection because he wished to soften the blow and to avoid unduly hurting or discouraging his young friend. Since, as the phrase *meus sodalis* shows, Caecilius was a friend of his, and since Catullus was very sensitive about hurting, even in a small degree, those whom he loved (see e. g. *c.* 12, esp. 10-17), the latter theory appears the better; moreover, as I shall show later, this theory is more nearly in harmony with certain other parts of the poem.

If then, the poem had been regarded by Caecilius as "finished" but by Catullus as still "unfinished," we can now find a possible approach to the problem of haste. If we may assume that Caecilius had sent his poem to Catullus in the hope of admiration and praise, rather than of criticism, and if he had indicated his intention of releasing the work to the public immediately, we can at once see why Catullus is in a hurry: he wishes to prevent premature publication. Caecilius was a young man (for whatever else *tener*, vs. 1, may mean, it certainly indicates the poet's youth); he was inexperienced; he had not felt, as Catullus doubtless had, the crushing force of critical condemnation. Catullus can visualize what will happen to this enthusiastic and promising young poet if his poem gets into the hands of the critics in its present form. This same consideration helps to explain Catullus' own gentleness in offering his *summatim* opinion that the poem needed further work. Thus he says to Caecilius, "Come, and come quickly!" And why did he not simply say, "Don't publish yet!" Again, it was in order to spare Caecilius' feelings and to avoid discouraging him, for the indirect hint is always less deflating than the direct statement.

This argument becomes more conclusive, and is more nearly consonant with the rest of the poem, if we assume that Catullus' poem is his *second* invitation to Caecilius. The abrupt, even if jocularly exaggerated, phrase *si sapiet viam vorabit* is more intelligible if Caecilius had refused an earlier invitation, or had put Catullus off, alleging some previous commitment. Perhaps in his first note Catullus had simply suggested that Caecilius come to see him, hoping that his position of relative importance in the world of poetry would be enough to bring the younger man to him in time. But Caecilius had sent a vague reply, saying that he was "busy" and would "hope to come some time soon." Possibly, too, he had sensed that something was wrong, since Catullus' note had not contained the anticipated praise; he may have reiterated his own opinion that his work was finished and ready for the copyist. Now Catullus is really concerned:

the poem must not go out as it stands; Caecilius must come at once, no matter how "busy" he may be. In this poem, then, he insists on haste, and to show that he really has something to say to Caecilius, he lays before him, gently but insistently, his opinion that the work is not as well done as Caecilius thinks.

And see, too, where our argument is leading us: we can now explain the presence of the *puella* in Catullus' poem. For what is she, if not the excuse which Caecilius had offered for not accepting Catullus' first invitation? ("Thank you for your invitation," says Caecilius, "I shall be glad to come one of these days. I'd come now except that I'm much engaged with a *puella*, and I don't feel that I can leave her right at the moment.") There is of course nothing new or startling about this suggestion; there could hardly be any other reason for the inclusion of the *puella*. But we have now managed, as editors hitherto have not, to connect her with the other elements in the poem and to show how she is part of a carefully integrated and unified scheme of thought.

What, then, of the passage (vss. 8-17) which deals with the girl's passion for Caecilius and with her poetic taste? Catullus says that she has been madly in love with Caecilius ever since she first read his *incohata Dindymi domina,* and that her having been so is proof of her superlative poetic judgment; she is indeed "more skilled in the art of poetry than Sappho's Muse" (*Sapphica puella Musa doctior*). Her passion is alleged as the reason for Caecilius' rejection of Catullus' first invitation; she was so madly in love with Caecilius that she could not bear to have him leave, even for the relatively brief trip (about 100 miles) from New Comum to Verona. Is all this intended merely as a compliment to the girl, as Kroll suggests? Does not this suggestion introduce a foreign element into the poem, and disrupt its unity? For must we not seek elsewhere, along lines of thought not thus far suggested by the poem itself, to account for Catullus' compliment? If we do this, we shall find ourselves debating whether or not the girl was herself a poetess (Kroll) and even what her social position was (Friedrich), questions which cannot be answered by anything in the poem or by anything connected in any immediate way with its train of thought. Furthermore, are these lines truly complimentary? They have a distinctly hyperbolous quality — the girl's wild entreaties to Caecilius not to leave, as if he were about to go to the ends of the earth, and not just to Verona, the ascription of her passion to her having read Caecilius' "unfinished" poem, the assertion that she knew more about poetry than Sappho, the "tenth Muse," herself. The exaggeration is patent; if these lines were a compliment, they were a very clumsy one, and altogether too susceptible of an ironic interpretation.

How then can we connect them with the basic thought of our poem, logically, and without violating its unity? We may elaborate the character of Caecilius' excuse, and say that he refused Catullus' first invitation not merely because he was engaged with a girl, but specifically because she had begged him not to leave. In this case, Catullus is here indirectly quoting his friend's reply, when he says that the girl has thrown her arms about his neck and begged him a thousand times not to go (vss. 8-10). Or Caecilius may have said only that his *puella* preferred him not to go, and all the rest — her wild entreaties — may be Catullus' own invention.

Let us leave it at that for the moment, and pass on to the two questions of the origin of the girl's passion, and of her poetic taste and judgment. For the first, one can hardly imagine Caecilius' having himself declared that the reading of his poem had set the girl's heart aflame (vss. 14-15). But he may well have asserted that his poem was an excellent piece of work, that he was proud of it, and felt that it was ready for publication. This very consideration, as we have seen, probably occasioned Catullus' concern, and motivated his own pointed declaration that Caecilius' poem was *incohata*. In this light, the lines may be seen to be Catullus' jocular reply to Caecilius' dangerously high opinion of his own work: "if it's as good as you say, perhaps it is the cause of that mad passion which your *puella* has conceived for you and which is now the cause of your refusing my invitation!" If this is true, then it is perhaps better to ascribe to Catullus, rather than to Caecilius, the picture of the girl's entreaties. Now the whole passage is a unit. Caecilius has refused Catullus' first invitation on grounds of his preoccupation with a girl, and has reiterated his opinion that his poem is a finished piece of work. Catullus laughingly puts the two

together, draws an amusing and exaggerated picture of Caecilius'
sweetheart beseeching him to stay, and declares ironically that
it must be that — "finished? no, my friend, unfinished!" —
poem that has been the cause of her passion.

As for the matter of the girl's poetic taste and judgment,
these can now be seen to be a natural outgrowth of Catullus'
hyperbolous description of her love. They are in effect a *reductio
ad absurdum* of the whole idea. Such passion — if the poem is
as good as Caecilius thinks — can be accounted for only on
grounds that the *puella* is a person of remarkable literary dis-
cernment, a very *Sappho rediviva.* The jest would be cruel
except for its good-natured and obvious humor; moreover it is
rescued from cruelty by the last line of Catullus' poem. The
oxymoron, *venuste incohata,* not only points up Catullus' opinion
that Caecilius' poem needs more work; in addition it makes very
clear his further opinion that that work is good, even if still
unfinished. It *is* an excellent poem, full of promise of eventual
venustas, but it must be worked over and polished before it is
released for the critics to pounce upon. By this interpretation
of the *puella* and the remarks which are made about her, we are
brought back, as we should be, to the central and critical thought
of the poem and to the circumstances and considerations which
occasioned the writing of it.

In the light of this interpretation of the poem, there will be
little difficulty in explaining the *cogitationes* of vs. 5 and the
amicus suus meusque of vs. 6. For the *cogitationes,* are, as they
ought to be, "thoughts." What thoughts? What thoughts indeed,
if not, as Baehrens again suggested, in a very hesitant way, the
thoughts of someone about Caecilius' poem, someone's criticisms
of that poem. To take the word in any other way completely
disrupts the unity of Catullus' poem, and leads to wild and
completely unfounded speculation (Ellis' "something political"
is a triumph of inconsequence). If our poem were made more
meaningful by some other interpretation, we might forgive,
although we should have to regret, its disrupted unity; but it is
not made more meaningful; it is simply made obscure and
puzzling. All that remains is to explain Catullus' choice of
words. *Cogitationes* is rather vague and general, and suggests
nothing about the nature or content of the "thoughts." For

this there are two reasons. The general term is indirect, and therefore less likely to hurt and discourage Caecilius; it is thus of a piece with *venuste incohata* and the jocular, although emphatic, demand for haste. Further, the content of the thoughts is adequately suggested, or at least suggested as far as Catullus cares to at this point, by the rest of the poem, and particularly by the repeated *incohata*. After reading the poem, Caecilius cannot have been in much doubt as to what was in store for him at Verona.

As for *amicus suus meusque*, who again could this be, if not Catullus himself? He is certainly the "someone" whose "thoughts" he wished Caecilius to hear. There is no problem of Latinity here; the parallels in support of this interpretation are just as convincing as those on the other side. This being so, what is to be gained by disrupting the unity of the poem by introducing a third party? He merely raises the unnecessary question as to why Catullus, in a matter involving the judgment of poetry, should be reporting the thoughts of someone other than himself. It is certainly clear that Catullus did have an opinion about Caecilius' work; in point of fact, he writes in his poem about very little else. The "obscure" phrase *amicus suus meusque* is not really obscure at all; it is indirect, to be sure, and for the same reason that *cogitationes* is indirect. It is also mildly jocular. Its indirection and its jocularity are both for the purpose of reassuring Caecilius.

Now we can reconstruct the occasion for the poem, and tell its whole story. Caecilius has sent Catullus a copy of his *Magna Mater*, giving him the impression that he considers it a finished job, ready for publication. Catullus reads it, and becomes concerned. The poem shows great promise, but if it is released in its present form, it will be bound to bring down the critics on Caecilius' head, and possibly to hurt and discourage him. He invites Caecilius to come to see him, hoping that he need do no more than that. But Caecilius misses the point of the invitation, and replies that he can't come, since he is at the moment absorbed in a love-affair. Disappointed, too, that he had not received praise for his work, he reiterates his opinion that it is ready for publication. Now Catullus writes *c.* 35, telling Caecilius that he really must come, and quickly; he has certain "thoughts" which he wants Caecilius to hear. His poem is excellent — so good, in fact, that the reading of it must have been the cause of that tremendous passion which Caecilius' lady has conceived for him, and which is holding him at New Comum. She is a girl of real taste! But he must come anyway; his work is charming but — unfinished. Thus we can see our poem for what it is, a graceful invitation and offer of help. Its prevailing note is a sensitive kindness, coupled with unswerving honesty. Catullus is anxious not to hurt his young friend and not to see him hurt by others. Caecilius has real promise; he must not be discouraged by over-harsh criticism. At the same time he must be told the truth, that his *Magna Mater,* however excellent and indicative of real ability, is far from finished, and must be carefully reworked before it will be acceptable as good poetry.

UNIVERSITY OF MICHIGAN. FRANK O. COPLEY.

XII

Frank O. Copley
Catullus, *c.* 38

Extracted from the Transactions of the American Philological Association, Vol. LXXXVII, 1956.
Printed in U. S. A.

XI.   Catullus, *c.* 38

FRANK O. COPLEY

UNIVERSITY OF MICHIGAN

The theory that this poem was written "near the end of the poet's life" (Heyse, Schwabe, Baehrens) and even "on his death-bed" (Ellis, Merrill, Duff [*Lit. Hist. Rome*,[3] 233]) has persisted for a long time, in spite of occasional protests (e.g. from Kroll and Friedrich). Like much that has been written about Catullus, the theory has no basis in objectively demonstrable fact. It is pure conjecture, sprung probably of someone's desire to have a "last poem" for the collection, and pieced together out of Simonides' reputation as a writer of dirges and the expression *male est . . . Catullo*, which could mean "Catullus is ill," especially to one who was looking for a deathbed poem.

If the theory had confined itself solely to the matter of approximate dating, it could have been dismissed as interesting and possible, but not especially significant. Unfortunately, the very process by which it was pieced together has led to misunderstanding, and even to grotesquerie: we are asked to believe that Catullus, the least egotistic of all the Roman poets, thought to lighten his last hours by reading a eulogy upon himself, composed by Cornificius. Even Propertius never indulged in such Trimalchionics; he at least wrote his *magne poeta iaces* himself. As if this were not enough, the excessive concentration upon detail that has muddied the stream of Catullan criticism at many another point has done its work here, too, with the result that even so perspicacious and sensitive a scholar as Kroll has given the poem up as only partially comprehensible.[1]

Let us put aside all thoughts of last poems and dying poets, forget all minutiae, and read the poem through as it stands, all by itself. We need make only two assumptions: (1) that the poem, like any good lyric, is a unit, centered on some single thought and con-

---

[1] "C. ist in tieftrauriger Stimmung, deren Anlass das Gedicht nicht verrät; denn es ist ein wirklicher Brief, dessen Anlass Schreiber und Empfänger wohl kannten und der von dem Rechte, nur anzudeuten, starken Gebrauch macht" (*c.* 38, intro. note).

fined within the range of that thought; (2) that it contains within itself all that we need to know in order to understand it.[2]

Reading it like this, and with these assumptions, we can hardly miss the central thought, for it is entirely clear: Catullus is in deep distress, and is bitterly disappointed because his friend, Cornificius, has not sent him the *consolatio* that was customary in such cases. In order to have complete understanding we need only to know what the nature of the poet's distress was.

The opening lines do not make this immediately clear, for the expression *male est* is ambiguous: it may refer either to physical illness or to emotional stress.[3]   At this point we might concede Kroll's contention[4] that the poem has the onesided character of a true letter, for no doubt Cornificius knew at once what was wrong, and we do not — at once.

But let us look again at the whole poem, and see if clarification cannot be found.   It should be axiomatic in the lyric — at least in the Catullan lyric — that when meaning is obscure we should look to the concluding line or lines for help.[5]   Here, if anywhere, the poet makes his point; here he closes the circle that circumscribes his poem.   *C.* 38 ends with the line *maestius lacrimis Simonideis*; a correct understanding of these words should give us the clue that we need.

To turn the line into English is simple enough: Catullus asks for something "sadder than the tears of Simonides."[6]   The "something" (paulum nescioquid locutionis) is a *consolatio*, as vs. 5 shows (qua solatus es adlocutione).   That a *consolatio* should dwell on themes of sadness should not surprise us; we need only recall Cicero's remark to Caecina, commemorarem non solum veterum, sed horum etiam recentium vel ducum vel comitum tuorum gravissimos casus, etiam externos multos claros viros nominarem; levat enim dolorem communis quasi legis et humanae condicionis recordatio,[7] and to

---

[2] I should not wish to be misunderstood here.   Catullus writes for the Roman world of the fifties, B.C., and naturally assumes that his readers know that world.   Obviously we must learn of it, too, as far as we can, if we are to become competent readers of his poetry.   But *beyond this* the poems are self-contained: Catullus' contemporaries did not need notes to comprehend them.

[3] See Kroll, *ad loc.*   There are abundant parallels for both meanings: see the dictt. s.v. *male.*

[4] Above, note 1.

[5] See my remarks on *c.* 35: *AJP* 74 (1953) 152–53.

[6] It seems almost incredible that anyone should have proposed any other meaning for the line, yet see Baehrens *ad loc.*

[7] *Ad fam.* 6.6.12.

put with this Sulpicius' famous letter to Cicero himself[8] and such passages as Lucr. 3.1024–45 and Hor. *Od.* 2.9.9–17.   The idea that we have no right to grieve, when other and greater men have suffered as much or more than we, is one of the commonest themes of the ancient *consolatio*.[9]   It is in this sense and for this reason that Catullus asks Cornificius for "something sad."   He hopes to lessen his own suffering by comparing it to the greater suffering of others.

But what kind of suffering was meant?   The answer to this question is to be found in *lacrimae Simonideae*.   Here the key word is not *lacrimae*, which may or may not be Catullus' imperfect translation of Θρῆνοι.[10]   *Lacrimae* is as ambiguous as *male est*, for either physical suffering or emotional stress might be the cause of "tears." The key is rather to be found in the name of Simonides himself. If this name was to be anything but confusing (and is Catullus the man to deliberately confuse his reader?) it must convey a clear-cut and unequivocal idea; to put it in psychological terms, it must elicit an instant and single response, as *Shakespeare* would elicit "plays," *Keats*, "lyric," or *Milton*, "Paradise Lost."   Now there seems to be no disagreement as to the idea that the name of Simonides would suggest to the ancient reader: it is the idea of death and of songs of lament for death.[11]

The occasion for the poem and the nature of Catullus' distress are now quite clear.   Catullus is not ill; he is not suffering from *Liebesgram*,[12] for the name of Simonides suggests neither of these kinds of pain.   Rather, it is death that has caused him to remark *male est . . . tuo Catullo.*   Could it then be the poet's own (impending) death, as has been so often conjectured?   If, as I proposed earlier, we rule out the mawkish picture of Catullus gloating over his own eulogy, and think of him rather as fortifying himself for death by meditating on the courage of other, greater, dying men, this remains a possibility.   Yet somehow the idea seems far-fetched, and

---

[8] *Ad fam.* 4.5, esp. paragraph 4.

[9] See the article *Consolatio ad Liviam* in *RE*, esp. col. 938.

[10] Baehrens *ad loc.*: "per 'lacrimas' C. ad verbum vertit graecum Θρῆνοι, non nimis feliciter. . . ."   I have been tempted at times to wonder whether an anthology of Simonides' Θρῆνοι, under the title Δάκρυα Σιμωνίδου, might have been in circulation in the ancient world: cf. the Ἀηδόνες of Heraclitus: *A.P.* 7.80.

[11] The editors almost universally quote Quintilian 10.1.64, Praecipua tamen eius in commovenda miseratione virtus, ut quidam in hac eum parte omnibus eius operis auctoribus praeferant; and Aristides the Rhetorician 1.127, ποῖος ταῦτα Σιμωνίδης θρηνήσει; τίς Πίνδαρος; see also Ellis, intro. note.

[12] So Kroll and Friedrich.

not quite the one that the name of Simonides would have suggested. Simonides' songs were for the *survivors* of the dead, to console them for their loss.[13]   It would seem then natural, logical, and above all simple, to conclude that Catullus is suffering at the death of someone who had been close to him, and that he wished Cornificius to send him a *consolatio* for his loss.   The theme of the poem may then be partially expressed in the following paraphrase: "Cornificius, Catullus is broken-hearted and heavy with a sorrow that increases with every passing hour.   Have you — so little a thing! — no word of solace for me?   Please: one word; sadder than the tears of Simonides!"

One matter yet remains to be cleared up.   This is the phrase *sic meos amores* (vs. 6).   Here again it is over-attention to detail and failure to view the poem as a whole that have caused trouble.   If we look at *mei amores* in isolation, we are of course reminded of passages in Catullus in which these words mean "my beloved," "my darling";[14] some editors, with a conscientious eye on parallels, have accepted this meaning and conjectured that Catullus was referring to Juventius or to Lesbia.[15]   Yet we dare not disrupt the unity of the poem by injecting a third party, such as Lesbia or Juventius, here: the reader has not been prepared for it; the theme of the poem does not suggest it — all this quite apart from the fact that no relation between Cornificius and either Lesbia or Juventius has ever been so much as hinted at in any other of the poems.   If Catullus had meant *mei amores* to mean either of these two individuals, or for that matter, any other person, he would have had to add a note to his poem to that effect; otherwise the ancient no less than the modern reader would have been led astray.   As for taking *mei amores* to mean Catullus himself, or Cornificius himself, somewhat as *amicus suus meusque* (35.6) means Catullus himself,[16] this would inject a light, ironic touch which would violate the emotional, if not the logical unity of the poem.

But if *mei amores* does not mean "my beloved" then it does mean "my love," "my affection" — sc. for you, Cornificius.   Parallels for this meaning are rare in Catullus — in fact, no exact parallel is to be found.   The nearest is 13.9, at contra accipies meros

[13] See note 11.
[14] E.g. 15.1; 21.4; 40.7–8; cf. *sui amores* 10.1–2; 45.1; 64.27, and *tui amores* 6.16–17.
[15] See Baehrens and Ellis *ad loc.*
[16] See Friedrich, *ad loc.*; cf. *AJP* 74 (1953) 159.

amores, where *amores* clearly means "love" or "affection." But examples are not lacking in other authors,[17] and a study of the word *amor* in *ThLL* makes it certain that this meaning is entirely normal and natural. The singular is of course far more common than the plural, and we may be tempted to wonder why, in this apparently isolated instance, Catullus chose the plural. One obvious reason at once suggests itself: *Meos amores* at this point is metrically possible; *meum amorem* is not. There may have been other reasons as well, such as euphony, or the fact that there was some subtle difference, which now escapes us, between the meaning ·of the singular and of the plural, and which was of significance at precisely this point.

However, the final arbiter must be the poem itself, and here the meaning "love," "affection" is demanded as the only one that lies within the compass of the poem and does not violate its unity. Its theme is Catullus' sorrow and his chagrin at Cornificius' apparent lack of sympathy. These two ideas, which are really two aspects of one idea, are the only ones that are expressed anywhere else in the poem, and they find their most intense single expression in *irascor tibi* (vs. 6). After this outburst, what else can *sic meos amores* mean but "(is it) thus (you repay) my love?" Any other meaning would be illogical, disruptive, and — what would probably have been worst in Catullus' eyes — clumsy and tasteless.

One final point: who was it that had died? To this we can give no answer. The poem is not concerned with the identity of the deceased, but with Catullus' grief and Cornificius' failure to respond properly to it. We are bound to think of Catullus' brother, and perhaps it was indeed he. Also, perhaps not. It could have been any one of the many people for whom Catullus felt deep affection. If he had wanted us to know who had died, he would have told us. As things stand, it simply does not matter.

[17] *Meos amores*: Tib. 1.2.59–60; 1.3.81; *amores* alone, or with other modifiers, in the required sense: Hor. *Epod.* 15.23; Prop. 1.8.45; 1.9.1; 1.15.19.

XIII

Eduard Fraenkel
Vesper adest

49

VESPER ADEST

(Catullus LXII) *

To Sir John Beazley
on his seventieth birthday, 13 September 1955

Vesper adest : iuvenes, consurgite : Vesper Olympo   1
expectata diu vix tandem lumina tollit,
surgere iam tempus, iam pinguis linquere mensas :
iam veniet virgo, iam dicetur hymenaeus.
    Hymen o Hymenaee, Hymen ades o Hymenaee !   5

Cernitis, innuptae, iuvenes? consurgite contra :
nimirum Oetaeos ostendit noctifer ignes.
sic certest; viden ut perniciter exiluere?
non temere exiluere : canent quod vincere par est.
    Hymen o Hymenaee, Hymen ades o Hymenaee !   10

Non facilis nobis, aequales, palma parata est :
adspicite, innuptae secum ut meditata requirunt.
non frustra meditantur : habent memorabile quod sit.
nec mirum, penitus quae tota mente laborant.
nos alio mentes, alio divisimus aures;   15
iure igitur vincemur : amat victoria curam.
quare nunc animos saltem convertite vestros :
dicere iam incipient, iam respondere decebit.
    Hymen o Hymenaee, Hymen ades o Hymenaee !

Hespere, quis caelo fertur crudelior ignis?   20
qui natam possis complexu avellere matris,
complexu matris retinentem avellere natam
et iuveni ardenti castam donare puellam.
quid faciunt hostes capta crudelius urbe?
    Hymen o Hymenaee, Hymen ades o Hymenaee !   25

---

* Journal of Roman Studies 45, 1955, 1-8.

Hespere, quis caelo lucet iucundior ignis?
qui desponsa tua firmes conubia flamma,
quae pepigere viri, pepigerunt ante parentes
nec iunxere prius quam se tuus extulit ardor.
quid datur a divis felici optatius hora?   30
    Hymen o Hymenaee, Hymen ades o Hymenaee!

Hesperus e nobis, aequales, abstulit unam

          * * *

namque tuo adventu vigilat custodia semper.
nocte latent fures, quos idem saepe reverters,
Hespere, mutato comprendis nomine Eous.   35
at lubet innuptis ficto te carpere questu.
quid tum, si carpunt, tacita quem mente requirunt?
    Hymen o Hymenaee, Hymen ades o Hymenaee!

Ut flos in saeptis secretus nascitur hortis,
ignotus pecori, nullo convolsus aratro,   40
quem mulcent aurae, firmat sol, educat imber,
multi illum pueri, multae optavere puellae:
idem cum tenui carptus defloruit ungui,
nulli illum pueri, nullae optavere puellae:
sic virgo, dum intacta manet, dum cara suis est;   45
cum castum amisit polluto corpore florem,
nec pueris iucunda manet nec cara puellis.
    Hymen o Hymenaee, Hymen ades o Hymenaee!

Ut vidua in nudo vitis quae nascitur arvo,
numquam se extollit, numquam mitem educat uvam,   50
sed tenerum prono deflectens pondere corpus
iam iam contingit summum radice flagellum,
hanc nulli agricolae, nulli coluere iuvenci;
at si forte eadem est ulmo coniuncta marito,
multi illum agricolae, multi coluere iuvenci: 55
sic virgo, dum intacta manet, dum inculta senescit;
cui par conubium maturo tempore adepta est,
cara viro magis et minus est invisa parenti.

Et tu ne pugna cum tali coniuge, virgo.
non aequum est pugnare, pater cui tradidit ipse,   60
ipse pater cum matre, quibus parere necesse est.
virginitas non tota tua est, ex parte parentum est,
tertia pars patris est, pars est data tertia matri,
tertia sola tua est: noli pugnare duobus,
qui genero sua iura simul cum dote dederunt.   65
    Hymen o Hymenaee, Hymen ades o Hymenaee!

The scene which we are going to watch unfolds gradually. We are listening first to a group of young men talking excitedly together, then to a group of equally excited young women. It is evening, shortly after sunset; a rich wedding feast is coming to its end; the arrival of the bride is imminent. In the large room or hall the two groups have been dining at some distance from one another, the men near to the open door, the women farther inside : they cannot directly observe the rising of the evening star, but have to infer it (7, *nimirum*) from what they see the young men doing. At this preparatory stage, before the actual singing of the choirs begins, the young men cannot distinctly hear the voices of the girls at whom they are looking (12) : the din among the company is overwhelming . When the young women, after some flurried consultation (6 ff.) and a quick last minute rehearsal (12 ff.), are ready, they intone their first stanza (20) ' Hespere, quis caelo fertur crudelior ignis ? ' etc. What we have heard up to this point was not to be taken as singing but as snatches from the talk of the young people. Whether at lines 5 and 10 and 19 they are supposed to hum, by way of preparation or anticipation, the ritual refrain ' Hymen o Hymenaee' we cannot decide; it seems, however, more likely that in these places the refrain belongs, as it were, to the poet rather than to the choirs and merely serves to separate the words of the young men from those of the young women [1].

With l. 20 begins the singing competition. The parts of the women and those of the men are arranged in strict correspondence. The five lines of the first stanza of the girls, 20-24 (not counting the refrain), are answered by the five lines 26-30. The initial line of the young men, 26, differs only in a single, though decisive, phrase from that of the girls, and also in what follows a close parallelism is noticeable both in the form of the sentences|and in many expressions. There is no doubt 3 that the next two stanzas also were linked together by a symmetrical structure, but this symmetry can no longer be observed, since a lacuna in the archetype of our manuscripts has swallowed

[1] Some such division mark was required; for it could never have occurred to Catullus that his text might be presented in the form in which we see it, for instance in the Oxford text, with IUVENES and VIRGINES above the initial lines of the stanzas and quasi-stanzas.

7

up all but the first line, 32, of the stanza of the girls and the beginning of the stanza of the youths. In the third pair of stanzas there is again a marked correspondence, as will be seen from a comparison of l. 39 with 49, of 42 with 53, of 46 f. with 57 f., and above all of 45 with 56, where only the last two words differ. But the symmetry of the two stanzas as a whole is somewhat loosened : after l. 58 the refrain is not repeated (the reason will be discussed later on), and the stanza of the girls (minus the refrain) consists of nine lines [1], whereas its counterpart consists of ten. After silencing their rivals, the young men carry on to the end.

Before we examine the poem more closely, a word must be said about the foundations on which the text is based. All our manuscripts of Catullus derive from a single copy, now lost, that re-emerged at the poet's birthplace, Verona, towards the end of the thirteenth century [2]. Only for the text of the poem that concerns us here, LXII, do we possess a manuscript independent of V(eronensis); for this poem was incorporated in a florilegium written in the ninth century, the codex T(huaneus), so called after its former owner, the historian and eminent bookcollector de Thou (Thuanus), Scaliger's and Casaubon's friend. T alone preserves the indubitably genuine line 14, *nec mirum*, etc. Further, the readings of T are at several points, though not of course always, clearly superior to those of V, a salutary warning to editors of Catullus not to practise at all costs a ' conservative ' criticism where we have nothing but V to go upon.

The following remarks are not meant to be a substitute for a running commentary. What is intended here is a discussion

---

[1] Most editors (but not Ellis and Lafaye) assume the loss of a line after 41. I would not deny the possibility of such a loss, but the only argument in favour of it which I have found mentioned is the *petitio principii* of a consistent and mechanical symmetry. I therefore agree with Wilamowitz, *Hellenist. Dichtung* II, 278 (although I do not share his view on the function of the refrain), in believing that nothing is missing in this stanza.

[2] Cf. R. Sabbadini, *Le scoperte dei codici latini e greci* I (1905), 1 f. The jurist and poet Lovato Lovati (1241-1309; see the sketch in Sabbadini, *o. c.* II [1914], 105 f.), the ' decano dei preumanisti padovani ' (Giuseppe Billanovich, *I primi umanisti e le tradizioni dei classici latini*, Fribourg, 1953, 21), already possessed a copy of Catullus, as will be demonstrated by Guido Billanovich; in the meantime see the hint given by Giuseppe Billanovich, *o. c.* 41.

of one or another point of detail that seems to be in need of some comment or particularly worth noting. After this preparation we shall try to reach an understanding of the poem as a whole.

Catullus has been careful to avoid any definite localization. Neither *Olympo* at 1 nor *Oetaeos ignes* at 7 must be taken in a geographical sense [1]. The use of Ὄλυμπος = 'the sky' is well known; *Oetaeus* [2] had become to the Roman poets, presumably after some Hellenistic model, a common epithet of *Hesperus*, to be used at random. For the history of the identification of the evening star and the morning star and the use made of it by Catullus, Cinna, and the author of the *Ciris* (later than Ovid's *Metamorphoses*) it is now sufficient to refer to Pfeiffer's note on Callimachus fr. 291 (vol. I, 270). To reject at the end of l. 35 Schrader's 'brilliant and celebrated emendation' (Housman) *Eous* and to swallow *eosdem* (V, *eospem* T) is a sign of an iron digestion.

At the end of l. 9 the Veronensis had ' quo uisere parent '[3]. The last two words were corrected to ' vincere par est ' by Girolamo Avanzi and Battista Guarino, the great Veronese Guarino's son; the emendation *par est* was afterwards confirmed when the readings of the Thuaneus were made known. In the place of *quo* T provides the obviously correct *quod*. A conservative critic keeps *visere* (V and T), translates ' they will sing something we may well give an eye to ', and soothes his conscience by quoting from Aeschylus κτύπον δέδορκα.

l. 16 ' iure igitur vincemur : amat victoria curam '. The rhythm as well as the|syntactical structure and a stylistic device 4 (*vincemur ... victoria*) of this line recur in an early poem of Catullus' great admirer Virgil, *Ecl.* 3, 59 ' alternis dicetis : amant alterna Camenae '; cf. also ibid. 10, 3.

At l. 17 the readings *nunc* (*non* V) and *conuertite* (*committite* V) show the superiority of T; so does at 40 *conuolsus* (*conclusus* or *contusus* V).

---

[1] The correct view has often been stated. I mention the point to put the reader on his guard against the confusion in Ellis's commentary.

[2] Cf. Rehm, P-W VIII, 1255 f., Wilamowitz, *Hellenist. Dichtung* II, 179, n. 1.

[3] Neither Kroll in his short app. crit. nor Schuster (1949) in his extensive one mention V's reading, *parent*.

At the beginning of the stanza the rest of which is lost the girls blame Hesperus for having robbed them of one of their companions, the bride (32): 'Hesperus e nobis, aequales, abstulit unam'. Possibly we have here an echo of a passage from one of Sappho's wedding songs, but this cannot be proved [1]. In the initial lines of the following stanza Hesperus must have been praised in answer to the girls' accusation. When our text begins again (33) the nice point is made that Hesperus, so far from being himself a thief (abstulit), keeps off the thieves, for when he rises in the evening he summons the men of the custodia to do their duty, and in the morning it often happens that he, being one and the same as Lucifer, surprises burglars:

> namque tuo adventu vigilat custodia semper.
> nocte latent fures, quos idem saepe revertens,
> Hespere, mutato comprendis nomine Eous.

As is but natural, people in the ancient world were very much afraid of rogues on the move in the hours of darkness. Thus to them daybreak meant above all getting rid of the fear of thieves and robbers. This feeling is characteristically expressed in some lines of the Hecale of Callimachus (fr. 260, 63-5, Pf.), which now, thanks to one of Pfeiffer's brilliant discoveries, can be read in their genuine form,

> καδδραθέτην δ' οὐ πολλὸν ἐπὶ χρόνον, αἶψα γὰρ ἦλθεν
> στιβήεις ἄγχαυρος, ὅτ' οὐκέτι χεῖρες ἔπαγροι
> φιλητέων· ἤδη γὰρ ἑωθινὰ λύχνα φαείνει.

At l. 33 the word custodia calls for a brief comment. It is not very likely that Catullus should have thought of those minor Roman officials whose strict title was 'tres viri capitales' and who are commonly known as 'tres viri nocturni' [2]. What he

---

[1] The passage in question is Sappho fr. 95 Bergk (120 Diehl, 104 Lobel and Page), Ἕσπερε πάντα φέρων ὅσα φαίνολις ἐσκέδασ' Αὔως κτλ. In the following line Lobel could perhaps have spared the first of his daggers, for φέρεις ὄιν, φέρεις αἶγα might be accounted for in the manner suggested by Wilamowitz, 'Textgeschichte der griech. Lyriker', Abhdlgn. Gött. Ges. d. Wiss., Phil.-hist. Kl. N. F., Bd. 4, 3, 1900, 72. But the end of the fragment is a puzzle. What puzzles me most is whether ἀποφέρεις τῇ μητρί can mean 'you take away from the mother' as well as 'you bring back to ...'. So we cannot even be quite certain that the fragment comes from an epithalamium.

[2] The view that custodia denotes the 'tres viri nocturni' seems to have been held by the earlier commentators; see e. g. Valpy's note and the rejection of that

probably did have in mind is the night-watch, the φυλακή, employed in Hellenistic towns. In some parts of the Greek world it was called ὥρα[1], and under this name it figures in the famous folk-song which used to be ascribed to Sappho,

> δέδυκε μὲν ἀ σελάνα
> καὶ Πληιάδες, μέσαι δὲ
> νύκτες, παρὰ δ' ἔρχετ' ὥρα κτλ.

Quite recently evidence for the existence of such a φυλακή in the Athens of the early Hellenistic period has come to light in a fragment of New Comedy, P. Oxy. 2329, 26.

At l. 36 f. the young men sing :

> at lubet innuptis ficto te carpere questu.
> quid tum, si carpunt, tacita quem mente requirunt ?

They are teasing the girls, but nevertheless there is in their words a tactful restraint. The same idea is expressed more directly in the lyric wedding poem, 61, 31 ff.,

> ac domum dominam voca   5
> coniugis cupidam novi,
> mentem amore revinciens
> ut tenax hedera huc et huc
> arborem implicat errans.[2]

view in Friedrich's commentary. That is at any rate more sensible than Baehrens's reference to the ' sensus amatorius ' (reproduced, along with Friedrich's note, by Lenchantin) or Friedrich's wild suggestion (' der Stern wacht selbst ') or the classification of the *Thesaurus* IV, 1558, 42, under the heading ' in re militari '. Kroll says ' die Wache wird ausgestellt ' and leaves it at that.

[1] *Etym. M.* 117, 20; cf. Liddell and Scott, 9th ed., p. 2111.

[2] Wilamowitz, *Hellenist. Dichtung* II, 285, endeavoured to change the character of this stanza. Accepting Bonnet's punctuation (mentioned in Riese's commentary, who, as against it, compares ll. 176 ff., in Ellis's Oxford text, and by Lafaye, who adopts it), he removed the comma after *novi* and placed it at the end of the preceding line (31), after *voca*. Kroll in his second edition (see also ' Nachträge ', p. 297), Lenchantin, and Schuster followed suit. It looks then as if the text in this rearranged form were henceforth to become the vulgate. I reject the new punctuation and what it implies. To say nothing of its artificiality, it disrupts the connexion between ' mentem amore revinciens ' and the rest of the stanza, ' ut tenax ... errans '. According to the traditional punctuation, which I accept, *mentem* means the mind of the bride, and it is, of course, the bride, symbolized by the ivy, of whom it is said that her mind is being bound fast in love; it is also implied that she is embracing, clinging to him, the male, the tree (*tenax ... implicat*). If we take together ' coniugis novi mentem revinciens ', we make the final clause with its typical imagery all but meaningless.

The rich and delicate beauty of the next stanza, ll. 39-48, speaks for itself [1]. One problem, however, that arises from these lines must be briefly discussed; it concerns their possible relation to Sappho. The origin of the moving fragment (Sappho 94 Bergk, 117 Diehl, 105 (c) Lobel and Page),

οἴαν τὰν ὐάκινθον ἐν ὤρεσι ποίμενες ἄνδρες
πόσσι καταστείβοισι, χάμαι δέ τε πόρφυρον ἄνθος ...,

cannot be determined with certainty; Ahrens (*De Graecae linguae dialectis* I, 264) and Lobel doubt whether it comes from Sappho. But it should at least be admitted that Sappho has a very strong claim. The lines are not unworthy of her, and the author to whom we owe them, Demetrius περὶ ἐρμηνείας, quotes from her poems (counting neither this fragment nor other anonymous fragments that have been ascribed to Sappho) six times; three of these quotations come from the Ἐπιθαλάμια. If Catullus, when he wrote ' ut flos in saeptis secretus nascitur hortis ' etc., had in mind οἴαν τὰν ὐάκινθον ἐν ὤρεσι κτλ., he recast his model freely, which is exactly what those who are familiar with his ways would expect. The flower in the well-protected garden is as different from the wild hyacinth on the hills as is ' tenui carptus ... ungui ' (43) from πόσσι καταστείβοισι and *defloruit* from χάμαι ... πόρφυρον ἄνθος. And yet the feeling behind the two passages seems to be kindred. Personally, I am confident that Catullus adapted the same model a second time, and in a context which makes its Sapphic origin almost certain. We must pause for a moment to settle this point.

Gaston Boissier said of Catullus and Caelius : ' Ils eurent bien des reproches à se faire tant que dura leur liaison avec Clodia; lorsqu'elle fut finie, ils commirent la faute impardonnable de ne pas respecter le passé et de manquer aux égards qu'on doit toujours à une femme qu'on a une 'fois aimée '. This verdict does honour to the chivalrous spirit of the French humanist. But Catullus, alas, was long past the proprieties of chivalry when he poured out words the smart of which he felt far more deeply himself than the woman ever could :

---

[1] It is not without interest to compare the pattern of ll. 42-4 with that of 64, 146-8; the *sublimitas*, to which the repetition of certain words is subservient, is equal in both passages.

cum suis vivat valeatque moechis,
quos simul complexa tenet trecentos,
nullum amans vere, sed identidem omnium
    ilia rumpens;

nec meum respectet, ut ante, amorem,
qui illius culpa cecidit velut prati
ultimi flos, praetereunte postquam
    tactus aratro est.

After the hideous vilification in the stanza 'cum suis vivat' the following stanza, the last of the poem (XI), strikes an entirely different note : we hear the voice of sincere, though despairing, love. In happier days the poet had called her 'quam Catullus unam plus quam se atque suos amavit omnes' by the name of Lesbia, to testify to their common admiration| for Sappho. He had written for her the poem in which his jealousy expressed itself in a free version of Φαίνεταί μοι κῆνος. And now, in another poem written in the same Sapphic metre, he transformed once more the picture of the lines οἴαν τὰν ὑάκινθον ... χάμαι δέ τε πόρφυρον ἄνθος. The cruelty in the details of 'praetereunte postquam tactus aratro est', in keeping with his own fresh experience, is nearer to πόσσι καταστείβοισι than the gentler modification in the wedding song, 'tenui carptus ... ungui', where, however, the idea of convolsus aratro also played its part. Lesbia could be relied upon to recognize the allusion to Sappho and recall the time when she with Catullus enjoyed reading her poems.

The details of the picture in l. 51 f., 'sed tenerum ... flagellum', and the suggestive rhythm of these lines affect the reader profoundly. This is one of the passages in Catullus which make us understand why Virgil admired him so much.

We now come to a point which, apparently small, provides in fact a clue to the correct understanding of the whole poem. At the beginning of l. 59 most editors [1] have altered the et of manuscripts into at. This inconspicuous change is altogether destructive. There existed, we may almost say from time im-

---

[1] But et is retained by e. g. Is. Vossius, Ellis, Riese, G. Giri (De locis qui sunt ... corrupti in Catulli carminibus, Turin, 1894, 268), Merrill, Lafaye, Lenchantin. How enduring the influence of a convention can be may be seen from T. Heyse, who prints Et tu but translates 'Doch du ...'.

memorial, a manner of denoting the transition from a paraenetic tale or a general maxim to its application to the case in hand by means of the phrase καὶ σύ or οὕτω καὶ σύ, 'and so you (too) ...' [1]. That is precisely what we find here. In the preceding lines the young men had established the maxim

> cum par conubium maturo tempore adepta est,
> cara viro magis et minus est invisa parenti.

This plain truth silences the girls completely, for what could they possibly reply ? They have prepared and rehearsed their performance with the utmost care, have employed wit as well as sentiment and bravely carried their case to its extreme consequences. But their argument, however skilfully presented, proves hopelessly out of place, οὐδὲν πρὸς τὸν Ὑμέναιον. If they were right, there ought to be no wedding at all. So the girls, for all their fine effort, are doomed from the outset : the boys must win. *They* have come to the wedding wholly unprepared, but now they make up for their laziness by a remarkable presence of mind : point for point in the song of the girls is taken up and, through a process of true παρῳδεῖν, turned into its opposite. When the young men have worked up their mischievous reply to the climax of 'cum par conubium', etc., they know that they have carried the day; so they do not even pause to repeat the refrain, but turn straight to the bride, who, we may assume, has entered the hall a moment before, and put it to her to make proper use of what they have just demonstrated, 'and so you, too, do not struggle ... ',

> et tu ne pugna cum tali coniuge virgo.

It has often been said that *Vesper adest*, in contrast to the preceding epithalamium, *Collis o Heliconii*, gives a picture of a

---

[1] Sufficient examples of simple αἶνοι concluded by this formula of application are quoted *Rhein. Mus.* 73, 1920, 366 f. [see vol. I 235]. Here I add a few passages from early poetry in which the same formula is used in addressing a person who is to apply to himself the lesson of a preceding general maxim. Homer, *Il.* 9, 513, Hesiod, *Erga* 27, Theognis 99 (in the last two cases the transition is made by σὺ δέ, where δέ has its 'continuative' force), Pind., *Ol.* 12, 13 ff. (where καὶ σύ is replaced by καὶ τεά ... τιμά). At Bacchyl. 13 (12), 66, καὶ σὺ κτλ. after the general maxim introduces not an advice but a report. Finally a Hellenistic example: Theocr. 29, 1 f. The famous line Virg., *Ecl.* 10, 69, 'omnia vincit Amor; et nos cedamus Amori', is a perfect instance of the pattern with which we are concerned.

Greek wedding; many scholars have even gone so far as to see
in the poem a translation of a Greek work [1]. Others have asserted that it contains some Roman elements, without, however,
proving their assertion [2]. And yet it is | perfectly easy to clear 7
up at least one decisive issue. In the Greek world it was,
generally speaking, the custom that on the day of the wedding
a feast took place in the house of the bride's parents; the couches
of the men and those of the women were set in separate parts
of the room; the bride, who was, of course, present at the meal,
had her place among the other women [3]. Now it is obvious
that the setting of Catullus LXII shows on the whole the characteristic features of a Greek, as distinct from a Roman, wedding.
Nevertheless it is presupposed that the bride has not taken
part in the feast; only some time after its end is her arrival
expected. To account for this oddity and still to save for the
Catullan poem a spotless Greek character scholars have resorted
to strange subterfuges, one of them telling us that the bride,
after having dined with the others, has withdrawn to her room
— to change her dress for the honeymoon ? — and is now
expected back [4], while another [5] does not hesitate to use, in a
matter of Greek customs, this Latin poem, which he, like other
scholars before him [6], terms a translation from Sappho ('die

[1] This view is still found in Kroll's introductory note ('nichts, das nicht grie-
chischem Brauch entspräche; da auch die geographischen Andeutungen nach Grie-
chenland weisen [about this error see p.91 above], so ist klar dass C. ein griechisches
Original überträgt'). However, in the appendix to his re-edition (1929), p. 297,
he mentions Wilamowitz's correction. I need hardly add that Kroll's commentary
as a whole is very valuable.

[2] G. Friedrich (p. 281 of his commentary) says ' wir bemerken in dem Gedicht
echt römische Züge ', but all that he adduces to prove it is the topic of ' vitis ulmo
coniuncta marito ', which will be discussed presently. A much sounder scholar,
Arthur L. Wheeler, professed the same conviction when in his book ' Catullus and
the Traditions of Ancient Poetry ', *Sather Classical Lectures* IX, 1934, 190, he said
that in this poem allowance should be made ' for a possible admixture of Roman
elements ', but he no more than Friedrich came to grips with the problem.

[3] Lucian, *Symp.* 8, αἱ γυναῖκες ὅλον τὸν κλιντῆρα ἐκεῖνον ἐπέλαβον, οὐκ ὀλίγαι
οὖσαι, καὶ ἐν αὐταῖς ἡ νύμφη πάνυ ἀκριβῶς ἐγκεκαλυμμένη ὑπὸ τῶν γυναικῶν περι-
εχομένη. For further evidence see e. g. K. F. Hermann-Blümner, *Griech. Privat-
alterthümer* 271 f., Daremberg-Saglio III, 1650, P-W VIII, 2129 f.

[4] Riese in his introductory note: ' als die (vom Mahl, an dem sie teilgenommen
[Lukian conv. 8] aufgebrochene) Braut wieder aus ihrem Gemach erscheint ...'.

[5] C. Robert, *Hermes* 35, 1900, 659.

[6] Not, however, Isaac Vossius, of whom Riese, l. c., says that he was ' der
erste, der das Gedicht als aus Sappho übersetzt ansah '. Vossius, whose annotated

P

Sapphoübersetzung des Catull '), as a decisive testimony against the circumstantial evidence in our Greek sources [1]. We need not waste more words on such improbabilities; the facts as they lie before us are quite simple. An indispensable element in the Roman wedding ceremonies was the solemn *deductio* of the bride into the bridegroom's house [2]; her and her procession's arrival [3] forms the picturesque centre of Catullus' lyric epithalamium, written for the wedding of an aristocratic Roman couple. When Catullus in poem LXII wrote (l. 4) ' iam veniet virgo ', he borrowed, not indeed the whole *deductio* with its splendid procession, but a detail of it and transposed it into a scene where, if this scene were to be interpreted in terms of actual life, it would be inconsistent with the rest. The apparent inconsistency disappears as soon as we realize that the poem *Vesper adest* present to us a wedding such as could not be celebrated anywhere in the ancient world. The place of this epithalamium is neither in Greece nor in Rome but in a poetic sphere of its own. It owes some basic elements of its setting, above all the type of the feast, either to Greek life or to Greek poetry or to both, but it also employs freely some non-Greek elements. That this freedom in blending Greek and Roman materials, with the result that many situations can be located neither on the bank of the Tiber nor on that of the Ilissus nor in Alexandria nor anywhere else on the map of the earth, that this freedom had from very early days been a characteristic privilege of a good deal of Latin poetry could be shown without much difficulty. But here we are concerned with *Vesper adest*, and we want to find out, if possible, what induced the poet to bring in the heterogeneous feature of ' iam veniet virgo ' and all it implies. A moment's

---

edition (London, 1684) I have before me, did nothing of the kind; he merely adduced several fragments of Sappho to illustrate Catullus.

[1] Kroll regarded Robert's argumentation as conclusive. Wheeler, *o. c.* 274, n. 70, is sceptical, but instead of going into the matter (he could have found here a striking instance of ' the Roman elements ') he contents himself with saying that Robert's and Kroll's ' assertion is not certain '.

[2] Pomponius, *Dig.* 23, 2, 5, 'deductione enim opus esse in mariti [non in uxoris] domum, quasi in domicilium matrimonii '.

[3] The conservative obstinacy of Ellis, who at l. 77 clings to the final stroke of the MS reading *adest* (despite 95 f., 110, 120, and 122), is now repeated in Schuster's Teubner edition of 1949.

reflection will show that to Catullus the topic of l. 32, ' Hesperus e nobis, aequales, abstulit unam ' whether he derived it from Sappho [1] or from some other source, must from the outset have been a fundamental item in the singing competition since it would lead up to a perfect antithesis. It is also obvious that to say ' e nobis abstulit unam ' would be impossible if the bride was supposed to be present, surrounded by the other girls. So she had to be removed, and removed she was by the introduction of the Roman motif of ' iam veniet virgo ', inconsistent though that was with the Hellenizing background of the common feast. From | this introduction the poet derived the further advantage 8 of an additional dramatic feature : the whole action was intensified by its beginning with the expectation of the bride's arrival and its concluding with some sentences directly addressed to her shortly after she had entered the room.

It is with less certainty that we can judge the origin of the much disputed ' vitis ... ulmo coniuncta marito '. There can be no doubt that in Greek lands, even in λεπτόγεως Attica, the vines were sometimes fastened to trees; it will be sufficient to look up in any dictionary the instances of ἀναδενδράς (quoted as early as Isaac Vossius ' note on l. 50) [2]. But the custom of ' wedding the vines to a tree ' (by no means a poetic phrase : the prescription ' arbores facito uti bene maritae sint vitesque uti satis multae adserantur ' can be read in the elder Cato's dry handbook *de agri cultura*, 32, 2) was and is far more common in the rich plains of Italy. It is therefore unlikely that this feature in the poem should be derived from a Greek model [3].

Finally it may be permissible to venture the opinion that the jestingly exaggerated display of arithmetic in regard to the

---

[1] If it were the case that ' Hesperus ... abstulit unam' depends on Ἕσπερε πάντα φέρων κτλ., we should have to conclude that Catullus made the important change from the timeless φέρεις to the past *abstulit*.

[2] In general cf. V. Hehn, *Kulturpflanzen und Hausthiere*, 6th ed., 73, Hermann-Blümner, *Griech. Privataltert*. 108.

[3] That the wedding of the vine points to Italy rather than to Greece has often been said, cf. e. g. B. Schmidt's edition, *Proleg*. LXXV f., H. Magnus, *Bursians Jahresb*. 97, 1899, 217, Friedrich's commentary, p. 281. The *petitio principii* in Kroll's note on l. 49 ('das mehrfache Vorkommen bei römischen Dichtern wie Hor. Epod. 2, 9, *adulta vitium propagine altas maritat populos* weist auf hellenistische Vorlagen') is of a piece with his view on the absence of the bride.

three shares in the bride's virginity (62-4) seems to be in keeping
with that peculiar outlook of the Romans which annoyed Horace
so much [1].

Many years ago the true character of this poem was outlined
in a brief but masterly appreciation by Paul Maas [2]. He strongly warned against reconstructions of Sappho's epithalamia based
on inferences from the poem of Catullus, whose autonomy he
emphasized. Some passages, it was true, recalled Sappho,
but only as free variations (' sie sind nicht mehr als Anklänge ').
In particular Maas warns us not to ascribe to Sappho a feature
that is fundamental to the poem of Catullus, namely the manner
in which justice is done alike to the men's and to the women's
point of view. Eight years later (1924) Wilamowitz published
his interpretation of Catullus LXII, *Hellenist. Dichtung* II,
277 ff. [3]. As regards the links with Sappho, Wilamowitz's
view agrees entirely with that of Maas [4]. Moreover, he insists
on the ideal character of the poem [5]. As distinct from LXI,
it bears no relation to any particular wedding; it moves in the
free sphere of poetry. As Wilamowitz points out, it is difficult
to believe that either in Greece or in Rome two such choirs
should have taken part in a wedding feast. I would add that the
central idea of a singing competition and the role of the refrain
as a means of articulating the sections of the poem seem to indicate the same influence of the poetry of Theocritus and his
followers which we notice in the song of the Parcae in LXIV.
Lovers of Catullus may disagree about the relative merits
of his two wedding poems, LXI and LXII. Many will prefer

---

[1] *Ars. P.* 325 ff., ' Romani pueri longis rationibus assem discunt in partis cen-
tum diducere ', etc.

[2] P-W IX (1916), 132 (' Hymenaios '). His statement that Catullus LXII is
' bedeutende und einheitliche Poesie ' compares favourably with E. Norden's verdict
(*Römische Literatur*, 4th ed., 1952, 37), ' eine blosse Studie: Sappho in moderne
Technik umgesetzt, wahrscheinlich schon nach Vorgang eines hellenistischen
Dichters '.

[3] For the importance of Wilamowitz's studies on Catullus see *JRS* 38, 1948,
32 [below, p. 572].

[4] See especially p. 280, ' Wir lernen also, dass Catull keineswegs ein sapphisches
Gedicht übersetzt, sondern aus ihren Hochzeitsliedern hier und da hernimmt was
ihm gefällt, daneben auch von Kallimachos '.

[5] So also Wheeler, *o. c.*, 187 and 215.

the lyric poem on account of its wealth of realistic detail, its vigorous humour, its precious information about very ancient rituals, and its winged and gay rhythms, which somehow call to mind another song, ' Quant' è bella giovinezza, che si fugge tuttavia ! ' There are others to whom the softer notes of LXII will appeal with equal force. A scholar must not pretend to be a judge on such matters. I will rather conclude with saying that *Vesper adest* has one important characteristic in common with all that is best in Roman poetry : it could never have come into being without the Greek seed, and at the same time it owes its strength, its freshness, and its particular flavour to the soil of Italy out of which it grew.

XIV

J. P. Elder
Catullus' *Attis*

CATULLUS' *ATTIS.*

Though most students of Catullus and of Latin poetry in
general speak of the *Attis* in superlative terms, few have seriously
attempted to treat this poem as original poetry.[1] Its fate too
often has been: *laudatur et alget.* Possibly this neglect has
arisen from the backing which Wilamowitz gave to the unsupportable suggestion that in this work Catullus was translating or
closely imitating an imaginary Alexandrian prototype.[2] At all
events, in evaluations of Catullus' imaginative powers and of his
formal creative talents,[3] the poem is usually passed by with a
few stock compliments, and most of the comments on it are confined to matters of text, grammar, or the Cybele-Attis cult.[4]

---

[1] Two notable exceptions are G. Allen, *The Attis of Caius Valerius
Catullus* (London, 1892), and W. Y. Sellar, *The Roman Poets of the
Republic* (3rd ed., 1905), pp. 461-62. Considerable help, too, in this line
may be had from G. Friedrich, *Catulli Veronensis Liber* (Teubner,
1908), pp. 295-314.

[2] Wilamowitz, "Die Galliamben des Kallimachos und Catullus,"
Hermes, XIV (1879), pp. 194-99, conjectured that in his *Attis* Catullus
was translating a poem by Callimachus of which two lines, he claimed
(following the suggestion of O. Schneider, *Callimachea,* II [Teubner,
1873], p. 698), are still preserved by Hephaestion. In his "Attis,"
Hellenistische Dichtung (Berlin, 1924), pp. 291-95, Wilamowitz modified
his earlier view to allow as Catullian the middle of the poem. The
evidence, if it may be called that, is this: Hephaestion, 12 (ed. M.
Consbruch [Teubner, 1905], p. 38), describing the development of the
galliambic metre from Ionic tetrameter catalectic, remarks that the
metre is also called μητρῳακόν because the "newer" poets had used it
when writing of the Great Mother. To illustrate the metre, he cites
without mention of author two "famous" galliambic lines, neither of
which mentions Attis. The scholiast on this passage (Consbruch, *op.
cit.,* p. 246) says that "Callimachus also used this metre." Any attempt
to link the poem to other possible Alexandrian models is equally unsupportable.

[3] It is regrettable that A. L. Wheeler in his excellent *Catullus and the
Traditions of Ancient Poetry* (Berkeley, 1934) omitted a study of this
poem. Little help is to be found in G. Lafaye, *Catulle et ses Modèles*
(Paris, 1894), pp. 82-89 since he followed Wilamowitz so closely.

[4] It should be noted that Catullus is much more interested in this
poem in the rites of the cult than in the forms of the myth. On myth
and cult, see H. Hepding, *Attis, seine Mythen und sein Kult* (Giessen,
1903); H. Graillot, *Le Culte de Cybèle* (Paris, 1912), especially pp.

394

Such points surely merit the most careful study. Yet the work possesses many of the qualities which are commonly associated with great poetry; it is an exact and intense expression of a significant and moving theme, put in a form of high technical excellence. A study of the ideas and construction of the poem, therefore, would certainly appear to be merited.

This paper is directed toward such a study, and aims to suggest answers to three of the basic questions which should be asked about the poem. What idea or concept was the poet seeking to express in the work? Why did such an idea appeal to him? And with what technical and formal devices did he seek to express that idea? In such a subjective field, it need hardly be said, one cannot pretend to any dogmatism.

First, what was Catullus' aim in this poem? As I interpret the work, it is the dramatization of a mental state or, to put it another way, the sympathetic delineation of a mind undergoing a psychological experience of a most powerful sort. And Catullus' Attis, in my opinion, is not the original Attis of the myth but an ordinary man who by emasculation becomes a priest of Cybele. The poem presents a study of two moods of such a man. The first is one of wild and dominant fanaticism which culminates in a terrible self-sacrifice; the second is one of awakening and bleak despair when Attis realizes what he has done, what he now is, and recalls the world to which he may never now return. In brief, it is a study of fanatic devotion and subsequent disillusionment.

Why did such a study appeal to Catullus? I should say at once that I share Professor Havelock's distaste [5] for the school of literary criticism which, relying on those weary handmaids, history and psychology, believes that a poet's verses are best understood against a factual background of biography. Not only may such a "literal" approach inhibit our critical appreciation of the poet's imaginative powers and of the extent to which his own virtuosity is dictator, but, in many cases, the biographical "facts" are not facts at all, but simply conjectural cobwebs.[6]

101-3; F. Cumont, *Les Religions orientales dans le Paganisme romain* (Paris, 1929), pp. 43-68. I am indebted to Mrs. Milton Ryberg for much suggestive information on this cult.

[5] E. A. Havelock, *The Lyric Genius of Catullus* (Oxford, 1939), pp. 79-85.

[6] Thus, if one were to suggest that both Attis and Catullus through

Thus in the case of the *Attis* we can safely enough assume that Catullus had witnessed the rites of Attis in Bithynia (in 57-56?) and probably marvelled at a power which moved the frenzied worshippers *Veneris nimio odio* to such limits. Emasculation is obviously a subject full of attraction and horror for all human beings.[7] Certainly, too, like many educated Romans of his day Catullus must have watched with keen interest the worship of the Great Mother in Rome itself,[8] though, like Lucretius, Caecilius, Varro, or Maecenas, he could safely express this interest only in a literary way. Such personal observation may well explain the poet's original curiosity about this strange and bizarre cult and account for his knowledge of its rites. It is quite another matter, however, to explain why he chose to picture with such vivid contrast the high enthusiasm and the deep disillusionment of a human being who entered into this inhuman practice. The sympathetic reconstruction of poetic impulses is ticklish business; fortunately, it may not be a business of any great moment. But one element in the composition of the *Attis* we should not overlook—the poet's desire to indulge his own virtuosity. Surely the poet who could often express the most passionate thoughts in the calmness of high art was fully aware of the opportunities which such a subject offered his artistic talents. The chances for such a display in such a work undoubtedly attracted him to the theme. One cannot successfully probe too deeply into the distinction of form from content, but some aspects of formal excellence, in their subtle union with content, merit attention. In the *Attis* this is particularly true of those formal devices by which the poet created the effect of wild orgiastic speed and those by which he helps to convey the unforgettable picture of Attis' two states of mind. To a study of these technical devices we shall now turn.

To account for the speed and orgiastic abandon which stamp

an unworthy form of devotion had unfitted themselves for any other love, and that consequently this theme appealed to Catullus, not only may he actually be underrating the poet's artistic imagination by such a " literal " circumscription, but he has arbitrarily dated the composition of the poem on no evidence at all.

[7] Cf. S. Freud, *New Introductory Lectures on Psycho-Analysis* (transl. W. Sprott, New York, 1933), pp. 122-3 and 170.

[8] See Graillot, *op. cit.*, pp. 70-107.

the poem, one should first turn to the metre itself.[9] The preponderant number of short syllables, especially in the last half of the line, lends to the poem the air of swiftness which matches the quick enthusiasm of the worshippers, while the imperious caesura, preceded with striking contrast by the insistent long syllables, furnishes the fateful and heavy regularity of the tympana themselves. This orgiastic effect is heightened by the careful use of alliteration [10] and assonance, as in the line

typanum, tubam Cybelles, tua, mater, initia (9)

or in

dea, magna dea, Cybelle, dea, domina Dindimei (91).

The atmosphere of wild speed is also built up in other ways. The short cola and asyndeton are effective; so, too, are the great number of verbs of motion. The same purpose seems to have governed the poet's choice of adjectives. One is reminded of Southey's assonant participles in his description of the fall of the water at Lodore. Most of Catullus' adjectives either depict haste, like *celer, citatus,* and *rapidus,* or else frenzy, like *vagus,*[11] *rabidus,* and *furibundus.*

When we pass to an examination of the technical ways by which the poet helped convey his impressive picture of Attis' two moods, a number of points need attention. First, the struc-

---

[9] We do not know whether the galliambic metre was an Alexandrian invention, though most scholars assume that it was; cf., however, R. Ellis, *A Commentary on Catullus* (2nd ed., 1889), p. 252, n. 1. The only ancient galliambics known, beside those quoted by Hephaestion (see note 2) are: four fragments by Varro (E. Bolisani, *Varrone Menippeo* [Padova, 1936], frags. 80, 142, 143, 288), two by Maecenas (W. Morel, *Fragmenta Poetarum Latinorum* [Teubner, 1927], p. 102), and one by an unknown author (Morel, *op. cit.,* p. 174). On the metre itself, see G. Allen, *op. cit.,* pp. 126-54; R. Tyrrell, "Grant Allen on the Attis of Catullus," *C. R.,* VII (1893), pp. 44-5; E. Thompson and G. Dunn, "The Galliambic Metre," *C. R.,* VII (1893), pp. 145-8; E. Thomas, "Attin annotavit illustravit, anglice reddidit Grant Allen," *Rev. Crit.* (nouvelle série), XXXV (1893), pp. 284-6; T. Goodell, "Word-accent in Catullus's Galliambics," *T. A. P. A.,* XXXIV (1903), pp. 27-32.

[10] For some interesting views on the effect of recurrent sounds, see J. L. Lowes, *Convention and Revolt in Poetry* (Boston, 1919), pp. 243 ff., and D. A. Stauffer, *The Nature of Poetry* (New York, 1946), pp. 88-9.

[11] *Vagus* in line 4 depicts frenzy; in lines 13, 25, 31, 86, motion.

ture of the poem is noteworthy.   Narrative is kept to a minimum.
The sudden opening reminds one of the *Shield of Heracles* or
of some of Theocritus' shorter idylls or epyllia [12] or of Callimachus' *Hecale* or *Bath of Pallas*. Description, used with great
economy and usually for dramatic purposes, is confined to such
key elements as the savage sea over which the " mad crew were
borne," the furious enthusiasm of the devotees as they ascend
Mount Ida, the frozen wastes of Cybele's dark realm, and the
golden beauty of the sunrise that restores consciousness to the
worshippers. The description of Attis himself, as he was and
as he became, serves but to emphasize the dramatic contrast. For
once he was " the flower of the gymnasium, the glory of the
wrestler's ring, whose threshold was warmed with many visitors,
whose home was garlanded with fair wreaths." [13] This general
picture, thoroughly Greek, was enough; no individualization was
wanted here, for this is the picture of any man become Attis.
Then we see the new Attis, the now *notha mulier*, sketched with
the fewest of strokes—*niveis manibus, teneris digitis, roseis
labellis, tenerum Attin*. As for his companions, abruptly introduced in Hellenistic fashion in line 11 and forgotten before the
poem's close, they merit no description at all. So, too, similes
are few and functional. Of the three, *velut exules* (line 14)
bears an ironical reference to lines 59 and 60; the other two, in
lines 33 and 51, imply eventual mastery and enslavement under
Cybele. From the structural point of view, the chief emphasis
is given to the speeches, so that against the lightly drawn background described above we may focus all our attention upon
Attis' own feelings and moods. And the two speeches, reflecting
the two moods of devotion and of despair, are thrown into a
sharp contrast by the sudden and delicate beauty of the verses
on the sunrise:

> sed ubi oris aurei Sol radiantibus oculis
> lustravit aethera album, sola dura, mare ferum,
> pepulitque noctis umbras vegetis sonipedibus   (39 ff.).

This is a contrast which not only intensifies each separate mood
but also fuses them into a total picture of great power. Such

[12] Nos. 6, 8, 24, 25.
[13] Lines 64-6.

an equation of night with frenzy and of dawn with sanity is reminiscent of passages in the *Iliad* and in the *Ajax*.[14]

One of the poet's most interesting devices for showing us the tortured agony of the awakened Attis is the variation in the gender of Attis after the emasculation. Usually, of course, he is feminine. But now and then, in significant spots, he emerges masculine. Thus in line 45 when, freed momentarily from his madness with the coming of dawn, he reviews his own acts, he is *ipse*.[15] But a few lines later, when he addresses in his hopelessness his fatherland in Roman style, the word is *allocuta*. The masculine points back to his previous state; the feminine realistically depicts his present state. So in the speech itself he describes himself as masculine when he left his homeland (*quam miser relinquens*, line 51), but he acknowledges his present state elsewhere by applying feminine adjectives to himself. So, too, the goddess subtly recognizes the revolt in Attis' own mind by calling him masculine when she bids the lion drive him back into submission: *face ut hunc furor agitet* (line 78) . . . *qui fugere imperia cupit* (line 80). And in our last picture of Attis, *ille demens fugit in nemora fera* (line 89), we are left with a hint of that inner struggle which he is destined in occasional periods of sanity to feel for the rest of his life.

In his metrical variations, too, Catullus has shown great sensitivity to content. Consider, for example, lines 22 and 23 in Attis' first speech of enthusiasm:

> tibicen ubi canit Phryx curvo grave calamo,
> ubi capita Maenades vi iaciunt hederigerae.

In the first, one hears the slow music of the curved reed; in the second, one feels the orgiastic abandon of the Maenads.[16] Or note the utter weariness of the devotees in the close of this line:

> itaque, ut domum Cybelles tetigere lassulae   (35)

---

[14] Cf. *Iliad*, XXIII, 212-32, and *Ajax*, 21, 217, 258, 660, 672.

[15] I have followed the Oxford text of R. Ellis, *Catulli Carmina*. Friedrich, and Kroll (*C. Valerius Catullus* [Teubner, 1929]), have adopted the emendation *ipsa*, which here quite misses the point.

[16] Friedrich, *op. cit.*, p. 303, notes that the first half of lines 21-23 closes with a monosyllabic word, which thus heightens the mood of frenzy.

or the wavering, feminine, fluctuation of Attis expressed in the short syllables of:

> ego mulier, ego adolescens, ego ephebus, ego puer   (63).

On the whole, the first speech contains more short syllables than the second, which is what one would expect from a contrast of the thought of each. The second speech closes with a line memorable for its long syllables, by which the poet emphasizes the culmination of the emotional crisis:

> iam iam dolet quod egi, iam iamque paenitet   (73).

One of the most marked features of the poem is the extensive use of repetitions, a feature common, though to a less degree, to many other of Catullus' poems.[17] The eye has certainly largely displaced the ear in our modern literary communication, despite the radio.[18] But not so in Catullus' time, and we must not miss the force of pictures for the ear in a poetry written for recitation. In lines 62-71 of Attis' second speech, *ego* occurs thirteen times, an iterative device here used to reinforce the highly personal character of the speech. But more striking is

[17] E. g. Catullus uses the irregularly recurring refrain in several poems: In no. 61, *Virginem, o Hymenaee Hymen, / Hymen o Hymenaee* 4 times (with the first word wisely varied); and *Te volente. quis huic deo / comparier ausit* 3 times; and *Prodeas nova nupta* (with *abit dies* preceding in 3 cases; cf. also line 192) 5 times; and *Io Hymen Hymenaee io, / io Hymen Hymenaee* 11 times. In no. 62: *Hymen o Hymenaee, Hymen ades o Hymenaee!* 8 times. In no. 64: *currite ducentes subtegmina, currite, fusi* 13 times. In three short poems he commences and closes with the same line (nos. 16, 36, 57). Or he often suggests a theme by repeating words from another poem; cf. 2, 1 with 3, 4; 8, 5 with 37, 12; 21, 2-3 with 24, 2-3 (cf. 49, 2-3); 23, 1 with 24, 5; 41, 4 with 43, 5. And the device of repeating one or two words within the same poem in the same metrical position is surprisingly common in both his short and long works; cf. *obdura* in 8, 11 and 19 (cf. also line 12); *venisti* in 9, 3 and 5; *sive* in 11, 2 and 5 and 7 and 9; *cenabis bene* in 13, 1 and 7; *eone nomine* in 29, 11 and 23; *Sirmio* in 31, 1 and 12; *pueri integri* in 34, 2 and 3; *renidet ille* in 39, 4 and 6; *omnium* in 49, 5-7; *concubine* in 61, 125 and 128 and 130 and 133; variations of *tum Thetidis* in 64, 19-21; *-ore Theseu* in 64, 69 and 133; *-ore Theseus* in 64, 73 and 110; *Gallus* in 78, 1 and 3 and 5; *quid carius est oculis* in 82, 2 and 4; *formosa est* in 86, 1 and 5; *quid facit is* in 88, 1 and 3; cf. *niveis . . . artus* with *niveos . . . artus* in 64, 303 and 364.

[18] Cf. Stauffer, *op. cit.*, pp. 13 ff.

the repetition of words in the *same* metrical position.[19] Now this is a device not at all common in earlier writers. Naturally there is some correspondence of sounds in the strophes and antistrophes of Greek choral odes;[20] now and then one finds such repetitions by the same character within a few lines in the three tragedians,[21] and some instances of repetitions in the *same* metrical position may be found in the poems of Solon,[22] Theocritus,[23] and Bion.[24] Several examples occur in Euripides' ode to the Great Mother in his *Helen*[25] and in the *Hymn to the Idaean Dactyls.*[26] Callimachus appears to be the poet most fond of this practice.[27] Still, the device is rarely found and, though one may argue that the exigencies of the galliambic metre, which is certainly contrary to the genius of the Latin language, may explain some of this repetition, the amount of it in the *Attis* is so large that it would appear to be consciously done. And this iteration in the *same* metrical position involves key words: *Attis, Cybele, citatus, animus,* and *nemora.* This sort of repetition is not used here for liturgical purposes, for the *Attis* is anything but a hymn, nor is the repetition mere ornamentation. Rather, its function

[19] As pointed out in my "The Art of Catullus' Attis," *T. A. P. A.,* LXXI (1940), pp. xxxiii-xxxiv. My suggestions there made on epyllion and hymnal elements in this poem now seem to me largely unsupportable. J. W. Mackail, *Latin Literature* (Scribners, 1895), p. 57, noting the repetition of *identidem* in the same metrical position in 11, 19 and 51, 3 calls it "a stroke of subtle and daring art."

[20] E. g. *Antigone* 585 and 596, and 614 and 625.

[21] Cf. F. Schroeder, "De iteratis apud tragicos graecos," *Diss. Philol. Argentoratenses,* VI (1882), pp. 84-5 and 123-4.

[22] Cf. forms of ἄλλος in Solon, 13 (no. 1 in E. Diehl, *Anthologia Lyrica Graeca* [1936], pp. 23-29), lines 17, 29, 39, 47, 49, 51, 53, 57, 67.

[23] Cf. forms of Διόνυσος closing the verse in no. 26, lines 6, 9, 27, 37; Πενθεύς opens lines 10, 16, 18; χαίροι opens lines 33, 35.

[24] Cf. ὄλβιος ἦν in no. 8, lines 2, 4. 7.

[25] Cf. μάτηρ in lines 1301 and 1320, and ματρός in lines 1340 and 1356.

[26] *I.G.,* XII, 9, no. 259; lines 8 and 23, and 25 and 30 as edited by J. Powell, *Collectanea Alexandrina* (Oxford, 1925), pp. 171-3.

[27] E. g. Ζεῦ σὲ in Hymn 1, lines 6, 7, and 45; Ἀπόλλων in Hymn 2, lines 34, 42, 51, 61, 68, and 93; forms of Φοῖβος in Hymn 2, lines 44, 47, 55, and 65; forms of Λητώ in Hymn 4, lines 39, 60, 68, 204, 246, and 326; Ἀστερίη in Hymn 4, lines 37, 197, 224, 225, 244, 300, and 316; Ἀθαναία in Hymn 5, lines 5, 16, 33, 43, 55, 57, 69, 88, 96, 99, 133, and 137; forms of Ἐρυσίχθων in Hymn 6, lines 32, 65, 81, and 85; forms of ἐλαίη in Iambi, lines 224, 233, 262, 266, 271, 276, and 280.

5

in this poem is to help convey the picture of a unique and morbid state of mind, by returning the reader forcefully and frequently to key themes.[28]   The following cases merit attention:

super alta vectus *Attis* celeri rate maria	(1)
simul haec comitibus *Attis* cecinit notha mulier	(27)
comitata tympano *Attis* per opaca nemora dux	(32)
ibi Somnus excitum *Attin* fugiens citus abiit	(42)
simul ipse pectore *Attis* sua facta recoluit	(45)
tenerumque vidit *Attin* prope marmora pelagei	(88)

typanum, tubam *Cybelles*, tua, mater, initia	(9)
Phrygiam ad *domum Cybelles*, Phrygia ad nemora deae	(20)
itaque, ut *domum Cybelles* tetigere lassulae	(35)
ait haec minax *Cybelle* religatque iuga manu	(84)
dea, magna dea, *Cybelle*, dea, domina Dindimei	(91)

Phrygium ut nemus *citato* cupide pede tetigit [29]	(2)
hilarate aere *citatis* erroribus animum	(18)
quo nos decet *citatis* celerare tripudiis	(26)
ibi Somnus ex*citum Attin* fugiens citus abiit	(42)
alios age in*citatos*, alios age rabidos	(93)

agite ite ad alta, Gallae, Cybeles *nemora* simul	(12)
famuli solent, ad Idae tetuli *nemora* pedem	(52)
egone a mea remota haec ferar in *nemora* domo	(58)
ubi cerva silvicultrix, ubi aper *nemori*vagus	(72)
face uti furoris ictu reditum in *nemora ferat*	(79)
facit impetum: ille demens fugit in *nemora fera*	(89)

stimulatus ibi furenti rabie, vagus *animis*	(4)
hilarate aere citatis erroribus *animum*	(18)

---

[28] *Attis, animus, nemora, redimita, itaque ut* and *citus abiit* could stand metrically in several other positions. Words forming a bacchius, however, like *Cybelle, citato* and *acuto* must stand, I admit, just before the caesura.   But Catullus could have avoided this in the case of *Cybelle* by using the form *Cybele* (as he did in lines 12, 68, and 76, where it stands each time in the same metrical position).   The recurrences of *Attis* were noticed by T. Means, "Catullus LXIII," *C. P.*, XXII (1927), pp. 101-2, who suggests that "The word 'Attis' (or 'Attin') finds itself in that position in the line which is as neutral as possible" to show that he was neither masculine nor feminine.

[29] Note that forms of *citatus* suggest also the sound *Attis*.

abit in quiete molli rabidus furor *animi*   (38)
miser a miser, querendum est etiam atque etiam, *anime* (61)
ferus ipse sese adhortans rapidum incitat *animo*   (85)

devolvit ile *acuto* sibi pondere silicis   (5)
sectam meam exse*cutae* duce me mihi comites   (15)
ubi sacra sancta *acutis* ululatibus agitant   (24)

adiitque opaca silvis *redimita* loca deae [30]   (3)
mihi floridis corollis *redimita* domus erat   (66)

itaque ut relicta sensit sibi membra sine viro   (6)
itaque, ut domum Cybelles tetigere lassulae   (35)

ibi Somnus excitum Attin fugiens *citus abiit*   (42)
roseis ut huic labellis sonitus *citus abiit*   (74)

sed ubi oris aurei Sol radi*antibus oculis*   (39)
ibi maria vasta visens lacrim*antibus oculis*   (48)

abit in *quiete molli rabidus* furor animi   (38)
ita de *quiete molli rapida* sine rabie   (44)

This study has emerged from a belief that, perhaps because
of Wilamowitz's support of the view that Catullus was translating Callimachus in this poem, the work as original, creative
poetry has been too much neglected. Too frequently in estimates
of the poet's imagination and artistic powers, the *Attis* has
counted for little. Yet it deserves a better fate, and so in this
paper suggestions have been advanced as to what idea, moulded
from Catullus' own poetic fancy and discipline, and reflecting
his personal interest, may have drawn him to this subject. Such
conjectures about the psychology and art of an ancient poet,
being at best chiefly subjective, are always open to criticism and
correction. But the examination of the technical devices, the
" tricks " of poetry, lies in a surer field, and it is to be hoped
that this study of noteworthy formal elements in the *Attis* may
attract the reader's attention in the case of Catullus' other poems
to those devices which enabled this poet so often to recreate his
feelings and experiences " in the tranquillity of a perfect art."

JOHN P. ELDER.

HARVARD UNIVERSITY.

---

[30] Note the contrast in meaning in the two verses.

XV

M. C. J. Putnam

The art of Catullus 64

THE ART OF CATULLUS *64*

By Michael C. J. Putnam

FAVORABLE criticism devoted to the longer poems of Catullus is still comparatively rare. Recent signs manifest a worthy trend away from the hitherto frequent attempt to divide Catullus into two parts, one supposedly *doctus* and consequently an admirer of Alexandrian models and disciplines, the other by contrast witty and clever, the recipient of μανία, in fact the spirit whose lyric fancies offer such endless delight. Yet this heresy persists in a different guise, more damaging to an appreciation of Catullus, in the tendency to disown the long poems as obscurely motivated, foreign to the more successful aspects of his genius. We are allowed to admire Catullus, author of the short, brilliant essays in individualism, while his longer works (though sometimes, especially in the case of *63*, interesting in themselves) seemingly impersonal and built on the shaky foundations of tradition and imitation, are relegated to a secondary position and scorned as abnormal or at least exceptional.

Yet to ignore almost half his production can scarcely result in a unified picture either of a poet's mind at work or of his personality. If an examination of Catullus' long poems were only to result in shedding light on the imagination which poured forth the lyrics, it would serve not only a useful but an instructive purpose. But such a goal remains here only a corollary to a search for the unique beauties which one of these, poem *64*, possesses in its own right. In other words, we offer here, for one work of Catullus, an analysis comparable to that recently accomplished for the poetry of William Blake, showing, in fact, that his longer works, far from being dull asides or at best lengthy footnotes mirroring the taste of the time, are the offspring of a poet whose special powers can be traced throughout everything he produced.[1]

The result is a twofold plea for unity, unity first of *64* within itself, and unity between it and the shorter poems.[2] If *64* is, as has been maintained, a series of narrative sections strung loosely together by means of the most tenuous and superficial bonds, then we should certainly without further ado dismiss the poem as a piece of made-to-order Alexandrian work, a demonstration, as it were, on the part of Catullus that he too could write in a genre popular with his fellow *neoteroi*. Poem *64* ,we are often told, is written in a form (though even this fact is subject to doubt) which may have been prevalent during the so-called "Alexandrian" period, and therefore it goes without saying that it exhibits the worst side of the poetry we associate with Callimachus' contemporaries, wherein subject is molded to fit genre and imagination corrupted to the uses of virtuosity. The opposite is in fact the case. There is no meaningless artificiality here. Rather the whole is consciously calculated and specifically pointed, with Catullus' own directness, toward a grand design.

The long poems, and especially *64*, contain in the elaborate design which epic allows the same situations and emotions from which the lyrics grew. Catullus' genius is personality.[3] Inspiration for him is always drawn immediately out of confrontation with the events of life. Unlike Milton, Catullus was a poet who could never divorce himself from his themes. The end of *63* offers a case in point when the poet prays:

> dea magna, dea Cybele, dea domina Dindymei,
> procul a mea tuus sit furor omnis, era, domo:
> alios age incitatos, alios age rabidos.

In spite of his seeming protest to the contrary, the strength of imagery here repeated from the body of the poem proves beyond a doubt Catullus' own deep participation in this work. The writing of both *63* and *64* appears detached because the stories center upon remote mythology. But in fact they are the heightened imaginative efforts of a poet who left his mark on every line and who, though deliberately disavowing actual participation in the story, tells his reader by no less obvious means than in the lyrics that these are writings of the most personal sort. The longer poems change names, places, and dates; they do not alter either poetic or personal intensity. Catullus speaks through characters, but very much for himself. As John Livingstone Lowes found of Coleridge, we seek to discover Catullus' mind at work even in his longer poems and at the same time find Catullus as a person around every corner. Briefly, these poems are a very important part of Catullus' production, and no general interpretation which omits an examination of them can be completely successful.

Unity of emotion finds its twin, of course, in unity of imaginative expression. Thus we will have frequent recourse to other poems to observe the imagination which created *64* at work elsewhere on similar topics and in a similar manner.

We assume also at the start that *64* is no Hellenistic poem in the deprecatory sense of the word, meaning a superficial exercise containing little or no meaning beyond its form. It manifests only a few structural techniques in common with the poets of Alexandria, such as use of the

ὀμφαλός pattern for digressions (and even this is as old as Homer).[4]
Rather the language of *64* is simple, straightforward, and intense, only
rarely redundant or overelaborate. In a sense *64* gives an even truer
portrait of Catullus than do some of the polymetric and elegiac poems,
especially those which attempt to falsify and reverse the true situation
(a common Catullan habit).[5] In *64*, because the poet is writing epic, he
can give his thoughts a freer rein than usual just because he is writing
under the mask of symbolic poetry.

During the course of *64* certain almost prose-like statements about
love which the elegiacs offer are elaborated into long descriptive parallels
which embody in epic story the skeleton of their tortured utterances.
Though *72* is a poem to which further references will be made below, it
deserves quotation in full here since, in brief compass, it displays many
of the tensions which form the core of the subsequent discussion of *64*:

> Dicebas quondam solum te nosse Catullum,
>   Lesbia, nec prae me velle tenere Iovem.
> dilexi tum te non tantum ut vulgus amicam,
>   sed pater ut gnatos diligit et generos.
> nunc te cognovi: quare etsi impensius uror,
>   multo mi tamen es vilior et levior.
> qui potis est? inquis. quod amantem iniuria talis
>   cogit amare magis, sed bene velle minus.

Like *72*, *64* exhibits, par excellence, the opposition of past and present,
ideal and real, ever at hand in Catullus and here spread out in narrative
detail. This leads to the belief that Lesbia and the poet's brother are also
very much involved in the story as it unfolds. In a word, poem *64* shows
Catullus writing of himself in the figures of Ariadne and Aegeus, and of
the way he had hoped his relationship with Lesbia would evolve in the
story of Peleus and Thetis.[6] With the present disguised under symbolic
forms, it is true autobiography and consequently it says more than any
other of his poems because it can do so with impunity.

I. Divisions; Scene on the Shore and First Flashback

The poem divides essentially into two parts. It opens with the first
meeting of Peleus and Thetis, leading the reader to believe that the tale
of their love and marriage forms the bulk of the poem. Yet in the midst of
the opening description, only fifty lines after the poem begins, Catullus
digresses, by describing the coverlet on the marriage bed, into the tale
of Ariadne's desertion by Theseus. This, with its various ramifications,
takes up more than half the poem. Thereafter the happy wedding descrip-

tion returns, to balance the sadness of the previous episode. Even now all does not remain serene, for the song of the Fates follows, singing bliss to the happy pair, bliss enhanced and yet impaired by their son, the warlike death-dealing Achilles. Once more happy allusions to the *concordia* of the newly founded home surround the bitter lines, but the poet's point is clear. The ideal is never reached, even in the union between Peleus and Thetis, which to ancient authors was above all others the most perfect.[7] The story and the song now over, the work concludes with a few lines of moralizing wherein the virtues of the past are contrasted with present vices, lines which stand as commentary to the two diverse episodes which preceded.

Leaving the opening verses to be discussed along with those which follow the digression, we shall begin with the tale of Ariadne. We find her first in line 52 as she looks out from the sounding shore and beholds Theseus sailing away, unloving and oblivious. She, on the other hand, is in the grip of love for Theseus which even then she cannot suppress.[8] So sudden is her disillusionment that her mind refuses to acknowledge what her eyes admit as fact. She is aroused from a sleep which is *fallax*, because it lulled her into a confidence as false as her lover:

> immemor at iuvenis fugiens pellit vada remis
> irrita ventosae linquens promissa procellae.

The sound of *iuvenis* seems to be reiterated in *ventosae*, just as *linquens* picks up the sense of *fugiens*.

The picture of departure haunted Catullus, meaning to him on most occasions little short of desertion, and in the opening lines Catullus finds the opportunity to enhance this theme. He exploits the situation of Ariadne to the fullest. The winds which bear the youth away are the very ones which waft his promises into the air. As she repeats later in her speech, Theseus gave her *promissa* with *blanda voce*, in alluring and seductive tones but signifying nothing more than mere words. They were (according to lines 59 and 142, both of which utilize the metaphor of winds) *irrita*, a deadly accusation in Catullus' mind.[9] Like his oaths, Theseus' promises were only meant to gain the sensual satisfaction of the moment, remaining invalid for the future (line 148). To adapt the words of Catullus to Lesbia, he was indeed *nullam amans vere*.

Likewise the shore, which finds her deserted on its lonely waste, is a reflection in nature of the situation of her pitiful heart. She has cut herself off from love and home and family only to be surrounded by the girdling sea. The island is *sola* as she is and deserted.

It is not difficult to find other instances of Catullus' commenting on a similar fate. Attis, the victim of the madness of Cybele, is foreign to anything in *64*, but the Attis who awakens to find his madness fled, and with it all that was true and human, is a figure who has much in common with Ariadne. The mere parallels in the way the poet represents their external situations are interesting. We would expect the descriptions of each to begin coinciding at the moment of Attis' awakening, and so they do. In 63.42 Catullus relates that

> ibi *Somnus excitam* Attin fugiens citus abiit; . . .

much as he pictures Ariadne (64.56):

> utpote fallaci quae tum primum *excita somno* . . .

The lines which follow find Attis gradually becoming aware of the full implications of his recent deeds (63.45–47):

> simul ipsa pectore Attis sua facta recoluit,
> liquidaque mente vidit sine quis ubique foret,
> animo aestuante rusum reditum ad vada tetulit . . . ,

yet in much the same manner Ariadne yearns for Theseus. *Vidit* of 63.46 (with *visens* of 48) recalls 64.55. The verses which precede Attis' speech (63.48–49):

> ibi maria vasta visens lacrimantibus oculis,
> patriam allocuta maestast ita voce miseriter . . . ,

offer a situation not far different from 64.60:

> quem procul ex alga maestis Minois ocellis,

or from the recurrence of this very same description shortly before Ariadne begins to speak. Each is *miser* and each gives vent to suffering in words which reveal its full extent.

But verbal reminiscences alone — and many more could be adduced — do not tell us why the poet offers so much common ground between Attis and Ariadne, why two such supposedly disparate figures should be depicted in such a similar way. The answer can lie nowhere but in the realization that the circumstances and thoughts of each are very much a part of Catullus himself, and therefore are to be conveyed in like fashion. Each wakes from sleep to bitter truth. Each betakes himself to the shore, which becomes not a symbol for arrival (in the opening lines of *63* the shore is not even mentioned), but of separation from true love. Attis laments the loss of home and family through the excessive *furor* of devotion; Ariadne, while manifestly blaming Theseus, bewails almost exactly the same fate, since she herself has been the victim of mad passion to the detriment of all that remains true and steadfast.

Moreover the phraseology in these lines devoted to Ariadne bears a marked resemblance to the totality of poem *30*. Alfenus, after promising much to the poet, had betrayed and deserted him. He stands to Catullus as Theseus to Ariadne. The numerous parallels between the two poems,[10] many of which may be no more than clichés of situation, come suddenly to life with the reflection of 30.5,

> quae tu neglegis ac me miserum deseris in malis . . . ,

in 64.57, where Ariadne

> desertam in sola miseram se cernat harena.

In malis becomes *in sola harena* because of the epic setting. Otherwise the situations are noticeably similar. Only the emotions aroused in the reader by the pitiful case of Ariadne are heightened by the beauty of the shore scene, as the horror of her desertion is magnified by her loneliness.

It is not, however, to any stray example, such as *30*, that we turn in search of a completely parallel episode in Catullus' life which might have aroused in him the feelings of Ariadne. We look not to the Alfenuses, numerous as they may have been, but to Lesbia, to whom, alone of those mentioned in his poetry, he could ascribe the actions and feelings of a Theseus. This was the great emotion of his life. He describes in *64* Lesbia's desertion of him in epic terms. Lesbia is the one who has fled his embraces only to leave him *miser* with lovesickness.[11] The similarity between this event and the situation described in 64.58ff. is too close to be mere coincidence. Catullus is very much a part of Ariadne.

The irony of circumstance in these lines is thoroughly apparent. When Theseus sails away *celeri cum classe*, we think on Attis' arrival in Phrygia *celeri rate* and ponder the fact that Theseus' desertion is like the madness which drove Attis away from home. Likewise, Ariadne should arise happy on her wedding day. Instead she wakens to find no love at all.[12] These verses contrast in particularly effective fashion with the very opening section of the poem. Line 35 tells how

> deseritur Cieros, linquunt Pthiotica Tempe . . .

The same words used here to describe the home at Pharsalus, crowded with a throng joyously assembled for the marriage rites, recur in the picture of the abandoned Ariadne.[13] The result is direct and deliberate verbal irony to emphasize the distinction between true and false.

We meet another theme from the contrasts within the lines themselves, namely the difference between external and internal value. We had previously read of the waves of care on which Ariadne was tossed. Her sensations are depicted more explicitly in lines 68–70:

> sed neque tum mitrae neque tum fluitantis amictus
> illa vicem curans toto ex te pectore, Theseu,
> toto animo, tota pendebat perdita mente . . . ,

and the imagery is expanded in the lines which follow. She is passionately in love with Theseus with a desire which stems from her whole being, *toto ex pectore*.[14] By contrast, the heart of Theseus is labeled in the course of the poem both *immemor* (line 123) and *immite* (line 138).[15] He is bent on reaping the sexual rewards of the moment while she suffers the true feelings of love. The result is that lines 63 to 67, where her disheveled appearance is described, because they are framed by the similarity of thought in lines 62 and 68–70, bring out the contrast created by the juxtaposition. Ariadne cares nothing for her physical state. Externally all is disorder. Yet she seems what she is, as her heart yearns truly for Theseus.

This contrast between exterior and interior, a familiar one appearing in many guises throughout the poetry of Catullus, makes no more vivid appearances than in 64. Ariadne cries in lines 175–76 (and the words pick up her previous thoughts at lines 136–37):

> nec malus hic celans dulci crudelia forma
> consilia in nostris requiesset sedibus hospes!

The cruel counsels lurk beneath an exterior which tempts toward love. She was carried away by outward charm to hope for inner spiritual values where in fact there were none. The revelation about Lesbia came gradually to Catullus as the elegiacs show, and the tone of *8* clearly suggests that he wanted to postpone acceptance of it until denial was impossible. But Ariadne is the Catullus to whom all is clear. Recognition to her is instant on all levels. It takes place in the seconds which separate sleep from waking. The speech which Ariadne then delivers is the epitome of Catullus' own disillusionment.

In the first twenty lines devoted to the story of Ariadne, then, Catullus prepares the reader for much that is to follow and reveals at the same time his own personal feelings.[16] The very first adjective applied to any aspect of her plight, *fluentisono*, is an apparent coinage of the poet's. But he soon associates both the floods and the sounds with Ariadne in a way which makes the word a precursor of the description which follows. The ebb and flow, as part of the wave imagery, also become internal (line 62); yet we have seen how the turmoil of the sea affects her externally as well (lines 67–68). Again a few lines later the metaphorical usage reappears when the poet in his own person adds the aside (lines 97-98):

> qualibus incensam iactastis mente puellam
> fluctibus, in flavo saepe hospite suspirantem!

The roar of the beating waves resounds for one last time in the shrill cries of Ariadne bewailing her fate and telling how she began (line 125)

> clarisonas imo fudisse e pectore voces.[17]

With line 73 Catullus commences to tell the story from the start. From here to line 121, where we return to Ariadne on the shore, we are treated to a long flashback, beginning with Theseus' departure from Athens to kill the Minotaur and ending with Ariadne's relinquishment of family and home to take flight with Theseus. As always in Catullus, the voyage means more than geographical wandering. It symbolizes change through departure, the leaving of one kind of life for another. Here it gives scope to what may have been to Catullus merely the agony caused by Lesbia's infidelity. Perhaps we may find the source of the poet's continual return to this picture in his brother's death-journey to Troy. Whatever the case may be, *64* rises and falls on the theme of the journey, which is itself a reflection of the happiness and pain of love.

Here the focus of events upon the earlier stages of Ariadne's love adds to the poignancy of her plight while at the same time preparing the way for the speech in which she concentrates all her bitterness. The figure of Theseus is sketched with a few strokes.[18] His arrival in Crete found him only the *flavus hospes* (line 98), the hero whose boldness, coupled with her brave assistance, overcame the Minotaur. It is rather to her love for Theseus that Catullus primarily devotes himself, showing her as the lover capable of supreme devotion. The imagery of lines 86–90, when compared to like passages in *61*, proves her ripeness for marriage. But in *61* both the husband and wife are at some point called *cupidus*.[19] In *64* not a word is uttered of such a desire on the part of Theseus. It is Ariadne who views her lover *cupido lumine* (line 86), and who later implies that any eagerness Theseus may have had was but the moment's fancy.

Once again Ariadne is the mouthpiece of the poet himself, for rarely does Catullus speak of a desire on Lesbia's part for him.[20] Mention of his for her forms part of *70* and is the core of *107*, where Catullus applies the word *cupidus* to himself three times in the course of five lines. Any such yearning, first suggested in poems like *107*, finds its complete expression in the speech of Ariadne in *64*. In *107* Lesbia returned to the poet, who was beginning to despair of her devotion. In *64*, Theseus has departed for good.

From the word *cupidus* we may turn to other means by which the poet pictures Ariadne's love. As usual for Catullus, the senses play a role of great importance, especially the eyes. Through her eyes Ariadne first conceives (line 92) the flame of love which burns her to the very marrow. After this brief description couched in highly erotic imagery (especially lines 91–93), the poet has so fallen under the spell of, nay, become part of Ariadne's situation, that he suddenly turns and speaks to Cupid and Venus, addressing them in the second person as he had Theseus in line 69, where he was also thinking quite personally of Ariadne's suffering (lines 94–96):

> heu misere exagitans immiti corde furores
> sancte puer, curis hominum qui gaudia misces,
> quaeque regis Golgos quaeque Idalium frondosum. . . .

Line 95 reflects the sentiment of 68.17–18, where Catullus, looking wistfully at his own past, boasts:

> multa satis lusi: non est dea nescia nostri,
> quae dulcem curis miscet amaritiem.

In fact the whole surrounding passage in *68* is a variation on this situation in *64*. When Catullus was, like Ariadne, in the spring of life, 68.16 says, he was much under the power of Venus; yet now, he goes on, all joys are taken from him. The superficial source of the waves of fortune, on which he complains to Manlius he is tossed, is soon revealed as the death of his brother. Yet we know from the second part of *68* that he has also been meditating on Lesbia's infidelity, since he tries desperately to make light of it. Even though he makes no mention at all of Lesbia in *68a*, the *fluctus fortunae* may find a secondary application to Lesbia's faithlessness. So young Ariadne also experienced the *gaudia* of love with Theseus, only to find herself betrayed.

Epic description returns once more in line 105, this time devoted to the battle with the Minotaur. Little more need be said, Catullus hints in line 116, to fill the gap between this heroic achievement and the desertion on Dia. Yet he adds four interesting lines (117–120) narrating

> . . . ut linquens genitoris filia vultum
> ut consanguineae complexum, ut denique matris,
> quae misera in gnata deperdita laeta (batur),
> omnibus his Thesei dulcem praeoptarit amorem. . .

This is a familiar Catullan situation, but it deserves mention here. Ariadne left father, sister, mother, in fact home and family love on account of her passion for Theseus. Such also is the situation in which Attis finds himself when he says

> patria o mei creatrix, patria o mea genetrix
> ego quam miser relinquens. . . .

Each has given way to the violence of a passion which in its joy is fleeting while lasting with pain. Each has renounced the steadfast, lasting *pietas* of home, the love which exists between parents and children, between brother and brother. This is the spiritual side of the love which Catullus bore Lesbia, as he defines it in *72*. It is also the way he felt, as we shall later see, toward his own brother. The perfect love would have been ideally a union between this spiritual *pietas* and sexual passion. As it was, he learned that the combination could never be achieved, since the love he felt toward his brother could not be found in Lesbia, lacking as she did the *fides* and *pietas* which formed its very foundation.

Line 121 returns to where line 72 had left off. The description now leads directly into the beginning of Ariadne's lament,[21] and the imagery of these ten lines merely recapitulates and enhances the description at the beginning of her story. She rages. She is *tristis* and *maesta*, words applicable to love as well as grief. And the imagery utilized to depict her sorrow before she speaks recurs at her speech's end (line 202), thereby framing the whole. Once more the sad voice and the suffering of violent revelation recall Attis. Ariadne's words are, or at least so she thinks, her last complaints, *extremae querellae* (line 130).[22] She assumes she is in the very throes of death — and for purposes of this particular moment in the action she is indeed dying. When Bacchus arrives the mood changes completely, to be sure, but it is the story of Theseus' desertion which is the real subject of this section of the poem, not the arrival of the new lover. It is no coincidence that she later describes her complaints as those (lines 196–97)

> quas ego, vae misera, extremis proferre medullis
> cogor inops, ardens, amenti caeca furore.

Catullus is able to make the external situation justify and fit the internal feelings. What might even be called her *Liebestod* from love for Theseus is one with the tragic end she thinks she will have, left alone on a deserted island, a prey to birds and beasts. Her lips are already beginning to grow numb with cold as she begins.

II. ARIADNE'S LAMENT

> sicine me patriis avectam, perfide, ab aris,
> perfide, deserto liquisti in litore, Theseu ?
> sicine discedens neglecto numine divum,
> immemor a! devota domum periuria portas ?

From these initial questions, the reader learns of her seduction from home and why it is now quite clear to Ariadne that Theseus is carrying *devota domum periuria*, harbingers of the curse which she puts on him at the end. The repetition of *perfide*, with which the indictment opens, is, by standards Catullus sets elsewhere, overwhelming.[23] Theseus has no *fides*, cares not a whit for his promises (as line 144 reaffirms). The *deserto litore* of the first question seems to lead to the *neglecto numine* of the second. Theseus has lost all respect for the *numen divum*, the very accusation Catullus hurls against Lesbia in 76.3–4 when he asserts that he

> nec sanctam violasse fidem, nec foedere nullo
> divum ad fallendos numine abusum homines, . . .

Ariadne's curse is, however, to be fulfilled (line 204):

> annuit invicto caelestum numine rector; . . .

What was *neglecto* is in reality *invicto*, and any failure to worship the divinity of the gods will be punished by an all-too-vivid presentation of their power. Ariadne's accusation takes the reader from Crete to Dia and from Dia to Athens. As Theseus carried Ariadne from home and proved perfidious,[24] so now the results of the crime will be visited on his own father.

Ariadne's tone changes in the next two questions (lines 136–38). They are in the nature of pleas, no longer threatening. Will nothing bend his cruel purpose, she asks (as she does later in 175–76) ? Will he offer her no clemency from his pitiless heart ? The difference between what might have been and what actually is, a difference inherent in her questions, becomes now explicit as she sets off the *quondam* of the past (line 139) against the *nunc* of the present (line 143).[25] We recall the same distinction in 72. Even in 70 the thrice repeated *dicit* emphasizes the fact that Lesbia *said* she preferred to marry Catullus more than anyone else. But her *dicta* were likewise of little import.

This contrast of time present with time past leads the poet, as Ariadne, into six lines (143–48) of meditation on the infidelity of man:

> nunc iam nulla viro iuranti femina credat,
> nulla viri speret sermones esse fideles;

> quis dum aliquid cupiens animus praegestit apisci,
> nil metuunt iurare, nihil promittere parcunt:
> sed simul ac cupidae mentis satiata libido est,
> dicta nihil metuere, nihil periuria curant.

We will later draw in more detail comparisons between the Ariadne-Theseus episode and the description of the present ill times with which the poem concludes. Suffice to quote here lines 398 and 405–6, where Catullus inveighs against the lack of justice in the modern world, saying that men

> iustitiamque omnes cupida de mente fugarunt, . .
> omnia fanda nefanda malo permixta furore
> iustificam nobis mentem avertere deorum . . .

The phrase *cupidae mentis* of line 147 is echoed in *cupida de mente* of 398. The reader cannot but recall the situation of Ariadne in the later line. She is the image which corresponds to the generalizations with which the poem ends.

The next nine lines divide into two sections, 149–53 and 154–57. The first group returns to narration and to a direct address of Theseus. Ariadne's love for him triumphed over all other forms of affection. In order to save him, she even killed her own brother, and in return she is offered to beasts of prey and will lie unburied. Ariadne digresses at line 154 to speculate upon the origin of Theseus, who, she thinks, must be the offspring of a lioness or a Scylla to perform such actions against her.

The chief commentary on these thoughts is poem 60, where the poet also addresses some unknown person (it may or may not be Lesbia) who has failed him in his hour of need. I quote the entire poem:

> Num te leaena montibus Libystinis
> aut Scylla latrans infima inguinum parte
> tam mente dura procreavit ac taetra,
> ut supplicis vocem in novissimo casu
> contemptam haberes, a nimis fero corde ?

The parallels between the first three lines of this poem and 64.154–56 are both numerous and vivid. There is a close connection between Catullus' thoughts on his own *novissimo casu* and Ariadne's meditation on her supposedly imminent death (*extremo tempore*, line 169, contrasts with *tempore primo* two lines later). Ariadne considers herself about to be *dilaceranda feris*, with the result that her mind (or the poet's) immediately turns to the image of Theseus and the *leaena*. Reality has become metaphor. She is to be torn apart by wild animals, but Theseus is the spiritual beast who in leaving her caused her death. The lioness gives him birth, but it is of the deserter's mind (*mente*, 60.3) and heart (*corde*, 60.5) that the poet is speaking. It is his soul which is animal-like while his form is fair. The adjectives attached to the two nouns are also important. The mind is called *dura*. Its hard and unbending quality is reflected in the phrase *sola sub rupe* (64.154). The heart, in its turn, remains *fero*, an epithet which serves as commentary on the ambiguity latent in the whole section.[26]

Though there may be some connection between the *novissimo casu* of Catullus in 60 and the *casu acerbo* from which Manlius suffers in 68.1, the Laudamia-Protesilaus episode later in 68, to which we shall return in greater detail, offers an even closer parallel. In 68.105–7, for example, Catullus, very much involved in the feelings of Laudamia, mentions the Trojan war which drew Protesilaus away from her:

> quo tibi tum casu, pulcerrima Laudamia,
> ereptum est vita dulcius atque anima
> coniugium: . . .

This situation is not at all unlike that proposed by 64.157 when Ariadne asks Theseus if he is the kind of person

> talia qui reddis pro dulci praemia vita ?

Ariadne gave sweet life (*dulci vita*) to Theseus and he leaves her. Protesilaus leaves Laudamia even though he is *vita dulcius* to her. The *casus* is the same. Moreover the reversal pattern we have seen above is illustrated by the verb *eripui* in 64.150. She snatched Theseus from the jaws of death only to have him desert her in the same manner as Protesilaus departed from Laudamia (*ereptum est*, 68.106).[27]

Ariadne in her pain now cries out that even if it had not been in Theseus' heart to marry her because he feared the hard commands of a stern father (lines 160–63),

> attamen in vestras potuisti ducere sedes,
> quae tibi iucundo famularer serva labore,
> candida permulcens liquidis vestigia lymphis,
> purpureave tuum consternens veste cubile.

Ariadne would have come home to Theseus at least as servant if not as wife. The phraseology is quite unusual, displaying in Ariadne incredible devotion and the utmost submission to a stronger force, the weakest feminine impulse yielding to the adamant masculine. The thought here **briefly** expressed forms one of the basic ideas of 63, which seems to

R

represent certain salient aspects of the temperament of Catullus. The servitude demanded of Attis in *63* is even greater than that which Ariadne offers here, since it involves renouncing masculinity for abject slavery, whereas Ariadne need only be reduced to the lowest position for one of her own sex. Nevertheless the Catullus who, disguised in the form of Ariadne, proposes herself as servant for Theseus, is the same Catullus who, transformed imaginatively into Attis, will be the perpetual devotee of the Magna Mater. In other words the mistress/servant feeling, here experienced by Ariadne, finds its heightened and extreme expression in the emasculation of Attis.[28]

A complete change of thought occurs as Ariadne says (lines 164–66):

> sed quid ego ignaris nequiquam conquerar auris
> externata malo, quae nullis sensibus auctae
> nec missas audire queunt nec reddere voces ?

This passage is important, and typically Catullan, in two ways: first, it shows the dependence of his intense feelings on the senses, especially seeing and hearing; and second, it specifically draws attention to the need, in such a situation as Ariadne's, of the consolation of speaking and replying. There is no hope, she later cries (lines 186–87):

> nulla fugae ratio, nulla spes : omnia muta,
> omnia sunt deserta, ostentant omnia letum.

Desertion is a motif naturally present, but the key Catullan phrase is *omnia muta*. This imagery is particularly linked with death, as we may see for example in 96.1 and 101.4, especially the latter, where, thinking on his brother, Catullus cries,

> et mutam nequiquam alloquerer cinerem.

Likewise the world around Ariadne is dead. The pointedly repeated *nequiquam* in 101.4 and in 64.164 adds further poignancy to the vain uselessness of her cries, just as *mutam* coupled with *alloquerer* in *101* tells the reader that the poet for his part will speak, but will hear no reply from his beloved brother, for whom sympathy is now fruitless.

Merely the fact that his brother cannot reply to him in *101* and 65 makes it all the more important that he answer the *dicta* of Ortalus in the latter poem. Whatever they were, they deserve reply. Just as Ariadne must complain in vain to the unknowing breezes, so Catullus insists to Ortalus that (65.17):

> . . . tua dicta vagis nequiquam credita ventis.

Very similar imagery, but this time the crucial *nequiquam* will not be true. The poet can and must make answer. When, however, at the end of her speech Ariadne cries to the Eumenides, *meas audite querellas* (line 195), we realize that literally no one can hear and give help and sympathy, except the unseen furies whose help is vengeance for the dead, not life for the suffering.[29]

She is, in fact, *externata* with evil (the same word associated with the ardor of love in line 71). There is no person present to convey the active and manifest sympathy necessary in such a time of trial. In one poem of great suffering, *38*, Catullus had asked Cornificius for a brief *allocutio*. No matter how sad, anything would be comforting. Even such solace was denied Ariadne.[30]

The feelings which overcome Ariadne at this point form the heart of the remainder of her speech. In lines 171–76 she prays to Jupiter, wondering why all this has come upon her. Lines 177-81 return to the interrogative technique used earlier:

> nam quo me referam ? quali spe perdita nitor ?
> Idaeosne petam montes ? at gurgite lato
> discernens ponti truculentum dividit aequor.
> an patris auxilium sperem ? quemne ipsa reliqui
> respersum iuvenem fraterna caede secuta ?

This time she addresses herself instead of Theseus and asks whither she can turn now for help and consolation since the island offers none. She might return to Crete (though in truth she knows that the crime of her brother's death irrevocably bars such a recourse). In fact, as also for Attis, the sea is the great dividing line between true home and false, between lasting happiness and happiness for the moment leading to greater sorrow. The shore is the closest both characters can come to renewing what each now realizes is the only steadfast type of love.

The only thing she can do now is to call on the invisible furies to avenge her wrongs. The curse which comprises the final lines of her speech is important for the episode which follows.[31] In no other version of the legend is the curse of Ariadne connected with the death of Aegeus. Superficially this is the poet's way of linking two seemingly disparate events. More important, however, it helps to show the reactions of two people to one figure who betrays them both, of lover to lover separated by infidelity, and of father and son separated (as Aegeus thinks) by death. Catullus is no little part of both characters.

It will be seen that, taken as a whole, Ariadne's lament centers primarily around her own reactions to the departure of Theseus. But the beauty of the piece lies not in any over-reaching concepts which unify the whole, even though we retain the picture of the deserted Ariadne forever before our mind. Rather it is the series of approaches which she takes to her position which interests us. Around the idea of desertion (in which the loss of *fides* and *iustitia* was of equal importance with the loss of *amor*) the poet has written short elegiac and lyric comments, some four lines, some ten, none of them exactly like any other, but all looking back to the same initial situation and viewing it from various emotional angles. And the descriptions, which interweave among these thoughts, he has taken away from any prosaic setting in Rome or Verona or anywhere else, and placed where they will have the most imaginative effect upon the reader.

In brief, the portrayal of Ariadne, beautifully as it is crafted, is distinctive because of her special relationship with Catullus. Let others find in her speech the latent influence of writers from Homer to Lucretius. Every poet is born to tradition and conversant with his predecessors and contemporaries. Yet the source hunter should go no further. Ariadne expresses in the veiled terms which epic invites the struggles and aspirations which were Catullus' own.

III. Theseus and Aegeus

The curse of Ariadne ends at line 201, as she calls down punishment upon Theseus. And Jupiter, by making the universe tremble, acknowledges that the prayer will be fulfilled. To accomplish this and have the lover's forgetfulness redound to his own suffering, the poet once more turns back the clock to the time when Aegeus gave his final speech of farewell to his son departing for Crete. As the curse of Ariadne depended on the mind of Theseus (the word *mens* appears twice in lines 200–1), so also does its accomplishment (lines 207–9):

> ipse autem caeca mentem caligine Theseus
> consitus oblito dimisit pectore cuncta,
> quae mandata prius constanti mente tenebat, . .

The last line is all but repeated in line 238 at the end of Aegeus' speech. Yet the emphatic stress on Theseus' remembering and then forgetful mind in lines 210 and 238 serves to return the reader's thoughts to Theseus' treatment of Ariadne and to help forge a connecting link between the two episodes.

After a brief mention of the crucial *dulcia signa*, which Theseus forgets to raise upon return as he had been ordered, the digression begins. It presents at the outset the familiar Catullan picture of departure:

> namque ferunt olim, classi cum moenia divae
> linquentem gnatum ventis concrederet Aegeus,
> talia complexum iuveni mandata dedisse: . . .

Here the relationship is between father and son, the son leaving to go off on an adventure (this part of the story parallels the departure of Protesilaus in *68*, and of Ptolemy in *66*). We should recall here that in Catullus' own life there were two departures of paramount importance, different in outward detail, yet on the spiritual side, judging from the poet's reaction to them, interwoven and complicated. The first was the departure (such it must have been) of the brother and his subsequent death in the East. The second was the unfaithfulness of Lesbia. The Protesilaus-Laudamia episode in *68* combines these so intimately that it is sometimes hard to distinguish to whom the poet is applying his feelings, to the dead brother or the deserting Lesbia. Both themes are one in *68*. In *64* they are dealt with in separate sections. In the Ariadne episode it was Catullus' relationship with Lesbia which we saw was of paramount importance. The next event, shorter though it is, remains no less crucial. This time death is the outcome. I suggest that in it the poet is reflecting on his lost brother and, with himself as Aegeus, is speaking words not of hope for return, but of sadness looking to eternal separation.

Even before the speech begins these feelings are conveyed. If we turn to the imagery of the lines quoted above, *linquo* is a verb around which the thoughts of Catullus are much centered. It appears in line 117 when Ariadne is also leaving her parents. And since the word *complexum* (though a noun in one case, a participle in the other) appears in the lines subsequent to each, the poet was probably thinking back to the first passage. It could even be said that the whole emotional cast of the Theseus-Aegeus episode results from an enlargement of the thoughts contained in those lines devoted to Ariadne. Nor, when we think on Theseus' previous conduct and the imagery the poet attaches to it, does the phrase *ventis concrederet* leave much doubt as to the ultimate outcome of the story.

Let us take Aegeus' speech essentially line by line. The opening apostrophe —

> gnate mihi longa iucundior unice vita —

maintains a clear likeness to Catullus' frequent claim that he considered Lesbia dearer than life. Yet such an equation utilizes a comparative adjective only twice elsewhere. The first instance occurs in 68.106 where Laudamia realizes that the *coniugium* torn from her was *vita dulcius*.[32] The other passage is 65.10–11, where the poet is talking of his brother:

> numquam ego te, vita frater amabilior,
> aspiciam posthac ? . . .

This is the first of a series of comparisons we will make with 65 in elucidating the Aegeus passage, and the first where the brother is specifically mentioned.

With line 216,

> gnate, ego quem in dubios cogor dimittere casus,

the imagery begins to border on the sensual. Nor should we forget the simile of 68.119–24 when discussing line 217:

> reddite in extrema nuper mihi fine senectae, . . .

In *68*, Catullus is attempting to describe the extreme passion of love in terms of a relationship which has nothing at all to do with sex. And, even though in the first instance an aged sire has been reunited with his son while in the second a newborn grandson relieves his grandsire of the "vulture," the feeling which the grandfather experiences through contemplation of his daughter's late-born child is exactly that which Aegeus undergoes when he beholds his son returned to him in his late old age.[33]

Aegeus continues in line 218:

> quandoquidem fortuna mea ac tua fervida virtus
> eripit invito mihi te, cui languida nondum
> lumina sunt gnati cara saturata figura, . . .

Though *fortuna* is one of the key words in *68*,[34] it also appears in one other crucial spot, 101.5–6:

> quandoquidem fortuna mihi tete abstulit ipsum,
> heu miser indigne frater adempte mihi, . . .

The word *abstulit* (and also perhaps *adempte*) may find its parallel with the lines from *64* in the word *eripit*, but the surrounding words are more than chance occurrences, i.e., the phrase *quandoquidem fortuna* is repeated in the same metrical position in each passage, and the personal pronouns *mihi tete* of *101*, though linked with *mea ac tua*, are even closer to *mihi te* of 64.219.

The lines which follow are highly ambiguous, and without doubt consciously so. Especially words like *languida*,[35] *cara*, and *saturasset*, in terms of Catullan usage, can be applied to either mad passion or old age and death. *Luctus* is capable of a kindred double meaning. When, in line 226, Aegeus mentions *nostros . . . luctus nostraeque incendia mentis*, he is not only describing grief at parting but also the very pangs of love.[36] To define further the depth and quality of Aegeus' emotions, Catullus emphasizes, as he does in every other similar situation, the yearning eyes of the lover. Even here, then, in a basically spiritual relationship, the depth of the love the father bears his son is denoted in sensual as well as spiritual terms. The repetitions we have adduced from *101* and *65* show that the poet probably had his brother in mind. It remains only to say that Catullus considered himself almost in the place of father toward his brother. The death of his brother, as several passages in *68* reveal, marks the end of their *domus*.[37] Just as his brother's death for Catullus, so also now the death of Theseus would mean that Aegeus' family no longer exists: *domus* symbolizes continuity of tradition as well as personal affection.

Omitting lines 221–22 for the moment, let us continue with lines 223–24, where Aegeus cries in sorrow:

> sed primum multas *expromam mente* querellas
> canitiem terra atque infuso pulvere foedans, . . .

Though the objects involved are different — one refers to Aegeus' cries of woe, the other to poetic production cut off in sorrow and then continued by it — the situation is extraordinarily close to that of *65*, in the opening lines of which Catullus states that, because of his brother's death

> nec potis est dulcis Musarum *expromere* fetus
> *mens* animi, . . .

He can no longer produce the *dulcis fetus* of the Muses, verses of love and happiness,[38] but rather he must sing *maesta carmina* (65.12) while he mourns in the midst of his great sadness (*maeroribus*, 65.15). These plaints for the dead brother are surely akin, as the repeated imagery suggests, to the lament which Aegeus utters in his grief (*maesto*, line 210).

The community between the two poems would stop there were it not for the simile which follows. The songs Catullus sings in mourning are (65.13–14)

> qualia sub densis ramorum concinit umbris
> Daulias, absumpti fata gemens Ityli . . . ,

like those which Philomela sang for her son Itylus, torn from her. By thus depicting in *65* the relationship with his brother in parental terms,

Catullus reveals clearly the psychological impetus behind the whole Aegeus-Theseus episode. The poet is experiencing over again the death of his brother. Aegeus utters the cries of woe and performs the acts of a funeral even before anyone has died. Instead of giving Theseus a joyous sendoff, wishing him the best of fortune, he clothes him with the blackness of death, for he, as poet, knows beforehand what the real outcome of the journey will be.

Hence it is not unexpected that throughout this episode Catullus exhibits his habitual intensity about going and returning. Its most vivid manifestation occurs in lines 236–37 as Aegeus bids his son, upon safe return, to raise a white sail

> quam primum cernens ut laeta gaudia mente
> agnoscam cum te reducem aetas prospera sistet.

The poet means that upon his son's return the life of the old man will again become prosperous and livable.[39] For this reason when, in the lines which follow, Aegeus thinks that Theseus no longer lives, he takes his own life.

Catullus' feelings for his brother, as exhibited in *68*, are all but the same. He realizes that true *gaudia* have gone out of his life since his brother's death. And, along with all *commoda*, he has lost his ability to create poetry. And in each case, as we have said, Catullus focuses his strongest emotions upon a journey. To describe the departure (and at least hoped-for return) of Theseus, Catullus uses imagery which recurs frequently in such lyrics as *9* and *31* to express the pleasure of arrival and the joy of seeing someone else come back after an absence.[40] Aegeus offers the first hint of this theme in line 221 as he cries,

> non ego gaudens laetanti pectore mittam, . . .[41]

The emotions which Catullus centers on words such as *laetus*, *gaudium*, and their cognates can also be illustrated elsewhere within *64* itself by appealing to lines 33–34, where the poet describes the royal home and its guests as follows:

> . . . oppletur laetanti regia coetu:
> dona ferunt prae se, declarant gaudia vultu.

There happiness is the order of the day. And the context is not only that of marriage, but specifically the arrival of the invited to throng the house. And though the wedding guests are not returning home, as is Theseus, the emotions caused by arrival are in each case evoked in similar fashion.

Through such vocabulary, the poet describes his own sensations

aroused by the phrase *te reducem.* Catullus feels strongly about the return
of Veranius in *9* and of himself in *31.* Where return could never be
achieved, the loss was irretrievable, as in the case of his brother, whom he
now subconsciously (or even consciously) involves in the figure of the
forgetful Theseus.

The lines which follow Aegeus' speech are most crucial because they
unify the two sections of the digression.[42] It is the similarity between the
actual situations of Aegeus and Ariadne which first strikes the reader.
Aegeus stands at the topmost bastion of his citadel looking out over the
sea (lines 241–42):

> at pater, ut summa prospectum ex arce petebat,
> anxia in assiduos absumens lumina fletus, . . .

This very kind of prospect confronted Ariadne, as she gazed seaward in
longing for her beloved.[43] To show Aegeus catching sight of the ship,
the poet employs the very same word he had utilized when describing
Ariadne's first glimpse of Theseus (*conspexit*, lines 86 and 243), and
many other words, such as *anxius, luctus,* and *assiduus,* recur in both
passages.[44] But there is no need to elaborate connections of this sort, for
the similarity of situation is undeniable: two people are both standing
on eminences looking out to sea and losing, or about to lose, someone
beloved.

The most obvious connecting link between the two episodes is the
curse of Ariadne and its effects. The words which Theseus had once
uttered to Ariadne and the *mandata* of Aegeus to Theseus are essentially
parallel. Both depend on memory. In the first part emphasis lies on the
promissa (line 59) of the *immemor iuvenis* (line 58). Line 123 renews this
same stress on the *immemor pectus* of Theseus, and of course Ariadne
picks up the idea again in her speech (lines 134–35).[45] But the hero's
fallibility is exhibited most pointedly in lines 207–9:

> ipse autem caeca mentem caligine Theseus
> consitus oblito dimisit pectore cuncta,
> quae mandata prius constanti mente tenebat,

while his father repeats like words, urging (lines 231–32):

> tum vero facito ut memori tibi condita corde
> haec vigeant mandata, nec ulla oblitteret aetas; . . .

Catullus makes the forgetful mind the explicit link between the two
passages when he says of Theseus in lines 247–48:

> . . . qualem Minoidi luctum
> obtulerat mente immemori, talem ipse recepit.

It is surely now clear that in the figure of Theseus, whose *mens immemor* caused both Ariadne's trials and Aegeus' death, Catullus manifests the double suffering caused him by Lesbia and by his brother. The very words of Ariadne, in her final appeal to the Furies, reflect concisely this twofold result of Theseus' actions:

> vos nolite pati nostrum vanescere luctum,
> sed quali solam Theseus me mente reliquit,
> tali mente, deae, funestet seque suosque.

It takes the same kind of character, she observes, to kill one's parent as it does to depart from her. *Reliquit* and *funestet* are to her nearly one and the same. Likewise the same grief as she receives from his departure he will suffer from his father's death. In other words, Ariadne knows that the quality which Theseus most lacks is *pietas*, which he has shown neither in his love for her nor in his devotion to his father.

The phrase *seque suosque* has a pronounced Catullan ring (the contexts of 58.3 and 79.2 show varying uses of it). The genuine, more enduring relationship is that of father to son. Theseus' feelings for Ariadne were merely passing, even though Ariadne's passion was intense and strong. As we have seen from *68*, Catullus hoped ideally to combine the physical with the spiritual in love. It was not only by forgetfulness but also by his unusual impiety that Theseus could, at one and the same time, destroy both Ariadne and his own father, both lover and parent.

The much discussed lines in *72*:

> dilexi tum te non tantum ut vulgus amicam,
> sed pater ut gnatos diligit et generos . . . ,

find their archetype in epic form in the affection shown for Theseus by Aegeus. It is the same as that which the poet felt for his brother, and accounts for the superficially odd comparison in *72*. It was possible that Lesbia might be able to realize for him the combination which formed his ideal love, and apparently she did so, but only for a time. It is certainly true that in his happiness the poet could not, or rather did not need to, formulate the twofold aspect of what he sought in love. Only the suffering brought about by Lesbia's infidelity could make this clear, even to him.[46]

To those who urge that *64* contains nothing of the true Catullus because he was not one to veil his feelings in such a manner, we could reply with many arguments. The most interesting for our present purposes is to appeal to the Laudamia-Protesilaus simile in *68* (lines 73–130), to which occasional references have already been made. This simile is a little epic like *64*, though a good deal shorter. Yet we know that there the poet *is* telling his own story, and it is easy to trace his mind at work during its progress. Suffice to say that Protesilaus is the connecting link in *68* as Theseus is in *64*, for he not only leaves (deserts, Catullus would say) Laudamia as Lesbia did the poet, but he also dies in Troy like Catullus' brother. *68* therefore offers Protesilaus as an example of the same combination of double suffering which Theseus caused, and fuses in the character of Laudamia Catullus' own intense and individual love for Lesbia and for his brother. It thus merges in one episode that to which in *64* Catullus devotes two separate sections, unified in the end by similarity of conception and exposition.

The numerous connections, then, between the two sections of the digression are both external and internal. The poet deliberately emphasizes the external by means of plot and crucial imagistic repetition. We may find the true bond, however, only within the mind of the poet, in his ideas about love and in the aspects of his own feelings which he elaborates through his characters. Ariadne, disappointed of her ideal lover, looks back as Attis looked back, to the true home of the past. Also, in Aegeus' love for Theseus, we find epitomized Catullus' quest for *pietas*, for the true love between human beings, the deeply felt devotion which is only remotely connected with the sensual. But this quest fails. Aegeus' love for his son and Theseus' subsequent forgetfulness, her mother's love for Ariadne and the daughter's flight, are similar disasters. As Catullus says often of Lesbia, it was she

. . . quam Catullus unam
plus quam se atque suos amavit omnes, . .

The phrase gains all the more meaning when compared with Ariadne's and Aegeus' plight.

Lines 249–50 return to the opening picture of Ariadne. The digression has gone full circle and, with outward picture and inner metaphor, the poet returns to the initial emotion. Then the spell is broken. A mood bordering almost on death is replaced by life. Bacchus comes with his rowdy throng, seeking the love of Ariadne. Once more all is young, vigorous, full of joy. Perhaps this is the scene which the poet meant originally to have depicted on the coverlet. He does, after all, compare Ariadne to a Bacchant in line 60, and there is not much difference in sound from her *heu* to the *euhoe* shouted by Bacchus' followers. We have

7+C.P.

shown why it would not be difficult for Catullus to be carried away by the picture of the deserted heroine to the point of telling a tale which he had not otherwise planned to include in his narrative. But this is mere speculation. The arrival of Bacchus changes our mood entirely and prepares us for a return to the initial picture of the poem, the happy circumstances attending the wedding of Peleus and Thetis.

IV. PELEUS AND THETIS

The sections of the poem which surround the Ariadne digression deal with Peleus and Thetis. The song of the Fates begins with line 303, and everything up to that point, save the long interlude, consists of a description of the marriage, the circumstances under which Peleus and Thetis first met, when and how the ceremony took place. The narrative divides into two almost equal sections, lines 1–49 and 265–302. The mood of each is the same, and forms such a complete contrast with that of the digression that we cannot but seek the reason for it. For Ariadne all is empty, dark, and above everything else *muta*, yet for the happy pair throngs of people, including the gods themselves, mob the house, filling it with sounds of joy. The black silence of utter despair which surrounds the deserted Ariadne is juxtaposed with the bright shining happiness of the ideal wedding.[47]

Ostensibly, then, the common bond between the two tales is marriage, the one happy in its consummation, the other ill-fated in its sad conclusion. But there is more than this. Let us first examine the atmosphere in which the poet evolves the tale of Peleus and Thetis.

It begins, characteristically enough, on a mountain top. Like the *phaselus* of *4*, whose voyage covers both Catullus' own special journey and the universal course of human life, the Argo was born once long ago on the crest of Mr. Pelion. Thence the Argonauts set out on their journey to capture the Golden Fleece. The ship is fleet and Athena lends her aid with a favorable breeze. It ploughs the sea, which grows hoary (*incanuit*, line 13) with the churning, and out of the whitening deep the Nereids peep to look at the strange sight.[48] It was on this occasion that Peleus saw Thetis (lines 16–18):

> illa, atque (haud) alia, viderunt luce marinas
> mortales oculis nudato corpore Nymphas
> nutricum tenus exstantes e gurgite cano.

Images of whiteness and shimmer are connected by Catullus above all others with happiness, and these of the sea are the first of many instances in *64*.[49] A setting similar to this recurs during the epilogue of the poem. In the opening lines Catullus depicts the specific occasion when men saw the nymphs of the sea rising nude from the water, resulting in the union between mortal and divine which this section of the poem stresses as a prime consideration of the heroic age. At the poem's conclusion, he generalizes from the particular to describe the times in broader terms (lines 384–86):

> praesentes namque ante domos invisere castas
> heroum, et sese mortali ostendere coetu,
> caelicolae nondum spreta pietate solebant.

There is no doubt that Catullus has here in mind the opening part of the poem, the joyous meeting of Peleus and Thetis in that ideal age when men were righteous and the gods consequently did not hesitate to show themselves to the sight of mortals.

The atmosphere of the voyage, carried on as far as need be, is dropped after line 18. The desired result has been achieved. Peleus is *incensus amore* for Thetis (like Bacchus for Ariadne in line 253, a brief inroad of the gods in an otherwise quite mortal story). Thetis does not disdain *humanos hymenaeos*, and above all the *pater ipse*, Jupiter himself, blesses the match. The idea is important for Catullus, and he reiterates it in lines 26–27. There is no hint of jealousy on the part of Jupiter as the legend usually has it. Rather he sanctions the union, thereby throwing into greater relief the love between the happy couple.

For this reason it is important to compare lines 21 and 26–27 with the sentiments of 70.2 (Lesbia had said that she would prefer to marry the poet even more than Jupiter) and 72.2, where Lesbia protests that she would love Catullus even if Jupiter himself sought her.[50] When Catullus addresses the hero in lines 26–27 as

> Thessaliae columen Peleu, cui Iuppiter ipse,
> ipse suos divum genitor concessit amores . . . ,

he surely means to portray Peleus as surpassing, even if just for an instant, Jupiter in his happiness. It was Jupiter who, in giving up his love for Thetis, allowed Peleus to fulfill his desire. This is the ideal, just as the opening lines of *70* and *72* express in personal terms what Catullus' view of perfect love was. Momentarily he is greater than Jupiter because Lesbia loves him, just as Peleus, in the bliss of his marriage with Thetis, seems almost equal to the chief of the gods.[51] The second halves of both *70* and *72* take up the real, what actually comes of the dreams (on Catullus' part) and expression (on Lesbia's) of perfection, dreams which are shattered by the reality of her vulgarity. The reference to Jupiter, as an aspect of the perfect marriage defined by the short poems, offers a further hint that the contrasting section of *64*, devoted to Ariadne, is indeed the reenactment of the second halves of both *70* and *72*, the truth of reality after the fleeting hope of gaining the ideal goal. This hope finds a strikingly vivid, truthful, and Roman portrayal in *61*. The episode of Peleus and Thetis is its epic counterpart.

The poet is so taken with the picture he has drawn that he bursts in with an aside of his own (lines 22–23):

> o nimis optato saeclorum tempore nati
> heroes, salvete, deum genus!

When Catullus does this in epic statement, as at the end of *63*, it means much as a disclosure of his personal involvement. Here once more the thought reflects that of the closing lines of the poem. This was the great age of mankind, this the *optatum saeclorum tempus* in which men married happily and the gods blessed the union. Peleus will be happy (lines 25–26):

> teque adeo eximie taedis felicibus aucte,
> Thessaliae columen, Peleu, . . .

In much the same words the Fates begin their song to Peleus.[52] It would seem that Catullus can, like the Parcae, detach himself and admire the beauty and happiness of Peleus' love. The question with which he concludes the opening section (lines 28–30) almost implies amazement at the good fortune of the lovers. Could such a thing really happen to a mortal? the poet asks, repeating the *te* of direct address in lines 25, 28, and 29. He can separate himself from this love and admire. He can only partake in Ariadne's sadness.

The scene changes in line 31, and the generalized statement of line 22 becomes the particular. The poet's universal feelings about the age become centered on the special event about to take place. The six lines which follow (lines 32–37) paint a portrait which could without exaggeration be called Catullus' ideal setting, uniting the beauty of home with the pleasure of arrival, which in this case is doubly gratifying because of the future wedding. All Thessaly crowds the house (lines 32–34):

> advenere, domum conventu tota frequentat
> Thessalia, oppletur laetanti regia coetu:
> dona ferunt prae se, declarant gaudia vultu.

Much of the imagery recurs shortly. It was even of his *ianuae frequentes* that Attis thought, as symbolizing his lost home. The throngs of people mean as much to the poet as the joy which they display.

Catullus places the reader as an onlooker upon the threshold who is to behold the palace receding (line 43) in its brightness.[53] It gleams with gold and silver. The ivory glistens, the goblets flash. Indeed (line 46),

> tota domus gaudet regali splendida gaza.

The house has become for the moment a person, capable of displaying the same emotion as the guests. Exactly such an emotion Catullus imputes to a personified and rejoicing Sirmio at the end of *31*. Nor are the events dissimilar, for he is also arriving home, back to his beloved peninsula. He has left the fields of Bithynia to return, and his home displays obvious pleasure at the advent of its master, just as the house of Peleus glories in the arrival of the wedding visitors.[54]

So begins the poem. From the top of Pelion to the meeting of the lovers to the bright colors on the wedding couch, all the scenes are delightful. The poet conveys thus his own happiness, and makes the outer situation mirror the ideal beauty of such a perfect union among lovers. When the poet returns to this picture, after the digression on Ariadne, the mortal guests are departing and the gods beginning to arrive. The poet is true to his initial statement that the event shows the unity of gods and men. After a beautiful simile comparing the departing mortals to the sea at dawn ruffled by the rising winds which, in turn, make the waves glimmer as they recede into the distance (sight and sound could scarcely be unified imaginatively to greater effect), the poet turns to the gods. Chiron is the first to arrive (like the Argo, *e vertice Pelei*) bringing *silvestria dona* (lines 280–83). The imagery lends much to the atmosphere already established, but also adds a new note of youth and bloom, preparing the reader for the wedded joys to be described in the song of the Fates. Once again it is upon the house that Catullus, resorting to words of sound to convey the excitement of a lovely odor, centers his feelings (line 284):

> . . . permulsa domus iucundo risit odore.

Catullus maintains this mood up to line 302, as the home of Peleus gradually grows green with the gifts of nature brought by the divine guests.

Even here, however, the bliss of the wedding does not remain unbroken, for the appearance of Prometheus, which has never been adequately explained, somehow breaks the enchanting spell, as the description of Achilles does again later. Critics seize rather lamely upon two minor versions of the Peleus and Thetis myth which make Prometheus the person who warns Jupiter that whoever marries Thetis will beget a son stronger than himself. The lines devoted to him run as follows (294–97):

> post hunc consequitur sollerti corde Prometheus,
> extenuata gerens veteris vestigia poenae,
> quam quondam *silici* restrictus *membra* catena
> persolvit pendens e verticibus praeruptis.

The description seems needlessly verbose unless one compares the lines where Catullus describes Attis' act of emasculation (63.5–6):

> devolsit ili acuto sibi pondera *silice*,
> itaque ut relicta sensit sibi *membra* sine viro, . . .

Not only are the italicized words repeated, but there are parallels between *persolvit* and *devolsit*, *restrictus* and *relicta*, *pendens* and *pondera*. It is as if the poet himself wanted to appear at the wedding, a bit of the present in the happiness of the past, to show just what the evil power of woman is.[55]

Thus far it is basically atmosphere and mood which the poet has sought to convey. He has been building up a setting for the song of the Fates, who make their appearance in line 303.

V. THE SONG OF THE FATES

The song of the Fates is of course the wedding hymn itself, and should be designed to elaborate the future happiness of Peleus and Thetis and magnify their glories. Yet, at the same time, it takes one of their proudest boasts, their future son Achilles, and identifies him (despite the heroic attributes attached to him) with the bloody brutality of war. Moreover, the song stands apart from the symmetry of the whole.

The song itself, however, is finely symmetrical, and close analysis shows that it is constructed in the characteristic form of a digression. It starts off in lines 328–37 with a further allusion to the ideal love. The personal frame of reference gives way to abstract statement in lines 334–37, where the *domus* is said to roof over the two lovers and yet is conjoined symbolically with *amor* of the next line — the house symbolizes the structure of love. Just as the house *contexit*, the love *coniunxit*.[56] The result is a compact noteworthy for its concord.[57] These same thoughts are resumed at the end of the song (lines 372–81). The lovers are urged: *optatos . . . coniungite amores* in a *felici foedere*. There is no worry that Thetis will be *discors* (line 379).

Just as the Peleus-Thetis episode surrounds the Ariadne digression, a happy event framing a sad, so these groups of ten lines each, which begin and end the song, form a distinct contrast with the intervening section. This deals with Achilles, the tragic offspring of the happy pair. The reader at first wonders why Catullus adds this episode. (He warns of its violently contrasting nature by the mere outward technique of the digression, which resumes the feelings of joy at the end without allowing any excessively bitter taste to remain.)

However, there is no doubt that the poet is carried away by the picture he is creating. Our sympathy never lies with the hero Achilles. He is fearless, brave, and fleet of foot (how finely the poet gives metaphorical expression to the Homeric epithet in lines 340–41!).[58] No hero can compare with him, when the Phrygian fields are steeped with gore.[59] The poet seems almost sarcastic in the next stanza (lines 348–51) when he says that the mothers recognized his *virtutes* as they beat their breasts during their sons' funerals. The situation reminds us of Aegeus in line 224. Just as the reader's mind is scarcely centred on the *fervida virtus* of Theseus there, so also our sympathy rests with the aged women in their grief, and not with the ruthless hero.

Catullus gives symbolic form to this characteristic in the effective simile which follows (lines 353–55):

> namque velut densas praecerpens messor aristas
> sole sub ardenti flaventia demetit arva,
> Troiugenum infesto prosternet corpora ferro.

Similar imagery was used in 48.5 to depict an overwhelming number. The *aristae* are the bodies of the Trojans whom Achilles mows down indiscriminately.[60] The hot sun places the warriors in the prime of life, while the violence of the scene is enhanced by the verb *prosternet*.[61]

The imagery in the next stanza changes from land to water, but the same ironic tone still remains. It is now the wave of the Scamander which bears witness to his *magnis virtutibus* (line 357). The river bears the bodies. But the poet does not allow us to forget the reaping imagery of the previous stanza, because the carnage is pictured as rife with *caesis . . . corporum acervis* — slaughtered piles of bodies which, like heaps of grain, block the passage of the river and warm it with gore.

And the final witness to Achilles' prowess, the one particularly gruesome achievement singled out from the nameless heap, is the death of Polyxena, a murder especially "heroic," the poet ironically implies, because accomplished after the hero's death (lines 362–64):

s

253

> denique testis erit morti quoque reddita praeda,
> cum teres excelso coacervatum aggere bustum
> excipiet niveos perculsae virginis artus.

The tomb is as lofty as the river is deep,[62] and the previous imagistic strand is again carried on as the *acervi* of the slaughtered foemen become the tomb *coacervatum*. The image is so skillfully wrought by the poet that the reader's eye climbs the tomb — which instead of being polished or round becomes a heap of blood-red carnage — only to find the white-limbed virgin on the top, sacrificed to the ideal of heroism which lives in spirit though dead in the flesh. The poet elaborates further on the picture (lines 368–70):

> alta Polyxenia madefient caede sepulcra
> quae, velut ancipiti succumbens victima ferro,
> proiciet truncum summisso poplite corpus.

The lofty tomb is soaked in her blood. She is both an offering sacrificed on an altar and a victim of war. The word *ferro* recalls the *infestum ferrum* which Achilles himself had used (line 355), and the fact that it is *anceps* but adds to the ambiguity, for the war ax of the Romans was also usually double-bladed. She is just one more body among the other dead, only more pathetic than the rest. So ends the Achilles digression, and with it we return to the happy bridal couple.

One can only guess why the Achilles passage was written at all. The triumph of brutality over gentleness is another way of expressing the contrast between vulgarity and chastity which is nothing new to Catullus. The purity of the virgin is only further emphasized when put in contrast with the overwhelming masculine rage of Achilles. The plough always defeats the flower. Perhaps there is another reason. Troy means one event of special importance to Catullus — the death of his brother. When he thinks of the Trojan war in *68* the result is a repetition of the lines earlier in the poem on the sad loss of the brother. The atmosphere is much the same in each case. The men are summoned away from home to battle around the walls. The Parcae knew of the results beforehand (68.85) as they sing of them in *64.* And in the end only *sepulcra* remain. Out of all the virtues (*omnium virtutum*: 68.90) the only thing left is *acerba cinis*, and the bitterest is that of Catullus' brother. This is what Troy and the Trojan war meant to him. *64* touches upon the prowess of Achilles in epic terms, but the personal events of his own life may well be at the root of Catullus' elaboration.

At any rate, the song of the Fates is bitter and sorrowful. It is a lament for the loss of purity and the former contact men had with the gods.

Though Achilles is associated with the glorious marriage of Peleus and Thetis, nevertheless the brutality of his actions somehow helps bridge the gap between the ideal/past section of the poem and the real/present. He is part of the heroic age, yet the brilliance of his deeds is tainted by a certain unheroic quality. Unnecessary blood was shed in his honor. Though by no means specifically referring to civil war, the poet seems almost to create the same aura in picturing the murderous deeds of Achilles as he does through the description of the shedding of fraternal blood in the poem's conclusion. Certainly Polyxena becomes an almost symbolic Ariadne, sacrificed to the brutality of the heroic/masculine soul. And in this respect she is a figure of Catullus himself, the feminine flower of *11* sheared by the violence of the plough which, caring nothing for its beauty, cuts it heedlessly down.

Whatever the connection, Achilles' delight in the shedding of blood and the horrors of war leads directly into the lines which commence the description of the present in the poem's epilogue (lines 397–99):

> sed postquam tellus scelere est imbuta nefando
> iustitiamque omnes cupida de mente fugarunt,
> perfudere manus fraterno sanguine fratres, . . .

The word *imbuta* implies the drinking up of gore, a fact the poet specifies a few lines later with the phrase *sanguine fratrum* (and *perfudere* has an ironic connection with *perfundat* in line 330). Hence the sadness which the reader feels in the song of the Fates is deliberately made explicit, for it also, like the lament of Ariadne, is a commentary on the evils of the times.

VI. Epilogue and Conclusion

The two sections into which the epilogue divides, lines 382–96, detailing the attendance of the gods in the ceremonies of mankind during the heroic age, and lines 397–408, picturing the present ways of the world, which through evil have driven the gods far hence, seem strangely un-Catullan in theme at first and much more akin to certain passages in the *Georgics* where Virgil inveighs against the civil wars. But so strong and clear is the stamp of Catullus upon these verses that we cannot help finding therein an epic statement of his own thoughts. The heroic age contrasts with the present decay, and it is in terms of sexual purity or foulness that the poet interprets the division. The gods were accustomed to visit the houses of men when they were *castae*, and to show themselves willingly before *pietas* was spurned. Nemesis and Minerva, Mars and

7*

Bacchus, all joined in religious worship and daily life. Afterwards the
earth was imbued with *scelus*, and *iustitia* was put to flight. This seems
to be the only deliberate reference to civil war.[63] The lines which follow
detail in abundance the manifold sexual aberrations in which Catullus
found the key to the degradation of the times. A father desires the death
of his son in order to marry the son's bride. A mother loves her son, to
the defilement of the household gods. *Pietas* has become *impietas* (lines
403–4), *fanda* are confused with *nefanda*, justice is no longer at hand
(line 406).

The relationships are all perverse, all involving parents and their
children, as if to Catullus this were the worst type of offense against
moral purity. When the intense spiritual affection between parents and
children is violated for mere sensual ends, the worst of evils has occurred.[64]
The mother bears the burden of a double impiety — she is first called
impia (line 403) because of her relations with her son and then (line 404)
because she had no hesitation to *divos scelerare parentes*. The total picture
has much in common with the father's accomplishments in 67.23–24:

> sed pater illius gnati violasse cubile
> dicitur et miseram conscelerasse domum.

Again it is noteworthy that the *domus* possesses a twofold nature: it is
the *cubile* of 67.23, a symbol of sensual pleasure, yet it also stands for the
divos parentes of 64.404. This spiritual quality of reverence and awe is
also concentrated on the *penates* of 9.3 and *lar* of 31.9. The father hence
performs a double breach of piety by his unnatural act in 67, for he is
said not only to *violasse cubile* of his son but also to *conscelerasse domum*, to
have violated the symbol of true relations between parents and children.
To make the idea even clearer, Catullus calls the house *miseram*, as if it
were a person in actual pain at the act of force. He adds that it was only
an *impia mens* (line 25) which could have perpetrated such a deed, and
cries later in sarcasm (line 29):

> egregium narras mira pietate parentem.

The *mira pietas* of the father could not be better scorned than by the
explicit description of his crime that follows.

And all this, though lacking deliberate application, suggests Theseus'
treatment of Ariadne, not in regard to the seduction (hardly a crime in
the Roman calendar), but to his subsequent lack of *pietas* and *iustitia*.
The ideal past can in no way be found in the all-too-real present. Like
the bronze age, as delineated in Hesiod's pessimistic progress, the gods
no longer deign nor desire to partake in the ways of men (lines 407–8,

reflecting 384–85). When *pietas* is spurned, the result is not limited to a new lack of worship for the gods. Piety no longer exists on the human level, because men fail to be chaste in their dealings with each other.

The body of the poem, leading up to the lines of the epilogue, reveals exactly the same distinction that divides the final verses, and only when the analogy is pressed does the poem fall into a unified whole. The steadfast happiness of Peleus and Thetis, which contrasts with the infidelity of Theseus, is the product of that ideal age pictured in the first part of the epilogue. In the story of Ariadne we find the poet describing himself, but in so doing he becomes an example of the spirit of his own times. The very point which Ariadne makes in lines 143–48, with specific reference to Theseus, is here generalized into the lack of justice which pervades the modern world.

Indeed, Catullus found himself constantly surrounded by, and fighting against, that degeneracy of which the vulgarity of Lesbia was but a small part. Perhaps a brief word of further explanation is in order for such a claim. There is no denying that Catullus was very much a part of the press of life which swirled around him, but this in no way categorizes him as a cleverly gifted *debauché*. That he enjoyed life and described some of its more sordid aspects does not necessarily mean that he ordered his own existence in the manner he imputes to others. Indeed he protests against this very accusation when he says, in his oft imitated statement,

> nam castum esse decet pium poetam
> ipsum, versiculos nihil necesse est.

He also gives abundant evidence that his age was marked, amid its countless expressions of individuality, by the longing and search for some *modus vivendi* which transcended day-to-day life. The ideal, which was ever before his eyes but only briefly seemed attainable, takes its shape in this poem in the relationship between Peleus and Thetis.

The final lines are thus another unifying factor for the whole poem. They are of a rare sort for Catullus. To moralize was not his usual bent, even though here was one of the few occasions in his poetry where he could suitably do so. We have seen Catullus' deep involvement in the characters of Ariadne and Aegeus and traced his violent reaction to the figures of Theseus and Achilles. The organic links between the various episodes of the digression are found in the experience of the poet. Yet it is the final lines which make clear the design of the poem as a whole, and show exactly what goal the poet had in mind by the abrupt juxtaposition of two such seemingly diverse stories. The moralizing is for a purpose and is in order. The particular structure of *64* almost demands it for completion.

The fact that the Theseus-Ariadne episode adorns the marriage couch is scarcely an argument against the time differentiation which we have proposed. It is not the actual chronological sequence of events which is important, for this is gradually lost sight of in the vivid contrast which arises between the two episodes. The mere fact that the poet breaks into the happy story of Peleus and Thetis with a tale of profound sadness is proof enough that his thoughts were centred not on external temporal regularity, but rather upon the internal emotional effect which the juxtaposition caused. It is only by visualizing the resulting contrast as the tension between ideal and real that the full effect of the poem's balance is achieved.

Moreover, it is just because Catullus never states his direct involvement that he can write the final lines at all. If he were telling the tale of his own woes without the facade of epic to hide the personal intensity, he could never sit back and moralize. Yet unless we realize Catullus' own participation in the character of Ariadne and grasp the fact that it is indeed his own present story he is unfolding, the ending makes sense only as a prosaic moralistic appendage. As it is, this is the only place in the whole of Catullus where he could point a moral of such a sort, and its appropriateness is not only undoubted but demanded, because it unifies the poem and makes clear the design of the whole.

The ending is like a coda which draws together the many themes of a gigantic musical exposition. Catullus may seem here to sacrifice some of his usual Mozartian combination of tenderness, delicacy, and innate passion (the veil of suffering is hard to penetrate) for a Wagner-like quality of movement which depends not on lyric themes, but rather on the effect of a large and sweeping design. Since time is of little import, this poem seems mere rhetoric to those bent on interpreting it as part of a past tradition. E. A. Poe, in words limited because their direction was toward his own age, found the long poem an impossibility and documented his argument by casting a somewhat prejudiced eye on the *Iliad*, a poem which seemed to him only a series of lyrical efforts loosely joined together. Yet the admitted goal of many among the greatest of the Romantic poets (and Catullus is a "romantic," both through his own personality and through the temper of his age) was to write a long poem. The composition of short poems, beautiful in their fleeting selves, was often considered only an apprenticeship for things more grand in conception and outlook. *64* is, in a certain sense, to Catullus what *Hyperion* and *Prometheus Unbound* are to Keats and Shelley. It contains within it somewhere reflections of almost every major subject which interested him. Yet, great as are the long poems of the Romantics, Catullus here surpasses them with a sustained level of achievement which they did not maintain outside their lyric efforts.

The restless spirit of Catullus is revealed here as nowhere in his shorter poems, a spirit always yearning for a perfection which could never be achieved and at the same time partaking to a heightened degree in human emotions. Catullus could only rarely accept things as he found them, but rather propelled himself into an unceasing inquiry for what was better. In the manner of Baudelaire, he was a poet very much involved in both the sapphires and the mire of life, who yet demanded exterior exactness in everything from personal charm to the appearance of a manuscript, as a token of inner beauty. These are the two sides of the coin for Catullus. Such dichotomies also exist for Lucretius, whose self-imposed pattern ever fell victim to his personality and creative powers. In a very different and much more worldly manner, Cicero's idealism was likewise constantly shattered by the buffets of reality. *64* is the final expression of this tension in Catullus. In fact nothing less than the complete scope of the poet's own imagination is the central unifying core for the poem. To read it thus is to treat the work not as an obscure byproduct but as the copestone of Catullus' genius.

Nor are we justified in assuming that the epyllion could never be a vehicle for personal statement (an argument which seems to imply that Catullus could only be himself when writing in shorter verse forms).[65] Indeed, the trend of recent scholarship seems to suggest that the epyllion was not a stereotyped genre, incapable of flexibility to suit circumstances, if indeed it was a fixed genre at all. Yet, assuming that it was, it is often taken for granted that the epyllion, being perhaps a Hellenistic form, could never be used, however subtly, to express personal feelings, and that a poem such as *64* must be the result only of Alexandrian trends in a poet.

We have attempted to prove the opposite. This is not to say that there are no Alexandrian elements in *64*. Catullus could not and surely did not want to ignore tradition blindly. Nor, however, was he a poet to be bound by it when its appeal to him was not of a personal nature. Even those who seek to find the influence of Alexandria upon *64* are forced to admit how uncharacteristic the poem most often is. It is neither excessively learned nor obscure. It does not tell a story for the sake of knowledge displayed, but, on the contrary, turns two mythological tales into moving personal documents where personal intensity triumphs over any inherited stylistic devices inimical to the creation of fine poetry. If with 64 Catullus is making further acknowledgement of his debt to Alexandria, it is a very strange manner of expression indeed. Far from choosing the epic genre because it offered opportunity for mere literary exercise, he found that only here could he state his own situation as he now lived it, and as he hoped he might have but did not, in terms first veiled and then painfully clear.

This raises another point: if the poem is such a personal document, why did not the poet write in autobiographical fashion and tell his own tale in the first person ? It would be easy to answer this by saying that Catullus was carried away by the situation of Ariadne and, merging his own feelings with hers, used her as a mask for himself. But I think that another issue could also be raised in response, the origin of the subjective love-elegy.

If the genres of Latin literature are viewed in terms of what we still possess, it is only by means of the love-elegy that Catullus in his own person could have given a lengthy description of exactly what his situation was toward Lesbia. But this genre was probably not yet developed. Catullus himself may have been in the process of evolving it.[66] We find the germs of the subjectivism in all his epigrammatical poems, and it reaches a new peak of development in 76. The union of autobiography with myth, one of the trademarks of Propertius, appears in 68. But much of the interest of the myth in 68, as opposed to the subjective description, is that it tells the truth about the poet's present situation whereas the surrounding frame of reference is happy and past, false in relation to the present. He was not ready to, or perhaps could not, reinterpret the present by myth as Propertius does.

The only way Catullus could describe his situation in detail, and not in the bitter brevity of epigram, was through the long epic tale. Such a recourse as 64 would have been needless to the Augustan poets. To Catullus it was absolutely necessary, because it was only by the disguise of symbols that he could be autobiographical at such length. Epic statement remained the only means open to him, as he was still in the process of pioneering the genre which later Latin authors would find ideal as a mode in which to express personal feelings.

NOTES

1. The most recent work of any length on 64 is F. Klingner, "Catulls Peleus-Epos," *SBAW* 1956, No. 6, 1–92. Klingner's basic theme, to defend the long poems of Catullus, is akin to that presented here, but his argument looks pri-

marily to the changes Catullus has rung on traditional themes, not to the *ingenium* of the poet himself.

For a survey of other recent treatments see J. P. Boucher, "A propos du Carmen 64 de Catulle," *RevEtLat* 34 (1956) 190–202, to which add C. Murley, "The Structure and Proportion of Catullus LXIV," *TAPA* 68 (1937) 305–17. Murley quotes (p. 305) the criticism of Kroll on the Hellenistic appearance of the poem as based on four factors: the use of inserts, emphasis on the emotions of the characters, pedanticism, and metrical tendencies such as the frequent use of spondaic lines. That the poem is a translation of a Hellenistic original is an opinion proposed as early as 1866 by A. Riese, "Catulls 64 Gedicht aus Kallimachos übersetz," *RhM* 21 (1866) 498–509.

On William Blake see Northrop Frye, *Fearful Symmetry: A Study of William Blake* (Princeton 1947).

2. Its supposed lack of unity is perhaps the main stumbling block to an appreciation of the poem. See A. L. Wheeler, *Catullus and the Traditions of Ancient Poetry* (Berkeley 1934) who, p. 132, abandons "the effort to find some internal connection between the tales." Also cf. Wilamowitz, *Hellenistische Dichtung* (Berlin 1924) 2.301; E. A. Havelock, *The Lyric Genius of Catullus* (Oxford 1939) 77–78 and 187 n.32.

3. For a penetrating study of the unified artistic presence behind the short poems see J. P. Elder, "Notes on some Conscious and Subconscious Elements in Catullus' Poetry," *HSCP* 60 (1951) 101–36. A treatment which concentrates particularly on unity of style is H. Bardon, *L'Art de la Composition chez Catulle* (Paris 1943).

4. See O. Friess, *Beobachtungen über die Darstellungskunst Catulls* (Diss. Würzburg 1929) 12–13.

5. Poem *8* is the clearest example.

6. D. L. Slater, in his lecture on *The Poetry of Catullus* (Manchester 1912) makes the equation between Lesbia and Theseus, and the idea was elaborated in parts of the dissertation of L. L. Sell (*De Catulli carmine LXIV quaestiones*: New York 1918). Though Sell's initial idea is in the spirit of this exposition, the cargo of dubious additions it carries with it obscures its basic worth (see the review by B. L. Ullman in *CP* 16 (1921) 404-6, and Wheeler (above, n. 2) 267 n.28).

7. A history of various treatments of this marriage is given by R. Reitzenstein, "Die Hochzeit des Peleus und der Thetis," *Hermes* 35 (1900) 73–105. John Finley in *Pindar and Aeschylus* (Cambridge, Mass. 1955) reveals the essence of Pindar's treatment of the myth (see esp. p. 48), which seems to offer much common ground with that of Catullus.

8. Her feelings are *indomitos*, the very word Catullus uses to describe himself in relation to Calvus in 50.11.

9. Cf. 65.17–18. On Theseus' meaningless *dicta*, cf. 76.7–8 and 70.4, where once again the metaphor of winds is utilized.

10. *Immemor*: 30.1 and 64.58; *prodere*: 30.3 and 64.190. The theme of perfidy goes through both poems: 30.3, 6, 11; 64.132–133, 182, 191, etc. *Fallax* and *fallere* appear in 30.3–4, 64.56, 151; *iubebas*, 30.7 and 64.140; *obliviscor*, 30.11 and *64 passim* (e.g., 208). For the figure of the winds, see, along with the note immediately preceding, 30.10, and for the *facta* of Theseus and Alfenus cf. 30.6, 9 with 64.192, 203.

11. The word *fugit*, for example, appears in 8.10 and 37.11.

12. Cf. 61.11–12 (where Hymen almost symbolizes the bride) with 64.56–57.

13. E.g., *liquerit*, l. 123 (and cf. ll. 59 and 133).

14. With which cf. 76.22.

15. And cf. ll. 94 and 245.

16. The lines are not without their own beauties of craftsmanship. Consider, for example, the sounds of lines 59–60. The *pro* of *promissa* links with the opening syllable of *procellae*. The promises are equivalent to the breezes. But the breezes, like the wave imagery, are real as well as metaphorical. The *procul* of line 60, repeating the sound of *procellae*, tells the reader that the breezes of Theseus' fraudulent promises are indeed those which are wafting him far from her sight. And, as if to complete the circle, the final syllables of *procellae* are repeated in *ocellis* which ends the next line. The result of Theseus' perfidy is now literally apparent to her.

17. With the imagery cf. ll. 320–21.

18. The one adjective applied twice to Theseus, *ferox* (lines 73 and 247) is scarcely more than an epic epithet.

19. Cf. 61.32 and, by transference, 61.54. With the imagery of 64.86–90, cf. especially 61.58 and 62.21–22.

20. He may, of course, be reading it into a passage such as 2.7.

21. There are clear references to lines 121–23 in 133–35, e.g., the word *litus* occurs in 121 and 133; *liquerit* (line 123) becomes *liquisti* (line 133), *immemori* (line 123) *immemor* (line 135), and *discedens* appears in 123 and 134.

22. With which cf. *extremo tempore* (l. 169).

23. Cf. l. 174. For Theseus' perjury see also ll. 143, 146, and 148.

24. In her anger Ariadne surely means the word *avectam* (line 132) to have the connotations of forceful abduction, even though the previous description said nothing to that effect.

25. The same time scheme is used in poem *8*, among others. Though *quondam* warns the reader that Ariadne is looking at a happiness which is past, the theme of hope goes through the whole passage (e.g., ll. 144, 177, 180, 186, etc.).

26. One might compare, for its similarity of context, the imagery used by Dido in *Aeneid* 4. 366–67. This is picked up again and reversed in *Aeneid* 6.471, where it is she who is now like a *Marpesia cautes* toward Aeneas.

27. For similar uses of the verb *eripio* see 64.219, 65.8, etc. A comparison with the opening verses of *68* sheds further light on these lines from *64*. In line 149 Ariadne used the familiar water imagery to describe the trials of Theseus, caught in the very whirlpool of death. In such a way the poet describes Manlius' sea of troubles in 68.3–4. We would seek no further for comparisons — the image is indeed a common one — did not the phrase *spumantibus undis* of 68.3 appear also in 64.155 (and the lines show more resemblances than this). Though in *68* the poet is describing a survivor cast up on the shore while the comparison in *64* refers to a man sinking, nevertheless the metaphorical trials of the sea, in which Theseus earlier found himself, have now become Ariadne's.

28. This change from masculine to feminine, which I hope to examine more fully in a separate study, is most apparent in the long poems but occurs, under various guises, also in the shorter works (e.g., *11*).

29. In line 170, combining the breezes once more with her sense of hearing, she cries that fortune grudges ears to her wails: "fors etiam nostris invidit questibus auris." Words entrusted to the winds are useless (the similarity of sound between *aurae* and *aures* abets the ironic contrast between ll. 164 and 170).

30. Virgil offers a close commentary on these lines in the passage where

Anchises first greets Aeneas upon their meeting in the Underworld (*Aeneid* 6.687–94). Aside from many minor repetitions, l. 689 is repeated almost word for word from 64.166, with the appropriate change from *missas* to *notas*. Lines 692–93 also contain Catullan reminiscences, this time reflecting the opening line of *101*. Just as Aeneas comes to Anchises, so Catullus arrives to offer the last *munus* of love (and death) to his brother.

31. Without going into a detailed analysis here, we may observe that it is a comparison with Ariadne's situation and curse which demonstrates the unity behind the lyric *schema* of *50*. Cf. 64.54 with 50.11; 64.57 and 50.9, and especially 64.190–97 with 50.18–21.

32. The similarities between this passage in *68* and the opening lines of the speech of Aegeus are manifold. *Iucundior vita* parallels *vita dulcius*, *casus* is repeated in 64.216 and 68.105, and the verb *eripio* appears in 64.219 and 68.106.

33. It is noteworthy that the only appearances of the word *nuper* in Catullus are here (64.217) and 65.5, where Catullus is thinking on his brother recently dead.

34. Cf. 68.1, 13.

35. For the sensual connotations attached to *languidus*, see its use in 25.3 and 67.21 and the appearance of *languor* in 58b.9. For *saturasset*, cf. 68.83.

36. Both these images had been used previously to describe Ariadne's love. Line 71 tells that she suffered from *assiduis luctibus* when Theseus arrived in Crete, and line 97 shows her *incensam mente*.

37. The poet makes the connection explicit by using images of burial for each — the one literal, the other metaphorical (cf. 68.22, 94, 97, 99).

38. There is a similar use of *dulcis* in 64.210.

39. E. T. Merrill, *Catullus* (Cambridge, Mass. 1951) *ad loc.* claims for the word *aetas* only the meaning *tempus*.

40. The "journey" poems of Catullus show how frequently these words are associated with the joy of return, e.g., *laetus* (9.11, 31.4, 46.8, etc.) and *gaudeo* (31.12–13, etc.).

41. The phrase *laeta gaudia mente* is also employed of similar circumstances shortly after in line 236.

42. Lines 238–45 also offer an interesting example of the poet's mind at work. As Aegeus looks out from the citadel, the poet tells how he was (line 242): "anxia in *assiduos* absumens *lumina fletus*, . . ." In much the same words he portrays his own love-sick state in 68.55–56: "maesta neque *assiduo* tabescere *lumina fletu* / cessarent . . ." The lines which follow in *68* are a simile which has the twofold effect of describing both the poet's tears and the assuaging help which Manlius gave him. Yet the words of the opening lines of the simile are not unlike those which describe Aegeus' suicide (*praeceps* appears in 64.244 and 68.59; *vertice* in 64.244 and 68.57; *iecit* is parallel to *prosilit* in 64.244 and 68.58, and *scopulorum* to *lapide* in the same lines). What makes a subconscious (or even conscious) connection between these two sets of lines more plausible is the simile which preceded this description in *64* by a few lines, where the commands of Aegeus, at first remembered faithfully by Theseus, are said to leave him in the end (ll. 239–40): ". . . ceu pulsae ventorum flamine nubes / *aereum* nivei *montis* liquere cacumen." This is an elaboration of one of Catullus' favorite comparisons dealing with the lack of constancy in love. Yet in line 240 we have two crucial words repeated from 68.57: "qualis in *aerii* perlucens *vertice montis* . . ." The close juxtaposition in the repetitions in actual description and in simile must surely be

more than fortuitous. The feelings of love experienced by Catullus and Aegeus are once more described in terms of the same imagery, and here we have a chance to show the poet's mind at work upon the same imagistic pattern in two quite different poems.

43. The connection is most explicit in line 127, where Catullus tells how Ariadne climbed the sheer mountains "unde aciem (in) pelagi vastos protenderet aestus, . . ." So also Attis, while standing on the edge of the sea, begs in pitiful prayer to be told whither he should direct his eyes to find his fatherland (63.55–56).

44. *Anxius*, ll. 203, 242; *luctus*, ll. 71, 226; *assiduus*, ll. 71, 242. The word *anxius* appears often elsewhere in descriptions of love, e.g. 68.8.

45. And we recall that the same images of fleeting feeling and forgetfulness, which she uses in ll. 142–43, recur when applied to Theseus' obedience to the commands of Aegeus.

46. See F. O. Copley, "Emotional Conflict and its Significance in the Lesbia-Poems of Catullus," *AJP* 70 (1949) 22–40.

47. Poem *61* comes close to picturing in fact what must have been to Catullus the perfect marriage. But even throughout it are scattered occasional remonstrances to the happy couple concerning the preservation of marital bliss, as if the poet knew the pitfalls and was worried that the picture he was sketching could scarcely endure.

48. The same image suggested by *incanuit* is continued in *candenti e gurgite* (l. 14) and *e gurgite cano* (l. 18).

49. For other examples of imagery of whiteness in a happy setting cf. 68.148, 107.6.

50. In both 72.2 and 64.28 the verb *teneo* is used with the same sexual ambiguity.

51. A similar profession, this time made by the poet himself, is found in the opening lines of *51*.

52. Cf. ll. 25–26 with 323–24.

53. A very similar effect is achieved again in l. 273.

54. This event is similar to that Catullus expects when, in 35.3–4, he summons Caecilius to leave Novum Comum and come to Verona (cf. the sound of 35.4: "Comi *moenia Lari*umque litus" with that of 64.36: "Crannonisque domos ac *moenia Lari*ssaea").

55. One might compare with this the appearance of Shelley in stanzas 31ff. of *Adonais*.

56. Cf. also ll. 329, 331, 372–73.

57. Line 335 (and cf. 76.3 and 87.3–4).

58. Ellis (on l. 341, p. 335) quite rightly compares also Pindar *Nem.* 3.51.

59. *Campi*, a reading suggested by Statius to fill the gap in line 344, is especially apt in the light of 46.4.

60. For further instances of *carpo* see 62.36, 37, 43.

61. And we also recall the use of *substernens* in ll. 332 and 403.

62. With *alta madefient* of l. 368 cf. *alta tepefaciet* of l. 360.

63. L. Herrmann, "Le poème 64 de Catulle et Virgile," *RevEtLat* 8 (1930) 211–21, maintains that the last lines of *64* do indeed refer to contemporary events, a valuable corrective to former opinion.

64. Catullus emphasizes his point by repeating line endings such as *parentes* (ll. 400, 404), *nati* or *nato* (ll. 401, 403).

65. As does, e.g., C. J. Fordyce in a review of E.V. Marmorale, *L'Ultimo Catullo*, in *Class. Rev.* N.S. 4 (1954) 132.

On the epyllion see Walter Allen, Jr., "The Epyllion," *TAPA* 71 (1940) 1–26, and the salutary criticism of it by C. W. Mendell, "Epyllion and *Aeneid*," *Yale Cl. St.* 12 (1951) 205–26. For a more detailed history of the whole problem see L. Richardson, Jr., *Poetical Theory in Republican Rome* (New Haven 1944), and J. F. Reilly, "Origins of the Word 'Epyllion'," *CJ* 49 (1953) 111–14, with full bibliography.

66. On this much-debated problem, see A. A. Day, *The Origins of Latin Love-Elegy* (Oxford 1938), esp. 107–11, and E. Paludan, "The Development of Latin Elegy," *Classica et Mediaevalia* 4 (1941) 204–29, who agrees with those who find the origin in Catullus. One should, however, approach this judgment with caution, as G. Luck, *The Latin Love Elegy* (London 1959) 58 warns. Wheeler (above, n. 2) ch. 6, argues, quite rightly, that if Catullus had had the developed genre before him he would have made use of it.

XVI

Wendell Clausen

Callimachus and Latin Poetry

Callimachus and Latin Poetry

Wendell Clausen

THE POETIC TRIUMPH of Callimachus—I borrow my metaphor from the poet who styled himself the "Roman Callimachus"— took place, long after his death, in Rome. It was altogether impressive. Cinna, Calvus, Catullus, Gallus, Virgil, Propertius—their imaginations were captivated by Callimachus; but for his poetry and the esthetic attitudes expressed or implied in it, much of what they wrote could not have been written; and Latin poetry would be very different. I do not mean to say that Callimachus had been a negligible figure in his own time and city. Clearly he had not: he counted for something in the Library, though he never became its head, and in the Court; he exerted a considerable influence on Euphorion, and some influence on two better poets, Theocritus and Apollonius. An important figure, then, but no literary dictator, as we may be tempted to assume from the posthumous ascendancy which he enjoyed in an alien literature and from his own acrimonious statements. Callimachus' attitude is at once polemical and defensive. The most complete *apologia* for his poetic career he wrote towards the end of his life, as a preface to the second edition of the *Aetia*,[1] his major work, which he must have intended as a kind of substitute for an epic. He had been attacked—and violently attacked, if we may judge from the violence of his retort—by Posidippus and Asclepiades and some others, though apparently not by Apollonius. Now old poets are not passionately disturbed by criticism unless they feel themselves vulnerable to it. Callimachus' famous refusal to write an epic surely implies a widely held view that poets ought to write epics and perhaps even some expectation on the part of those in high places. His opinions had no decisive effect on Greek poetry during his own lifetime or after his death. For over against the *Europa* of Moschus and the poetry of Parthenius (of which I shall have more to say later) we can set the titles and fragments of many epics: epics about monarchs or war-

[1] See R. Pfeiffer, *Hermes* 63 (1928) 339.

T

lords, epics on mythological themes, epics concerning the history of a people or a region, τὰ Μεσσηνιακά, τὰ 'Αχαϊκά, or the like.[2]

My chief purpose in this paper is to explain—in so far as that can be done simply; for the subject is not a simple one—the sort of influence Callimachus had on Latin poetry, and especially on the poetry or poetic career of Virgil. But first I must give some account of Callimachus himself, not because I can say much that is new about him, but because, if I do not, some part of what I have to say about Latin poetry may be unclear.

I

Callimachus' view of poetry is stated (as I have already remarked) most completely and maturely in the elegant and rancorous denunciation of his enemies—Telchines, literary troglodytes or worse—which he prefixed to the second edition of his *Aetia*. I paraphrase:

> The Telchines murmur against me because I have not written a continuous poem in many thousands of verses about kings and heroes. But the shorter poems of Mimnermus and Philetas are better than their long. Let the crane delighting in Pygmies' blood fly far, from Egypt to Thrace; let the Massagetes shoot their arrows far against the Medes; poems are sweeter for being short. Judge poetry by its art, not by the surveyor's chain. Thundering belongs to Zeus, not to me.

And now I translate:

> When first I set a writing-tablet on my knees, Lycian Apollo spoke to me: "Poet, raise your victim to be as fat as possible, but your Muse, my friend, keep her thin.

> . . . ἀοιδέ, τὸ μὲν θύος ὅττι πάχιστον
> θρέψαι, τὴν Μοῦσαν δ' ὠγαθὲ λεπταλέην.

> And I tell you this besides: Walk where wagons don't travel; don't drive your chariot in the tracks of others or on a wide road, but on an unworn way, even though it be narrower." I obeyed him; for I sing for those who like the shrill echoing song of the cicada, not the braying of asses.

[2] See K. Ziegler, *Das hellenistische Epos* (Leipzig 1934).

Then follow the poignant lines on Callimachus' old age. This statement he placed before the original preface or proem to the *Aetia*, which he had written as a young man (ἀρτιγένειος, according to the Florentine scholiast): his famous Hesiodic dream of being initiated a poet on Helicon. Here is a personal, retrospective statement, deeply-felt: a poet's testament.

One cannot read very much of Callimachus without being impressed, or perhaps depressed, by his learning. But it would be a mistake to dissociate his poetry from his pedantry. Callimachus was not a poet and a scholar; he was a poet because he was a scholar, a γραμματικός, a man whose business was literature. And such, I think, must have been Callimachus' own view; for in his treatise against Praxiphanes he praised Aratus ὡς πολυμαθῆ καὶ ἄριστον ποιητήν [fr. 460 Pfeiffer]. The earlier literature of Greece had now been collected in the great library at Alexandria, and men came to know the exquisite delight of writing books about books. Now a scholar-poet could con and compare texts; pluck a ἅπαξ out of Homer and define it in a context of his own making, perhaps to spite another scholar-poet; employ an obscure variant of a myth or legend, the while deftly signaling to an alert reader his awareness of other variants as well; subtly modify an admired metaphor or simile; set an old word and a new one together in an elegant collocation. As Callimachus, for example, does, in *Hymn* 1.90, αὐτὸς ἄνην ἐκόλουσας, ἐνέκλασσας δὲ μενοινήν: ἄνη occurs in Aeschylus, *Sept.* 713, μενοινή in Apollonius, 1.894; the chiastic arrangement calls attention to what the poet has done, to his cleverness. Earlier Greek poets had made use of their predecessors, too—that is, after all, what we mean by a literary tradition—but not in quite the same way. Sophocles, for example, intended his allusions to the *Choephoroe* to be intelligible to everyone who saw the *Electra*; for otherwise something of the force of his own play would be lost. Earlier Greek poetry supposed a large group of hearers rather than a small group of readers. The poetry of Callimachus and others like him could be appreciated by only a very few readers as learned or nearly as learned as themselves. Theirs was a bibliothecal poetry, poetry about poetry, self-conscious and hermetic.

It is easy enough to understand why these umbratile poets were drawn to the composition of didactic poetry. For in such poetry they had everywhere the chance to show off their erudition and to demonstrate by how much their manner excelled their matter. Hence their choice of inert or apparently intractable subjects to versify. Their aim was to shine, not to persuade; and in their poetry breathed no Lucretian fire. The *Aetia* is didactic in character; and to the *Phaenomena* of Aratus, written (Callimachus asserts, *Epigr.* 27) in the style of Hesiod, Ἡσιόδου τό τ᾽ ἄεισμα καὶ ὁ τρόπος he gives his unstinting approval; χαίρετε λεπταί / ῥήσιες, Ἀρήτου σύμβολον ἀγρυπνίης; so might he have praised his own poetry. The attitude of Callimachus to Hesiod and Homer has sometimes been misunderstood: for Callimachus Hesiod was imitable, Homer inimitable. Callimachus did not condemn Homer, though apparently Parthenius did (it is not unusual for a disciple to be more extreme than his master); rather Callimachus condemned those who imitated Homer, who copied the epic form, not realizing that it was by now empty and obsolete, and who slavishly repeated Homer's phrases: poets like Creophylus of Samos in an earlier time, for whom to be mistaken for Homer was the highest possible compliment [*Epigr.* 6]:

> Ὁμήρειον δὲ καλεῦμαι
> γράμμα· Κρεωφύλῳ, Ζεῦ φίλε, τοῦτο μέγα.

Callimachus was determined not to be mistaken for anybody else, not even for Hesiod. To later poets Hesiod was the exemplar of didactic as Homer was of epic poetry; and Callimachus found Hesiod more to his liking. Hesiod's poems were relatively short as, in Callimachus' judgment, poems should be; and they recounted no long, involved tales of heroes and battles. Perhaps Callimachus took the cryptic, bitter words of the Muses to the shepherds [*Theogony,* 26–8]:

> ποιμένες ἄγραυλοι, κάκ᾽ ἐλέγχεα, γαστέρες οἶον,
> ἴδμεν ψεύδεα πολλὰ λέγειν ἐτύμοισιν ὁμοῖα·
> ἴδμεν δ᾽, εὖτ᾽ ἐθέλωμεν, ἀληθέα γηρύσασθαι—

perhaps Callimachus took these words as a criticism of epic poets, notoriously careless of the truth. The *Theogony*—and I think it was the *Theogony* that most interested Callimachus—dealt with the truth, or with the true causes of things (αἴτια); it was learned, if naïvely so—but its very naïveté would have appealed to Callimachus' sophistication; above all, as Wilamowitz has remarked, Hesiod's was a personal voice. It was Hesiod who provided Callimachus with a means of describing his own source of inspiration, a matter of deep concern to so late and self-conscious a poet. While keeping his flock under

Helicon, Hesiod met the Muses; they gave him an olive branch (the visible symbol of poetic inspiration) and breathed into him the divine power of song, that he might sing of things that had been and would be, and of the gods who are forever. While still a young man Callimachus dreamt he had been wafted to Helicon and there met the Muses, who told him of the causes of things (αἴτια). (The details of the scene are uncertain, because only a fragment of the text survives.) The old bard of Ascra seems to describe an obvious encounter with the Muses—strange things do happen to shepherds in lonely places; but one verse [10], ἐννύχιαι στεῖχον περικαλλέα ὄσσαν ἱεῖσαι, suggests nighttime, and the meeting was later interpreted ἀλληγορικῶς, as a dream. At any rate, Callimachus, drowsing perhaps in a suburb of Alexandria, could only dream of encountering the Muses on Helicon. This scene served as an introduction to the Aetia: what did it signify? That Callimachus challenged comparison with Hesiod—of what use is a model that cannot be surpassed?—and that Hesiod, not Homer, was the poet to emulate. A personal, allusive, polemical introduction; in a word, Callimachean.

II

A poet writing in the style of Homer may be expected to begin as Homer did, with an invocation to the Muses and an epitome of the tale he means to tell. Ennius did not: he began his Annales with the description of a curiously personal experience, a dream in which Homer's ghost appeared to him. Homer expounded the Pythagorean doctrine of metempsychosis: his soul (he informed Ennius) had once passed into a peacock's body, but had now passed into Ennius' body; and Ennius awoke, alter Homerus, capable of unfolding the epic story of Roman greatness. So much, or rather so little, is certain; for only a few fragments of this initial scene have been preserved. Where did the scene take place? On Helicon? On Parnassus? (Ennius had accompanied Fulvius Nobilior on his Aetolian campaign in 189, and Nobilior, Roman-like, had brought the Muses home with him.) Or—and this has been suggested—in Ennius' rooms on the Aventine hill? Did Ennius meet the Muses or merely invoke their aid? Did he drink of Hippocrene?

Most scholars have seen in this introduction to the Annales an allusion to the proem of the Aetia, but a few have denied this, most

recently an Italian scholar,[3] anxious to vindicate the Italian character
of Ennius' genius. Now nothing that Callimachus wrote was better
known than his dream of poetic initiation on Helicon: ἃ μέγα Βαττιάδαο
σοφοῦ περίπυστον ὄνειαρ . . . [Anth. Pal. 7.42.1]. Ennius was a literary
man, a philologist—dicti studiosus he called himself [Ann. 216]; he
had grown up in a Greek-speaking part of Italy, and was concerned
his whole life through with Greek poetry: he could not have begun his
Annales as he did without having the famous dream of Callimachus
in mind. To imagine that he could is, as Otto Skutsch has remarked,[4]
"to imagine that a modern literary man could write of a scholar's
pact with the devil, without being aware of Goethe's Faust." In all
that has been written about the initial scene of the Annales—and
there is very much[5]—I miss an essential question. It is this: why
should Ennius allude to Callimachus' dream at the beginning of the
Annales, τὰ 'Ρωμαϊκά, a long discursive epic about the vicissitudes of a
people, about kings and battles? Was this not precisely the sort of
poem Callimachus had condemned? Ennius' purpose, I believe, was
polemical and anti-Callimachean: he designed to confute Callimachus, alter Hesiodus, in something like Callimachus' own oblique
style. Ennius was as self-conscious a poet as Callimachus, and as
preoccupied with his art. Ovid's facile judgement on the two—
[Battiades] quamuis ingenio non ualet, arte ualet [Am. 1.15.13–14]:
Ennius ingenio maximus, arte rudis [Trist. 2.424]—is unfair to both, but
more unfair to Ennius than to Callimachus. Ennius stands at the
beginning of a poetic tradition, a tradition which he helped to shape—
not, like Callimachus, near the end of one; if his art is rude, it is so
mainly because he was struggling with a language that had not, like
Greek, been long subdued to the uses of poetry. It may seem odd that
Ennius began his Annales as he did, with a cryptic, literary polemic.
Perhaps it is; but in the introduction to Book 7, to the next part of the
poem that he published, we find him similarly engaged with literary
polemic [Ann. 213–15]:

> scripsere alii rem
> uersibus quos olim Fauni uatesque canebant,
> cum neque Musarum scopulos . . .

---

[3] G. Marconi, Riv. di Cult. Class. e Medievale 3 (1961) 224–245.
[4] The Annals of Quintus Ennius (London 1953) p. 10.
[5] For a convenient summary see J. H. Waszink, Mnem. Ser. IV, 3 (1950) 214–240; see also
the same author's "retractatio," Mnem. Ser. IV, 15 (1962) 113–132.

Apparently Ennius did not mention the poet he was attacking, Naevius, by name. This is the tone, as Leo long ago remarked,[6] that we know from Callimachus; and, as Leo acutely observed, the words *Musarum scopulos* refer to the dream at the beginning of Book 1.

Ennius, then, knew the poetry of Callimachus, or at least some part of it—I suspect that Virgil was the only Roman poet who ever read the *Aetia* all the way through. And Ennius alluded to the proem of the *Aetia* for his own reasons, private reasons, one is tempted to think; for he could hardly have expected his Roman readers to grasp the significance of his allusion. But Callimachus had little or no influence on Latin poetry until the generation of the New Poets. Ennius in his *Saturae* and Lucilius owe something to his *Iambi*, it has been argued,[7] and Lucilius something besides to his poetic example; but evidence for these claims is slight and inconclusive; and the *Iambi* was, in Latin poetry, one of Callimachus' least consequential works. Sometime before he committed suicide in 87 B.C., Lutatius Catulus rendered one of Callimachus' epigrams (41) into Latin; but this, the diversion of an idle hour, should not be taken as evidence of any serious interest in Callimachus' major poetry or in his esthetic views. Catulus was a Roman aristocrat with a taste for Greek poetry, an elegant amateur. He would have read many Greek epigrams; one, by Callimachus, pleased him especially, and he made a version of it. Meleager's *Garland* had been published a few years before the death of Catulus; he could have read the epigram there, or it might have been shown him by a Greek friend like Antipater of Sidon, himself an epigrammatist. In all probability Catulus had never read any of the *Aetia;* had he tried to do so, he would have liked it little enough and found the oblique polemic all but incomprehensible. There is, besides, no reason to suppose that Catulus felt any aversion to old-fashioned epic; his literary circle included a certain Furius, a writer (so it would seem) of such poetry, *Annales*.

It is a mistake, not uncommon in our literary histories, to employ the terms "Hellenistic," "Alexandrian," "Callimachean" interchangeably. The poetry of Catulus, Valerius Aedituus, Porcius Licinus, and Laevius might be called Hellenistic; but it had little to do with the New Poetry, which is Callimachean in its inspiration. Callimachus was brought to Rome, I am quite convinced, by Parthenius of Nicaea,

[6] *Geschichte der römischen Literatur* (Berlin 1913) 164–165.
[7] By M. Puelma Piwonka, *Lucilius und Kallimachos* (Frankfurt/M. 1949).

and arrived there with all the force and charm of novelty. I do not mean necessarily that no Latin poet had heard of Callimachus, or that there were no manuscripts of his poetry in Rome, though perhaps there were none; I mean rather that Parthenius made Callimachus important to some Latin poets. The main source of our knowledge of Parthenius is Suidas. Parthenius was taken prisoner when the Romans defeated Mithridates, and became the property or prize of Cinna—εἰλήφθη ὑπὸ Κίννα λάφυρον; and was later freed because of his learning—διὰ παίδευσιν. Presumably Parthenius came to Rome not long after 73 B.C., the year the Romans captured Nicaea; and presumably the Cinna who is not further identified was a relative of Helvius Cinna, author of the *Zmyrna*; or perhaps there is some conflation of details in the account given in Suidas. Parthenius: mentor or friend of Cinna and Gallus and Virgil, and very likely of Catullus and Calvus as well, literary epigone of Callimachus and Euphorion—I do not understand why those who have written recently on the New Poetry make so little of him: Quinn in his *The Catullan Revolution* (1959), Wimmel in his *Kallimachos in Rom* (1960), Fordyce in his edition of Catullus (1961), unless I am mistaken, do not even mention him. Otis in his *Virgil: A Study in Civilized Poetry* (1964) does recognize his importance. It may be that literary young men of the time began to read and appreciate Callimachus on their own with no prompting. But the suddenness and intensity of their interest would be hard to explain; and I doubt that even a Cinna or a Catullus could have understood Callimachus without some tutoring.

Cinna labored for nine years to be as obscure as Euphorion, and apparently succeeded; Catullus greeted his *Zmyrna* on publication with Callimachean enthusiasm (95).

> *Zmyrna mei Cinnae nonam post denique messem*
> *quam coepta est nonamque edita post hiemem,*
> *milia cum interea quingenta Hortensius uno*
>
> .   .   .   .
>
> *Zmyrna cauas Satrachi penitus mittetur ad undas,*
> *Zmyrnam cana diu saecula peruoluent.*
> *at Volusi Annales Paduam morientur ad ipsam*
> *et laxas scombris saepe dabunt tunicas.*

The art of this poem is minute. There are, or rather were, eight

verses, divided into two sections of four verses, each section beginning
with the title of Cinna's poem. I confine my remarks to the second.
Two rivers are named, the Satrachus and the Po: *Satrachi* stands
immediately before the caesura in the first hexameter, *Paduam*
immediately after the caesura in the second; and both hexameters
conclude with similar phrases: *mittetur ad undas, morientur ad ipsam.*
And in the second pentameter there is an echo, intended I think, of
the first:

> *Zmyrnam cana diu saecula peruoluent*
> *et laxas scombris saepe dabunt tunicas.*

A polemical poem in the Callimachean style was not meant to be
merely a confutation; it was meant to be simultaneously a demonstration of how poetry ought to be written. Catullus wrote one
other such poem, also attacking the wretched Volusius and his
Annales: 36, *Annales Volusi cacata carta*, which has not quite been
recognized for what it is. The *Zmyrna*—to return to 95—will be read
by the banks of the distant Satrachus and live for many ages: the
Annales of Volusius will provide much wrapping-paper for mackerel
and perish by the mouth of the Po. (Volusius must have come from
nearby: otherwise the emphatic reference would have no point,
Paduam . . . ad ipsam; and the name is common on inscriptions from
that part of Italy.) Catullus pays his friend an elegant compliment, as
commentators have noticed: his poem will be read even by the remote
river which it celebrates. But there is, I think, a piquancy commentators
have not noticed in the oblique comparison of the two rivers: the
broad familiar Po with its mud and flotsam, the exotic Satrachus,
deep-channelled, swift and clear—such is the implication of the
adjective *cauus*; Lucan (2.421–2) applies it to the Tiber and its tributary
the Rutuba where they flow swiftly down from the Apennines.
Callimachus had used a similar metaphor for long and short, or bad
and good, poetry at the end of *Hymn* 2. Envy (Φθόνος) sidles up to
Apollo and whispers an anti-Callimachean opinion into his ear;
Apollo kicks Envy, and replies (108–12):

> Ἀσσυρίου ποταμοῖο μέγας ῥόος, ἀλλὰ τὰ πολλά
> λύματα γῆς καὶ πολλὸν ἐφ' ὕδατι συρφετὸν ἕλκει.
> Δηοῖ δ' οὐκ ἀπὸ παντὸς ὕδωρ φορέουσι μέλισσαι,
> ἀλλ' ἥ τις καθαρή τε καὶ ἀχράαντος ἀνέρπει
> πίδακος ἐξ ἱερῆς ὀλίγη λιβὰς ἄκρον ἄωτον.

What was the *Zmyrna* about? The incestuous passion of Smyrna or Myrrha for her father Cinyras, her metamorphosis into a tree, and the subsequent birth of Adonis from her, or its, trunk. Precisely the sort of tale—erotic, morbid, grotesque—that appealed to Parthenius, as we may guess from the fact that he wrote *Metamorphoses*, and as we can tell from his Περὶ ἐρωτικῶν παθημάτων, the helpful collection of stories he put together for Gallus. One of these παθήματα, 11, deals with Byblis and her incestuous passion for her brother Caunus, which Parthenius himself had written about. He quotes, as a teacher might, his own verses: six verses, two of them σπονδειάζοντες, with an αἴτιον at the end: Καλλιμάχου τό τ᾽ ἄεισμα καὶ ὁ τρόπος. These are the verses, which have been curiously neglected by literary historians:

> ἡ δ᾽ ὅτε δή ῥ᾽ ὀλοοῖο κασιγνήτου νόον ἔγνω
> κλαῖεν ἀηδονίδων θαμινώτερον, αἵ τ᾽ ἐνὶ βήσσῃς
> Σιθονίῳ κούρῳ πέρι μυρίον αἰάζουσιν·
> καί ῥα κατὰ στυφελοῖο σαρωνίδος αὐτίκα μίτρην
> ἀψαμένη δειρὴν ἐνεθήκατο, ταὶ δ᾽ ἐπ᾽ ἐκείνῃ
> βεύδεα παρθενικαὶ Μιλησίδες ἐρρήξαντο.

Six verses, divided into two sections of three verses, each section ending with a σπονδειάζων. ἡ δ᾽ ὅτε δή ῥ᾽ ὀλοοῖο in verse 1 is answered by καί ῥα κατὰ στυφελοῖο in verse 4; θαμινώτερον in verse 2 is balanced by ἐνεθήκατο in verse 5, a word of the same metrical quality in the same position, and both words are followed by similar phrases: αἵ τ᾽ ἐνὶ βήσσῃς, ταὶ δ᾽ ἐπ᾽ ἐκείνῃ. There are two proper names: Σιθονίῳ at the beginning of verse 3 and Μιλησίδες immediately after the caesura in verse 6.[8] I would not go so far as to say that Catullus had these verses in mind when he was writing 95—there is, after all, no way of dating Parthenius' poem precisely; but I do think it likely that the technique of 95 owes something to the example of Parthenius, if

---

[8] E. Rohde failed to appreciate the symmetry of Parthenius' verses or the delicacy and restraint of the narrative, and supposed that some words were lost after ἐνεθήκατο (*Der griechische Roman*³, p. 102, n.): "noch hat man nicht einmal gehört, dass die B., nachdem sie 'an eine feste Eiche den Gürtel knüpfend, ihren Hals hineingelegt hatte,' auch wirklich *gestorben sei* . . ." There is a passage which resembles this in a poem written by one of Parthenius' pupils, Virgil, *Georg.* 4.457–61:

> illa quidem, dum te fugeret per flumina praeceps,
> immanem ante pedes hydrum moritura puella
> seruantem ripas alta non uidit in herba.
> at chorus aequalis Dryadum clamore supremos
> implerunt montis . . .

one may judge from these verses. And what could be more appropriate, if Parthenius, as I suspect, did inspire Cinna?

The Satrachus (or Σέτραχος) occurs only four times in ancient poetry: in Lycophron (448), which hardly matters; in Nonnus (13.459), who connects it with the legend of Adonis, as Haupt long ago pointed out (*Opusc.* 1.73); in Catullus, alluding to Cinna's poem; and in Parthenius (fr. 24 Martini). I translate part of the note in the *Etymologicum Magnum*:

> '... there was a mountain named Aoion, from which two
> rivers flowed, the Setrachus and the Aplieus; and one of these
> [Setrachus] Parthenius called Aoos.'

Aoos was another name for Adonis; and it appears from fr. 37 that Parthenius had written about Adonis. This coincidence can hardly be fortuitous. It seems likely, to me at least, that Parthenius suggested the story of Smyrna as suitable for treatment in an epyllion, much as he later suggested stories for Gallus to use in his elegies.

Callimachus I have already discussed briefly; about Euphorion, *Callimachus dimidiatus*, I can be even briefer: so pitifully slight are the remains of his poetry. Evidently he modelled himself on Callimachus: he had Callimachus' interest in local legends, aetiology, geography, mythology, and more than Callimachus' interest in the epyllion. Euphorion, according to one scholar,[9] "popularized the criminal love-story, and concentrated interest on the heroine." This is plausible. There is an indicative fragment[10] that survives to us—Apriate, being pursued with lustful intent by the hero Trambelus, delivers herself of an erudite and disdainful speech, and then in a single hexameter hurls herself into the sea. The poet is not interested in narrative detail; he is interested rather in obscure mythological allusions and in the emotional state of his heroine; and his narrative style is consequently abrupt and elliptical, like that of Catullus in 64 or Virgil in the Aristaeus epyllion. Then there are Latin poems that do not survive to us, except for a few verses: the *Zmyrna* of Cinna, the *Io* of Calvus. Cinna and Calvus, *cantores Euphorionis*—for Cicero must have been referring to them, among others, poets who owed an excessive debt to Euphorion. And Cicero would have known: he had been a student

[9] A. M. Duff in the *OCD*, *s.v.* EPYLLION.
[10] Easily accessible in *Select Papyri* III, ed. D. L. Page (Loeb Classical Library), pp. 494–497.

of Hellenistic poetry in his youth. Euphorion was important to these poets because Parthenius made him so; it was Parthenius, I think, who introduced his friends and pupils to Euphorion.

In his note on *Bucolics* 6.72, Servius gives some account of the Grynean Grove, and then adds: *hoc autem Euphorionis continent carmina, quae Gallus transtulit in sermonem Latinum.* It may well be that Parthenius suggested the subject to Gallus for an aetiological poem, as he suggested subjects to him for his elegies. Parthenius himself had written a poem on a similar subject, the *Delos*. Stephanus of Byzantium (Γρῦνοι) preserves three fragments of this poem. One of these is curious and relevant. Γρῦνοι (Stephanus notes) is the name of a small town; the ἐθνικόν, or adjective, is Γρυνεύς or Γρυνηίς in the feminine; but he also knows of the form Γρύνειος in Parthenius' *Delos*: λέγεται καὶ Γρύνειος Ἀπόλλων ὡς Παρθένιος Δήλῳ. This is the form Virgil used in the sixth eclogue, 72: *his tibi Grynei nemoris dicatur origo;* and he later translated the phrase Γρύνειος Ἀπόλλων in *Aeneid* 4.345, *Gryneus Apollo*—commentators seem to have overlooked this—as (so Gellius 13.27 and Macrobius 5.17.18 tell us) he translated, or rather adapted, a verse of Parthenius in *Georgics* 1.437, *Glauco et Panopeae et Inoo Melicertae*: Γλαύκῳ καὶ Νηρῆι καὶ Ἰνώῳ (εἰναλίῳ Gellius) Μελικέρτῃ. According to Macrobius—and his information must be from an earlier source—Parthenius tutored Virgil in Greek.

Now (it may be asked) could a single Greek professor have made such a difference to Latin poetry? The question is more easily asked than answered. We are concerned with only a few poets, pupils or friends of Parthenius; and he may well have been a forceful and persuasive teacher: he won his freedom διὰ παίδευσιν. But (it is only fair to add) Parthenius' teaching alone could not have produced such a renovation—some have called it a revolution—in Latin poetry: he spoke to listening ears. No significant poetry had been written in Latin for several decades; and young poets—Cinna, Calvus, Catullus—living in a turbulent and rebellious age were not minded to write an old-fashioned epic about Roman history, *Annales*. Ennius, whatever his virtues, could only seem crude and outmoded to a generation conversant with the elegance of Hellenistic poetry and ambitious of rivalling it. They could not, like Callimachus, look back to a classical poetry in their own language; they had rather to look to Greek for that. Perhaps they felt some artistic kinship with Callimachus; they could appreciate his experiments with language, his technical refine-

ments, his passion for elegance; and like Callimachus, they were in a
defensive position. Their objection to epic poetry was not, I think,
merely esthetic, as it had been for Callimachus; it was moral as
well.

I have put this matter rather crudely; perhaps I can explain what I
mean by commenting briefly on Virgil's poetic career and especially
on the sixth Eclogue.

The *Liber Bucolicorum* is one of the few perfect books: each Eclogue
is enhanced somehow by its position—this effect was achieved, I have
no doubt, by a certain amount of rewriting; and, taken together, the
ten have an additional beauty and sense. For his own profession of
poetic faith Virgil reserved a place of prominence: the sixth Eclogue
introduces the second half of the book and defines the character of
the whole book. It has an obvious connection with the tenth Eclogue,
and a less obvious, but perhaps more important, connection with the
first (1–5):

> *Tityre, tu patulae recubans sub tegmine fagi*
> *siluestrem tenui musam meditaris auena,*
> *nos patriae finis et dulcia linquimus arua.*
> *nos patriam fugimus: tu, Tityre, lentus in umbra*
> *formosam resonare doces Amaryllida siluas.*

Meliboeus notices Tityrus, relaxed under a beech-tree, carelessly
meditating his thankful muse. They talk; and their talk is of the
violence and disorder of civil strife, the possibility of reconciliation,
and the infinite sadness of exile. A strange introductory poem,
recognizably Theocritean in manner, but yet quite unlike anything
Theocritus wrote: a suave and beautiful poem about a harsh and ugly
experience that Virgil had shared with his fellow-countrymen.

The sixth Eclogue also begins with a reference to war. Virgil
declines to praise the military record of Varus in epic style. The refusal
is Callimachean, translated into pastoral terms (3–8):

> *cum canerem reges et proelia, Cynthius aurem*
> *uellit et admonuit: "pastorem, Tityre, pinguis*
> *pascere oportet ouis, deductum dicere carmen."*
> *nunc ego (namque super tibi erunt qui dicere laudes,*
> *Vare, tuas cupiant et tristia condere bella)*
> *agrestem tenui meditabor harundine musam.*

No attentive reader can miss the echo of the first eclogue: *siluestrem tenui musam meditaris auena;* and commentators duly notice it. But surely it needs a word of explanation? For I do not suppose that Virgil was simply trying to unite the two halves of his book with this device. Why should Virgil remind his readers of the first Eclogue at the beginning of the sixth, in a Callimachean context? To write a Roman epic a poet had to celebrate war; he had to accept war as heroic. Virgil could not, at least not then; and his refusal to write about it— *tristia condere bella*—was not merely esthetic, it was also (as the reminiscence of the first Eclogue intimates) moral. Callimachus knew nothing of war; he knew only the vast, stagnant peace of the Ptolemaic empire; for him refusing to write an epic was a stylistic decision. But for Virgil and his contemporaries it was, I feel, something more: they knew what war was. Propertius 1.22.1-5:

> Qualis et unde genus, qui sint mihi, Tulle, penates
> quaeris pro nostra semper amicitia.
> si Perusina tibi patriae sunt nota sepulchra,
> Italiae duris funera temporibus,
> cum Romana suos egit discordia ciuis . . .

In the first Eclogue the adjective *tenui* is ornamental, necessary rather to the balance of the verse than to its sense—*siluestrem tenui musam meditaris auena;* the involved word order is suggestive of Hellenistic elegance. But in the sixth Eclogue *tenui* is more than ornamental—*agrestem tenui meditabor harundine musam;* it implies a concept of style; it is the Latin equivalent of λεπτός or λεπταλέος: μοῦσαν . . . λεπταλέην, λεπταί / ῥήσιες. His pastoral poetry, Virgil thus obliquely asserts, is Callimachean in character. Failure to recognize this has impaired the quality of much that has been written about the *Eclogues.*

Although the sixth Eclogue is primarily addressed to Varus, its chief figure is obviously Gallus. Because of this some readers have detected an awkwardness or lack of unity in the poem. Büchner, for example, describes the first twelve verses as "a detachable proem".[11] The failure in sensibility is not Virgil's; it is the modern reader's: unschooled in the Callimachean esthetic, he senses disunity where he ought to sense unity. The refusal to write an epic poem implied the intention of writing some other sort of poem: the refusal was always

[11] *PW,* zweite Reihe XV, 1219.

made in a poem. Apollo's epiphany as literary critic and the poet's
initiation on Helicon—these scenes are complementary, the one
explicitly, the other implicitly, programmatic; and they stood together at the beginning of the *Aetia*. Ancient readers would associate,
not dissociate, the two; and for such readers, and not for us, Virgil
wrote the sixth Eclogue. Here are Linus' words to Gallus (69–73):

> *hos tibi dant calamos (en accipe) Musae,*
> *Ascraeo quos ante seni, quibus ille solebat*
> *cantando rigidas deducere montibus ornos.*
> *his tibi Grynei nemoris dicatur origo,*
> *ne quis sit lucus quo se plus iactet Apollo.*

Apollo will be pleased with Gallus' poem about his grove: at this
point the reader may recall how little pleased Apollo was with
another sort of poem. Now with a summary *quid loquar*, at the beginning of verse 74, Virgil hurries Silenus' song and his own to a close.
This abrupt phrase has the effect of emphasizing what immediately
precedes; and the poet speaks again in his own person, as he did at the
start: *cum canerem reges et proelia*.

That the same poet who wrote *cum canerem reges et proelia*[12] wrote,
a few years later, *arma uirumque cano* is one of the surprises of Latin
literary history, although I do not find that historians of Latin
literature are at all surprised. The sixth Eclogue, as I have tried briefly
to show, is an uncompromising, if oblique, statement of the Callimachean esthetic; a reader at the time of publication could not have
anticipated that its author would one day write an epic—a didactic
or aetiological poem perhaps, or an epyllion, but not an epic. The
very fact of Virgil's poetry imposes on us and persuades us to see his
poetic career as an orderly progression from the lesser to the greater
work; it requires an effort of the imagination to understand that it
cannot have been so. Only when he was well along with the *Georgics*,
I suspect, did Virgil make up his mind, slowly and with some reluc-
tance, to write an epic; and perhaps under some compulsion—I mean
not the compulsion of an order which he would have to obey, but the

---

[12] Ancient scholiasts, not recognizing the allusion to Callimachus, took *cum canerem
reges et proelia* as a biographical statement and imagined that the youthful Virgil had
attempted unsuccessfully to write an epic before turning to pastoral; see *Vita Donati*, 19:
*mox cum res Romanas incohasset, offensus materia ad Bucolica transiit, maxime ut Asinium
Pollionem, Alfenum Varum et Cornelium Gallum celebraret* . . . Some modern scholiasts have
made this same mistake.

G.R.B.S.—4

even stronger compulsion of hope and expectation which he would want to satisfy.

There is much of Callimachus in the *Georgics*: its character is established by the epyllion and αἴτιον at the end and by the reference to Gallus; for I am certain there once was such a reference. But here and there one detects un-Callimachean ambiguities, notably in the proem to the third book, which begins in Callimachean style, but seems unclear, as if Virgil were no longer quite sure of his own intentions, or in these verses (2.173–6):

> salue, magna parens frugum, Saturnia tellus,
> magna uirum: tibi res antiquae laudis et artis
> ingredior sanctos ausus recludere fontes,
> Ascraeumque cano Romana per oppida carmen.

Here, in a single period, are joined an almost epic expression of pride in Italy and an allusion to Callimachus. (References to Hesiod in Virgil and Propertius are really references to Callimachus or his conception of Hesiod. You will recall the verses from the sixth Eclogue —*hos tibi dant calamos (en accipe) Musae,/Ascraeoquos ante seni* . . . —and my comments on Hesiod and Callimachus.)

The *Aeneid*, finally, is in many ways a strange epic; and there are indications that Virgil was not wholly content with it. He must have been out of his mind, he wrote, when he undertook such a task, and he wanted to burn it as he lay dying. Most likely it was illness or fatigue that caused this ultimate despondency, or an artist's dissatisfaction with an unfinished work; but, just possibly, some Callimachean scruples haunted Virgil to the end.[13]

HARVARD UNIVERSITY

September, 1964

[13] Read at the Fourth International Congress of Classical Studies in Philadelphia on August 28, 1964. I have added some footnotes and made a few small changes.

XVII

Eduard Fraenkel

Catulls Trostgedicht für Calvus

50

CATULLS TROSTGEDICHT FÜR CALVUS *

I

Der moderne Leser mag unwillkürlich dazu neigen sich 278
Catull als strahlenden Mittelpunkt vorzustellen und seine Dich-
tergenossen, Calvus, Cinna und die übrigen, als Satelliten. Was
jedoch das Verhältnis von Catull zu Calvus anlangt, so entspricht
diese Vorstellung jedenfalls nicht dem Bilde, das die beiden
Freunde und ihre unmittelbaren Zeitgenossen sich davon machen
mussten. Catulls wohlhabender Vater war zu seiner Zeit
wahrscheinlich der angesehenste und sicher einer der angesehen-
sten Bürger der alten und blühenden Stadt Verona. Das folgt
unbedingt daraus dass Caesar, wann immer die mit seiner Gal-
lischen Statthalterschaft verbundenen Amtsgeschäfte ihn nach
Verona führten, sein Quartier im Hause von Catulls Vater auf-
zuschlagen pflegte [1]. Aber dieser Mann war ein Provinziale.
Hingegen gehörte Catulls Freund C. Licinius Macer Calvus
jenem alten römischen Adelsgeschlecht an, ' das vielleicht unter
allen plebeischen das angesehenste und bedeutendste war ' [2].
Sein Vater, C. Licinius Macer, erregte bereits im Jahre 73 v.
Chr. als Volkstribun Aufsehen durch seine leidenschaftlichen
Reden gegen die Sullanische Verfassung und zugunsten der
Wiederherstellung der tribunizischen Rechte; aber ' wie auch
jene demokratischen Agitatoren die Flammen schürten, es half
eben nichts, da der Brennstoff fehlte ' [3]. Seine Praetur fällt
wenige Jahre vor die Ciceros (66 v. Chr.). Cicero, dem der

* Wiener Studien 69, 1956, 278-288.

[1] Sueton *Iul.* 73 *hospitio ... patris eius, sicut consuerat, uti perseveravit.*
[2] F. Münzer, *RE* XIII, 214; vgl. auch Münzer, *Römische Adelsparteien und Adelsfamilien* 9 f. und passim.
[3] Mommsen, *Röm. Geschichte* III, 9. Aufl., 97.

Mann tief unsympathisch war, lässt in seiner Charakteristik
der Reden des Macer immerhin ein erhebliches Talent und
eine ganz ungewöhnliche Sorgfalt in der Vorbereitung und
Ausarbeitung seines Materials erkennen. Seine Leistung als
Historiker wird von der neueren Forschung viel günstiger
279 beurteilt als von Mommsen und denen, die ihm gefolgt|sind [1].
Gleichwohl ist nicht zu verkennen dass an rednerischer und
künstlerischer Begabung wie in seiner gesamten Persönlichkeit
der Sohn Calvus den Vater weit in den Schatten stellt. Dass
wir uns von der Art seines Auftretens und seinem hinreissenden
Temperament noch eine wirkliche Vorstellung machen können,
verdanken wir der so anschaulichen wie liebevollen Skizze in
den Memoiren des älteren Seneca (*Controv.* 7, 4, 6 ff.). Calvus
ist im Mai 82 geboren [2]; ob er etwas älter oder etwas jünger war
als Catull [3], können wir nicht sagen. Aber auf einen etwaigen
Altersunterschied kommt nicht viel an; wichtiger ist es sich
gegenwärtig zu halten dass in dem Verhältnis der beiden jungen
Männer (beide sterben frühzeitig) mindestens zunächst, und
wahrscheinlich auch weiterhin, Calvus der Führende gewesen
sein wird. Zu der Zeit da der Veroneser Catull, vermutlich
gefördert durch Empfehlungen seines Vaters und durch Bezie-
hungen zu einflussreichen *conterranei* wie Cornelius Nepos,
anfing sich seinen Weg in der römischen Gesellschaft zu bahnen,
war der Sohn des im Jahre 66 verstorbenen Senators Licinius
Macer bereits eine stadtbekannte Persönlichkeit. Als Calvus
zum ersten Mal Caesars Günstling Vatinius angriff, war er noch
nicht 25 Jahre alt, und bald darauf hielt er jene Reden, von
denen einige noch zur Zeit des Tacitus klassische Schulstücke
waren. Alle Wahrscheinlichkeit spricht dafür dass die Initiative
zu dem von den beiden Freunden gemeinsam unternommenen

[1] Belochs knappe Bemerkungen, *Röm. Geschichte* (1926), 1 f., treffen genau
überein mit den Ergebnissen, zu denen Münzer in seinem gleichzeitig veröffentlich-
ten Artikel, *RE* XIII, 421-8, auf Grund einer eingehenden Prüfung der Bruchstücke
gelangt war.
[2] Heinzes Verteidigung (*Hermes* 60, 1925, 194 Anm. 3) des für Calvus und M.
Caelius Rufus von Plinius angegebenen Geburtsdatums hat mich überzeugt; Münzer, *RE* XIII 429, blieb skeptisch.
[3] Dass das bei Hieronymus für Catull überlieferte Geburtsjahr 87 ' nicht
die geringste Gewähr hat ', hat R. Helm, *Philol.* Suppl. 21, Heft 2, 1929, 39 gezeigt;
seine Argumente sind von P. Maas, *Class. Quart.* 36, 1942, 79 f., nicht aber von
M. Schuster, *RE* VII A 2356, genügend berücksichtigt.

unverschämten Pasquillenfeldzug gegen Pompejus, Caesar und ihre Anhänger von Calvus ausging. Ebenso wahrscheinlich, wenn auch bei der Dürftigkeit unseres Materials nicht beweisbar, ist es dass der frühreife und gesellschaftlich gesicherte Calvus schon Dichtungen veröffentlicht hatte noch ehe Catull an dergleichen denken konnte. Aber sei dem wie ihm wolle, aus den Versen Catulls spricht die Schwär|merei eines jungen Menschen, 280 der zu seinem Freunde bewundernd aufblickt. Das kleine Gedicht (53), das uns mitten in den Sturm der berühmten Reden gegen Vatinius versetzt, ist ein Muster der raffiniert kunstfertigen Einfachheit Catulls :

> Risi nescioquem modo e corona,
> qui, cum mirifice Vatiniana
> meus crimina Calvos explicasset,
> admirans ait haec manusque tollens :
> ' di magni, salaputium disertum ! '

Dies ist ein typischer αἶνος in jener uralten schlichten Form, bei der in wenigen knappen Sätzen nur gerade das berichtet wird, was zum Verständnis des stets in direkter Rede an den Schluss gesetzten Dictums unbedingt erforderlich ist [1]. Für den Anfang, wie für den Anfang von 56 (*O rem ridiculam...*), könnte man versucht sein an Einfluss des dem Catull gut bekannten Archilochos (χρῆμά τοι γελοῖον ἐρέω) zu denken. Aber dessen bedarf es nicht. Gerade so, einschliesslich der Anfangsstellung des Verbums, beginnt man in lebhafter Alltagsrede : ein Brief Ciceros an seinen Bruder (2, 12) fängt an *Risi nivem atram*. Der Bericht über den amüsanten kleinen Vorfall wahrt scheinbar vollkommene Objektivität; es ist ja nicht der bewundernde Catull, sondern der unbekannte Zuhörer, der seinem fassungslosen Staunen über die Redekraft des kleinen Kerls (*imponi se supra cippum iussit — erat enim parvolus statura* erzählt Seneca) einen so leidenschaftlichen Ausdruck gibt. Aber an Einer Stelle ist der Ton distanzierter Berichterstattung aufgegeben. Genau in der Mitte des aus einer einzigen Periode bestehenden Gedichtchens heisst es *meus... Calvos*. Darin ist mehr Wärme als in allen Superlativen der Welt. So sagt Horaz in der Mittelstrophe des einzigen Gedichtes in seinem

---

[1] Vgl. *Rhein. Mus.* 73, 1920, 367 ff. [siehe Bd. I 236 ff.].

8

vierten Liederbuch, in dem der Name des Maecenas vorkommt
(4, 11, 19), *Maecenas meus.* Und da hören die Leute nicht auf
(wie Wilamowitz sich auszudrücken pflegte) zu behaupten, das
Verhältnis zwischen Maecenas und Horaz sei damals nicht mehr
das alte gewesen !

Nur mit einem Blicke darf ich hier die beiden berühmten
Gedichte 14 und 50 streifen, so stark auch die Versuchung ist
sie eingehend zu besprechen. Der überströmende Enthusiasmus
281 am Anfang von 14, *Ni te plus oculis meis amarem* [1], *iucundissime* [2]
Calve, ist ganz echt, obwohl er hier auch als Folie für das Folgende dient. Was das Gedicht als Ganzes angeht, so scheint
die zweifache Orientierung, die für so viele der kleineren Catull-
gedichte bezeichnend ist, nicht immer gebührend gewürdigt zu
sein. Selbstverständlich ist dies ein Gelegenheitsgedicht im echten
Sinne. Man braucht nicht daran zu zweifeln dass Calvus dem
Freunde wirklich ein solches Saturnaliengeschenk ins Haus
geschickt hat. Eine so graziöse Abart des ‘ practical joke ’
würde im Freundeskreis mancher Oxforder Studenten ebenso
wenig überraschen wie bei anderen unter ihnen die sehr viel
handgreiflicheren Formen solcher Scherze. Unverkennbar hat
das Gedicht zunächst den Zweck dem Calvus Freude zu machen.
Aber ebenso unverkennbar dient es dem Zwecke eine ganze
Reihe von *pessimi poetae,* das heisst von Dichtern, die nicht mit
Calvus und Catull befreundet waren oder nicht zum Kreise des
Valerius Cato gehörten wie Catull, Ticida, Cinna, Furius Bi-
baculus und andere — dem Zwecke solche Poetaster (die V.
18 f. mit Namen genannten sind nur eine kleine Auswahl, wie
das folgende *omnia venena* [3] zeigt) tüchtig anzuprangern, in
den Augen des Calvus, vor allem aber in den Augen des Lesers.
Das Gedicht ist ein Dokument der Freundschaft, aber mindestens ebenso sehr eine Waffe in Catulls literarischen Fehden.
Im Gedicht 36 kommt auf das Mädchen und ihr unwahrschein-

---

[1] Vgl. dazu Krolls Bemerkung zu 58, 3 über den *sermo amatorius*; hinzuzuneh-
men ist Cic. *Brut.* 295 *hunc, quem tu plus quam te amas, Brutum.*

[2] Die Vorliebe der meisten Catullherausgeber für die Schreibung *iocundus,*
von der jeder weiss dass sie neben der andern inschriftlich und handschriftlich
belegt ist, vermag ich nicht zu teilen.

[3] Für diesen Gebrauch von *omnia* zur Ergänzung einer vorhergehenden Auf-
zählung s. F. Leo, *Analecta Plautina* III (Göttingen 1906), 19 [*Ausgew. Kl. Schr.*
I 180].

liches Gelübde [1] sehr wenig an, sehr viel aber auf die Invektive
gegen die *Annales Volusi*; dass dieses elegante Pasquill in dem
modernen Roman über die Wechselfälle in Catulls Liebesleben
immer noch seine Stelle behauptet, ist erheiternd.
Gedicht 50, *Hesterno, Licini, die otiosi*, trägt den Stempel
des unmittelbaren Erlebnisses. Wir dürfen ebenso sicher sein
dass Catull dies *poema* am Morgen nach dem *per iocum atque* 282
vinum betriebenen poetischen Zweikampf dem Calvus zuge-
schickt hat wie wir sicher sind dass Cicero, gereizt durch die
seine juristische Sachkenntnis verdächtigende Neckerei seines
jungen Freundes Trebatius, und triumphierend weil er, *etsi
domum bene potus seroque redieram*, ohne weiteres feststellen
konnte dass er Recht gehabt hatte, sogleich beim Anbruch des
nächsten Tages dem Freunde das graziöse und in einem liebens-
würdigen Kompliment für Trebatius gipfelnde Billet hat zu-
kommen lassen, das beginnt *Inluseras heri inter scyphos* (*Fam.*
7, 22) [2]. Und doch war Catulls Gedicht von Anfang an nicht
nur für Calvus bestimmt, sondern ebenso sehr für alle Leser
quot sunt ... quotque post aliis erunt in annis. Wäre nur an Calvus
als Empfänger gedacht, so wäre es ganz unsinnig ihm sechs
Verse lang (1-6) mit vielen Einzelheiten das zu erzählen was
er wenige Stunden zuvor selbst erlebt hat. Diese Einleitung
dient dem Leser, der aus ihr alles erfährt was er zum Verständnis
des Folgenden braucht. Damit ein Gelegenheitsgedicht zum
echten Gedicht wird, muss es von seinem äusseren Anlass eman-
zipiert und so durchgeformt werden dass es geschlossen und
autark in sich selbst ruht. Die Lebensmitte dieses kleinen
Gedichts ist Catulls hemmungsloses Entzücken über so viel
Geist und Anmut in dem Freunde. Die glückliche Aufregung
nach den beschwingten Stunden des Zusammenseins zittert
noch in allen seinen Nerven. Wie einem Verliebten ist ihm
zu Mute; er weiss es und schildert diesen Zustand mit ganz
leichter Übertreibung, ganz leisem Lächeln über sich selbst.

---

[1] 3-6 *nam ... vovit ... electissima* folgt der Sitte echter Gelübde: man weiht
das Erlesenste, das dann näher bestimmt werden kann, z. B. Eur. *Iph. T.* 20 f.
(Kalchas zu Agamemnon) ὅ τι γὰρ ἐνιαυτὸς τέκοι κάλλιστον, ηὔξω φωσφόρῳ θύσειν
θεᾷ. Das folgende *pessimi poetae scripta* kommt παρὰ προσδοκίαν.
[2] [Siehe oben, S. 77 f.]

II

Was wir bisher uns in Erinnerung gebracht haben, waren vollkommene kleine Gebilde. Jetzt wenden wir uns einem Gedichte zu (96), das als Gedicht nicht vollkommen ist, das aber vielleicht, wenn es gelingt es recht zu verstehen, uns in anderer Weise zu ergreifen vermag.

> Si quicquam mutis gratum acceptumve sepulcris
> accidere a nostro, Calve, dolore potest,
> quo desiderio veteres renovamus amores
> atque olim missas flemus amicitias,
> certe non tanto mors immatura dolorist
> Quintiliae, quantum gaudet amore tuo.

283 Die Gliederung ist ungelenk: das erste Distichon gehört ganz dem Kondizionalsatz, das zweite ganz dem illustrierenden Relativsatz [1], das letzte ganz dem Nachsatz. Es ist als hörte man die Scharniere leise knarren. Daneben halte man etwa das gleich lange Epigramm des jungen Virgil (*Catal.* 8), *Villula, quae Sironis eras*, und überzeuge sich, wie frei, trotz des für die klassische Form von Gedichten in elegischen Distichen geltenden Verbots des Enjambements über das Distichonende hinweg [2], dort eine durchaus nicht einfache Periode dahinströmt und wie elegant der abschliessende selbständige Hauptsatz innerhalb des letzten Hexameters beginnt. Die hier bei Catull zu beobachtende Mechanisierung des Satzbaus im Distichon ist bei ihm durchaus nicht vereinzelt. Die ersten sechs Verse von 76, *Siqua recordanti*, sind in dieser Hinsicht unserem Gedicht sehr ähnlich: ein Kondizionalsatz bis zum Ende des zweiten Distichons, und zwar derart gebaut dass Distichon I die positiven, Distichon II die negativen Elemente enthält; im dritten Distichon folgt der Nachsatz. Stilistisch nahverwandt, wenn auch gemäss seiner Länge sehr viel unerfreulicher,

---

[1] Mit Recht folgen die neueren Erklärer M. Haupt, *Opusc.* I 215, der gezeigt hat dass *quo desiderio* das vorhergehende *dolore* aufnimmt.

[2] Vgl. mein ' Kolon und Satz, I ', *Nachr. Gött. Ges.*, Phil.-hist. Kl. 1932, 198 ff. [Bd. I 74 ff.], auch darüber dass Catull noch nicht durchweg an die Regel gebunden ist.

ist der Brief an Hortensius (65). Für die syntaktische Analyse dieses Monstrums, wie W. Kroll es nennt, kann ich auf dessen Kommentar verweisen; nur glaube ich nicht wie er dass die Unbeholfenheit ' zum Teil durch die Lässigkeit des Briefstiles entschuldigt' ist. Ich sehe überhaupt darin kein Zeichen von Lässigkeit, vermute vielmehr dass das Drechseln dieser hölzernen Perioden Catull viel sauren Schweiss gekostet hat. Die Zeitgenossen haben vielleicht auch diese Produkte einer Kraftanstrengung bewundert; wir aber legen notwendig andere Massstäbe an. Nichts konnte den Sprachstil wie den Satz- und Versbau von Catulls Phalaikeen, Jamben und Hinkjamben übertreffen; in der Form seiner elegischen Distichen aber — und zum Teil seiner Hexameter — war er noch ein beträchtliches Stück von der Vollkommenheit entfernt, an die, soweit wir uns ein Bild machen können, erst das Auftreten Virgils die römischen Leser gewöhnt hat.

Etwas hölzern scheint für diesen Stil auch die Wiederaufnahme von *dolore* durch *quo desiderio* [1], und in der Verbindung *gratum acceptumve* [2] wirkt eins der beiden Glieder wie ein notdürftiges Füllsel [3]. Doch wir müssen endlich zur Hauptsache kommen, zum Inhalt.

Über das hinaus was das Gedicht selbst aussagt hat Lachmann die Grundlage des Verständnisses erweitert, indem er (in seinem Properz, 1816, zu 2, 11, 6, S. 141) feststellte dass das letzte Distichon, *certe ... amore tuo*, sich bezieht auf einen Vers des Calvus (16 Morel),

forsitan hoc etiam gaudeat ipsa cinis.

[1] Das ist eine Variante — und zugleich eine leichte stilistische Milderung — des Typus, den wir z. B. bei Terenz *Haut.* 20 *exemplum quo exemplo* ... finden; vgl. dazu Leo, *Anal. Plaut.* II (1898), 23 Anm. 1 [*Ausgew. Kl. Schr.* I 144 n. 1], Kühner-Stegmann II 283 f., Schmalz-Hofmann 710. Diese ' im Kurialstil ebenso wie in der literarisch anspruchslosen Erzählung' geläufige Struktur ' tritt in der Hochsprache mehr und mehr zurück'; ' die hohe Dichtung verschmäht diese Wiederholung als zu prosaisch' (Hofmann).

[2] Die bei Plautus ein paar Mal belegte Nebeneinanderstellung von *gratus* und *acceptus* ist in Prosa nicht selten, kommt aber, falls man sich auf das im Thesaurus, I 320 f. und VI 2, 2263, vorgelegte Material verlassen darf, in Versen sonst nicht vor.

[3] Das Füllsel ist hier jedoch viel weniger krass als 95, 2, wo der Pentameter mit Hilfe von *nonamque ... post hiemem* vervollständigt wird, obwohl der vorhergehende Hexameter mit *nonam post denique messem* schliesst.

Lachmann erschloss mit Recht dass dieser Pentameter aus dem von Properz bezeugten Trauergedicht [1] des Calvus auf Quintilia, offenbar seine Gattin, stammt. Andere haben dann erkannt dass das von Charisius zusammen mit diesem Pentameter aus den *carmina* des Calvus zitierte Bruchstück (15 Morel)

cum iam fulva cinis fuero

mit allergrösster Wahrscheinlichkeit dem selben Gedicht zuzu-
285 weisen ist, also zu einer Rede der Quintilia gehört. Der Sinn dieses Bruchstücks wird uns noch beschäftigen.

Danach sollte eigentlich das Verständnis von Catulls Versen und ihrer Beziehung auf das Gedicht des Calvus offen zutage liegen. Jedoch eine scheinbare Kleinigkeit — aber gibt es im Auffassen des Sprachlichen Kleinigkeiten? — hat alles verdorben. Das Gedicht sagt dass Quintilia tot ist, also Calvus ihre Liebe ein für alle Male verloren hat. Dass das aber nicht durch *missas* (V. 4) bezeichnet werden kann, haben die Gelehrten der Renaissance ganz richtig erkannt, denn sie besassen noch die beneidenswerte Fähigkeit sich in Sachen des lateinischen Sprachgebrauchs kein X für ein U vormachen zu lassen. Also schrieben sie *amissas*. Seitdem ist eine Sündflut von Conjecturen über das Partizipium hereingebrochen; die Proben etwa in Schwabes Apparat sind ganz ausreichend um unser Entsetzen zu erregen. Mit so vielen andern zweifelte auch Moriz Haupt nicht im geringsten daran dass hier eine Corruptel vorliege, ' da von freiwilligem Aufgeben nicht die Rede sein kann ' (*Opusc.* I 215); Baehrens stimmte ihm nachdrücklich zu. Dann aber kam die Periode jener durch dick und dünn apologetischen Texterklärung, in deren Arsenal die für ihre Zwecke unentbehrlichen Pseudoparallelen stets gebrauchsfertig bereitliegen. Demgemäss lesen wir in der ersten Auflage (1876) des Kommentars von R. Ellis : ' *missas*, ' *lost* ', as in Pseud. II. 3. 19 *Certa*

---

[1] Was die ' Vorstufen ' eines solchen Trauergedichts anlangt, so ist uns jetzt des Parthenios *Arete*, garnicht lange vor den Dichtungen des Calvus und Catull verfasst, etwas deutlicher geworden durch Pfeiffers eindringende Behandlung (*Class. Quart.* 37, 1943, 23 ff.) des von ihm als Bruchstück der *Arete* erkannten Genfer Papyrus 97, der bis dahin trotz dem Widerspruch von Wilamowitz den Aitia des Kallimachos zugewiesen war. Über die Einwirkung des Parthenios auf die Römer s. Pfeiffer S. 31. Durch Pfeiffers Entdeckung ist der Artikel ' Parthenios ' in der *RE* in einem wesentlichen Stücke überholt.

mittimus dum incerta petimus' [1]. Genau so steht es noch in
Lenchantins Kommentar (Turin 1933); G. Friedrich (1908)
sagt einfach ' *missas* steht statt *amissas*'. Auch W.
Kroll führt getreulich die Pseudolusstelle an, obwohl er an volle Synonymi-
tät von *missas* und *amissas* nicht recht glaubt, wie seine Anmer-
kung zeigt. Ihm bleibt im übrigen *missas* verdächtig, denn in
seinem sehr knappen kritischen Apparat erwähnt er ausser
dem seligen *amissas* (es figuriert auch noch in Schusters Teubner-
Ausgabe) noch eine, übrigens schlechthin phantastische, Conjectur. Uns kommt es hier auf das Verständnis Catulls an, aber
bei der Langlebigkeit solcher ' Parallelen ' lässt es sich nicht
vermeiden dass wir uns erst einmal die Stelle bei Plautus etwas
genauer ansehen. Der Sklave Pseudolus, versunken in das was
er selbst als *philosophari* bezeichnet (687), meditiert folgender-
massen über die blinde Torheit der Menschen (683 ff.) :

> stulti hau scimus, frustra ut simus, quom quid cupienter dari   286
> petimus nobis, quasi quid in rem sit possimus noscere.
> certa mittimus, dum incerta petimus; atque hoc evenit
> in labore atque in dolore, ut mors obrepat interim.

Trotz der verbreiternden Umsetzung des attischen Monologs
in den Klingklang eines Plautinischen Canticums vernehmen
wir hier immer noch den fast tragischen Unterton, den wir
jetzt vor allem aus eindrucksvollen Stellen Menanders kennen.
Certa mittimus : soll das heissen ' in unserer Jagd nach dem
Ungewissen verlieren wir das Gewisse ' ? Das wäre vielleicht
traurig, aber jedenfalls banal. Was der Dichter in diesem ernsten
Zusammenhange sagt, ist feiner und tiefer. Wir Menschen,
töricht wie wir nun einmal sind, und von dem eitlen Wahn besessen,
wir wüssten was uns frommt, lassen in unserer πλεονεξία das
gewisse Gute, das wir besitzen, zugunsten eines Ungewissen
mutwillig fahren. Oder um es mit Worten Demokrits (frg.
224) zu sagen : ἡ τοῦ πλέονος ἐπιθυμίη τὸ παρεὸν ἀπόλλυσι τῇ
Αἰσωπείῃ κυνὶ ἰκέλη γινομένη. Der Hund in der Aesopfabel
büsst zwar das Fleischstück, das er im Maule hielt, schliesslich
ein, aber das Entscheidende ist dass er es nicht irgendwie ' ver-
liert ', sondern, wie es noch in unserer späten Fassung ganz

---

[1] In der zweiten Auflage (1889) drückt er sich etwas vorsichtiger aus, lässt
aber die Hauptsache unverändert.

präzis heisst, ἀφεῖσα τὸ ἴδιον ὥρμησεν ὡς τὸ ἐκείνης ἀφαιρησομένη. Daran dass in der Wendung *certa mittimus* das Verbum nichts anderes bedeutet als ἀφίεμεν, kann nicht der leiseste Zweifel bestehen [1].

Der Passus also, der unserer Hoffnung, *mittere* könne uns den Gefallen tun gelegentlich auch für *amittere* einzutreten, Stab und Stütze sein sollte, hat sich als brüchiges Rohr erwiesen. Aber woher nehmen wir eigentlich das Recht ohne weiteres vorauszusetzen dass im vierten Verse des Catullgedichts nur vom Tode der Quintilia die Rede sein kann, oder, anders ausgedrückt, nur davon dass Calvus sie und ihre Liebe durch ihren Tod verloren hat ? Dass ein Mann vom Temperamente des Calvus seiner Frau beständig treu geblieben sei, wird niemand für sehr 287 wahrschein|lich halten, der im allgemeinen etwas Menschenkenntnis besitzt und der im besondern mit den Sitten der römischen Gesellschaft jener Zeit nicht ganz unvertraut ist. Wir Philologen sind ja aber erst dann wahrhaft glücklich, wenn wir auch für das was im Grunde kaum anders sein kann ein Zeugnis in Händen halten. In diesem Falle hat ein freundliches Geschick uns dieses Glück beschert. Auf Grund der eigenen Gedichte des Calvus sagt Ovid, *Trist.* 2, 431 f., *par fuit exigui similisque licentia Calvi, detexit variis qui sua furta modis.* Jetzt erinnern wir uns wieder an das Trauergedicht des Calvus. In ihm hatte er Quintilia, als sie noch am Leben war, zu ihm, Calvus, sagen lassen : *cum iam fulva cinis fuero,* ... Den Wortlaut des Nachsatzes herzustellen ist unmöglich; die Richtung aber, in der sein Gedanke sich bewegt haben muss, ist durch die Natur des menschlichen Herzens gewiesen. In dem ergreifendsten römischen Privatbrief, der uns — dank dem Fleiss und der Einsicht von Catulls Freund Cornelius Nepos — erhalten geblieben ist, schreibt Cornelia nach der Katastrophe ihres Sohnes Tiberius Gracchus an Gaius : *ubi mortua ero, parentabis mihi et invocabis deum parentem.* Quintilia wird in der von ihrem

---

[1] Was ich hier über *Pseud.* 685 (wo gleichfalls lange Zeit die aus der Renaissance stammende Conjectur *amittimus* in den Ausgaben stand) sagen musste, sollte sich für jeden, der sich überlegt, was *mittere* heissen kann und was nicht, von selbst verstehen. Übrigens ist es keine neue Weisheit. So hat z. B. Joh. Schneider, *De proverbiis Plautinis Terentianisque* (Diss. Berlin 1878) 27, den Sinn der Stelle ganz richtig erfasst, denn er vergleicht damit Hesiod frg. 219 Rz. νήπιος, ὅς τις ἑτοῖμα λιπὼν ἀνέτοιμα διώκει.

Dichtergatten ihr in den Mund gelegten Rede etwa gesagt
haben : ' wenn ich längst Asche bin, dann wirst du bereuen
was du mir mit deinen *furta* angetan hast '.   Die Wunde brennt
noch immer, und Catull bewährt sich dem Freunde als ein
Arzt, der mit Schonung, aber auch mit Sachkunde zu Werke
geht. Ganz ohne Wehtun kann es dabei nicht abgehn; nur muss
der Leidende spüren dass ihn eine gelinde Hand anrührt. Catull
darf nicht verschleiern dass Calvus damals, *olim*, willentlich
preisgegeben hat, *misit*, was er hätte festhalten sollen.   Er
weiss auch von den Schmerzen dessen der in sehnsüchtigem
Verlangen, *desiderio*, immer und immer wieder das längstver-
gangene Liebesglück nacherlebt.   Aber welche schlichte Zart-
heit liegt darin dass er an dieser Stelle kein hartes ' Du' äussert,
sondern mit ' Wir ' sich selbst in das Schicksal von Menschen-
irrtum und Menschenleid einschliesst :

> quo desiderio veteres renovamus amores
> atque olim missas flemus amicitias.

In dem Denkmal seiner Reue und wiedererwachten Liebe
hatte Calvus gesagt :

> forsitan hoc etiam gaudeat ipsa cinis.

Das zaghafte ' Vielleicht ' nimmt Catull auf.   Auch hier ist er 288
ganz ehrlich, macht sich und dem Freunde nichts vor, heuchelt
keine Gewissheit über ein Leben nach dem Tode.   Das ' Wenn '
am Anfang des kurzen Gedichts soll nicht vergessen werden.
Wenn es aber so ist dass eine Kunde von unserm Schmerz die
Dahingeschiedenen erreicht und zu rühren vermag, dann, Calvus,
ist eines ganz gewiss :

> certe non tanto mors immatura dolorist
> Quintiliae, quantum gaudet amore tuo.